ALSO BY MARK R. LEVIN

Men in Black

Rescuing Sprite

Liberty and Tyranny

Ameritopia

The Liberty Amendments

Plunder and Deceit

Rediscovering Americanism

Unfreedom of the Press

American Marxism

THE
DEMOCRAT PARTY
HATES AMERICA

MARK R. LEVIN

THRESHOLD EDITIONS

NEW YORK   LONDON   TORONTO   SYDNEY   NEW DELHI

Threshold Editions
An Imprint of Simon & Schuster, Inc.
1230 Avenue of the Americas
New York, NY 10020

Copyright © 2023 by Mark R. Levin

First Threshold Editions hardcover edition September 2023

THRESHOLD EDITIONS and colophon are trademarks of Simon & Schuster, Inc.

For information about special discounts for bulk purchases, please contact Simon & Schuster Special Sales at 1-866-506-1949 or business@simonandschuster.com.

The Simon & Schuster Speakers Bureau can bring authors to your live event. For more information, or to book an event, contact the Simon & Schuster Speakers Bureau at 1-866-248-3049 or visit our website at www.simonspeakers.com.

Interior design by Jaime Putorti

Manufactured in the United States of America

10 9 8 7 6 5 4 3 2 1

Library of Congress Cataloging-in-Publication Data has been applied for.

ISBN 978-1-5011-8315-7
ISBN 978-1-5011-8317-1 (ebook)

To my big brother, Doug, with my love and deepest admiration. You have always been selfless and humble. Your family adores you.

CONTENTS

THE
DEMOCRAT PARTY
HATES AMERICA

CHAPTER ONE

THE DEMOCRAT PARTY & AUTHORITARIANISM

This book is not intended to be provocative, but in the Democrat Party–centric parts of our society, it undoubtedly will be. That said, it is not written for Democrat Party officials, politicians, media, sycophants, activists, and surrogates. It is written for those patriotic Americans who fear for our country and its future. America is unraveling. Our founding and history are under assault. Our families and faiths are being degraded. Individualism has been substituted for groupism. Color blindness is now racist. Capitalism and prosperity are being devoured by economic socialism and climate-change fanaticism. Classrooms have become indoctrination mills for racism, segregation, bigotry, and sexual perversion, and teachers' unions are hostile to parental involvement in critical decisions about the health and welfare of their children.

In America, free speech and academic freedom are shrinking, and the police state is growing—as is monitoring and spying on citizens. The government is banning and regulating more and more household products, from incandescent lightbulbs to dishwashers,[1] while creating shortages and driving up costs of others. Crime is out of control on our streets, public transportation, and schools, while police budgets are slashed and many prosecutors and judges coddle violent criminals. Our borders are wide open to millions of foreigners who seek entry into the country, as drug and criminal cartels ship killer drugs into our country by the tons and brutalize migrants by using them as indentured servants and sex slaves. And the list goes on.

The Democrat Party is responsible for most of this and much more. It seeks to permanently control our governmental institutions, just as it dominates our cultural entities—from the media to academia, from entertainment to science. It seeks to delegitimize and eviscerate the Constitution—including the Bill of Rights, the Electoral College, the Supreme Court, separation of powers, etc.—which obstructs its ideological designs. It abuses the rule of law by targeting its political opponents for harassment, investigation, and prosecution. In the end, it seeks to imprison them.

On October 30, 2008, when Barack Obama shouted to a crowd that "[w]e are five days away from fundamentally transforming the United States of America," he was not kidding. On May 14, 2008, when Michelle Obama pronounced that "[w]e are going to have to change our conversation; we're going to have to change our traditions, our history; we're going to have to move into a different place as a nation," she meant it.[2]

The Obamas are not alone among Democrat Party apparatchiks in their contempt for the country. In fact, it is the rare top Democrat Party politician who regularly praises America and is sincere about it. They mostly trash-talk the country and smear millions of its people. The examples are too numerous to catalogue here. But it is a party that is built on the demands and propaganda of revolutionaries, demagogues, and malcontents, and has a horrifying history of supporting the most contemptible causes, including slavery, segregation, the Ku Klux Klan, eugenics, and even lynchings. Indeed, almost from the start, the Democrat Party rejected the principles and values of the American experiment. And today it is the home of another anti-American movement, American Marxism, with its various ideological appendages. The Democrat Party ruling class, elites, and activists are united in this revolution.

As the title of this book declares, the Democrat Party hates America. Indeed, if you want to "fundamentally transform" something, you clearly do not love it or even like it. As I have explained on my radio show, if someone says, "I wish I could fundamentally transform my spouse," then you obviously don't love or like your spouse. But what if you do not want to fundamentally transform America and love our country? Then it is important to speak the truth about those who seek to impose their will on the rest of us. When dealing with such a dire threat to our freedom, society, and way of life, we cannot dodge our responsibilities as citizens, especially in my case—when I have such large platforms to push back. It can be difficult and unpleasant to speak out and write a book such as this, given the predictable outrage and anger that will surely result from numerous individuals and quarters. Nonetheless, the time is late and the cause is too important to self-censor. So, let us step back and examine what is taking place and the central role of the Democrat Party.

Of course, it is necessary to expose the role of the Democrat Party's current leader, President Joe Biden, in undermining America. In a March 2023 speech to the Canadian parliament, Biden concluded his remarks, aimed mostly at further government-to-government space exploration with the Canadian government, in which he proclaimed: "Ladies and gentlemen, we're living in an age of possibilities. Xi Jinping asked me, in the Tibetan Plateau, could I define America. And I could've said the same thing if he asked about Canada. I said, 'Yes. One word—and mean it.

One word: *possibilities.*' Nothing is beyond our capacity. We can do anything. We have to never forget. We must never doubt our capacity. Canada and the United States can do big things. We stand together, do them together, rise together. We're going to write the future together, I promise you."[3]

Biden was not talking about the possibilities of entrepreneurship, capitalism, individual human initiative, etc., when speaking to Xi or the Canadian parliament. He was talking about the endless opportunities of an activist government—which means the expansion of his own power and that of the Democrat Party, the establishment of an all-powerful central government, a command economy, and the remaking of man's nature. Indeed, Biden rules as an autocrat. Biden has said that he wants his legacy to be as big as or bigger than Franklin Roosevelt's, who did in fact radically change the nature of the federal government and its relationship with the citizen.[4] And Biden is being urged to continue the transformation of America away from the founding ideals toward an Americanized Marxist model that I wrote about at length in *American Marxism*. Today, Biden is a reckless and stubborn autocrat who has frequent temper tantrums and screams and curses at his staff. He has also racked up a disastrous record both domestically and internationally.

Some wonder how Biden moved from a relatively nondescript politician to a radical leftist. In fact, for most of his life, Biden has been a political chameleon and an intellectual lightweight. When he entered the Senate, he immediately sided with the segregationists and racists and actively opposed the integration of public schools. When law and order became an important issue in the mid-1990s, he cosponsored a criminal justice bill that was tough on criminals. At one point he was a fiscal centrist by Washington standards and also supported some limits on abortion. He also backed border enforcement. None of that is true today.

Of course, Biden's conduct on the Senate Judiciary Committee, and the viciousness and dishonesty of his attacks on conservative nominees, was appalling, but it reflected the views and demands of his party. Moreover, Biden always saw himself as presidential timber, when most did not. His lies and deceit, including his habitual plagiarizing, including stealing words and phrases of speeches by Robert Kennedy and Neil Kinnock (British Labour Party leader), as well as his blatant lies about his academic record, helped derail his previous embryonic presidential campaigns. Today, his lack of character, cringeworthy outbursts, and obvious stage 5 dementia (of which there are seven stages)[5] are all but ignored or dismissed.

In 2020, however, the Democrat Party operatives saw Biden as their only hope to stop President Donald Trump from winning re-election. Trump was threatening their grip on power and the culture and undoing their ideological agenda. They rightly believed that Socialist Democrat (aka Marxist) Bernie Sanders could not win a general election. Therefore, the party, and its powerful surrogates, used its enormous infrastructure and resources, including party operatives, billionaire donors, activist media, academic scholars, the immense bureaucracy, the legal community, corporatists, labor unions, etc., to help the basement-dwelling Biden secure the Democrat Party nomination and install him in the Oval Office.

Indeed, it was the most radical elements within the Democrat Party and its powerful surrogates—Never Trumpers, and wealthy dark-money donors—that ran a "shadow campaign that saved the 2020 election" for Biden. In February 2021, *Time*'s Molly Ball reported that "[t]here was a conspiracy unfolding behind the scenes. . . . Their work touched every aspect of the election. They got states to change voting systems and laws and helped secure hundreds of millions in public and private funding. They fended off voter-suppression lawsuits, recruited armies of poll workers, and got millions of people to vote by mail for the first time. They successfully pressured social media companies to take a harder line against disinformation and used data-driven strategies to fight viral smears."[6]

These secret meetings became huge events. As Ball reported: "The meetings became the galactic center for a constellation of operatives across the left who shared overlapping goals but didn't usually work in concert. The group had no name, no leaders and no hierarchy, but it kept the disparate actors in sync."[7]

The group included a handful of the usual GOP and corporate establishmentarians, but the self-proclaimed alliance to protect the election was in fact a product of and driven by radical Democrats and party operatives. Although Biden campaigned in 2020 as a moderate Democrat and a "uniter," that was all illusory propaganda.

There were notable hints that Biden sold out to his party's most radical elements for their support during the election. In July 2020, Biden tweeted: "We're going to beat Donald Trump. And when we do, we won't just rebuild this nation—we'll transform it."[8] Another Democrat preaching the fundamental transformation of America.

In fact, during the 2020 campaign, left-wing media outlet *Vox* noted: "Former Vice President Joe Biden and progressive Sen. Bernie Sanders are teaming up to create joint 'unity' task forces that will have a direct hand in shaping Democratic policy and the party's agenda in 2020 and beyond. The group of 48 lawmakers, labor leaders, economists, academics, and activists signals what the Democratic Party platform might look like going forward. Each campaign selected representatives to serve on six policy-specific committees: climate change, criminal justice reform, education, the economy, health care, and immigration. Sanders's allies seem encouraged about the names on the task force, which include vocal proponents for progressive policies like Medicare-for-All and a Green New Deal, like Reps. Alexandria Ocasio-Cortez (NY) and Pramila Jayapal (WA). Sanders's former campaign manager Faiz

Shakir, who has been leading negotiations with the Biden campaign, told *Vox* that Biden's team has been very 'amenable and open' to working with progressives throughout the process. '[Biden] has some room to run in terms of building a more fleshed-out policy agenda to campaign upon,' Shakir told *Vox*. 'Because he hasn't fleshed it out as deeply as some other candidates over the course of the primary, that's an opportunity.'"[9]

When the policy project was completed, David Harsanyi, writing in *National Review*, declared: "Biden's joint 110-page policy wish list for the Democratic Party was co-written with the nation's most famous collectivist, Castro apologist Bernie Sanders. The document is jammed with policies that a moderate Senator Biden would never have embraced. 'The goals of the task force were to move the Biden campaign into as progressive a direction as possible, and I think we did that,' Sanders told NPR at the time. 'On issue after issue, whether it was education, the economy, health care, climate, immigration, criminal justice, I think there was significant movement on the part of the Biden campaign.' Mission accomplished. 'If I'm the nominee I can tell you one thing— I would very much want Bernie Sanders to be part of the journey,' Biden had noted. 'Not as a vice presidential nominee, but just in engaging in all the things that he's worked so hard to do, many of which I agree with.'"[10] Biden was now surrounded by Obama and Sanders extremists, among others, to ensure that their and now his anti-American Marxist agenda would be instituted.

Among those pushing Biden's radical agenda behind the scenes is a group of descendants of men and women who helped Franklin Roosevelt institute his New Deal. As reported by *Politico* in 2021: "At 6 p.m., two rows of elderly faces appeared on screen, staring into the camera: June Hopkins, Henry Scott Wallace, Tomlin Perkins Coggeshall and James Roosevelt Jr. If their names sound vaguely familiar it's because their relatives—Harry Hopkins, Henry

Wallace, Frances Perkins and Franklin Delano Roosevelt—formed
the nucleus of one of the most famous and influential Oval Office
rosters in American history. Ninety years later, these descendants
of the FDR administration have reconstituted his Cabinet. And
they have played their roles with a conscientious sense of purpose.
This is a meeting, not happy hour. No one drinks, and they begin
on time. . . . In a city of interest groups, 'the descendants,' as they
refer to themselves in frequent press releases and op-eds, are among
the more unusual. They are determined to polish the legacy of
America's 32nd president by pushing the 46th to embrace a legislative agenda as transformational as the New Deal. They want
Joe Biden to embrace the idea of an 'activist' government. They
want him to eliminate the filibuster. They spend hours parsing his
words for echoes of the stirring language that helped defeat the
Great Depression. And they devote their Wednesday night Zoom
meetings, where they have met nearly every week since last June,
to plotting ways to keep the comparisons to FDR alive, as if repetition might somehow will Biden's latent progressivism to life. . . .

   "The sudden impulse to compare the two men—or to take
issue with the impulse to compare the two men—has become
commonplace in Washington. You'll find the two men's names
side-by-side in headlines—more than 175 already this year. You'll
read about the way both men faced the threat of authoritarianism. You'll see 'New Deal' allusions in the coverage of Biden's
proposed infrastructure package. You'll forget there was ever a
time when the president wasn't on the cusp of 'transformational.'
The presidential candidate who ran for office on the promise that
'nothing would fundamentally change,' the six-term senator who
moved with rather than ahead of his party from one decade to the
next—is now, maybe, the next FDR."[11]

   Bernie Sanders agrees, having early on endorsed Biden for re-
election in 2024, comparing his radical record to Roosevelt's.

Indeed, Mike Allen, writing in *Axios* in March 2021, reveals that a private meeting was held with Biden and certain Democrat-supporting historians "around a long table in the East Room earlier this month, President Biden took notes in a black book as they discussed some of his most admired predecessors. . . . The March 2 session, which the White House kept under wraps, reflects Biden's determination to be one of the most consequential presidents. The chatty two-hour-plus meeting is a for-the-history-books marker of the think-big, go-big mentality that pervades his West Wing. . . . Biden's presidency has already been transformative, and he has many more giant plans teed up that could make Biden's New Deal the biggest change to governance in our lifetimes."[12]

Who were these historians?

"The session was organized by Jon Meacham, the presidential biographer and informal Biden adviser who has helped with big speeches from Nashville, and serves as POTUS's historical muse. Besides [Doris Kearns] Goodwin, participants included Michael Beschloss, author Michael Eric Dyson, Yale's Joanne Freeman, Princeton's Eddie Glaude Jr., Harvard's Annette Gordon-Reed and Walter Isaacson. . . . They talked a lot about the elasticity of presidential power, and the limits of going bigger and faster than the public might anticipate or stomach."[13] Several of these Biden "historians" are regular guests on cable TV, where they relentlessly condemn Donald Trump and other Republicans, without revealing their political association and activism.

What Biden has learned, what Roosevelt knew, and what the Democrat Party seeks is the importance of monopolizing the political system. Indeed, this is something Vladimir Lenin wrote about, insisted on, and instituted before, during, and after the Russian Revolution. The Democrat Party has, in fact, largely conquered America's cultural, educational, and media institutions, but there still remains significant resistance. Millions of

Americans reject its radical ideology, do not want to fundamentally transform America, and are now awake to what the Democrat Party is doing to destroy the country.

Of course, the Constitution is written to limit the centralization and monopolization of power—that is, the Democrat Party's present-day power grabs—and the Republican Party, while often anemic if not ignorantly contributory to the Democrat Party's ambitions, is, nonetheless, an impediment by its mere existence. That said, there remain active efforts within the Republican Party and mostly elsewhere to challenge the Democrat Party's growing tyranny. Clearly, power-sharing is not, and cannot be, part of the Democrat Party's agenda. Frankly, like autocratic parties everywhere, the Democrat Party is intolerant of opposition and insists on absolute control.

A democracy or republic consisting of multiple political parties competing for power is simply unacceptable to and incompatible with Marxism of any form or in any country, including the United States. Yet that is the unmistakable goal of the Democrat Party. As the late philosopher Raymond Aron explained, the party structure in America and other Western countries is based on the "legality of opposition" (a rare phenomenon in history), a constitutionally based "peaceful rivalry," the "legal exercise of power," the "temporary exercise of power," and the "legitimate method of exercising power."[14] Importantly, Aron adds: "The opposition accepts decisions which are taken legally by the government in power, or the majority, but if a time comes when these decisions endanger its most vital interests, its very existence, will they not try to resist? There are circumstances in which a minority chooses to fight rather than submit. . . . The smooth functioning of a western regime depends then essentially on what the competing parties propose to do. The fundamental problem of western democracy, the combination of national understanding and contestation, is easy or difficult to resolve according to the nature of the parties, the aims which they set themselves and the doctrines which they preach."[15]

However, writes Aron, "[w]hen a party, one party alone, has the monopoly of political activity, the state is indissolubly linked to it. In a multi-party regime in the west, the state boasts of not being circumscribed by the ideas of any competing parties; the state is neutral through the fact that it tolerates a plurality of parties. . . ."[16]

In the United States, it can now be said that the monopoly party is the Democrat Party. Indeed, the vast administrative state built mostly, albeit not exclusively, by the Democrat Party issues edicts, dictates, regulations, rules, fines, and penalties that serve the ideological purposes of the Democrat Party, whether the Democrat Party is in power or not. It requires the affirmative intervention of a Republican administration to roll back, stop, or fundamentally reverse the trajectory of administrative state decisions exercised on behalf of the Democrat Party. And most of the time their efforts fail, because the administrative state often seeks to sabotage Republican Party initiatives and policies, or a Republican president, through leaks, red tape, and internal countermands, thereby nullifying the decision of the electorate in a particular election cycle. Indeed, it can be said that the administrative state has essentially become a permanent appendage of the Democrat Party. Consequently, even though elections are held, the Democrat Party has a permanent hold on major aspects of the government and policy-making. The more powerful the central government becomes, with ubiquitous tentacles, unlimited resources, and increasing police powers, the more powerful the Democrat Party becomes. Hence, the Democrat Party works tirelessly to not only protect its administrative state fiefdom, but to constantly strengthen and enlarge it.

The Democrat Party is the party of the state.

As Aron describes it, "[i]n a one-party regime, the state is a party-state, inseparable from the party which monopolizes legitimate political activity. If, instead of a state of parties, a party-state exists, the state will be obliged to restrict freedom of political discussion. Since the state presupposes as absolutely valid the ideology of the monopolistic party, it cannot officially allow this ideology to be called into question. In fact, the restriction on freedom of political discussion varies in degree according to the regimes of a single party. But the essence of a single-party regime in which the state is defined by the ideology of the monopolistic party is not to accept all the ideas and to prevent some ideas relating to the party from being openly debated."[17] And this is where the Democrat Party has driven the nation. The power and control of the Democrat Party, and allegiance to it and to its ideology above all else, are the objective. This is evident in the media, social sites, entertainment, and academia.

Moreover, "[a]t least with regard to those who do not belong to the monopolistic party," declares Aron, "the party-state reserves for itself almost *unbounded possibilities of action*. Besides, if the monopoly is justified by the vastness of the revolutionary changes to be achieved, how can one ask the exercise of power to be moderate and legal? . . ."[18] [Italics are mine.] Exactly. Hence, Biden's talk to the Canadian parliament of endless "possibilities" and, therefore, the Democrat Party's endless intrusions into our lives and self-righteous justifications for it.

For those of us who love our country, and the principles and values on which it was founded, the Democrat Party has pushed and dragged the nation into a very dangerous and perilous place. Decades of usurpations of the Constitution, family, and faith, and abuses of power and governance in support of "progressive" or, more to the point, Marxist theories and models of ruling, are destroying our country from within. Moreover, the pace of the decay has quickened and the extent has broadened. And, of

course, through it all, the Democrat Party has become more powerful and omnipresent in our everyday lives.

In 2017, Freedom House (FH) (founded in 1941) released a
substantial report on modern authoritarianism focused primarily,
but not exclusively, on communist China and fascistic Russia. FH
is a well-intentioned nonprofit but center-left organization with a
very important mission. It describes itself as a group "founded on
the core conviction that freedom flourishes in democratic nations
where governments are accountable to their people; the rule of
law prevails; and freedoms of expression, association, and belief,
as well as respect for the rights of women, minority communities,
and historically marginalized groups, are guaranteed. We speak out
against the main threats to democracy and empower citizens to
exercise their fundamental rights through a unique combination of
analysis, advocacy, and direct support to frontline defenders of freedom, especially those working in closed authoritarian societies."[19]

Although focused mostly on China and Russia, I believe in many
significant respects the FH document reflects what is occurring in
the United States at the command of the Democrat Party and
the implementation of its various extra-constitutional, economic,
and political schemes. Moreover, since 2017, the situation in the
United States has become significantly worse and even dire. When
I apply, in part, many of the Democrat Party's aims and actions to
the FH analysis on China and Russia, the similarities are stunning.

As a general matter, FH declared that "[t]he 21st century has
been marked by a resurgence of authoritarian rule that has proved
resilient despite economic fragility and occasional popular resistance. Modern authoritarianism has succeeded, where previous
totalitarian systems failed, due to refined and nuanced strategies
of repression, the exploitation of open societies, and the spread of
illiberal policies in democratic countries themselves. The leaders
of today's authoritarian systems devote full-time attention to the

challenge of crippling the opposition without annihilating it, and flouting the rule of law while maintaining a plausible veneer of order, legitimacy, and prosperity."[20]

Frankly, I can think of no better description of the Democrat Party and Democrat Party rule. For example, the Democrat Party seeks to eliminate the Senate filibuster rule in order to pass legislation that will fundamentally alter innumerable aspects of our culture and society; add four more Democrat senators to the Senate to prevent the Republican Party from ever winning a majority in the Senate; add justices to the Supreme Court in order to control the ideological makeup of the Court for decades to come; and change the rules, processes, and outcomes of the popular vote throughout the nation to make it impossible for the Republican Party to win the presidency and majorities in Congress. The goal is to "cripple the opposition [the GOP] without annihilating it" and empower the Democrat Party into the distant future. And, of course, the Democrat Party's use of the Department of Justice, FBI, IRS, etc., against political opponents is the stuff of police-state autocracies. (More on this in Chapter 8 respecting President Trump.)

FH goes on: "Central to the modern authoritarian strategy is the capture of institutions that undergird political pluralism. The goal is to dominate not only the executive and legislative branches, but also the media, the judiciary, civil society, the commanding heights of the economy, and the security forces. . . ."[21]

Indeed, the Democrat Party pulled this off in California, which was once a reliably Republican state in presidential elections. California was the biggest barrier to the Democrat Party winning the presidency. Republicans won the state in nearly every presidential election between 1952 and 1988 (except for 1964). In large part, the Democrat Party succeeded in changing the state's immigration system, voting system, and redistricting. The Democrat Party now has supermajorities in the California legislature. Administrative agencies, departments, and commissions are populated with radicals loyal to the party, as is the judiciary. The Democrat Party–aligned teachers' unions have de facto control over the school systems and classrooms.

The FH description of the modern authoritarian strategy, however, is increasingly present and visible not just in California but throughout the country. The modern-day American media are effectively an appendage of and mouthpiece for the Democrat Party and its agenda; the public school systems are ruled by Democrat Party–aligned teachers' unions; the tenured college and university professors are overwhelmingly members of the Democrat Party and ideological propagandists for its agenda; billionaire George Soros is among several oligarchs who spend widely to support the Democrat Party and its radical causes; the Biden administration's "all-of-government" indoctrination by imposing Critical Race Theory (CRT) and the use of "woke" brainwashing throughout the federal bureaucracy; the regulatory imposition by such federal entities as the Securities and Exchange Commission (SEC) of Environmental, Social, and Government (ESG) investing in private businesses to help subsidize the Democrat Party's extreme political agenda; the use of Diversity, Equity, and Inclusion (DEI) commissars throughout society to enforce and promote the indoctrination, dehumanization, intimidation, and discrimination of individuals in service to the Democrat Party's political agenda; the Democrat Party working with federal law enforcement and intelligence agencies to monitor, censor, investigate, smear, and/or criminally charge political opponents ("Russian collusion," parents protesting at school board meetings, pro-life protestors at abortion clinics, Republicans challenging an election, etc.); and silencing free speech on the Internet to advance the election of Biden and other Democrat Party candidates; silencing differing views on government policy; and squelching out-of-favor scholars and experts (the "Twitter Files"), etc.

FH notes that "[t]he rewriting of history for political purposes is common among modern authoritarians. . . ."[22]

Of course, the purpose of American Marxism generally; the 1619 Project; the vilification of America's founders, the Declaration of Independence, and the Constitution; teaching CRT and other racist ideologies; the toppling of historic monuments and statues; changing names of schools and military installations; etc., is to weaken if not destroy allegiance to our country and knowledge of its real history, especially with younger generations of Americans. Marx would be proud. And the Democrat Party supports it all.

For example, the 1619 Project is nothing more than the cobbling together of racist, extremist propaganda about America's founding that was once rejected as the foolish screeds of outlier radical activists and academics. But with the support and financing of the *New York Times*—which in the past has supported Stalin, covered up the Holocaust, and helped install Castro in Cuba—it has been mainstreamed throughout school systems and the culture. As Peter W. Wood, president of the National Association of Scholars, explains: "The larger aim of the 1619 Project is to change America's understanding of itself. Whether it will ultimately succeed in doing so remains to be seen, but it certainly has already succeeded in shaping how Americans now argue about key aspects of our history. The 1619 Project aligns with the views of those on the progressive left who hate America and would like to transform it radically into a different kind of nation. Such a transformation would be a terrible mistake: it would endanger our hard-won liberty, our self-government, and our virtues as a people. . . ."[23]

FH highlights how elections are used to acquire and exercise autocratic power. "The toxic combination of unfair elections and crude majoritarianism is spreading from modern authoritarian regimes to illiberal leaders in what are still partly democratic countries. Increasingly, populist politicians—once in office—claim the right to suppress the media, civil society, and other democratic institutions by citing support from a majority of voters. The resulting changes make it more difficult for the opposition to compete in future elections and can pave the way for a new authoritarian regime." [24]

As the Heritage Foundation points out, the Democrat Party introduced the "For the People Act of 2021" (H.R. 1), which would have destroyed the American voting system and replaced it with a collection of schemes intended to empower the Democrat Party for decades to come. Heritage states: "H.R. 1 would federalize and micromanage the election process administered by the states, imposing unnecessary, unwise, and unconstitutional mandates on the states and reversing the decentralization of the American election process—which is essential to the protection of our liberty and freedom. It would implement nationwide the worst changes in election rules that occurred during the 2020 election and go even further in eroding and eliminating basic security protocols that states have in place. The bill would interfere with the ability of states and their citizens to determine the qualifications and eligibility of voters, to ensure the accuracy of voter registration rolls, to secure the fairness and integrity of elections, to participate and speak freely in the political process, and to determine the district boundary." [25]

Although it was defeated, it is being implemented in states in pieces and parts, and the Democrat Party has no intention of abandoning it.

FH explains that modern autocrats also resort to older tyrannical tactics: "While more subtle and calibrated methods of repression are the defining feature of modern authoritarianism, the past few years have featured a reemergence of older tactics that undermine the illusions of pluralism and openness. . . ." [26]

In the United States today, these tactics include the unraveling of the Bill of Rights, which exist to protect the individual from the federal government. Hillsdale College professor Paul A. Rahe observes that, for example, the individual protections set forth in the First Amendment of the Bill of Rights are under a frontal assault. Once again, the primary architects and instigators are Democrat Party leaders. Rahe writes: "Now we live in a brave new world in which there is a great deal of legislation in place that has a considerable impact on the free exercise of religion and that abridges freedom of speech, freedom of the press, and the right of the people to petition the government for a redress of grievances. The First Amendment has not been amended. It has not been repealed by the American people acting in a solemn fashion via the amending process provided for in the Constitution. But it is nonetheless well on its way to becoming a dead letter—thanks to the ambition of politicians, to the grand projects they pursue, and to a decision of the courts to strike a balance between the rights provided for by the First Amendment and other imperatives thought to be of greater or at least equal importance."[27]

"Modern authoritarianism," declares FH, "has a different set of defining features." They include "state or oligarchic control over information on certain political subjects and key sectors of the media, which are otherwise pluralistic, with high production values and entertaining content; independent outlets survive with small audiences and little influence."[28]

Elon Musk's exposé of the "Twitter Files" is a frightening example of what FH describes. As journalist Matt Taibbi wrote, after he reviewed a large cache of emails and texts between and among Twitter executives, the files "show the FBI acting as doorman to a vast program of social media surveillance and censorship, encompassing agencies across the federal government—from the State Department to the Pentagon to the CIA."[29] In fact, the Twitter Files, explains *The Federalist*'s John Daniel Davidson, "contain multitudes, but for the sake of brevity let us consider . . . the suppression of the Hunter Biden laptop story, the suspension of [Donald] Trump, and the deputization of Twitter by the FBI. Together, these stories reveal not just a social media company willing to do the bidding of an out-of-control federal bureaucracy, but a federal bureaucracy openly hostile to the First Amendment."[30] Twitter executives censored President Trump, conservatives, scientists, medical doctors and experts, Republican politicians, authors, and many more—often at the behest of the Biden administration and pressure from powerful congressional Democrats.

FH argues that "Majoritarianism is [a] signal idea of many authoritarians [who use it for] the proposition that elections are winner-take-all affairs in which the victor has an absolute mandate, with little or no interference from institutional checks and balances."[31]

Of course, this is evident in Democrat Party efforts to eliminate the Electoral College, which has as its purpose to select presidents and vice presidents based solely on the popular vote. This would result in Democrat Party–run metropolitan areas mostly on the East and West Coasts, where a significant and crucial population of the Democrat Party base reside, essentially controlling the outcome of these elections. No longer would states with smaller populations, rural areas, etc., have any effective say in the selection of presidents and vice presidents. Indeed, only nine states make up about 50 percent of the nation's population. Thus, representative government, where all areas of the country have a say in the conduct of the national government, would end. Tens of millions of people would be without meaningful input in governmental affairs—most of whom just happen to be Republicans and Independents. Representative government would be over for tens of millions of American citizens.

Moreover, to underscore what was pointed out earlier, the Democrat Party seeks to pack the Senate with more Democrats by adding Puerto Rico and Washington, D.C., as new states, producing four more Democrat senators; eliminating the Senate filibuster rule, thereby enabling a simple majority to make enduring changes to the country; and, expanding and packing the Supreme Court, thereby turning the Court and ultimately the law into a powerful ideological and political tool for enforcing Democrat Party dogma. These are the tactics and actions of a party seeing absolute power.

Meanwhile, even if the Democrat Party were to lose elections, as I explained, it has built a massive bureaucratic complex of departments and agencies, staffed by an army of nearly two million federal employees, the vast majority of whom are Democrats committed to the Democrat Party agenda, and whose purpose is to expand its own authority over the public and issue rules and regulations mostly supportive of the Democrat Party's ideological schemes.

FH notes that "[a] number of countries have undertaken a refashioning [rewriting] of history to buttress the legitimacy and aims of the current government."[32]

The revision of American history, to comport with the American Marxist agenda, is in full bloom, out in the open, and out of control. From the war against the nuclear family and the promotion of sexuality and perversion in public schools (starting in elementary school classes) to racial brainwashing and stereotyping in teacher training, seminars, classroom courses, textbooks, and the school libraries; resegregating students based on race; promoting economic socialism and "environmental justice" ("climate change" and anticapitalism); and, disemboweling America's founding, founders, Declaration of Independence, and Constitution, schools have become indoctrination mills operated by Democrat Party–affiliated teachers' unions on behalf of the Democrat Party and the American Marxist agenda.

Moreover, major media corporations celebrate, hire, and/or promote many of the most prominent radicals who preach anti-Americanism, racism, and false historical narratives on their large platforms. And these media outlets are aligned with the Democrat Party ideologically as well as in their employment practices, i.e., the hiring of prominent Democrats and those associated with them for news and commentary positions.[33] In fact, it is difficult to find any major issues where the Democrat Party and the overwhelming number of corporate media outlets diverge.

FH describes "[a] testament to the power of the democratic idea that authoritarian leaders around the globe have claimed the mantle of democracy for forms of government that amount to legalized repression."[34]

Hence, Joe Biden regularly frames arguments as between those who believe in democracy and those who promote autocracy. Fair enough, but he claims perversely that he is a democrat (lowercase "d") and that those who object to his power grabs are autocrats—a typical propaganda ruse employed by autocrats. Biden uses executive orders (EO) in violation of the Constitution's separation-of-powers doctrine (student loan cancellations) to destroy female athletic programs (in violation of Title IX), to defy immigration statutes, and to promote racial discrimination in the provision of federal funds and protection of equal rights ("equity" policies). Biden attempted to set up a "Disinformation Governance Board" (aka Ministry of Truth), and his FBI teamed with social media oligarchs to use the latter's platforms to censor, ban, and monitor those who questioned or disagreed with official government policies and to interfere in the 2020 election by, among other things, repudiating the Hunter Biden laptop story. The Biden Justice Department has threatened parents who protest at school board meetings—challenging CRT, pornographic material in school libraries, drag queen shows, the sexualizing of their children, and

other Democrat Party agendas taught to public school children—
and used armed SWAT teams to arrest pro-life protestors at their
homes for peacefully assembling at abortion clinics. Incredibly,
the FBI issued a warning about a growing overlap between white
nationalist groups and "Radical Traditionalist Catholics," such as
those preferring the traditional Latin Mass.[35]

FH writes about "[t]he illusion of pluralism. Yet just as with
other democratic institutions, modern authoritarians have mas-
tered the techniques of control over the electoral process, maintaining political dominance behind a screen of false diversity.
They have adapted in many ways to the age of the Internet and the
expectations of a better-informed public. In the most sophisti-
cated authoritarian states, professional political operatives—in
Russia they are called 'political technologists'—work just as hard
as their counterparts in the United States. Their goal, however, is
not to defeat opposition candidates in a competitive setting, but
rather to organize a system that creates the illusion of competition while squelching it in reality."[36]

 The Democrat Party has engaged in, and in numerous instances
implemented, obvious and blatant fraud-inducing techniques to
sabotage elections, and accused those who question these techniques as racist, supporters of voter suppression, and election
deniers. These efforts include eliminating voter identification laws;
eliminating signature and date requirements for absentee ballots;
universal mail-in voting; automatic voter registration; preregister-
ing voters under the age of eighteen; voter harvesting; voter drop
boxes; early voting; extended voting; illegal-alien voting in local
elections; the distribution of driver's licenses to illegal aliens; etc.
Since the objective of these recent changes to the election process
is intended to actually incorporate fraud into the law, it becomes
difficult if not impossible to establish "evidence of fraud." Hence,
if you ask about the outcomes of elections that use one or more

of these voting devices, especially in close elections, you are said to be "an election denier." And if a Republican state legislature takes steps to repeal or reform these notorious election devices, the legislature is accused by the Democrat Party and its surrogates of racism—"Jim Crow 2.0."[37]

Of course, FH had no intention of applying its formulation to the United States and particularly the Democrat Party. But it applies nonetheless. As I explained at length in *American Marxism*, the underlying ideology in the modern cultural revolution in the United States is, as Ludwig von Mises once wrote, "[t]he ideas of Marx, and his philosophy [which] truly dominate our age. The interpretation of current events and the interpretation of history in popular books, as well as in philosophical writings, novels, plays, and so forth, are by and large Marxist."[38]

As will become clear, today the Democrat Party is the political and institutional home for this ideology in its Americanized forms. This is due, in significant part, to the fact that long ago the Democrat Party evolved into an anti-American political and cultural entity. That is not to say there are no Democrat Party officials and, of course, party members who are patriots. However, they are increasingly the exception to the rule. At the highest levels of the Democrat Party are individuals who are dragging our nation into their "Marxist paradise."

People ask me all the time, "Why is this happening to our country? Don't these Democrat politicians and their friends care about our country?" The answer is *power*. The power to rule over the citizenry and remake not just society but mankind into the kind of image that these would-be masterminds prefer and demand. In other words, they do not share our values, beliefs, and principles. They have a totalitarian mind-set. This means the party must come before country, as the party is the means by which the country is to be conquered from within and ultimately ruled. It is essential to attaining, accumulating, retaining, and exercising power over the country. And it is the nature of autocratic parties around the world.

Of course, Americanism and Marxism are utterly incompatible. Americanism emphasizes unalienable, God-given individual rights; the right to life and liberty; natural law (that is, the existence of eternal truths and moral principles); a civil society (or social compact/contract) where there is equal justice under a just law and law and order to secure the safety and well-being of the citizenry; religious freedom; limited government; representative government; private property rights; free speech and the competition of ideas; freedom of association; the right to bear arms; etc. Marxism rejects these fundamental principles and values, and demands, in practice, the centralization of power over things small and large; control over the individual; conformity and obedience; uniformity of ideas and thought; and, an elaborate, intrusive, and far-reaching police state to enforce its rule. This also describes the nature and character of the Democrat Party.

The Democrat Party has become the political and operational organism through which American Marxism functions—just as earlier in our history it was the party of the Confederacy and slavery, segregation and the Ku Klux Klan, and Jim Crow. In more recent times, it has adapted and tailored Marxist ideology to American governance and politics. In so doing, the Democrat Party has adopted what some call a "passive" or "quiet" revolutionary approach—that is, as the late Italian communist Antonio Gramsci argued, "a long march through [America's cultural] institutions," where intellectuals (broadly defined) would populate these institutions, slowly but surely radicalize them, soften existing societal morals, and ultimately destroy the culture and restructure society.[39] Indeed, Gramsci asserted: "Socialism is precisely the religion that must overwhelm Christianity. . . . In the new order,

Socialism will triumph by first capturing the culture via infiltration of schools, universities, churches, and the media by transforming the consciousness of society."[40] Although Gramsci urged subterfuge and deceit, he did not oppose force or violence employed strategically and wisely. This is the Democrat Party's script.

The Frankfurt School and Herbert Marcuse's Marxist teachings have spread throughout our educational institutions as well. Marcuse, long considered a fringe figure, also argued for "working against the established institutions while working in them."[41] Both Gramsci and Marcuse believed that Marxist intellectuals needed to appeal to and work with society's disenchanted, disparate radical activists and groups, ethnic and labor organizations, as well as draw in the broader "working class" population by hook or by crook.

Saul Alinsky, a Marxist and Gramsci fan, wrote *Rules for Radicals: A Pragmatic Primer for Realistic Radicals*, based essentially on Gramsci's approach. Importantly, Alinsky was a key mentor to Hillary Clinton, who in 1969 wrote her ninety-two-page senior thesis on Alinsky at Wellesley College; and his writings were extremely influential with a young community activist, Barack Obama. Obviously, these are two of the most prominent Democrat Party leaders in the last thirty years. Of course, Obama was a short-term senator before quickly ascending to the presidency for two terms, and Clinton was a first lady, senator, secretary of state, and Democrat Party presidential candidate.

In the opening paragraph of his book, Alinsky writes: "What follows is for those who want to change the world from what it is to what they believe it should be. *The Prince* was written by Machiavelli for the Haves on how to hold power. *Rules for Radicals* is written for the Have-Nots on how to take it away."[42] He added: "To build a powerful organization takes time. It is tedious, but that's the way the game is played—if you want to play and not just yell, 'Kill the umpire.' What is the alternative to working 'inside' the system? A mess of rhetorical garbage about 'Burn the system down!' Yippie yells of 'Do it!' or 'Do your thing.' What else? Bombs? Sniping? Silence when police are killed and screams of 'murdering fascist pigs.' When others are killed? Attacking and baiting the police? . . . Lenin was a pragmatist; when he returned to what was then Petrograd from exile, he said that the Bolsheviks stood for getting power through the ballot but would reconsider after they got the guns!"[43]

Alinsky bluntly explained that "[a]ny revolutionary change must be preceded by a passive, affirmative, non-challenging attitude toward change among the mass of people." Alinsky called this the "reformation" of revolution and "practical revolution." I call it a sleazy deception of a steady but quiet Marxist revolution. Again, it also explains the approach of the Democrat Party.

Alinsky's rules for balkanizing and dividing society, undermining faith in America's institutions, and laying the groundwork for revolution have had a gravely deleterious effect on the nation's civility, rule of law, and tranquility. Here are his rules:

1. Power is not only what you have but what the enemy thinks you have.

2. Never go outside the expertise of your people.

3. Whenever possible go outside the expertise of the enemy.

4. Make the enemy live up to its own book of rules.

5. Ridicule is man's most potent weapon. There is no defense. It is almost impossible to counterattack ridicule. Also, it infuriates the opposition, who then react to your advantage.

6. A good tactic is one your people enjoy.

7. A tactic that drags on too long becomes a drag.

8. Keep the pressure on.

9. The threat is usually more terrifying than the thing itself.

10. The major premise for tactics is the development of operations that will maintain a constant pressure upon the opposition.

11. If you push a negative hard and deep enough it will break through into its counter side; this is based on the principle that every positive has its negative.

12. The price of a successful attack is a constructive alternative.

13. Pick the target, freeze it, personalize it, and polarize it.[44]

Obama was also mentored by Frank Marshall Davis. During the time Obama was in high school, college, and a community activist in Chicago, few people were as close to him as Davis. As Professor Paul Kengor recounts, "Davis joined Communist Party USA in Chicago during World War II (his Party number was 47544). He became extremely active in Party circles and even wrote for and was the founding editor-in-chief of the Communist Party publication there, the *Chicago Star*. He left Chicago in 1948 for Hawaii, where he would write for the Party publication there, the *Honolulu Record*. Those writings reveal a man fully loyal to the Soviet Union and the Communist Party line, and often bear an uncanny resemblance to Obama's own rhetoric, whether Davis was bashing Wall Street, big oil, big banks, corporate executives and their 'excess profits' and 'greed' and their 'fat contracts,' the wealthy and 'millionaires,' GOP tax cuts that 'spare the rich,' and on and on."[45]

Another leading influence in the Democrat Party is, of course, Sen. Bernie Sanders. Despite more recent efforts to mainstream himself, Sanders, who nearly won the Democrat Party nomination for president in 2020 and whose issue papers have served as the revolutionary blueprint for the Biden administration, has spent his entire life as a Marxist activist.[46] Although he is treated as a kind of elder statesman of the Democrat Party, his record in Marxist movements and activities, and in support of repressive communist regimes and causes, is so extensive, it would require far too many pages in this book to elaborate. That said, Sanders has praised genocidal communist regimes in the old Soviet Union, Cuba, Nicaragua, etc., called for the government takeover of most industries, and offered "a 21st Century Economic Bill of Rights" that could have been lifted straight from Joseph Stalin's 1936 Soviet Constitution.[47]

These are but a few of the "stars" in the Democrat Party. As you can see, this is a top-down, elitist-driven movement, just as Gramsci encouraged. For example, Clinton graduated from Yale Law School, Obama from Harvard Law School, and Sanders from the University of Chicago, hardly part of the proletariat. Again, no less than Vladimir Lenin, who led the Russian Revolution in 1917, believed in a top-down revolution as well, which he called "democratic centralization." Of course, there was nothing democratic about it. Most Russians were not communist revolutionaries when the czar was toppled. Lenin insisted that the masses must be led by the few and, of course, he was first among equals. Moreover, Lenin preached that the party must be the monolithic structure through which every aspect of society is managed. And that all citizens must adhere to the party program. He did not believe in the natural attraction of Marxist ideology to the masses but, instead, exercised the use of an iron fist to impose the party's agenda on the population. All public resistance must be broken; there could be no tolerance for opposition; and, all aspects of life were subject to the will and whims of the Communist Party–controlled state. Furthermore, truth and justice are to be defined by what serves the best interests of the party.[48]

To be clear, I am not arguing that every Democrat Party leader, operative, or surrogate is schooled in, or an adherent to, the fine points and details of Marx, Gramsci, Marcuse, Alinsky, Lenin, or anyone else. However, several among the elites, who have clawed their way to the very top of the power scale, are clearly informed by and familiar with these views. Others are collaborators or sympathizers with them, and are often surrounded by advisers and activists who are committed ideologues. Put another way, and more succinctly, the Democrat Party today is more Leninist than Jeffersonian, more Marxism than Americanism.

Inevitably, the Democrat Party's infinite cultural, economic, and political interventions, always in the name of the people and some virtuous and worthy cause, lead to the steady decline of liberty, to the steady rise of totalitarianism—and to the exploitation of the people. Fewer and fewer masterminds, with an ever-increasing army of bureaucrats and enforcers, reign over the citizenry and decide what is and is not good for them. The abuses of power are limitless, as are the justifications. And slowly but surely, the people get used to it, even vote for it, until one day its grip is too tight. Then it is too late. The police state is not known to retreat peacefully.

Moreover, the Democrat Party, as the state party, is supported by a state media that poses as a free press. The state media are no less devious and diabolical than the party they promote and like other propagandists, they are skilled at deceit and deception on behalf of the cause. More on this topic in Chapter 4.

Every time the Democrat Party wins an election, whether at the school board or mayoral level, or governorship or presidency, it becomes even more powerful and dangerous. Totalitarianism through the ballot box is not new. Even now, Democrat Party electoral victories further empower the administrative state and its appointed judicial oligarchs, who hold what is as close to permanent governing authority without checks or personal consequence as mankind has ever invented. Indeed, the Democrat Party makes the most of its electoral victories, both in its efforts to enshrine electoral changes that advantage it and to strengthen and expand the unelected part of the government that is appended to it. Increasingly, Republican Party victories, while deeply troubling and intolerable to Democrat Party officials, are seen as fleeting interludes in the long march to what is effectively the hardening of one-party Democrat control of the government. Nonetheless, like all autocratic parties, the Democrat Party and its media and other surrogates relentlessly pursue Republican victors with all manner of tactics and sabotage, for they must pay a huge personal and professional price for daring to challenge, let alone win, an election and disrupt one-party Democrat Party rule.

For example, Richard Nixon was forced to resign for doing far less than Franklin Roosevelt, John Kennedy, or Lyndon Johnson and their weaponizing of the IRS, FBI, and later the CIA; Ronald Reagan was pursued over the so-called Iran-Contra matter, which was nothing, compared to Barack Obama's $1.7 billion cash payment and nuclear deal with the Iranian regime; and, of course, the endless political and criminal pursuit of Donald Trump by the Democrat Party is unprecedented. In this, and virtually all else it does, the Democrat Party's loathing of America is limitless.

CHAPTER TWO

ANTI-BLACK RACISM & ANTI-SEMITISM

The Civil War was not only a breathtakingly bloody dispute between the North and the South, the Union and the Confederacy, and antislavery and proslavery forces, but a battle between the Republican Party and the Democrat Party—the latter conflict of which is rarely mentioned and certainly not emphasized. Indeed, for major elements of the Democrat Party, the Civil War did not end in 1865. It never ended. Despite the best efforts of its party apparatchiks, academic surrogates, and media propagandists to ignore, spin, or obscure the horrendous story of the Democrat Party's past—from the Ku Klux Klan and lynchings to segregation, Jim Crow laws, voter intimidation, etc.—the Democrat Party had a hand in all of it. In fact, Jefferson Davis, the president of the Confederacy, was a Democrat, as were virtually all the leaders and generals of the Confederacy. Confederate general Nathan Bedford Forrest, a Democrat, became the first grand wizard of the Ku Klux Klan after the Civil War, which he helped found to terrorize the newly freed slaves and gut Reconstruction, and which Republican president Ulysses S. Grant sought to destroy by deploying the U.S. Army. Grant's efforts were stymied after the Democrat Party won a majority in the House of Representatives, which cut his support.

A few decades later, among the leading so-called progressive intellectuals (American Marxists) of the late 1800s and early 1900s was Woodrow Wilson, a prominent Democrat who was president of Princeton University and would become governor of New Jersey. Wilson was an accomplished racist activist. "In his academic work on American history, Wilson was friendly to the Ku Klux Klan's mission of suppressing blacks, and he was forgiving of its terror tactics," explains Williamson M. Evers in *Education Weekly*.[1] "When he was the president of Princeton, Wilson expressed his pride that no African-American students had been admitted during his tenure."[2] As governor, in 1911 Wilson signed into law a eugenics bill titled "An ACT to authorize and provide for the sterilization of feeble-minded (including idiots, imbeciles and morons), epileptics, rapists, certain criminals and other defectives," which was later struck down by the New Jersey Supreme Court.[3]

What is eugenics? As current Princeton University professor Thomas C. Leonard writes, "Eugenics describes a movement to improve human heredity by the social control of human breeding, based on the assumption that differences in human intelligence, character and temperament are largely due to differences in heredity."[4] It was also fundamentally and inherently a horrific racist and bigoted justification for literally thinning out minority populations.

Wilson's backing for eugenics was common among progressives. Indeed, progressivism and eugenics were interdependent. "Progressive Era eugenics was, in fact, the broadest of churches," states Leonard. "It was mainstream; it was popular to the point of faddishness; it was supported by leading figures in the newly emerging science of genetics; it appealed to an extraordinary range of political ideologies, not just progressives; and it survived the Nazis. . . . Eugenic ideas were not new in the Progressive Era, but they acquired new impetus with the Progressive Era advent of a more expansive government. In effect, the expansion of state power meant that it became possible to have not only eugenic thought, but also eugenic practice."[5] Why? By their lights, what better way to improve society than to improve human heredity and socially manage reproduction. In fact, tens of thousands of Americans were sterilized against their will.

It is little noted that the American eugenics movement "influenced Adolf Hitler and his policies and ultimately contributed to the Holocaust. . . ." as reported by no less than PBS.[6]

In its report, PBS spoke to historian Daniel Kevles, who explained: "People tend to think that eugenics was a doctrine that originated with the Nazis, that it was grounded in wild claims that were far outside the scientific mainstream. Both of those impressions are fundamentally not true."[7]

Historian Jonathan Spiro added that "[t]he United States has the reputation of being on the forefront of scientific endeavor. When Adolf Hitler was in prison, he read Madison Grant's *The Passing of the Great Race*, wrote Madison Grant a fan letter saying, 'This book is my bible,' and when he wrote *Mein Kampf*, his autobiography, he said, 'We Germans must emulate what the Americans are doing.'"[8]

Grant, an American lawyer, wrote his book in 1916. It was the first book published by the Nazi regime. The book is a racist screed filled with pseudoscientific claims about the American superiority of the "Nordic race."

To be clear, the eugenics movement, and the "scientific" application of eugenics as creating a superior governing system, was promoted by the so-called Progressives and the Democrat Party, and led to the idea of creating a superior race of people by culling the population. Moreover, like most racists and racist theories, Grant insisted that historical and current events evolve around race rather than other social, economic, or cultural issues. The same emphasis on this dangerously perverse, racist ideological approach is the lens through which the American Marxist movements insist we view America today—but with a different set of victims. More on this in Chapter 3.

One of the most avid and influential advocates of eugenics was Margaret Sanger, the founder of Planned Parenthood, which has had deep ties to the Democrat Party for a century and has been funded with billions of federal taxpayer dollars for decades. Indeed, any present-day attempts to reduce the group's tax subsidies is met with howls of objections from congressional Democrats.

Who was Margaret Sanger? Sanger has been celebrated as an early feminist and "birth control pioneer." But she was much more than that. Sanger was an ardent racist. She spoke to the women's auxiliary of the Klan in New Jersey. She supported the forcible sterilization of "unfit" women. And Sanger made many documented racist declarations throughout her life. For example, she wrote: "Eugenics is . . . the most adequate and thorough avenue to the solution of racial, political and social problems."[9] She argued that "[b]irth control is not contraception indiscriminately and thoughtlessly practiced. It means the release and cultivation of the better racial elements in our society, and gradual suppression, elimination and eventual expiration of defective stocks—those human weeds which threaten the blooming of the finest flowers of American civilization."[10] Nonetheless, Planned Parenthood praised Sanger for decades, conferring its "highest award," the Margaret Sanger Award, on a long list of recipients, including Hillary Clinton, who proudly accepted it. Not until 2000 did Planned Parenthood begin to distance itself finally and reluctantly from Sanger's racial eugenics, but only after a torrent of criticism.

Like Sanger, for the longest time Wilson's racism was mostly blue-penciled or softened by historians, the media, and the Democrat Party until more recently because he was a crucial "progressive reformer" and hyper-globalist. He was also the first Democrat since Andrew Jackson in 1832 to win two consecutive presidential terms (1913–1921). The Democrat Party and its surrogates could not politically afford to abandon him, let alone condemn him. They were invested in him. After all, Wilson reestablished the federal income tax, created the Federal Reserve and Federal Trade Commission, was generally antibusiness and pro–organized labor, and so forth. In other words, Wilson was the truly first president, and a Democrat at that, to widely institute the kind of administrative-state governance, supposedly relying on "scientific" and expert knowledge, that progressivism demands. Moreover, for Wilson and his ilk, the inferiority of blacks was a scientific fact about which the administrative state should take note in its reengineering of society. That is, if you are going to establish a society in which the best and brightest are to be in charge, from Wilson's perspective, inferior races must be taken into account and denied such top positions or significant influence.

Furthermore, Wilson, like so many Progressive Era Democrats and intellectuals, believing blacks to be an inferior race, opposed black suffrage and supported various insidious efforts in predominantly southern states to limit their influence at the ballot box and in politics and society overall for essentially the same reason they supported racial eugenics—that is, they believed it was impossible for government to more expertly and perfectly manage society given the influences of a supposedly inferior race. Thus, they believed they were justified and even compelled to use social and economic regulation to minimize black influence.

Consequently, as president, Wilson overturned decades of racial progress made under prior Republican administrations, set-

ting back race relations for half a century. For example, Wilson
brought Jim Crow to the federal government and helped intro-
duce it to areas of the North and spread it throughout the country by resegregating federal departments and agencies, including
hiring practices, work areas, and even segregating restrooms and
lunchrooms. Beginning in 1914, Wilson required applicants for
federal civil service jobs to provide photographs for the first time
to block the hiring of blacks. Wilson appointed racists and segregationists to his cabinet and throughout the highest levels of the
federal government. Wilson fired black federal administrators, was
openly sympathetic to the Klan, opposed black suffrage, and not
only screened the racist movie *The Birth of a Nation* at the White
House (the movie was adapted from the book *The Clansman*),
but racist diatribes from his own book, *A History of the American
People*, were prominently featured in title cards in the movie.[11]

"The policy of the congressional leaders wrought . . . a
veritable overthrow of civilization in the South . . . in their
determination to 'put the white South under the heel of
the black South.'"[12]

"The white men were roused by a mere instinct of
self-preservation . . . until at last there had sprung into
existence a great Ku Klux Klan, a veritable empire of the
South, to protect the southern country."[13]

"Adventurers swarmed out of the North, as much the
enemies of one race as of the other, to cozen, beguile and
use the negroes. . . . In the villages the negroes were the
office holders, men who knew none of the uses of authority,
except its insolences."[14]

Progressive Era Democrats like Wilson rejected the Declaration
of Independence's references to individual unalienable rights,

transcendent natural law, eternal truths and values, and divine influence, which are the fundamental ideals undergirding American society and the establishment of our country. Why? Because the Declaration, properly understood, rejects both the progressive (Marxist) ideology and Democrat Party racism. In fact, the former explains, in part, why Barack Obama and Ketanji Brown Jackson shun the Declaration.

As Abraham Lincoln explained in his famous Lewistown, Illinois, speech on August 17, 1858: "'We hold these truths to be self-evident: that all men are created equal; that they are endowed by their Creator with certain unalienable rights; that among these are life, liberty and the pursuit of happiness.' This was their [the founders'] majestic interpretation of the economy of the Universe. This was their lofty, and wise, and noble understanding of the justice of the Creator to His creatures. Yes, gentlemen, to *all* His creatures, to the whole great family of man. In their enlightened belief, nothing stamped with the Divine image and likeness was sent into the world to be trodden on, and degraded, and imbruted by its fellows. They grasped not only the whole race of man then living, but they reached forward and seized upon the farthest posterity. They erected a beacon to guide their children and their children's children, and the countless myriads who should inhabit the earth in other ages. Wise statesmen as they were, they knew the tendency of prosperity to breed tyrants, and so they established these great self-evident truths, that when in the distant future some man, some faction, some interest, should set up the doctrine that none but rich men, or none but white men, were entitled to life, liberty and the pursuit of happiness, their posterity might look up again to the Declaration of Independence and take courage to renew the battle which their fathers began—so that truth, and justice, and mercy, and all the humane and Christian virtues might not be extinguished from the land; so that no man would hereafter dare to limit and circumscribe the great principles on which the temple of liberty was being built.

"Now, my countrymen, if you have been taught doctrines con-flicting with the great landmarks of the Declaration of Indepen-dence; if you have listened to suggestions which would take away from its grandeur, and mutilate the fair symmetry of its propor-tions; if you have been inclined to believe that all men are *not* created equal in those inalienable rights enumerated by our chart of liberty, let me entreat you to come back. Return to the fountain whose waters spring close by the blood of the Revolution. . . ."[15]

Wilson and the progressives saw America quite differently from Republican Lincoln, the "Great Emancipator," and our country's founders. In 1907, Wilson wrote:

So far as the Declaration of Independence was a theoreti-cal document, that is its theory. Do we still hold it? Does the doctrine of the Declaration of Independence still live in our principles of action, in the things we do, in the pur-poses we applaud, in the measures we approve? It is not a question of piety. We are not bound to adhere to the doc-trines held by the signers of the Declaration of Indepen-dence; we are as free as they were to make and unmake governments. We are not here to worship men or a docu-ment. But neither are we here to indulge in a mere rhetorical and uncritical eulogy. Every Fourth of July should be a time for examining our standards, our purposes, for determining afresh what principles, what forms of power we think most likely to effect our safety and happiness. That and that alone is the obligation the Declaration lays upon us. It is no fetish; its words lay no compulsion upon the thought of any free man; but it was drawn by men who thought, and it obliges those who receive its benefits to think likewise.[16]

And in a July 4, 1914, speech at Independence Hall, Wilson declared that "[t]here is nothing in [the Declaration] for us unless we can translate it into the terms of our own conditions and of our own lives. We must reduce it to what the lawyers call a bill of particulars. It contains a bill of particulars, but the bill of particulars of 1776. If we would keep it alive, we must fill it with a bill of particulars of the year 1914."[17]

Wilson's contempt for the principles undergirding the Declaration is embraced by leading Democrats today. For example, when asked if she believes in the Declaration's proclamation about natural rights during her confirmation hearing, Associate Justice Ketanji Brown Jackson answered, "I do not hold a position on whether individuals possess natural rights."[18] Jackson could not openly disavow the Declaration, lest she face a Republican filibuster in the Senate against her confirmation. Nonetheless, she, like Wilson and others, refused to endorse it.

The Declaration of Independence and the Democrat Party are fundamentally incompatible. For Wilson and progressives since, the supposed scientific ability of Marxist masterminds to manage and manipulate society, government, and economics necessarily requires controlling the individual and compelling his conformity and compliance with the "collective will" and the best interests of "the communal," as determined and dictated by the self-anointed ruling-class elites. Thus, it is necessary to dehumanize the individual or at least deemphasize him, which fundamentally reverses the very purpose of America's founding, and group individuals into various manageable categories based on economics, gender, religion, and, of course, race. Conformism and standardization replace free will, self-determination, and self-sufficiency. Traditions, customs, and institutions must be eradicated.

In 1913, Wilson wrote *The New Freedom*, in which he proclaimed: "We are in the presence of a new organization of society. Our life has broken away from the past. The life of America is not the life it was twenty years ago; it is not the life that it was ten years ago. We have changed our economic conditions, absolutely, from top to bottom; and, with our economic society, the organization of life. The old political formulas do not fit the present problems; they read now like documents taken from a forgotten age. The older cries sound as if they belonged to a past age which men have almost forgotten. . . ."[19] Obama, Sanders, Biden, et al. express these same sentiments as Wilson did.

As Associate Justice Neil Gorsuch pointed out in a recent Supreme Court decision, "Woodrow Wilson famously argued that 'popular sovereignty' 'embarrasse[d]' the Nation because it made it harder to achieve 'executive expertness.' In Wilson's eyes, the mass of the people were 'selfish, ignorant, timid, stubborn, or foolish.' He expressed even greater disdain for particular groups, defending '[t]he white men of the South' for 'rid[ding] themselves, by fair means or foul, of the intolerable burden of governments sustained by the votes of ignorant [black Americans].' He likewise denounced immigrants 'from the south of Italy and men of the meaner sort out of Hungary and Poland,' who possessed 'neither skill nor energy nor any initiative of quick intelligence.' To Wilson, our Republic 'tr[ied] to do too much by vote.'"[20]

The modern Democrat Party remains an authoritarian political and societal enterprise, for which its conceit and self-righteousness know few limits, and its self-appointed experts seek to lord over their fellow man. The rejiggering of society and social engineering are unending and increasingly intrusive, the practice and legalization of abuses of power are more ambitious and pervasive in order to impose and enforce increasingly unpopular and unjust rule, and constant turmoil and tumult are used to confound the public and promote fissures among the citizenry. Tyranny is thus planned and ultimately predictable. Again, in 2008, shortly before winning election to the presidency, Barack Obama declared that "we are five days away from fundamentally transforming the United States of America. . . ."[21] Transforming it into what? This sounds a lot like Wilson's "new organization of society" writings.

In 2016, at the Democratic National Convention, and announcing his endorsement of Hillary Clinton for president, Bernie Sanders shouted: "Together, we have begun a political revolution to transform America, and that revolution continues. Together, we will continue to fight for a government which represents all of us and not just the one per cent."[22] Exactly what kind of government does the "Democratic-Socialist" have in mind? In 2020, President Biden proclaimed that "we have an incredible opportunity to not just dig out of this crisis [COVID-19], but to fundamentally transform the country."[23] Again, transform it into what? This has been the Democrat Party's mantra for at least the past 130 years.

The Democrats of the earlier Progressive Era and the Democrats of the present day share contempt for the American experiment and the American people. In 2008, at a San Francisco fundraiser, Obama proclaimed that people in small-town America were "bitter, they cling to guns or religion or antipathy toward people who aren't like them or anti-immigrant sentiment or anti-trade sentiment as a way to explain their frustrations."[24]

The Declaration's essential, founding principles, especially the emphasis on the individual, conflict with the Democrat Party's political purposes and obsession with power, and always have. It naturally follows, therefore, that during much of American history, the Democrat Party has sought to pervert and dismember our governing document as well, the Constitution, and republicanism generally, inasmuch as the Constitution is a bulwark against the ideologies and motivations for which the Democrat Party stands and has stood. Among other things, prominent Democrats have denounced or usurped, at various times, the Constitution's checks and balances, separation of powers, federalism, the Electoral College, the Commerce Clause, and the Bill of Rights—or have trashed the Constitution entirely as an old document written by slaveholders. Today, the Democrat Party's denunciation of America's founders, the Constitution's framers, and American history itself has been relentless. More on this later in the book.

The Democrat Party's greatest hero is Franklin Roosevelt, largely due to his New Deal agenda and its highly successful transformation of the United States away from constitutionalism and capitalism toward a centralized, socialist state. Indeed, the Great Depression provided Roosevelt, more than any president until his time, with the opportunity to fundamentally alter the prism through which national governance was and would be viewed. Even more than Wilson, Roosevelt altered the role of the American government. Roosevelt created a labyrinth of agencies, departments, programs, subsidies, etc. Henceforth, human improvement and progress would be measured not by actual outcomes and success, but by the extent to which government could be expanded, personal and economic freedom could be curbed through legislation, regulation, and taxation—and, significantly, altering the relationship between the individual and the government. Again, more on this later. But for this reason, Roosevelt's reputation has been mostly spared criticism more than virtually any other public figure, dead or alive, for the racist, bigoted, lawless, and unconstitutional aspects of his true legacy. Indeed, the number of books and documentaries celebrating Roosevelt, and distorting his record, seem infinite.

Let us add some truth to Roosevelt's record. For example, in 1942, after Imperial Japan's attack on Pearl Harbor, Roosevelt issued Executive Order 9066, in which 120,000 Japanese Americans, including 70,000 United States citizens, were forcibly relocated by the U.S. Army to internment camps in remote parts of the country. They lost their homes, property, and liberties.[25] In fact, well before Japan's attack on Pearl Harbor, resulting in the United States entering World War II, the David S. Wyman Institute's Rafael Medoff explains that "[i]n a series of articles from 1923 to 1925, FDR railed against 'non-assimilable' immigrants from the Far East. 'Japanese immigrants are not capable of assimilation into the American population. . . . Anyone who has traveled in the Far East knows that the mingling of Asiatic blood with European or American blood produces, in nine cases out of ten, the most unfortunate results.'"[26]

In 1944, in *Korematsu v. United States*, the Supreme Court, the majority of whose members were appointed by Roosevelt, upheld the internment order in a 6–3 decision. Associate Justice Hugo Black, writing for the majority, said, in part: "Compulsory exclusion of large groups of citizens from their homes, except under circumstances of direst emergency and peril, is inconsistent with our basic governmental institutions. But when, under conditions of modern warfare, our shores are threatened by hostile forces, the power to protect must be commensurate with the threatened danger."[27] However, there was no threat that these Japanese Americans, including children and infants, posed any such danger.

In truth, Japanese Americans fought bravely during World War II. As the Densho Encyclopedia explains: "Much decorated for their valor and often cited as being part of the most decorated unit in World War II for its size and length of service, Japanese Americans served in the U.S. armed forces in disproportionate numbers, despite having their loyalties questioned after the Japanese attack on Pearl Harbor. Though they mostly served in the segregated 442nd Regimental Combat Team and its predecessor, the 100th Infantry Battalion, others served as translators and interpreters in the Military Intelligence Service."[28]

Who was Hugo Black, the justice who authored the *Korematsu* decision? Black rose through the Democrat Party ranks in Alabama, was a lawyer for the Ku Klux Klan in the 1920s (from which he later resigned, but whose leaders he continued to work with), and was elected to the United States Senate in 1926. He opposed the 1934 Wagner-Costigan antilynching bill and was an intensely loyal supporter of Roosevelt and the New Deal.[29] In 1937, Black was rewarded by Roosevelt as his first nominee to the Supreme Court. His overall record as a justice is mixed and disputed, as he was an activist for Roosevelt's economic socialism, but he also insisted on a strict interpretation of the Bill of Rights, but with notable exceptions—like the *Korematsu* decision. That said, Hugo Black Jr., Black's son, recalling the appeal of the Klan to his father, stated that "[t]he Ku Klux Klan and Daddy, so far as I could tell, had one thing in common. He suspected the Catholic Church. . . . He thought the Pope and the bishops had too much power and property. . . ."[30]

A Republican president, Ronald Reagan, signed into law the Civil Liberties Act of 1988, which provided a restitution payment of $20,000 to the 60,000 surviving Japanese Americans who had been unconstitutionally imprisoned in internment camps by Roosevelt. Reagan declared: "For throughout the war, Japanese-Americans in the tens of thousands remained utterly loyal to the United States. Indeed, scores of Japanese-Americans volunteered for our Armed Forces, many stepping forward in the internment camps themselves. The 442d Regimental Combat Team, made up entirely of Japanese-Americans, served with immense distinction to defend this nation, their nation. Yet back at home, the soldiers' families were being denied the very freedom for which so many of the soldiers themselves were laying down their lives."[31]

Importantly, these payments were made *directly* to those who were actually harmed by Roosevelt's racist directive, not to their progeny or individuals several generations removed from their internment.

It is, therefore, shameful that even today the Democrat Party, and its surrogates at Harvard and the University of North Carolina, would stoop to using racially discriminatory admissions policies specifically targeting Asian Americans for exclusion. In the recent Supreme Court decision in *Students for Fair Admissions, Inc. v. President and Fellows of Harvard College*, the Court by 6–2 (Justice Jackson recused herself respecting Harvard but voted with the minority by 6–3 respecting UNC), overturned their racist policies. Chief Justice John Roberts, writing for the majority, said in part:

> . . . [t]he Harvard and UNC admissions programs cannot be reconciled with the guarantees of the Equal Protection Clause. Both programs lack sufficiently focused and measurable objectives warranting the use of race, unavoidably employ race in a negative manner, involve racial stereotyping, and lack meaningful end points. We have never permitted admissions programs to work in that way, and we will not do so today.[32]

Thus, but for the Republican-appointed conservatives on the Supreme Court, these racist higher education policies would remain today—and be sanctioned by the Court's Democrats.

Indeed, in his concurring opinion, Clarence Thomas reminds us that Harvard, Yale, and Princeton instituted a similarly racist admissions policy in the 1920s against Jews. During this same period, Thomas notes that "Harvard played a prominent role in the eugenics movement. According to then president Abbott Lawrence Lowell, excluding Jews from Harvard would help maintain admissions opportunities for Gentiles and perpetuate the purity of the Brahmin race . . . "[33]

The Supreme Court's decisions was roundly condemned by Democrat Party officials, the Democrat Party media, and, of course, the universities. Biden proclaimed: "I strongly, strongly, disagree with the Court's decision . . . This is not a normal court."[34]

Looking back again, when Roosevelt's civil rights record toward blacks is scrutinized, it is not as generally described by historians and professors supportive of the New Deal and Roosevelt's socialist economic policies. In fact, it is deeply troubling. For example, Roosevelt established the Federal Housing Administration (FHA) in 1934. Its ostensible purpose was to insure mortgages, thereby promoting homeownership. However, it furthered racial segregation by specifically denying insurance in and around black neighborhoods. Incredibly, "the FHA was subsidizing builders who were mass-producing entire subdivisions for whites—with the requirement that none of the homes be sold to African-Americans. . . . The term 'redlining' . . . comes from the development by the New Deal, by the federal government of maps of every metropolitan area in the country. And those maps were color-coded by first the Home Owners Loan Corp. and then the Federal Housing Administration and then adopted by the Veterans Administration, and these color codes were designed to indicate where it was safe to insure mortgages. And anywhere where African-Americans lived, anywhere where African-Americans lived nearby were colored red to indicate to appraisers that these neighborhoods were too risky to insure mortgages."[35]

Roosevelt infamously and unceremoniously slighted the great black Olympian Jesse Owens. White athletes who had competed in the 1936 Berlin Olympics were later invited to meet the president at the White House. Owens, the star of those Olympics, was not. Owens complained that he was insulted. Asked if he was snubbed by Hitler at the Olympics (whom he had not met), Owens replied: "Hitler didn't snub me, it was FDR who snubbed me. The President didn't even send me a telegram." Owens campaigned for Roosevelt's Republican opponent, Alf Landon, when he returned from Europe.[36]

Even when the issue was the horror of lynching, Roosevelt refused to support federal antilynching legislation. In 1940, black heavyweight boxing champion Joe Louis endorsed Roosevelt's Republican opponent, Wendell Wilkie, explaining: "If Mr. Willkie is elected . . . he has promised in writing to put over the antilynching bill. Roosevelt has been in office for eight years and done nothing about that. The people in the North don't know how long is eight years."[37] Roosevelt feared he would lose Democrat Party support, especially in the South, and would not gain an unprecedented third term if he backed the bill. Therefore, it died, never to be successfully resurrected during the rest of his presidency. In that same year, Roosevelt refused to reintegrate the armed forces, which Wilson had resegregated.[38] The fact is that Roosevelt did little for the black community. Author Bruce Bartlett notes that "Roosevelt never used his political capital to do anything meaningful to help blacks. . . . [He] never spoke to the NAACP or gave a single speech devoted to black concerns, and even banned black reporters from White House press conferences."[39]

Rafael Medoff goes further, explaining that Roosevelt's personal prejudices appeared to influence his decision-making as well. He explained that "Roosevelt enlisted government resources to advance his ideas on racial engineering. In 1942, he commissioned three prominent anthropologists to study 'problems arising out of racial admixtures.' A senior White House aide instructed them: 'The President wishes to be advised what will happen when various kinds of Europeans—Scandinavian, Germanic, French-Belgian, North Italian, etc.—are mixed with the South American base stock.' Roosevelt also wanted to know, 'Is the South Italian stock—say Sicilian—as good as the North Italian stock—say Milanese—if given equal social and economic opportunity? . . . [If] 10,000 Italians were to be offered settlement facilities, what proportion of the 10,000 should be Northern Italians and what Southern Italians?'"[40] Even given all that was on Roosevelt's plate in 1942, he was focused on this.

What of Roosevelt's relationship with the Jewish community, which is often believed to have been admirable? Roosevelt had some prominent Jews advising him as president, including in his cabinet. But his more complete record respecting Jews has been censored in significant ways, or worse, embellished—even today in books and documentary films.[41]

In his March 1933 inaugural address, Roosevelt declared, in part: "We are stricken by no plague of locusts. Compared with the perils which our forefathers conquered because they believed and were not afraid, we have still much to be thankful for. Nature still offers her bounty and human efforts have multiplied it. Plenty is at our doorstep, but a generous use of it languishes in the very sight of the supply. Primarily this is because the rulers of the exchange of mankind's goods have failed, through their own stubbornness and their own incompetence, have admitted their failure, and abdicated. Practices of the *unscrupulous money changers* stand indicted in the court of public opinion, rejected by the hearts and minds of men. True they have tried, but their efforts have been cast in the pattern of an outworn tradition. Faced by failure of credit they have proposed only the lending of more money. Stripped of the lure of profit by which to induce our people to follow their false leadership, they have resorted to exhortations, pleading tearfully for restored confidence. They know only the rules of a generation of self-seekers. They have no vision, and when there is no vision, the people perish. The *money changers* have fled from their high seats in the temple of our civilization. We may now restore that temple to the ancient truths. The measure of the restoration lies in the extent to which we apply social values more noble than mere monetary profit."[42] (Italics are mine.)

The phrase "unscrupulous money changers" has been a damnable ethnic slur used against Jewish people since at least the twelfth century.[43] And given the significance of his first inaugural address, Roosevelt and his advisers knew this when they inserted the phrase twice in his speech.

Even more, Roosevelt's purposeful inaction during the Holocaust, to assist Jews being slaughtered by the millions, was contemptible and unconscionable. Medoff explains: "Here is the president who was regarded as a humanitarian, who portrayed himself as the champion of the little man, who had the power to save many Jews from the Holocaust but who—to quote Fowler Harper, the Solicitor General for the Interior Department in the 1940s— 'would not lift a finger' to help them. His was the administration that kept the immigration quotas 90% under-filled— meaning it could have saved 190,000 Jews under the existing quotas, without changing the immigration laws. His was the administration that sent planes to bomb German oil factories less than five miles from the gas chambers of Auschwitz, but refused to instruct them to drop bombs on the gas chambers, or the railway lines, even after receiving maps and detailed information about what was happening in the camp. His was the administration that refused to pressure the British to open the gates of Palestine so Jews could find refuge there."[44]

As I mentioned, Roosevelt had Jewish associates, however, notably the White House and particularly the State Department were populated with several infamous anti-Semites. At State, where the decisions about immigration and refugee issues were made, Roosevelt nearly always backed the bigots who blocked the migration of Jewish refugees into the United States from Germany and the rest of Europe during the height of the Holocaust. In fact, "[T]he US immigration quota from Germany was filled for the first time in 1939, and almost filled in 1940. In all other years of Nazi rule (1933–1945) the quota was not filled."[45] The person directly in charge of the visa process at State was Samuel Breckinridge Long, whom Roosevelt met and became good friends with when both served in the Woodrow Wilson administration. Long became a major donor to Roosevelt's presidential campaign in 1932 and was previously rewarded with an ambassadorship to Italy. "Long's dispatches to Washington from Rome praised the fascist Mussolini regime for its 'well-paved' streets, 'dapper' black-shirted stormtroopers, and 'punctual trains.'"[46] In his private diary, Long "described Hitler's Mein Kampf as 'eloquent in opposition to Jewry and Jews as exponents of Communism and chaos.'"[47]

Moreover, "Long regularly briefed . . . Roosevelt on his efforts to suppress [Jewish] immigration below the level allowed by existing law. In one diary entry from October 1940, Long mentioned meeting with FDR to discuss 'the whole subject of immigration, visas, safety of the United States, procedures to be followed,' and 'I found that he was 100% in accord with my ideas.'" Not until 1944, when Congress got wind of Long's doings and began to publicly raise concerns, was Long finally demoted and, ultimately, left the State Department.[48]

Throughout his life Roosevelt made blatantly bigoted private remarks about Jews. Although he is not alone among presidents in this regard, Roosevelt, as Medoff writes, "allowed his prejudices to influence his policies regarding America's response to the persecution of European Jewry."[49] Among other things, Roosevelt "blamed Polish Jews for anti-Semitism in Poland; spoke of the 'understandable complaints' of the Germans about the prominence of Jews in some professions; boasted to a colleague that '[w]e know we have no Jewish blood in our veins'; helped bring about a quota on Jewish students admitted to Harvard; and recommended that Jews be 'spread out thin' around the world so they would not dominate any particular economy or culture."[50]

Then there was Joseph P. Kennedy, the patriarch of the Kennedy clan and a powerful Democrat. He was a contemptible anti-Semite and pro–Third Reich, anti–Winston Churchill isolationist who undermined U.S. policy as ambassador to Britain. Eventually, Kennedy resigned as ambassador.

In the left-wing *Daily Beast*, Jacob Heilbrunn explains, with the help of David Nasaw's Kennedy biography, *The Patriarch*, that "[i]t was in Hollywood that Kennedy's mounting paranoia about Jews . . . manifested itself. Kennedy saw everything in terms of ethnic groups, partly as a result of his own upbringing in Boston. Nasaw explains that Kennedy suggested he would be 'Hollywood's white, or non-Jewish knight and rescue it from the suspicion that its pictures were not to be trusted because they were produced by men who through breeding and background were morally untrustworthy.' All his life Kennedy would remain convinced that Jews acted as a cabal to serve their common interests—a mind-set that would manifest itself most vividly in the run-up to World War II, when he blamed Jews for allegedly suborning . . . Roosevelt from pursuing the nation's best interests abroad.[51] There is a great deal more, but this is not a biography about Joe Kennedy.

About twenty years after Roosevelt's death, and less than sixty years ago, the 1964 Civil Rights Act—which essentially outlawed Jim Crow segregation and discrimination based on race, color, religion, sex, and national origin—was opposed by 69 percent of Senate Democrats (and supported by 82 percent of Senate Republicans) and opposed by 61 percent of House Democrats (and supported by 80 percent of House Republicans). Of those who voted no in the House, 74 percent were Democrats, and of those who voted no in the Senate 78 percent were Democrats.

The civil rights movement, and the federal government's actions in eventually supporting it—including the overwhelming majority of congressional Republicans—was compelled by the racist, segregationist practices and policies in the Democrat Party, which had continued one hundred years after the end of the Civil War. Among those who filibustered the legislation for some seventy days was West Virginia's Democrat senator Robert Byrd. Byrd spoke for over fourteen hours in a desperate, last-ditch effort to kill the bill. Yet Byrd would go on to serve as the Senate's Democrat leader from 1977 to 1989, including majority leader from 1977 to 1981 and 1987 to 1989, and minority leader from 1981 to 1987. He was chosen to serve in these powerful posts by his fellow Democrat senators. Byrd had come a long way. As a young man, he was a recruiter and organizer for the Klan in West Virginia.[52] When Byrd died, he was praised in glowing terms by the leading lights of the Democrat Party ruling class, including Joe Biden, Barack Obama, Bill Clinton, Hillary Clinton, and many other Democrat bigwigs. Several called him a "mentor," including Biden.

President Lyndon Johnson is credited for his support of the 1964 Civil Rights Act and the 1965 Voting Rights Act. Yet Johnson was notoriously and personally racist in many ways, including his constant use of the "N-word" throughout his lifetime, according to a long list of associates and staffers as well as audio recordings.[53] For example, in 1967, Johnson nominated Thurgood Marshall to the Supreme Court as its first black justice. Even so, Johnson biographer Robert Dallek writes that Johnson said he appointed Marshall rather than a less well-known black judge because "when I appoint a [N-word] to the bench, I want everybody to know he's a [N-word]."[54]

Moreover, up until 1957, Johnson biographer Robert A. Caro

notes that "[d]uring . . . twenty years [in Congress], [Johnson] had never supported civil rights legislation—any civil rights legislation. . . . [H]is record was an unbroken one of votes against every civil rights bill that had ever come to a vote: against voting rights bills; against bills that would have struck at job discrimination and at segregation in other areas of American life; even against bills that would have protected blacks from lynching."[55]

Although as Senate majority leader Johnson helped President Dwight Eisenhower pass the 1957 Civil Rights Act, he spent most of the year equivocating. Ultimately, Johnson succeeded in pressuring the Eisenhower administration to weaken the bill at the behest of his southern colleagues and by threatening to kill it altogether. He also needed to change his position on civil rights because he was seriously eyeing a run for the presidency in 1960.[56] Johnson was able to diminish the bill's enforcement strength and subsequently supported the bill, allowing him to have it both ways politically.

Conversely, in 1957, Republican Eisenhower, in an unprecedented presidential act, ordered federal troops to enforce the integration of Central High School in Little Rock, Arkansas, and upheld the Supreme Court's 1954 *Brown v. Board of Education* decision, which Democrat governor Orval Faubus had blocked. Eisenhower also signed into law his second civil rights bill, the 1960 Civil Rights Act.

The opposition among elected Republicans to the 1964 Civil Rights Act was small and insignificant. And those Republicans who opposed it, including Sen. Barry Goldwater, mostly did so not for racist beliefs, but reasons related to federalism—that is, the sorting out of which level of government had the authority to act. Obviously, they were wrong. That said, Goldwater supported the 1957 and 1960 Civil Rights Acts.

Even Wikipedia, whose co-founder says is now "propaganda

for the left-leaning establishment," [57] acknowledges the following about Goldwater: "Barry Goldwater was fundamentally a staunch supporter of racial equality. Goldwater integrated his family's business upon taking over control in the 1930s. A lifetime member of the NAACP, Goldwater helped found the group's Arizona chapter. Goldwater saw to it that the Arizona Air National Guard was racially integrated from its inception in 1946, two years before President Truman ordered the military as a whole be integrated (a process that was not completed until 1954). Goldwater worked with Phoenix civil rights leaders to successfully integrate public schools a year prior to *Brown v. Board of Education*." [58]

Wikipedia continues its praise of Goldwater: "Goldwater was an early member and largely unrecognized supporter of the National Urban League Phoenix chapter, going so far as to cover the group's early operating deficits with his personal funds. Though the NAACP denounced Goldwater in the harshest of terms when he ran for president, the Urban League conferred on Goldwater the 1991 Humanitarian Award 'for 50 years of loyal service to the Phoenix Urban League.' In response to League members who objected, citing Goldwater's vote on the Civil Rights Act of 1964, the League president pointed out that Goldwater had saved the League more than once, saying he preferred to judge a person 'on the basis of his daily actions rather than on his voting record.'" [59]

Moreover, it is noteworthy that the Civil Rights Acts of 1875, 1957, 1960, 1964, and 1965 were overwhelmingly supported by Republicans. Moreover, in 1982, President Reagan signed a twenty-five-year extension of the Voting Rights Act (the longest extension by far up to that time). In 1983, Reagan also signed into law the designation of Martin Luther King Jr.'s birthday as a national holiday.

As for Johnson, the truth is that he had less of an epiphany than a slap of political reality, realizing that most of the nation had already rejected the southern Democrat segregationists and it was in his political interests to do so as well.

People are imperfect, political parties are imperfect, and institutions are imperfect. This has been understood since Biblical times. Looking back at history through present lenses of moral and ethical understandings has its shortcomings. But the Democrat Party's problem is not about imperfection. Clearly, it has been among the most organized, systemic, and malignant political institutions behind racism, bigotry, and segregation throughout much of American history.

Indeed, the Democrat Party's institutional racism extended well into the 1970s. President Joe Biden, in the early to mid-1970s, as a senator, had a close relationship with several of the Senate's most notorious racists and segregationists, about which he brags to this day, including Mississippi senator James Eastland, who fought hard against the Civil Rights Act of 1964 and the Voting Rights Act of 1965. Biden worked closely with Eastland, among others, to thwart public school integration.[60] In 1977, Biden declared, unless there is "orderly integration . . . [m]y children are going to grow up in a jungle, the jungle being a racial jungle."[61]

When campaigning in the South for the Democrat Party's presidential nomination several decades ago, Biden often touted the praise he received from Alabama Democrat governor George Wallace, another leading racist and segregationist, as "one of the outstanding young politicians of America."[62] Biden knew who and what he was dealing with, yet he was comfortable embracing it. Moreover, Biden has a long history of racist and stereotypical remarks about blacks and other minorities, which he has openly and repeatedly voiced to this day.[63]

In his 2022 choice of Ketanji Brown Jackson for the Supreme Court, Biden said, in part: "For too long, our government, our courts haven't looked like America. And I believe it's time that we have a Court that reflects the full talents and greatness of our nation with a nominee of extraordinary qualifications and that we inspire all young people to believe that they can one day serve their country at the highest level."[64]

But Biden did not feel that way in 2003, when President George W. Bush nominated Judge Janice Rogers Brown, a black woman, to the U.S. Court of Appeals for the District of Columbia. As Marc A. Thiessen wrote in the *Washington Post*: ". . . . Biden wants credit for nominating the first black woman to the Supreme Court. But here is the shameful irony: As a senator, Biden warned President Bush that if he nominated the first black woman to serve on the Supreme Court, he would filibuster and kill her nomination.[65]

Judge Brown is the "granddaughter of sharecroppers, and grew up in rural Alabama during the dark days of segregation, when her family refused to enter restaurants or theaters with separate entrances for Black customers. She rose from poverty and put herself through college and UCLA law school as a working single mother. She was a self-made African American legal star. But she was an outspoken conservative—so Biden set out to destroy her."[66] Thiessen points out that "[w]hat Biden threatened was unprecedented. There has never been a successful filibuster of a nominee for associate justice in the history of the republic. Biden wanted to make a black woman the first in history to have her nomination killed by filibuster."[67]

Biden fought like a rabid dog to block Brown's nomination—though she was confirmed later—because he knew Brown would be in line to become the first black woman on the Supreme Court. Biden did not want such a historic appointment conferred on a Republican and he did not want the Republican Party to receive credit for making it.

Race and racism have always been central to the Democrat Party's existence. Given the atrocious history of the Democrat Party on race, described in abridged form here (it is actually much worse), how did the Democrat Party turn the tables on the Republican Party and successfully self-define as the party of civil rights, and define the Republican Party as racist, or at least convince blacks to align with and vote overwhelmingly for the Democrat Party?

There are several reasons for this. For starters, debunking the frequent and preposterous claim that the Democrat Party and Republican Party switched places in the 1960s and during the election of Richard Nixon as president requires attention. *National Review*'s Kevin D. Williamson made hash of this Democrat Party propaganda, calling it an "outright lie, the utter fabrication with malice aforethought." He summarized it this way: "The Democrats have been allowed to rhetorically bury their Bull Connors, their longstanding affiliation with the Ku Klux Klan, and their pitiless opposition to practically every major piece of civil-rights legislation for a century. . . . Even if the Republicans' rise in the South had happened suddenly in the 1960s (it didn't) and even if there were no competing explanation (there is), racism—or, more precisely, white southern resentment over the political successes of the civil-rights movement—would be an implausible explanation for the dissolution of the Democratic bloc in the old Confederacy and the emergence of a Republican stronghold there. That is because those southerners who defected from the Democratic Party in the 1960s and thereafter did so to join a Republican Party that was far more enlightened on racial issues than were the Democrats of the era, and had been for a century. There is no radical break in the Republicans' civil-rights history: From the abolition of slavery to Reconstruction to the anti-lynching laws, from the Fourteenth and Fifteenth Amendments to the Civil Rights Act of 1875 to the Civil Rights Acts of 1957, 1960, and 1964, there exists a line that is by no means perfectly straight or unwavering but that nonetheless connects the politics of Lincoln with those of Eisenhower. And from slavery and secession to remorseless opposition to everything from Reconstruction to the anti-lynching laws, the Fourteenth and Fifteenth Amendments, the Civil Rights Act of 1875, and the Civil Rights Acts of 1957 and 1960, there exists a similarly identifiable line connecting John Calhoun and Lyndon Baines Johnson. Supporting civil-rights reform was not a radical turnaround for congressional Republicans in 1964, but it was a radical turnaround for Johnson and the Democrats."[68]

So, what did happen? Among other things, as older black Americans passed on, so did their memories and generational ties to the Party of Lincoln. Moreover, the Great Depression was devastating for most Americans, especially poorer Americans, including black Americans. And the terrible recession that would lead to the Depression started in 1929–30, when Republican Herbert Hoover was president. Therefore, the Republicans shouldered much of the blame, and the Democrat Party succeeded spectacularly in politically exploiting the citizenry's economic misery.

In addition, there was a mass migration of blacks from the South to the North, where Democrat Party political machines existed in many of the large inner cities, which encouraged blacks to register as Democrats. If you wanted, say, a patronage job, you had to be a registered Democrat.

Furthermore, although the New Deal was rife with racism, both in certain structural aspects and implementation, blacks were able to participate in some educational, public works, and food programs. Roosevelt was also the consummate glad-hander who paid attention to outreach, albeit to only certain key black leaders. Consequently, in 1936, for the first time, more black Americans began voting for Democrats over Republicans. Democrat Roosevelt received more black votes than Republican Alf Landon for president.

Most significantly, as the early progressive (Marxist) intellectuals had urged, the Democrat Party began laying the foundation for economic socialism and, more broadly, cultural Marxism, redefining civil rights and human rights as economic issues and in economic terms. They also began the process of breaching constitutional firewalls, which served as barriers to their designs. Although Wilson and especially Roosevelt poured the foundation for this political and economic upheaval, the tipping point was reached in the 1960s with Lyndon Johnson's Great Society. As civil rights activist Joyce Ladner, writing for the Brookings Institution, stated: "[T]he [civil rights] victories of the movement, however decisive they seemed at the time, did not bring the long-term parity that activists and policymakers hoped for. Bread-and-butter issues such as unemployment, substandard housing, inferior education, unsafe streets, escalating child poverty, and homelessness supplanted the right to vote, eat at a lunch counter, and attend desegregated schools. As new issues arose, appearing and intensifying in ways that fell beyond the scope of the legislative and social reforms, the old civil rights model—one that relied mostly on judicial and protest remedies—seemed less and less effective in dealing with them."[69] Thus, having mostly achieved legal equality, the focus shifted to economic equality, which in turn has now moved to "equity"—that is, economic socialism and cultural Marxism.

In fact, in 1944, Roosevelt argued for what he titled "The Second Bill of Rights." Professor Cass Sunstein, who has made his rounds among Ivy League schools and served in the Obama administration, argued that "the second bill attempts to protect both opportunity and security, by creating rights to employment, adequate food and clothing, decent shelter, education, recreation, and medical care. The presidency of America's greatest leader, Franklin Delano Roosevelt, culminated in the idea of a second bill. It represented Roosevelt's belief that the American Revolution was radically incomplete and that a new set of rights was necessary."[70]

Roosevelt proclaimed that every American is entitled to:

The right to a useful and remunerative job in the industries or shops or farms or mines of the nation;

The right to earn enough to provide adequate food and clothing and recreation;

The right of every farmer to raise and sell his products at a return which will give him and his family a decent living;

The right of every businessman, large and small, to trade in an atmosphere of freedom from unfair competition and domination by monopolies at home or abroad;

The right of every family to a decent home;

The right to adequate medical care and the opportunity to achieve and enjoy good health;

The right to adequate protection from the economic fears of old age, sickness, accident, and unemployment;

The right to a good education.[71]

Roosevelt had to be aware of Soviet dictator Joseph Stalin's 1936 Constitution when developing his second bill of rights, as there is an obvious overlap between the two documents. For example, Stalin's Constitution provided, in part:

ARTICLE 118. Citizens of the USSR have the right to work, that is, are guaranteed the right to employment and payment for their work in accordance with its quantity and quality. . . .

ARTICLE 119. Citizens of the USSR have the right to rest and leisure. . . .

ARTICLE 120. Citizens of the USSR have the right to maintenance in old age and also in case of sickness or loss of capacity to work. This right is ensured by the extensive development of social insurance of workers and employees at state expense, free medical service for the working people and the provision of a wide network of health resorts for the use of the working people.

ARTICLE 121. Citizens of the USSR have the right to education. This right is ensured by universal, compulsory elementary education; by education, including higher education, being free of charge; by the system of state stipends for the overwhelming majority of students in the universities and colleges. . . .

ARTICLE 126. In conformity with the interests of the working people, and in order to develop the organizational initiative and political activity of the masses of the people, citizens of the USSR are ensured the right to unite in public organizations—trade unions. . . .[72]

Keep in mind that the early progressive intellectuals, including John Dewey, who was probably the most influential among them, were infatuated with the 1917 Russian Revolution and Stalin in the 1920s and 1930s.[73] Indeed, Dewey, who had an enormous influence on the direction of public education in America, wrote admiringly of Stalin's educational system—that is, Stalin's use of brainwashing.

Of course, in Karl Marx's 1848 *Communist Manifesto*, Marx famously published his "10 Planks" of policy, which included "a heavy progressive or graduated income tax; abolition of all rights to inheritance; centralization of credit in the hands of the state, by means of a national bank . . . ; gradual abolition of the distinction between town and country by a more equable distribution of the population over the country; free education for all children in public schools. . . ." Much of this has been and is being advanced by the Democrat Party.

As I have said many times and explained in *American Marxism*, progressivism is a form of Marxism. It is customized and tailored in a way to devour the American system and society by abusing liberty to promote tyranny and hijack the Constitution to enshrine its policy agenda. The overarching fundamentals enlist the ideas and goals of Marxism.[74] Indeed, in promoting Roosevelt's Second Bill of Rights, Sunstein declares: "Why does the American Constitution lack Roosevelt's second bill? Why hasn't it become a part of our constitutional understandings? . . . If [Richard] Nixon had not been elected, significant parts of the second bill would probably be part of our constitutional understandings today. In the 1960s, the nation was rapidly moving toward accepting a second bill, not through constitutional amendment but through the Supreme Court's interpretations of the existing Constitution. An appreciation of this point will drive home . . . the extent to which the meaning of America's Constitution depends on the commitments of its judges. Even more important, it will show that a belief in the second bill lies beneath the surface of our current constitutional understandings. With a little work of recovery, we can easily uncover it there. Parts of it are widely accepted already."[75]

Sunstein is well aware that Woodrow Wilson believed and argued that the judiciary was the most potent tool by which to transform America into the kind of society the American Marxists envision. Moreover, this provides some context for the Democrat Party's hatred of Nixon and obsession with forcing him from the presidency, with the active participation of its media surrogates.

In truth, Marxism permeates American society due to the

efforts of the Democrat Party and its proxies throughout the culture and society, including the media and academia. It is devouring America from within, as Italian communist Antonio Gramsci, German communist Herbert Marcuse, and Saul Alinsky had all advocated. And the propaganda in support of American Marxism and the Democrat Party is similar to this woeful PhD student's harangue: "Capitalism nurtures the continuation of racism, sexism, discrimination, and oppression, as they offer those among the privileged an advantage over subordinate groups. Race is a catalogue of descriptive differences—an ideology which construes populations as groups—sorting them into hierarchies of capacity, civic worth, based on perceived 'natural' characteristics attributed to them. 'Whiteness' is a descriptive quality that ensures the bearer of it is privileged over blacks, Latinos, or any race which is not white."[76] And, unfortunately, like this PhD student, an awful lot of young people are falling for it.

CHAPTER THREE

ANTI-WHITE RACISM & ANTI-SEMITISM

It is an empirical fact that anti-white racism now pervades our culture and society. It is not only fully embraced by the Democrat Party, it is responsible for promoting it. So are its surrogates in academia and the media. It is necessary to spend some time digging into the arguments of certain American Marxists behind this movement and the grave threat it poses to our country.

Although Karl Marx did not emphasize race when defining class struggles (in fact, he never defined what he meant by class despite incessantly referencing it), his American progeny did, in fact, link the two. Indeed, a little-noticed subterranean movement had been afoot since the early days of the Progressive Movement—the late 1800s and early 1900s—which promoted cultural Marxism and economic socialism. Among the most prominent among the movement's advocates were several black Marxist intellectuals, such as W. E. B. Du Bois. They argued that America's capitalist system was built on slavery and the exploitation of slaves by the white race. It should be noted, as Phillip

W. Magness, senior research faculty and director of research and education at the American Institute for Economic Research, writes in *National Review*, that Du Bois, who is celebrated in school textbooks and during Black History Month, as well as modern-day Marxist authors, "split from the avowedly anti-communist leadership of the NAACP. . . . He spent his final years gallivanting with Mao Zedong and touting the alleged credentials of Joseph Stalin as a leading anti-racist."[1]

Were Du Bois and his circle of Marxists right? Did capitalism promote slavery, and was America built on the exploitation of slaves? This is a frequently repeated narrative of modern-day Marxists as well. First, of course slavery is an undeniable fact of American history. However, so are the numerous efforts to abolish it.

Every northern state passed laws to abolish slavery in the first two decades after the Revolutionary War, either immediately or soon thereafter.[2] In 1800, Congress passed the Act Prohibiting the Importation of Slaves, which took effect in 1808.[3] Of course, slavery within parts of the United States persisted. By the time of the Civil War, the overwhelming number of slaves were held in the agrarian South. However, most white southern families did not own slaves. Less than 25 percent of the South was wealthy enough to own slaves.[4]

Second, the North did not rely on slavey to build its industrial capacity. Indeed, "[w]hile factories were built all over the North and South, the vast majority of industrial manufacturing was taking place in the North. The South had almost 25% of the country's free population, but only 10% of the country's capital in 1860. The North had five times the number of factories as the South, and over ten times the number of factory workers. In addition, 90% of the nation's skilled workers were in the North."[5]

Consequently, by "1860 the North had over 110,000 manufacturing establishments, the South just 18,000. The North produced

94 percent of the country's iron, 97 percent of its coal and—not incidentally—97 percent of its firearms. It contained 22,000 miles of railroad to the South's 8,500. The North outperformed the South agriculturally as well. Northerners held 75 percent of the country's farm acreage, produced 60 percent of its livestock, 67 percent of its corn, and 81 percent of its wheat. All in all, they held 75 percent of the nation's total wealth."[6]

Hence, the lesson is the exact opposite of what the American Marxists and Democrat Party preach—that is, capitalism and a free people create wealth, prosperity, opportunity, and, yes, colorblindness. Indeed, Nobel Prize laureate and economist, the renowned Milton Friedman, profoundly declared: "The great virtue of a free market system is that it does not care what color people are; it does not care what their religion is; it only cares whether they can produce something you want to buy. It is the most effective system we have discovered to enable people who hate one another to deal with one another and help one another."[7]

Of course, slavery is unconscionable. There is no excusing it. But capitalism did not drive slavery. Slavery has existed, and exists today, throughout the world and in noncapitalist societies. As Peter W. Wood, president of the National Association of Scholars, explains: "Slavery . . . was not an American invention, or a European one. It has existed in human societies for thousands of years. In north and east Africa, slave capture and trading were pursued on an enormous scale by Arabs. When Europeans encountered native kingdoms on Africa's Atlantic coast in the fifteenth century, they discovered slavery as a deeply embedded practice. That the Portuguese and the Spanish fostered this practice by creating a market for African slaves in the New World is among the great tragedies of human history. Other European powers eventually joined in perpetuating that tragedy."[8]

In his review of Nikole Hannah-Jones's 1619 docuseries, Magness points out that "[e]quating capitalism with the exploitation of workers certainly serves the purpose of designating chattel slavery as a capitalistic institution, but it is simply not an accurate—or even functional—definition of the concept. Ancient Roman slavery, medieval feudalism, Soviet-era gulags, and North Korean prison camps today would also qualify as 'capitalism' if we reduce the concept to exploitive worker conditions. . . ." Magness also explains that "Canada, Japan, several European states [were] of economies that underwent massive industrialization in the 19th century without the alleged benefits of slavery." He adds that "Brazil, which maintained a large slave economy for several decades longer than the United States did so without industrializing."[9] Indeed, Hannah-Jones, writes Magness, contends that "almost every economic fallacy and pejorative denigration imaginable describe economic development under market-based capitalism."[10] By this, she insists that slavery and capitalism are inextricably linked, and she proceeds from there to cheerlead for Marxism.

Perhaps someone should inform Hannah-Jones and other American Marxists that the greatest slave states that exist today do so under the banner of Marxism.

And what of post–Civil War America? Again, the accusation is that capitalism and American economic growth had been nurtured by racial discrimination and racial inequality—that is, capitalism "intersected" with slavery and racism. This theory has now been given a name—"racial capitalism." It is argued that racial capitalism is based on the theft, exclusion, and exploitation of people of color for the economic benefit of white people. In short, white supremacy is what undergirds America's economic system and its history.

More recently, the late professor Cedric J. Robinson, influential in radical circles but mostly unknown by the body politic, took Du Bois's views a step further in his book *Black Marxism: The*

Making of Black Radical Tradition. He argued that "[t]he development, organization, and expansion of capitalist society pursued essential racial directions, so too did social ideology. As a material force, then, it could be expected that racialism would inevitably permeate the social structures emergent from capitalism."[11]

UCLA professor Robin D. G. Kelley explains that for Robinson "capitalism emerged *within the feudal order* [rather than replacing it, as Marx wrote] and flowered in the cultural soil of a Western civilization already thoroughly infused with racialism. Capitalism and racism, in other words, did not break from the old order but rather evolved from it to produce a modern world system of 'racial capitalism' dependent on slavery, violence, imperialism, and genocide. Capitalism was 'racial' not because of some conspiracy to divide workers or justify slavery and dispossession, but because racialism had already permeated Western feudal society."[12] (Italics are mine.) In other words, anti-black racism is in the nation's DNA thanks in large part to capitalism.

Moreover, Robinson insisted, racial capitalism was not limited to the South. The claim is that the Industrial Revolution, which reached deeply into the North and was in many ways a product of the North, was built on the backs of blacks and their unequal and abusive treatment. Thus, whether from slavery in the South or industrial capitalism in the North, racism was and is endemic in capitalism and, therefore, throughout all corners of the country. Capitalism is, therefore, the economic tool by which the white-dominant society lords over and exploits blacks and other minorities to this day.

The attraction of Marxism, even in its altered forms, to Du Bois and Robinson, and numerous other self-proclaimed radicals and revolutionaries past and present, is now routinely taught in our public schools, colleges, and universities and enforced through Diversity, Equity, and Inclusion or DEI administrators, seminars, and training; advocated by elected Democrats and the

Biden administration; imposed through government regulations, grants, and executive orders; and, propagated in the media. It is even a growing ideology in major corporations and financial institutions—disguised and customized as the Environmental, Social, and Governance or ESG corporate movement.

Of course, identifying slavery and racism as essential elements of early and present-day capitalism gets it backwards. Capitalism is not to blame for mankind's evils or the institution of slavery generally, or its early institutionalization in parts of America. Indeed, it requires a rewriting of American history and a perverse view of the *free*-market system to blame capitalism for slavery. It was the Progressive Era—that is, the early American Marxists—that advo-cated the fundamentals of Marx, in which the "science" of eugenics and widespread racism thrived post–Civil War. As described in Chapter 2, it was a thoroughly anti-black racist movement that claimed to apply science to the ranking of a human hierarchy and Darwin's selection of the fittest, in which blacks consistently ranked at the bottom. Professor Thomas C. Leonard explains that "[i]n defining race, American race science was as protean as was evolutionary thought. Eugenics and race theorists used 'race' to refer to the human race as well as to the conventional division of humanity into 'white, black, yellow, brown, and red faces.'"[13]

Furthermore, in no rational understanding of capitalism, the foundational blocks of which emphasize individualism, liberty, and free will, does government-sanctioned enslavement or racial discrimination of fellow human beings for the forcible use or abuse of their labor coexist with the core principles of capitalism. And what goes unsaid is that the most egregious political and governing institution that embraced, promoted, and defended slavery, and post–Civil War racism, segregation, and inequality, was the Democrat Party, not some perverse concept of capitalism. Yet most of American Marxism identifies with the Democrat

Party, and vice versa. Why? Among other reasons, the Democrat Party fundamentally rejects capitalism as well.

Robert Reich, President Bill Clinton's radical secretary of labor and currently a professor at UC Berkeley, credits Biden with revitalizing what he calls "democratic capitalism." Of course, democratic capitalism is just another phrase for what Bernie Sanders calls "democratic socialism," with a few twists and turns. Reich's point, however, is that Biden has jettisoned market capitalism for Roosevelt's government-directed socialism.[14] In this, he is correct.

Let us briefly examine what Biden and the Democrat Party disparagingly refer to as "Reaganomics." In 1990, Martin Anderson, a Hoover Institution senior fellow and former Reagan adviser, explained in a *New York Times* opinion piece that "[w]e don't know whether historians will call it the Great Expansion of the 1980's or Reagan's Great Expansion, but we do know from official economic statistics that the seven-year period from 1982 to 1989 was the greatest, consistent burst of economic activity ever seen in the U.S. In fact, it was the greatest economic expansion the world has ever seen—in any country, at any time."[15] Anderson added that "[o]ne thing the Marxists got right: Economics is a powerful determining factor of history. But Marxists never dreamed it would be the economics of Ronald Reagan and all those capitalists that would prevail in the end."[16]

Did economic conditions for black Americans improve during Reagan's enormous economic boom? Unequivocally, yes. In 2004, American Enterprise Institute scholar Michael Novak observed: "In constant dollars, 1988 dollars, the total annual income earned by all 30 million U.S. blacks together rose from $191 billion at the end of 1980, to $259 billion by the end of 1988. That sum was larger than the GDP of all but ten nations in the world. The number of black families earning more than $50,000 per year much more than doubled, from 392,000 in

1982 to 936,000 in 1988. The median salary/wage of black males increased from $9,678 in 1980 to $14,537 in 1988 (in current dollars). Median means half earned more than that, half less, so more than half of all black males improved their income by more than 50 percent."[17]

And without instituting Democrat Party/Marxist punitive redistributive tax policies but, to the contrary, slashing taxes across the board, "Reagan . . . shift[ed] the burden of income tax upward from the poor and lower middle class—indeed from the whole bottom half of income earners. By 1988, Reagan had the lower half paying less than 6 percent of income taxes. The top-five percent, which before Reagan had been paying under 38 percent of all income taxes, by 1988 were paying nearly 46 percent. He had the top-ten percent of income earners paying a whopping 57 percent of all income taxes."[18]

Much more can be said about the Reagan years and their remarkable successes, but that is not the object of this book. Nonetheless, even an abbreviated look at the record exposes the lies obsessively and repeatedly disgorged by Biden, the Democrat Party, and its Marxist ideologues against Reagan and the capitalist system.

In addition, there are a host of socioeconomic reasons individuals succeed or fail as well as individual weaknesses and strengths, having absolutely nothing to do with race or racism, and yet determine outcomes. In fact, given the uniqueness of each person, equal outcomes or "equity," even in societies that are racially, ethnically, or otherwise largely homogenous and never experienced slavery, and even within the same families, are impossible. Indeed, the pursuit of such lofty egalitarian yet totalitarian objectives by governing institutions breeds tyranny, and is used to justify horrendous forms of persecution. You would think that over one hundred years of experience with Marxism's inhumanity has demonstrated even to the Democrat Party the genocidal nature of the ideology in its various applications and impositions.

Whether a person is a slave to a plantation or to a government, he is a slave. Ask the people who escaped, say, North Korea if they had lived as slaves. Yet the Democrat Party finds Marx's ideology more appealing than the vision of America's founders, whom they continuously revile. Moreover, unlike capitalism, slavery is baked into Marxism.

Writing in the *City Journal*, Coleman Hughes points out that there are "several historical examples in which capitalism inspired antiracism. The most famous is the 1896 *Plessy v. Ferguson* Supreme Court case, when a profit-hungry railroad company— upset that legally mandated segregation meant adding costly train cars—teamed up with a civil rights group to challenge racial segregation. Nor was that case unique. Privately owned bus and trolley companies in the Jim Crow South 'frequently resisted segregation' because 'separate cars and sections' were 'too expensive,' according to [research published in the *Journal of Economic History*.]"[19]

Again, the American Marxist has succeeded today in establishing the idea that a societal, cultural, and political intersection of racism and capitalism exists. There are at least two important conclusions resulting from this distortion: 1. Capitalism must be destroyed and replaced if racism is to be eliminated; and, 2. The white race is said to be responsible for the capitalist system and is the beneficiary of the system, and the society created around it, which is intended to sustain and perpetuate white domination and privilege. Therefore, it follows that the white race is the ultimate oppressor. Consequently, in order to end anti-black racism and white supremacy, inasmuch as the entire society is said to be irredeemably racist and white-race dominated, the society must be overhauled and ultimately overturned if justice and equity are to prevail. Therefore, the goal is no longer to end individual cases of racism or illegal discrimination, which are said to be distractive or irrelevant to a comprehensive solution to a systemic problem, but to terminate the country.

Furthermore, it is said that the white-dominant society imposes racial capitalism on blacks and other minorities to maintain its privileged and oppressor status in society, thereby institutionally creating unequal outcomes—*inequitable* outcomes—and is, there-fore, to blame for any real or perceived disparate economic and social results. This is the essence of Critical Race Theory (CRT), which pervades the ivory towers of academia, public school class-rooms, newsrooms, corporate boardrooms, religious institutions, and beyond. It has assimilated into nearly all aspects of the culture. I call this *civil rights Marxism*, which has co-opted the old civil rights movement. Justice per se has been replaced with so-called eco-nomic justice—that is, economic socialism and cultural Marxism.

On May 10, 2023, the vice president, Kamala Harris, spoke at the swearing-in of commissioners to the White House Initiative on Advancing Educational Equity, Excellence, and Economic Oppor-tunity for Hispanics. She said, in part: "[S]o many of us have come from movements that were about the fight for equality. We also understand there's a difference between equality and equity. Equity is everyone deserves to have rights and be treated equally. But equity understands that not everybody starts out on the same base. So, if you're giving everybody an equal amount, but they're starting out on different bases, are they really going to have the opportunity to compete and achieve? That's why we purposefully as an admin-istration, the president, myself, the secretary, and everyone in our administration are so dedicated to a specific principle which is that of equity."[20] This also explains, in part, the Democrat Party's rejec-tion of a color-blind society and capitalism.

Marx, like Harris and the rest of the Biden administration and Democrat Party, was not particularly a fan of "equality."

He believed it was a tool of the bourgeoisie to retain the status quo in society—where the proletariat were under the thumb of the bourgeoisie. Hence, he insisted on ultimately abolishing all "classes" and the existing society—that is, starting with a blank slate, thereby making way for the communist paradise.

This ideology has cost tens of millions of human beings their lives. For example, for Vladimir Lenin, Joseph Stalin, Mao Zedong, Pol Pot, Fidel Castro, et al., this meant annihilating entire "categories" of people—teachers, professors, lawyers, and mostly all professionals. It meant forcibly marching city dwellers into rural areas, where they would be compelled to farm, pick fruit, gather rice, etc. It meant nationalizing private property, seizing bank accounts, etc. In other words, as Kamala Harris explained, "not everybody starts out on the same base," and the Biden administration is "dedicated to a specific principle which is that of equity"—meaning, the government will use the law and its considerable resources to redistribute wealth, discriminate against certain individuals and groups, abolish merit, and ultimately control human behavior. When linked to race, as it is today, it means racial discrimination and quotas in school admissions, the hiring and firing of employees, segregating college dorm rooms and graduation ceremonies, dumbing down school curricula, sabotaging merit scholarship programs, and issuing presidential executive orders that, for instance, exclude white farmers and other "privileged" racial groups. Again, as Harris declared, "everyone in our administration are [sic] dedicated" to the promotion and institution of equity.[21]

Although the Supreme Court and other courts have struck down some of these hideous and unconstitutional policies, many of the Democrat-controlled institutions that have used them have announced their intention to circumvent the Court—at the Biden administration's urging.

Because of the emphasis on race as the basis for all behaviors and outcomes, and allegations of irreversible white racism based on skin color at birth, CRT and civil rights Marxism dehumanize the individual and groups of individuals. Ironically, the scholars and activists promoting this point of view use dehumanizing stereotypes not only to label white people but to describe black individuals and the black community. After all, in the end, Marxism of any kind is built on the false foundation of oppressor and oppressed class identification, which is said to exist in all non-Marxist societies.

Ibram X. Kendi, director of the Center for Antiracist Research at Boston University and a leading advocate for CRT, has written that "[t]o say that there is widespread racial inequity caused by widespread racism, which makes the United States racist, isn't an opinion, isn't a partisan position, isn't a doctrine, isn't a left-wing construct, isn't anti-white, and isn't anti-American. It is a fact."[22]

In fact, CRT scholars and activists dismiss all the societal efforts, economic programs, laws, court rulings, even the Civil War and the presidencies of Abraham Lincoln and Ulysses S. Grant, as well as Martin Luther King Jr.'s courageous activism and speeches, as little more than transparent and self-serving attempts by the white-dominant society, or those who go along with and help perpetuate white privilege (knowingly or otherwise), to paste over the incurably flawed American founding, the tentacles of which reach into all aspects of modern life now and into the future.

The civil rights Marxists also reject both the idea and pursuit of a color-blind society. Lest we forget, Peter C. Myers, visiting fellow at the Heritage Foundation, reminds us that "[f]or Frederick Douglass, the 19th century's greatest abolitionist and civil rights advocate, an abiding faith 'in reason, in truth and justice' sustained an expectation that 'the color line . . . will cease to have any civil, political, or moral significance' in America. In the most famous dissenting opinion in U.S. Supreme Court history,

Justice John Marshall Harlan provided a more focused expression of that sentiment, thus explaining his vote in *Plessy v. Ferguson* to invalidate a law mandating racial segregation on train cars: 'Our constitution is color-blind. . . . The law regards man as man, and takes no account . . . of his color when his civil rights as guaranteed by the supreme law of the land are involved.' . . .

In his brief for the plaintiffs in the landmark *Brown v. Board of Education* case, Thurgood Marshall argued, 'distinctions . . . based upon race or color alone . . . [are] the epitome of that arbitrariness and capriciousness constitutionally impermissible under our system of government.' Three score and seven years after *Plessy* came the most resounding statement of all, when the Rev. Martin Luther King, Jr., stood under the shadow of Abraham Lincoln and immortalized the moral vision of the civil rights movement by declaring, 'I have a dream that my four little children will one day live in a nation where they will not be judged by the color of their skin but by the content of their character.'"[23]

Today, civil rights Marxism preaches and demands the opposite. For example, Kendi has declared: "The only remedy to racist discrimination is antiracist discrimination. The only remedy to past discrimination is present discrimination. The only remedy to present discrimination is future discrimination."[24] Thus, the demand for "equity." Indeed, the movement has come up with a new term for condemning colorblindness: *color-blind racism*. A column by radical Dani Bostick, an educator and contributor to the Democrat Party–supporting *Huffington Post*, further illustrates the point. She asserts that:

> Colorblindness foists whiteness on everyone. It is another way of saying, "I view everyone as if they were white." Your default color for sameness is white.
> Colorblindness strips non-white people of their unique-

ness. Your default culture for sameness is white culture. When you encourage your child to be colorblind and view everyone as "the same," you are projecting white on people of [sic] who aren't white, negating their experiences, traditions, and uniqueness.

Colorblindness suppresses critically important narratives of oppression. Once you view everyone through a colorblind, white lens, you deny the reality that non-white people face. . . .

Colorblindness assumes everyone has the same experience here in America. When you fail to see color, you fail to recognize injustice and oppression. . . .

Colorblindness promotes the idea that non-white races are inferior. When you teach your child to be colorblind, you are essentially telling them, "If someone isn't white, pretend they look like you so you can be friends." Stripping people of a fundamental aspect of their identity by claiming not to see color is dehumanizing.[25]

Consequently, Myers explains, "[i]f racism is conceived in practical terms as a maldistribution of socioeconomic goods and ills, then its remedy must be conceived in terms of redistribution, not only of opportunities but also of outcomes. The proper function of preferential race-classifications would then be to effect the desired redistributions. . . . The minimum condition of a just society, in this view, is that no historically disfavored racial group would suffer any aggregate disadvantage in the incidences of the main goods and ills whereby we measure socioeconomic well-being. The ultimate expectation is that those goods and ills would be distributed among racial groups in rough proportion to their percentages of the societal population."[26] Thus, racism, equity, Marxism.

As the recent propaganda and intolerance of the Democrat

Party and American Marxists spread, which is intended to empower the former and enshrine the latter, and is aggressively promoted by the media, academia, and revolutionary activists, the truth is that the American people are nothing like how they are portrayed and stereotyped by the Democrat Party and their surrogates.

For example, looking at interracial marriage, in 2021 Gallup reports that 94 percent of Americans approve of interracial marriage, between white and black people, up from 4 percent in 1954. . . . "Americans in all age groups today are more supportive of black-white marriages than adults in the same age group were in the past, particularly among older adults. In 1991, 27 percent of U.S. adults aged 50 and older approved of interracial marriage, compared with 91 percent today."[27]

In addition, there has been a steady and significant rise in interracial marriages. In 2021, Pew Research reported: "In 2019, 11% of all married U.S. adults had a spouse who was a different race or ethnicity from them, up from 3% in 1967. Among newlyweds in 2019, roughly one-in-five (19%) were intermarried."[28]

Moreover, the number of Americans who identify as coming from multiple races has jumped. Pew Research notes: "According to the U.S. Census Bureau, Americans who identify as two or more races are one of the fastest growing racial or ethnic groups in the country, along with Asians. Roughly 6.3 million American adults—2.5% of the adult population—identified as being more than one race in 2019. The number has grown significantly since the census first allowed people to choose more than one racial category to describe themselves in 2000. Among adults who identify as more than one race, relatively few (2.1%) are Black and Asian."[29]

You would think that the evidence of Americans as an accepting, tolerant, and "live and let live" people would complicate things for the Democrat Party and American Marxists. You would be wrong. In fact, it encourages them to intensify and escalate their revolutionary campaign. Remember, for them this is about power: the party comes before country, and the revolution is top down.

DePaul University professor Jason D. Hill, who happens to be black, explains in his book *What Do White Americans Owe Black People: Racial Justice in the Age of Post-Oppression* that this ideology is "a vicious anti-reason and, therefore, anti-life phenomenon that robs human beings of a particular method of cognition. It deprives them of integrating fundamental principles to clear and lucid thinking that leads to intelligible and reasonable actions. It cuts away at the idea of objective reality and replaces it with an unbridled and amorphous, necrotic lump of feelings that are treated as tools of cognition . . . a convenient cover for any subjective and personal quest for power, violation of rights, and basic human lawlessness. Even the concept of law is regarded as an oppressive construct designed by those who wish to exercise dominion over the marginalized. . . . Today, in the form of not just these but in manifestations of cancel culture, cultural appropriation, and successful efforts to suppress offending speech, we are witnessing the wholesale death of our civilization. . . . Because this philosophy is an attack against individualism, reason, progress, and the notion of truth itself, its deadliest consequence is a form of moral inversion of human beings."[30]

Of course, this is totalitarian in mind-set and practice. It is an undeniably racist application of Marxism, pure and simple. And it is extremely dangerous. If it continues to take hold throughout America's culture and society, and the federal government uses its lawmaking power to enforce it, and the private sector uses its hiring, wealth creation, and distribution decision-making to impose it, this cancerous ideology will destroy the norms, traditions, and comity that form the bases of a civilized society. Indeed, it will all come crashing down, perhaps violently. After all, this is the true yet often unstated intention of its advocates.

Incredibly, despite untold numbers of books, essays, seminars, training manuals, classes, etc., insisting that there exists a white-dominant society, white privilege, white oppression, and so forth, many proponents of civil rights Marxism insist that this perverse and hateful ideology is not built on anti-white racism. Of course, this an utterly preposterous attempt at deception. In fact, if the ideology and its toxicity are disputed, denounced, or opposed, the criticism itself is said to reinforce the evidence of white supremacy and privilege. The circuity and irrationality of the ideology are inescapable. It is a delusion. But delusions can be powerful attractions, and their quest a disastrous journey.

Professor Lynn Uzzell, visiting assistant professor of politics at Washington and Lee University, explains that "[t]he definition of racism has undergone a radical change in a short time. [For example], [a]ccording to the new eighth-grade curriculum for the Albemarle County (Va.) School District, racism now means: 'The marginalization and/or oppression of people of color based on a socially constructed racial hierarchy that privileges white people.' Perhaps the most jarring aspect of this new definition is that it is no longer race-neutral. It is now impossible, by definition, for white people to be the victims of racism. The definition itself constructs a 'racial hierarchy' whereby only people of color may be victimized, and only 'white people' may marginalize or oppress. . . . Since the 'marginalization and/or oppression of people of color' is no longer committed by word, thought, or deed, but is based instead on an inescapable 'socially constructed racial hierarchy' that *always* 'privileges white people'—it means that white people are engaging in racism simply by being white (and hence privileged) within this impersonal system of marginalization and oppression. A person of color is a victim of racism, by definition. A person identified as white is a racist, by definition. . . ."[31]

Uzzell notes that Hannah-Jones, the lead author of the roundly criticized 1619 Project, which is primarily a collection of "anti-white screeds" and historical distortions, has a long background in vile anti-white racist tantrums. "In a letter to her college paper, [Hannah-Jones] alleged: 'The white race is the biggest murderer, rapist, pillager, and thief of the modern world.' Not only were white people in America's past 'barbaric devils,' but the 'descendants of these savage people' continue to harm 'the Black community' to this day. . . .'"[32] This sounds a lot like racists Louis Farrakhan and Leonard Jeffries.

What does this have to do with the Democrat Party? Everything.

As described earlier, race and racism have been core characteristics and hideous weapons of the Democrat Party's pursuit and maintenance of power from its earliest days. Capitalism and constitutionalism, with their emphasis on the individual and freedom, as well as limitations on central planning and social engineering, have been inconvenient obstacles to the Democrat Party's objectives for its entire existence. Democrat Party intellectuals, leaders, and activists have told us this since at least the Progressive Era. Therefore, abandoning the old civil rights movement for civil rights Marxism, and abandoning anti-black racism for anti-white racism, was not as difficult a transition as one might otherwise imagine. In essence, the Democrat Party has and does reject *Americanism*, meaning the fundamental principles upon which our nation was founded—and not only capitalism, but the Declaration of Independence and the Constitution. This is the common thread that ties the old anti-black Democrat Party of Woodrow Wilson to the current anti-white Democrat Party of Joe Biden.

Indeed, Biden is a clear example of the Democrat Party's transition from anti-black racism to anti-white racism, and its abandonment of capitalism for economic socialism. Today, Biden repeatedly uses anti-white racism as a self-righteous cudgel with which to attack his political opponents and the Republican Party, promote his radical domestic agenda, and curry favor with the numerous and growing Marxist elements that make up the Democrat Party base and activists. In fact, Biden positions himself as some kind of savior of American democracy, the nation's soul, and civil rights icon who stands bravely against white supremacy.

When running for president in 2020 and speaking at a National Action Network event hosted by Al Sharpton—whose own background is littered with racist and anti-Semitic episodes[33]—the same Biden whose legacy includes significant relationships with segregationists, infinite bigoted statements, and years of fighting racial integration, declared: "The bottom line is we have a lot to root out, but most of all the systematic racism that most of us whites don't like to acknowledge even exists. We don't even consciously acknowledge it. But it's been built into every aspect of our system." He continued, "[b]ecause when your schools are substandard, when your houses are undervalued, when your car insurance costs more for no apparent reason, when poverty rates for black Americans is still twice that of white Americans, . . . there's something we have to admit. Not you—we—white America has to admit there's still a systematic racism. And it goes almost unnoticed by so many of us."[34]

Of course, the unmentioned irony of Sharpton's past history of anti-Semitism and white racism, Biden's anti-black racism and support for segregation, and the loathsome story of the Democrat Party went without comment.

In 2021, when signing an "Executive Order on Racial Equity," Biden said that "[o]ne of the reasons I'm so optimistic about this nation is that today's generation of young Americans is the most progressive, thoughtful, inclusive generation that America has ever seen. And they are pulling us toward justice in so many ways, forcing us to confront the huge gap in economic . . . inequity between those at the top and everyone else, forcing us to confront . . . systemic racism and white supremacy."[35] In 2022, Biden tweeted that "[w]hite supremacy is a poison running through our body politic. We need to say as clearly and forcefully as we can that the ideology of white supremacy has no place in America."[36]

Biden has spent decades fine-tuning his skills as a poisonous demagogue and political opportunist—and exploiting race since his earliest days in the Senate. When Biden speaks repeatedly of white supremacy, he does not mean such horrendous organizations as the Ku Klux Klan or neo-Nazis. He is speaking of systemic white-on-black discrimination and society-wide enshrined white privilege, which he claims exists in America today. By his own words, Biden hates America.

Biden proves the point that in order to be a politically successful Democrat, especially if you want the Democrat Party nomination for president, you must despise our country. You must lie about it. You must denounce it. You must smear it. And if you want to be reelected and create an FDR-like legacy for yourself, you must attack the nation's long-standing institutions, its history, its founders, its economic system, its sovereignty, and multimillions of its people—first black and now white. Being the consummate political chameleon, having spent half a century as a Washington, D.C., politician, Biden, even in his feeble state, is more than up to the task. However, he is hardly alone, as a long line of equally unconscionable and unscrupulous Democrat Party apparatchiks, also egomaniacal in ambition and the pursuit of power, stand ready to pounce.

Here Biden is again, this time at the unveiling of a heart-wrenching documentary about the torture and murder of Emmett Till: "It was one of the great honors of my career, the Emmett Till Anti-Lynching Act, making lynching a federal hate crime. You know, folks, lynching is pure terror, enforcing the lie that not everyone belongs in America and not everyone is created equal. Pure terror to systematically undermine hard-fought civil rights. Innocent men, women, children hung by a noose from trees. Bodies burned, drowned, castrated. Their crimes? Trying to vote. Trying to go to school. Trying to own a business. Trying to re-preach the gospel. False accusations of murder, arson, robbery. Lynched for simply being Black, nothing more. With white crowds, white families gathered to celebrate the spectacle, taking pictures of the bodies and mailing them as postcards. Hard to believe, but that's what was done. *And some people still want to do that.*[37] (Italics are mine.)

Biden's "some people" without identifying who he means is deranged and dangerous rhetoric. Way over the top. Yet this kind of hate speech is regular fare on Democrat Party–supporting media platforms and in academic institutions, as it was during the days of segregation. This is similar to his his unhinged attack on then Republican presidential candidate Mitt Romney in December 2015, when he said to a racially mixed crowd: "[Romney] said in the first 100 days, he's going to let the big banks once again write their own rules. Unchain Wall Street! They're gonna put y'all back in chains."[38]

As Fox News reported, on May 15, 2023, during a commencement speech at Howard University, a historically black college, Biden began by talking about "America's battle with racism from the time of its inception, saying, 'We know American history has not always been a fairy tale. From the start, it's been a constant push and pull for more than 240 years, between the best of us—the American ideal that we're all created equal—and the worst of us, a harsh reality that racism has long torn us apart. It's a battle that's never really over,' he said, adding, 'But on the best days, enough of us have the guts and hearts to stand up for the best in us, to choose love over hate, unity over disunity, progress over retreat.' Biden then zeroed in on white supremacy, saying,

'To stand against the poison of white supremacy as I did in my Inaugural Address.' He then called it 'the most dangerous terrorist threat to our homeland.' The audience erupted in applause."[39]

Biden has never acknowledged or apologized for his racism or support for segregation. And the Democrat Party–supporting media provide cover for him.

Biden and the Democrat Party have adopted the ideology, language, and agenda of anti-white racists and racism, the intersection of racism with capitalism, CRT, and outright Marxism. As president, Biden is using the tools of government and the presidency to spread and impose this ideology throughout the federal bureaucracy, the culture, and society.

In fact, as the *Washington Examiner*'s Paul Bedard explained, in the Democrat Party's 2020 eighty-page draft platform, in which it lays out its mission and beliefs as a political organization, "whites are mentioned 15 times, all critical, including three references to white supremacy or supremacists and one to white nationalists. The document doesn't capitalize white as it does Black, Latinos, Asian Americans, and Native Americans. . . . Typical in it is the reference to the wage gap between whites and minorities, which the party document said 'is hurting our working class and holding our country back.' The theme in much of the document is that America is divided between whites and minorities, the situation is unfair and needs to be remedied, and that most issues, even military court-martials, are in a racial crisis."[40]

Here are the fifteen references to whites:

1. We will never amplify or legitimize the voices of bigotry, racism, misogyny, anti-Semitism, Islamophobia, or white supremacy.

2. Median incomes are lower and poverty rates are higher for black Americans, Latinos, Native Americans, and

some Asian Americans and Pacific Islanders, compared to median white households.

3. And there is a persistent, pernicious racial wealth gap that holds millions of Americans back, with the typical white household holding six times more wealth than the typical Latino family and 10 times more wealth than the typical black family.

4. The wage gap between black workers and white workers is higher today than it was 20 years ago.

5. It takes a typical black woman 19 months to earn what a typical white man earns in 12 months—and for typical Latinas and Native American women, it takes almost two years.

6. Even before the COVID-19 pandemic, the uninsured rate was nearly three times higher for Latinos and nearly twice as high for black Americans as it was for whites.

7. Black children are far more likely than white children to suffer from asthma.

8. Latinos, Native Americans, Asian Americans and Pacific Islanders, and black Americans are diagnosed with diabetes at higher rates than whites.

9. Black women are more than three times as likely to die from complications of pregnancy and childbirth compared to white women.

10. President Trump's words and actions have given safe harbor and encouragement to bigots, anti-Semites, Islamophobes, and white supremacists.

11. The extreme gap in household wealth and income between people of color—especially black Americans, Latinos, and Native Americans—and white families is hurting our working class and holding our country back.

12. We will confront white nationalist terrorism and combat hate crimes perpetrated against religious minorities.

13. Each year, the United States spends $23 billion more on schools in predominantly white districts than in non-white districts.

14. We will root out systemic racism from our military justice system, where black service members are twice as likely as white ones to face court-martial.

15. Our counterterrorism priorities, footprint, and tools should shift accordingly, including to respond to the growing threat from white supremacist and other right-wing terrorist groups.[41]

Of course, it is impossible to know how the cherry-picked information and allegations were amassed. Nonetheless, we know that the stated purpose is to tear down the country, attack capitalism, and spread anti-white racism.

Coleman Hughes caught Ibram Kendi in several questionable assertions and even big whoppers, when Kendi made similar claims about "white privilege" and capitalism. Hughes explained: "[Kendi] correctly notes that blacks are more likely than whites to die of prostate cancer and breast cancer, but does not include the fact that blacks are *less* likely than whites to die of esophageal cancer, lung cancer, skin cancer, ovarian cancer, bladder cancer, brain cancer, non-Hodgkin's lymphoma, and leukemia. Of course, it should not be a competition over which race is more likely to die of which disease—but that's precisely my point. By selectively citing data that show blacks suffering more than whites, Kendi turns what should be a unifying, race-neutral battle ground—namely, humanity's fight against deadly diseases—into another proxy battle in the War on Racism."[42]

Hughes further notes that when Kendi asserts that the "'black unemployment rate has been at least twice as high as the white unemployment rate for the last fifty years' because of the 'conjoined twins' of racism and capitalism . . . why limit the analysis to the past 50 years?" Hughes cites a Pew Research article that shows "the black-white unemployment gap was 'small or nonexistent before 1940,' when America was arguably more capitalist—and certainly more racist."[43]

Moreover, Alan Berube of the liberal Brookings Institution examined recent Census information and found that although there is an income gap between whites and blacks, "[F]rom 2013 to 2018 most major metropolitan areas registered estimated increases in black median household income that exceeded those for white households. In Phoenix, for instance, the typical black household's income rose 29% (from just under $40,000 to more than $51,000), compared to a 12% increase for the typical white household (from $63,000 to $71,000). Across the 20 metro areas with the largest black populations (where sample sizes are larger), 15 registered a larger estimated rise in median black income than median white income."[44]

And there is more. Although "the Bureau of the Census on household income inequality show that in 2017 the bottom 20 percent of households had an average income of $13,258, other . . . data from the Bureau of Labor Statistics (BLS) show that these same households spent $26,091 on consumption—two times more than their income. Households in the second

20 percent income group spent 11 percent more than their Census income. The Census also reports that the top 20 percent of households had average income of $221,846, but BLS reports they consumed . . . $116,998."[45]

"The bottom quintile can consume more than twice its Census income only because the Census does not count two-thirds of transfer payment as income for those who receive them. The Census reports that the top 20 percent of households averaged 16.7 times as much income as the bottom 20 percent can be reconciled with the BLS report that they only consumed 4.5 times as much by adding the value of the transfer payments received to the income of the bottom 20 percent and subtracting the taxes paid by the top 20 percent." In fact, "[i]n 2017, federal, state, and local governments redistributed $2.8 trillion, 22 percent of the nation's earned household income, with 68 percent of those transfer payments going to households earning in the bottom 40 percent."[46]

Keep in mind, the level of government spending since 2017, and especially during Biden's ascendency to the White House, has exploded, making the amount of government redistribution of household income, and the extent to which it is transferred to the bottom 40 percent, much larger.

Looked at another way, a comprehensive study conducted by Just Facts concluded that "after accounting for all income, charity, and non-cash welfare benefits like subsidized housing and food stamps—the poorest 20 percent of Americans consume more goods and services than the national averages for *all people* in most affluent countries. This includes the majority of countries in the prestigious Organization for Economic Cooperation and Development (OECD), including its European members. In other words, if the United States poor were a nation, it would be one of the world's richest."[47]

For the civil rights Marxists, however, it is ideologically

critical that all fingers point to race, and by that they mean the "white-dominant society," "racial capitalism," etc., as the culprit for "inequity" and injustice. Racial and economic progress are measured against the impossibility of their ideological radicalism. For them, injustice and inequity abound, and there is always some event, some statistic, some outcome that serves as conclusive evidence of their righteousness and society's derangement. Yet what of the home environment, family structure, education, geography, immigration, and so forth? Do they not have an impact on an individual's life and personal outcomes? And, of course, the endless promise and pursuit of "equity" or equal outcomes is a fantasy by which all Marxist societies deceive, entice, and ultimately control their populations, eventually through a brutal police state.

Indeed, the situation has become so depraved that the "white-dominant culture" is blamed for black-on-black acts of violence. For example, here is Van Jones, CNN commentator and former Obama administration official, insisting that the murder of Tyre Nichols, who was black, by five black police officers is due to the training the black officers received, which is based on white societal racism toward black people. Jones declared that "[f]rom the [Rodney] King beating to the murder . . . of George Floyd, American society has often focused on the race of the officers—so often white—as a factor in their deplorable acts of violence. But the narrative 'White cop kills unarmed black man' should never have been the sole lens through which we attempted to understand police abuse and misconduct. It's time to move to a more nuanced discussion of the way police violence endangers black lives. Black cops are often socialized in police departments that view certain neighborhoods as war zones. In those departments, few officers get disciplined for dishing out 'street justice' in certain precincts— often populated by black, brown or low-income people—where there is a tacit understanding that the 'rulebook' simply doesn't apply. Cops of all colors, including black police officers, internalize those messages—and sometimes act on them. In fact, in black neighborhoods, the phenomenon of brutal black cops singling out young black men for abuse is nothing new. At the end of the day, it is the race of the *victim* who is brutalized—not the race of the violent cop—that is most relevant in determining whether racial bias is a factor in police violence. It's hard to imagine five cops of any color beating a white person to death under similar circumstances. And it is almost impossible to imagine five *black* cops giving a white arrestee the kind of beat-down that Nichols allegedly received."[48]

Therefore, the Nichols murder is due to the psychological indoctrination of police officers by a white system of justice, which influenced the lawless behavior of the five black police officers toward the black victim. Of course, this is imbecilic psychobabble.

Moreover, if you are not white and your views do not conform to the Marxist ideology and anti-white racist narrative, then you may be of black or brown pigmentation, but you are of a racist white outlook. Wajahat Ali, an author, playwright, contributor to the *New York Times*, and regular guest on MSNBC, said as much about former governor Nikki Haley when she announced her run for the presidency. He said, "To quote Zora Neale Hurston, not all skin folk are kinfolk. Nikki Haley instead is the Dinesh D'Souza of Candace Owens. She's the alpha Karen with brown skin. For white supremacists and racists, she is a perfect Manchurian candidate. Instead of applauding her, I'm just disgusted by people like Nikki Haley who know better, whose parents were the beneficiaries . . . of the 1965 Nationality Act, which passed thanks to those original BLM protesters and the Civil Rights Act. Her father came here because he was a professor, he taught at a historically black college in South Carolina. That's how she became the proud American that she is. And yet, what does she do, like all these model minorities, which, by the way, is a strategy of white supremacy, to use Asians in particular as a cudgel against black folks? Instead of pulling us up from the bootstraps and pulling others from the bootstraps, we're thought to take your boot and put it on the neck of poor browns, immigrants, refugees and black folks. That's what she did in her ad. So, I see her and I feel sad . . . because she uses her brown skin as a weapon against poor black folks and poor brown folks, and she uses her brown skin to launder white supremacist talking points. The reason why I feel sad, because no matter what she does . . . it will never be enough. They will never love her."[49]

Amazing how much hate, racism, and bigotry is spewed by deranged Democrats and their surrogates in the name of anti-racism.

The fact is that systemic white racism, the supposed evil at the core of American society, therefore, must be eradicated. Biden and the Democrat Party are doing all they can to exploit this hateful ideology and use the instrumentalities of government and political propaganda to advance it, under the guise of a new civil rights movement. Indeed, they are as blatant in promoting racism and resegregation as Woodrow Wilson and the Democrat Party were during much of the last century in promoting anti-black racism and segregation.

Biden and the Democrat Party were ready to impose their ideological will on the public immediately after Biden's inauguration. And no longer do they bother going through Congress and the legislative process. Biden signed an executive order hours after his swearing-in that stated, in part: "Affirmatively advancing equity, civil rights, racial justice, and equal opportunity is the responsibility of the whole of our government. Because advancing equity requires a systematic approach to embedding fairness in decision-making processes, executive departments and agencies must recognize and work to redress inequities in their policies and programs that serve as barriers to equal opportunity."[50]

What Biden intended by this presidential fiat would become crystal clear. Remember, CRT demands that new racial discrimination is necessary to address past racial discrimination. Loyola Marymount University professor Evan Gerstmann, writing in *Forbes*, has noted that there is "a recent trend toward the [Biden administration] excluding white people, and sometimes Asian Americans, from access to government relief funds and other benefits. These exclusions go well beyond traditional affirmative action plans. . . . [T]he Biden Administration has pursued this new approach most doggedly, across a broad array of relief funds, with billions of dollars being marked as off-limits to white business owners and farmers regardless of need."[51]

Rav Arora in the *City Journal* put it this way: "According to this framework, race, rather than individual circumstance, is the definitive marker for economic need. The effects of historical discrimination are presumed to be so immense that any black American, regardless of economic position, is eligible to jump ahead of the line for governmental assistance. Neither wealth nor education nor skills can attenuate a black individual's ancestral connection to the horrors of slavery, Jim Crow, or other forms of past institutionalized racism. In this paradigm, blacks are hostages to history. What could be a more dehumanizing view? . . . [T]he Biden administration has extended racial preferences . . . to virtually any individual not born into the inflexibly oppressive 'white' caste. Thus, farmers or restaurant owners of Indian, Taiwanese, and Filipino extraction—among the highest-earning groups in America—qualify for government assistance, but not poor white farmers in Appalachia."[52]

For example, the Small Business Administration (SBA) processed and distributed nearly $29 billion in funds allocated under the American Rescue Plan Act of 2021. The SBA distributed funds on a supposedly first-come, first-served basis. But during the first twenty-one days the agency gave grants to priority applicants only. Priority applicants were restaurants that are at least 51 percent owned and controlled by women, veterans, or the "socially and economically disadvantaged." "Socially disadvantaged" means someone who has been "subjected to racial or ethnic prejudice" or "cultural bias" based on his immutable characteristics. Indeed, Biden's SBA injected explicitly racial and ethnic preferences into the priority process, asserting certain applicants are socially disadvantaged based solely on their race or ethnicity—that is, to the exclusion of white-owned businesses. Not surprisingly, the Sixth Circuit Court of Appeals ruled that the federal government cannot allocate limited COVID-19 relief funds based on the race and sex of the applicants.

Moreover, under the same law passed by congressional Democrats and signed by Biden, "the Secretary [of Agriculture] shall provide a payment in the amount of up to 120 percent of the outstanding indebtedness of each socially disadvantaged farmer or rancher. . . ." The Department of Agriculture interprets "socially disadvantaged" to include farmers or ranchers "who are one or more of the following: Black/African American, American Indian, Alaskan native, Hispanic/Latino, Asian or Pacific Islander." As the court describes it: "the loan forgiveness program is based entirely on the race of the farmer or rancher."[53] The court struck down the racist part of this law as well.

Furthermore, as Betsy McCaughey, a former Republican lieutenant governor of New York, explains in the *New York Post*, Biden's student loan cancellation, recently overturned by the Supreme Court in *Biden v. Nebraska*, in addition to being unconstitutional, was defended by the administration "as a way to close the 'wealth gap' between races, citing data showing that 20 years after starting college, the average black borrower still owes 95% of the loan, while the average white borrower has paid off all but 6%. . . . [O]lder people who are white will find it harder to get an appointment with a doctor who takes Medicare. Biden is forcing physicians to categorize their patients by race and demonstrate they have an 'anti-racism' plan to combat health disparities. To meet that test, black patients will be in demand; white ones not so much. Doctors who insist on treating patients as individuals rather than by race will be punished with lower payments. . . . Fannie Mae's new Equitable Housing Finance Plan will help with appraisals and closing costs—but only if you're black. If you're a white company owner who sells to the federal government, get ready to lose business to a competitor who identifies as 'underserved,' 'marginalized' or 'disadvantaged'—all euphemisms for identity groups. The Biden bureaucracy gives preference to minorities in federal procurement."[54]

On February 16, 2023, with virtually no fanfare, Biden doubled down on his government-wide racist policies by signing another executive order—a second massive equity dictate—described as an "Executive Order on Further Advancing Racial Equity and Support for Underserved Communities through the Federal Government." Among other things, it declares that the federal government will "establish equity-focused leadership across the federal government; deliver equitable outcomes through government policies, programs, and activities; deliver equitable outcomes in partnership with underserved communities; create economic opportunity in rural America and advance urban equitable development; advance equitable procurement; further advance equitable data practices."[55]

The order also defines, among other things, "equity" to include "Black, Latino, Indigenous and Native American, Asian American, Native Hawaiian, and Pacific Islander persons and other persons of color; members of religious minorities; women and girls; LGBTQI+ persons; persons with disabilities; persons who live in rural areas; persons who live in United States Territories; persons otherwise adversely affected by persistent poverty or inequality; and individuals who belong to multiple such communities."[56] Specifically excluded from the list of favored Americans are most heterosexual, white males.

Beyond the racist federal regulations, rules, and mandates, Biden and the Democrat Party seek permanent changes to the electoral process to ensure the Democrat Party holds power for extensive periods of time without interruption. Thus, Biden and other Democrats use deceit and racial propaganda to try to both rally support for and camouflage their true electoral schemes. For example, in July 2021, in a speech intended to promote the Democrat Party's effort to nationalize election laws and enshrine its power over the federal government for generations, Biden gave one of his many demagogic speeches, in which he proclaimed, in part, that America has a long history as a racist hellhole. "From denying enslaved people full citizenship until the 13th, 14th, and 15th Amendments after the Civil War; to denying women the right to vote until the 19th Amendment 100 years ago; to poll taxes and literacy tests, and the Ku Klux Klan campaigns of violence and terror that lasted into the '50s and '60s . . ."[57]

Of course, the American people have confronted and do confront, and the American system is built to adjust and reform, what Biden described. But what is always missing from Biden's tirades is, again, the role the Democrat Party played in so much of this. The Democrat Party supported slavery and segregation and opposed the Emancipation Proclamation, the 13th Amendment (abolishing slavery), the 14th Amendment (due process and equal protections for blacks), and the 15th Amendment (giving blacks the right to vote). The Democrat Party was reluctant to give women the right to vote; created poll taxes, literacy tests, and other forms of intimidation to prevent blacks from voting; was tied closely to race-based eugenics and the Ku Klux Klan; and for decades refused to support a federal law outlawing lynching. This is the Democrat Party's obscene history.

More from Biden: "The 21st century Jim Crow assault is real. It's unrelenting, and we're going to challenge it vigorously. While this broad assault against voting rights is not unprecedented, it's taking on new and, literally, pernicious forms. It's no longer just about who gets to vote or making it easier for eligible voters to vote. It's about who gets to count the vote—who gets to count whether or not your vote counted at all. It's about moving from independent election administrators who work for the people to polarized state legislatures and partisan actors who work for political parties."[58]

"To me, this is simple," Biden declared. "This is election subversion. It's the most dangerous threat to voting and the integrity of free and fair elections in our history. Never before have they decided who gets to count . . . what votes count. . . . So, hear me clearly: There is an unfolding assault taking place in America today—an attempt to suppress and subvert the right to vote in fair and free elections, an assault on democracy, an assault on liberty, an assault on who we are—who we are as Americans."[59]

Despite Biden's constant and reckless race-baiting and pathological lying, nobody who is qualified to vote is prevented from voting. More on this later in the book.

In addition to demanding that Congress pass the power-grabbing Democrat Party voting bill, Biden was taking aim at states that were reforming their own election laws after the 2020 election and ensuring election integrity, such as Georgia, with no intention of suppressing any American's vote. Biden and the Democrats rallied the media, corporations, and others to promote a boycott of the state. Major League Baseball even moved its all-star game out of black-majority Atlanta. The Republican Georgia legislature was condemned as taking steps to suppress the black vote. Of course, this was another flat-out lie.

Writing in the *Daily Signal*, Heritage Foundation voting rights expert Hans von Spakovsky looked back at the 2022 midterm election in Georgia. Here is what he found: "In a propaganda campaign over the past two years that would impress Russian President Vladimir Putin, Biden and [Stacey] Abrams [Democrat candidate for governor of Georgia] falsely claimed that new Georgia election reforms such as an ID requirement for absentee ballots were 'Jim Crow 2.0' and deliberately intended to 'suppress' minority voters. . . . [A] survey from the Survey Research Center of the School of Public & International Affairs at the University of Georgia found that precisely 0% of black respondents said that they had a 'poor' experience voting in 2022, compared to 0.9% of white voters. . . . In fact, 96.2% of black voters said their voting experience was 'excellent' or 'good,' compared to 96% of whites, a statistically insignificant difference. Georgia voters were asked to compare their voting experience in the 2022 midterm congressional elections to the 2020 presidential election. State legislators passed the election reform bill, SB 202, in 2021 and its new provisions were in effect for the 2022 elections. Biden claimed the new law was 'Jim Crow 2.0.' Over 19% of black voters said their voting experience was 'easier' and 72.5% said there was 'no difference,' for a total of 91.6%. That compares to 13.3% of white voters who said they had an 'easier' experience in 2022 and 80.1% who said they saw 'no difference,' for a total of 93.4%. . . . 68.7% of black voters reported that they had no wait time at all, or had to wait less than 10 minutes. Another 27.3% said they waited only 10 to 30 minutes. That means that 96% of black voters voted within 30 minutes of getting to a polling place. The comparable number for white voters was 95.2%."[60]

The point is that Biden and the Democrat Party, helped by their media surrogates and corporatists, spent months pushing a malicious ruse against the Republican Party and Republican-controlled Georgia legislature, for the purpose of preventing legitimate election reforms aimed at averting voter fraud. More on the Democrat Party's voting scheme later in the book.

Biden is not alone among Democrats in his inflammatory and exploitive advocacy of civil rights Marxism and anti-white racism. I cannot think of a single national Democrat who has denounced any aspect of this un-American and hateful ideology. It now runs through the political veins of the Democrat Party, as anti-black racism did in the last century. Its surrogates in the teachers' unions, professoriate, media, Hollywood, corporate boards, etc., are all in. It is enforced throughout the economy by corporatists, activist shareholders, and government oversight and regulatory agencies (such as the Securities and Exchange Commission) and through Environmental, Social, and Governance (ESG) rules and policies; it is imposed on the rest of society through Diversity, Equity, and Inclusion (DEI) personnel employed by the thousands as enforcers and propagandists in human resource departments, in public and private workplaces, educational institutions, government departments, etc.

Although the Democrat Party has recalibrated its modern racist targets, like Democrats of old, it remains the party of anti-Semitism. In fact, as the Democrat Party's Marxist core continues to metastasize, so does its anti-Semitism. For example, the current leader of the House Democrats, and Speaker-in-waiting, Hakeem Jeffries, strongly defended his bigoted, anti-Semitic uncle Leonard Jeffries, when Hakeem Jeffries was a leading activist in college. CNN reports that Leonard Jeffries "faced widespread backlash in the early 1990s after comments he made about the involvement of 'rich Jews' in the African slave trade and 'a conspiracy, planned and plotted and programmed out of Hollywood' of Jewish executives who he said were responsible for denigrating Black Americans in films. 'Dr. Leonard Jeffries and Minister Louis Farrakhan have come under intense fire,' wrote Hakeem Jeffries in February 1992. 'Where do you think their interests lie? Dr. Jeffries has challenged the existing white supremacist educational system and long-standing distortion of history. His reward has been a media lynching complete with character assassinations and inflammatory erroneous accusations.'"[61] Hakeem Jeffries also smeared black critics of his uncle: "The House Negro of the slavery era and the black conservative of today are both opportunists interested in securing some measure of happiness for themselves within the existing social order. In both cases, the social order has blacks occupying the lowest societal echelon."[62] For years, Hakeem Jeffries has flatly lied about his past support for his uncle's vile anti-Semitism. But all is forgiven and forgotten, as Democrats have lined up in his defense.[63] After all, power is their aphrodisiac, and absolute power is their aim.

Scholar and author Victor Davis Hanson explains in *National Review* that "[t]he new anti-Semitism that grew up in the 1960s was certainly in part legitimized by the rise of overt African-American bigotry against Jews (and coupled by a romantic affinity for Islam). It was further nursed on old stereotypes of cold and callous Jewish ghetto storeowners (e.g., 'The Pawnbroker' character), and expressed boldly in the assumption that black Americans were exempt from charges of bias and hatred. . . . By the late 1970s, Israelis and often by extension Jews in general were demagogued by the Left as Western white oppressors. Israel's supposed victims were romanticized abroad as exploited Middle Easterners. And by extension, Jews were similarly exploiting minorities at home. . . . Soon it became common for self-described black leaders to explain, to amplify, to contextualize, or to be unapologetic about their anti-Semitism, in both highbrow and lowbrow modes: James Baldwin ("Negroes are anti-Semitic because they're anti-white"), Louis Farrakhan ("When they talk about Farrakhan, call me a hater, you know what they do, call me an anti-Semite. Stop it. I am anti-termite. The Jews don't like Farrakhan, so they call me Hitler. Well, that's a great name. Hitler was a very great man"), Jesse Jackson ("Hymietown"), Al Sharpton ("If the Jews want to get it on, tell them to pin their yarmulkes back and come over to my house"), and the Reverend Jeremiah Wright ("The Jews ain't gonna let him [Obama] talk to me"). Note that Jesse Jackson and Al Sharpton both ran as Democrat candidates for president. Sharpton officially visited the Obama White House more than one hundred times, and Wright was the Obamas' longtime personal pastor, officiated at the couple's wedding and the baptism of their daughters, and inspired the title of Obama's second book."[64]

Hanson notes that "marquee black leaders—from Keith Ellison to Barack Obama to the grandees of the Congressional Black Caucus—have all had smiling photo-ops with the anti-Semite Louis Farrakhan, a contemporary black version of Richard Spencer or the 1980s David Duke. Appearing with Farrakhan, however, never became toxic, even after he once publicly warned Jews, 'And don't you forget, when it's God who puts you in the ovens, it's forever!' . . . In that vein, Michigan's new congresswoman, Rashida Tlaib, assumed she'd face little pushback from her party when she tweeted out the old slur that Jewish supporters of Israel have dual loyalties: Opponents of the Boycott, Divest, and Sanctions movement, which targets Israel, 'forgot what country they represent,' she said. Ironically, Tlaib is not shy about her own spirited support of the Palestinians: She earlier had won some attention for an eliminationist map in her office that had the label 'Palestine' pasted onto the Middle East, with an arrow pointing to Israel. Similarly, Ilhan Omar—like Tlaib, a new female Muslim representative in the House—used to be candid in her views of Israel as an 'apartheid regime': 'Israel has hypnotized the world, may Allah awaken the people and help them see the evil doings of Israel.' On matters of apartheid, one wonders whether Omar would prefer to be an Arab citizen inside 'evil' Israel or an Israeli currently living in Saudi Arabia or Egypt."[65]

And, of course, many present-day Democrat Party anti-Semites view the Jewish people as part of the white-dominant, white-privileged, oppressor white race. Hanson points out: "The new, new anti-Semites do not see themselves as giving new life to an ancient pathological hatred; they're only voicing claims of the victims themselves against their supposed oppressors. The new, new anti-Semites' venom is contextualized as an 'intersectional' defense from the hip, the young, and the woke against a Jewish component of privileged white establishmentarians—which explains why the bigoted are so surprised that anyone would be offended by their slurs."[66]

In early September 2016, writes Rabbi Yaakov Menken, managing director of the Coalition for Jewish Values, in the *Observer*, "[T]he Obama administration reacted angrily to a video in which Israeli Prime Minister Benjamin Netanyahu pointed out that the Palestinian Authority intended to be *Judenrein*, ethnically cleansed of Jews. The State Department willfully distorted Netanyahu's remarks, asserting he was promoting Israeli settlements, and reiterating its false claim that those settlements are illegal. In other words, the Obama administration twisted a statement about Arab bigotry against Jews into a perceived injustice against Arabs. Later that same month, Obama delivered his final address to the United Nations General Assembly. 'And surely, Israelis and Palestinians will be better off if Palestinians reject incitement and recognize the legitimacy of Israel,' he said, 'but Israel recognizes that it cannot permanently occupy and settle

Palestinian land.' While his words may sound to the untrained ear as if Obama were striving for balance, these two phrases could not be further apart."[67]

Apparently, the Jewish people are the only indigenous people Obama, the Democrat Party ruling class, and their ilk do not recognize. "Jews lived in the area Jordan labeled the 'West Bank' continuously for the past 3,000 years," writes Menken, "save for brief periods when they were massacred, and the survivors were forced from their homes—most recently by the Jordanian Army in 1948. To now call the Tomb of the Patriarchs and the Temple Mount 'Arab land' tacitly endorses Arab ethnic cleansing of Jews."[68]

In fact, Obama was disastrous for the state of Israel, as he was for the United States. He denied Israel arms for a period when it was under attack; he signed an agreement with the terrorist Iranian regime that ensured its acquisition of nuclear weapons and threatened Israel's existence; he directed his secretary of state, John Kerry, to abstain rather than vote "no" on another anti-Semitic UN resolution against Israel; he attempted to unseat Israel's elected prime minister, Benjamin Netanyahu, and treated him disrespectfully when he visited the White House; and, much more.

Biden has picked up where Obama left off, reversing President Trump's pro-Israel policies. He negotiates with the Iranian regime in secret, reportedly promising tens of billions in financial relief and acceptance of Iran's substantial advances in developing nuclear weapons; he bypassed the Taylor Force Act, which prevented United States' funding of the Palestinians unless they stopped using the money to reward the families of Palestinian terrorists for murdering Jews (Taylor Force was a former U.S. Army officer who was part of a Vanderbilt University tour group who was stabbed to death in a terror attack that left ten others wounded in an old section of Tel Aviv); he delivered hundreds of millions of dollars to the Palestinian Authority; and much more.[69]

And Biden has done next to nothing to address the growing anti-Semitism in the Democrat Party or on Democrat Party–supporting college and university campuses.

In *Newsweek*, Kenneth Marcus, chairman of the Louis D. Brandeis Center for Human Rights Under Law, recently wrote: "The Biden White House had announced last spring (and even before that), that the Education Department's Office for Civil Rights (OCR) would deliver an important proposed regulation in December 2022. The regulation is supposed to implement the Executive Order on Combating Antisemitism, which former President Donald Trump had signed in 2019. This order had been a major milestone, codifying important rules under which Jewish students receive civil rights protections in American colleges and schools. . . . [T]he Biden administration announced that the proposed regulation would be delayed another 12 months, until December 2023."[70]

The Biden administration decided to move up its announcement, Marcus explained in the *Jewish Press*. However, the move was "deeply troubling," because "the administration appears to be retreating from a longstanding commitment to issue regulations on combating antisemitism. Instead of issuing a new regulation that strengthens protections for Jewish students, the administration is promising only to issue informal guidance to remind institutions of their existing commitments."[71] In other words, Biden appeased the anti-Semitic elements in his party and like-minded Democrat Party surrogates and groups. Like Lyndon Johnson, who succeeded in watering down the 1957 Civil Rights Act, Biden has done the same with anti-Semitism in colleges and schools.

The editors at *National Review*, in an editorial titled "Time for Democrats to Address Their Anti-Semitism Problem," explained that "[a]nti-Jewish attacks did not spring forth in a vacuum. Increasingly, the American Left has gone beyond mere criticism of the Jewish State (of the sort that is made against other nations) and adopted the kind of virulent strain of anti-Israel rhetoric that was once mercifully relegated to far-left college campuses. In this environment, Squad members Ilhan Omar, Alexandria Ocasio-Cortez, and Rashida Tlaib can falsely accuse Israel of being an 'apartheid state' and of employing U.S. military aid to target civilians and children—a new spin on an old blood libel—and experience almost no rebuke from their own party."[72]

The editors continued: "The intense opprobrium saved for Israel, and spared authoritarian nations such as China and Iran, betrays the progressive left's moral corruption. And rather than react in dismay, *New York Times* progressive columnist Michelle Goldberg lamented that attacks on Jews might undermine the Palestinian political cause. Rather than distance themselves from violence conducted by their allies, former Bernie Sanders surrogate Amer Zahr implored progressives in a video and tweet to 'stop condemning anti-Semitism.' He said, 'You are not helping. You are playing their games. It's a distraction.' Instead, he urged followers to say 'Free Palestine—and nothing else!' Zahr needn't worry. Most progressive politicians who did bother denouncing the recent wave of violence against Jews diluted their rebukes by also condemning rising Islamophobia, creating the impression that advocates of both sides of the Israeli–Palestinian debate were engaging in violence—which is, needless to say, a myth."[73]

Indeed, for American Marxists and the Democrat Party, anti-Semitism fits neatly into their political and ideological narrative. "There is little political upside for Democrats to call out the Squad. Polls show a party that has lurched leftward and become increasingly antagonistic towards the Jewish State," write the *National Review* editors. "As Ayaan Hirsi Ali recently noted, the Israeli–Palestinian conflict feeds into many of the progressive left's ideological biases: 'the narrative of the oppressor versus the oppressed, of the colonizer versus the colonized, of the genocide perpetrator and system of supremacy.'"[74]

And do Democrat Party leaders condemn what is taking place among their ranks? "When it comes to Ilhan Omar and Co., where is Nancy Pelosi? Where is Chuck Schumer or Dick Durbin? To this point, nowhere to be found. It is, of course, true that neither Left nor Right has a monopoly on anti-Semitism. These days, however, one party is increasingly under the sway of a noxious, all-encompassing hostility to the Jewish State."[75] The Democrat Party is not only tolerating anti-Semitism, it is promoting it.[76] Not so with the Republican Party.

Nonetheless, the Democrat Party, once again, attempts to project upon the Republican Party and others the bigotry and hatred that have always defined it, in one form or another. This is typical of arrogant autocratic parties and regimes, which use propaganda to distract and manipulate events. Jonathan S. Tobin, editor in chief of the *Jewish News Service*, responded to an effort by a Democrat-aligned writer to paint former president Donald Trump and the Republican Party as the real home of anti-Semitism. "To the contrary," writes Tobin, "[Trump] was not only the most pro-Israel president ever but surpassed his predecessors in opposing antisemitism on college campuses and had closer ties to Jews than any other previous president via his family and close associates. The claims that he never condemned right-wing extremism or had endorsed the neo-Nazis who marched in Charlottesville, Va., in August 2017, which continue to be voiced on the left, were simply untrue. The argument that Trump somehow encouraged antisemites on the far-right with his trolling of his critics and foes on Twitter, as well as in speeches, was pure partisanship. It's also hypocritical since it's the sort of charge that is never applied to liberals, like Biden, who are also prone to hyperbolic and dishonest attacks on their opponents."[77]

Tobin declares: "The reality of contemporary politics is the GOP is a lockstep pro-Israel party where philo-Semitism is the norm. The opposite is true of the Democratic Party, whose intersectional left-wing's embrace of critical race theory has driven growing hostility to Israel and support for ideologues in the Black Lives Matter movement that embrace the idea that Jews are 'white' oppressors. And rather than isolating their extremists, the party's progressive wing and pop-culture and media cheering sections have embraced them."[78] Tobin explains that for many on the left, "their goal is to redefine antisemitism in a way so as to label the demonization of Israel and the Jews as legitimate discourse rather than hate speech."[79]

Indeed, Biden has a history of treating the State of Israel, the only Jewish state in the world, and established after World War II and the Holocaust, as a second-class country. He speaks down to its elected leaders, when those leaders are members of the Likud Party—Israel's largest political party for the last quarter century. It is also Israel's most prominent conservative party.

On June 22, 1982, Sen. Biden confronted then Israeli Prime Minister Menachem Begin during his Senate Foreign Relations committee testimony, threatening to cut off aid to Israel when Begin refused to accept Biden's demands on how to run his country. Begin looked directly at Biden and said: "Don't threaten us with cutting off your aid. It will not work. I am not a Jew with trembling knees. I am a proud Jew with 3,700 years of civilized history. Nobody came to our aid when we were dying in the gas chambers and ovens. Nobody came to our aid when we were striving to create our country. We paid for it. We fought for it. We died for it. We will stand by our principles. We will defend them. And, when necessary, we will die for them again, with or without your aid."[80]

Today, Biden is at it again. Like his former boss, Obama, Biden is actively undermining Israeli Prime Minister Benjamin Netan-

yahu, his coalition government, and the State of Israel, as it faces
down the Iranian terror state and its nuclear weapons development and Palestinian terrorists. The *Wall Street Journal* editorial
board recently asked: "Why does President Biden go out of his
way to snub, criticize and give marching orders to the government
of Israel? At least rhetorically, the President and his Administration treat Prime Minister Benjamin Netanyahu and his governing
coalition worse than they do the ruling mullahs in Iran....Tom
Nides, Mr. Biden's departing Ambassador to Israel, chimes in that
the U.S. must speak up to stop Israel from 'going off the rails.'"[81]

The *Journal* notes that Biden's "Israel policy has been coun-
terproductive. U.S. aid to anti-Israel international bodies has
resumed, and all of [Judaea and Samaria] and East Jerusalem is
treated as 'occupied territory.' This is now a liberal article of
faith, but how does it advance peace to indulge Palestinians in
the belief that Jews are interlopers in Judea and at the Western
Wall?"[82]

Biden is selling out Israel in pursuit of another treacherous
nuclear deal with Iran that allows Iran to complete its nuclear
arms program, and in which Biden and the Obama holdovers surrounding him, arrogantly claim and stupidly believe they can dip-
lomatically manage the region. Hence, Netanyahu, who insists
that Iran must never produce a single nuclear weapon—and is
prepared to go to war to stop that genocidal terrorist regime—is
viewed by Biden as the problem.

Biden has not and never will treat another country, especially
an ally, with the kind of condescension and disdain he singularly
saves for Israel and its democratically elected government. And
despite his self-aggrandizing lies, in which he claims a decades-
long record of supporting the Jewish state, his motives are sinister
and his contempt is obvious. In this, his record may well exceed
Franklin Roosevelt's legacy toward the Jewish people.

• • •

As the Democrat Party's want for ever more control intensifies, and its hate for America becomes even more pronounced, it will look increasingly like autocratic parties, past and present, around the world. The Marxist model best fits its aims because Marxist rhetoric is more easily made appealing to "the masses," as is the promise of a paradisiacal society supposedly replacing the irredeemably amoral society inherited by present-day Americans. Moreover, their progress is never measured by promises kept, but by more promises made.

The Democrat Party will also continue to aggressively denounce and degrade capitalism, which rewards individual accomplishments, merit, and freethinking and is, thereby, a huge impediment to their effort to centralize power and decision-making. It will further extol CRT's oppressor-oppressed Marxist-based racism, which breeds jealousy, anger, and hate toward the existing "white-dominant society;" and, anti-Semitism within the Democrat Party will further fester and become increasingly belligerent and bellicose, which is a sign of the evil nature of such parties and, ultimately, regimes throughout the centuries.

This is the unmistakable path the Democrat Party is on. And it is the path down which it is driving the rest of the country.

CHAPTER FOUR

LANGUAGE CONTROL & THOUGHT CONTROL

Dr. Joost A. M. Meerloo, probably unknown to most Americans, but well known in psychiatric circles, was a practicing psychiatrist for over forty years. "He did staff psychiatric work in Holland and worked as a general practitioner until 1942 under Nazi occupation, when he assumed the name Joost to fool the occupying forces, and in 1942 fled to England (after barely eluding death at the hands of the Germans). He was chief of the Psychological Department of the Dutch Army-in-Exile in England. . . . Meerloo specialized in the area of thought control techniques used by totalitarian regimes."[1]

In his book *Delusion and Mass Delusion*, Meerloo explains that "[t]otalitarian or dictatorial thinking is a remnant of archaic times. Objective verification of ideas is rejected since no reality beyond the dictatorial opinion exists. The deviant point of view is considered dangerous for the weak. Free thought is experienced as a thwarting, hostile force. The critical word, the deviating attitude, the non-conformism of one man threatens the clan.

The individual is only permitted to think with the tribe. Archaic thinking follows what we might call an imperialistic strategy. It lulls people to sleep, it resists their consciousness and critical confrontation, it suppresses all individual creativity. Totalitarian thinking is identifying thinking; it takes account only of totalities and never of parts. Specific and particular forms have no value. Only the recurrent and expected is accepted. Man remains one with his people, his land, his race. Human evolution, however, breaks the bond between man and his world and places him in opposition to it."[2]

If we are to be honest with ourselves, this is where our culture is heading, or is already parked.

For example, it is difficult to forget this exchange between Republican Tennessee senator Marsha Blackburn and Supreme Court nominee Kentanji Brown Jackson:

"Can you define the word 'woman'"?

"Can I provide a definition?" Jackson responded.

"No, I can't," Jackson declared, before adding: "I'm not a biologist."[3]

Thus, the first black woman ever nominated to serve on the Supreme Court, and celebrated as such by Joe Biden, the Democrat Party, and the media, and who now serves on the Court, refused to define the word *woman* even though she obviously knew the answer. But what explains such nonsense? Jackson, Biden, and the same Democrats who refuse to use the word *woman* in certain contexts have no problem using the word when it comes to celebrating "International Women's Day," "Women's History Month," "The Violence Against Women Act," "a woman's right to choose," or, of course, "the first black *woman* to serve on the Supreme Court." Moreover, not one Senate Democrat or prominent Democrat anywhere found Jackson's testimony embarrassing, troubling, or disqualifying. On the contrary, she was defended.

As Associate Professor Magda Stroinska at McMaster University in Hamilton, Canada, explains in her essay "Language and Totalitarian Regimes," "[t]otalitarism promotes persuasion by means of altering people's perception of reality. . . ." She also explains that communist regimes used the means of propaganda and mass deception based on a fiction.[4] In other words, language is weaponized to serve the purposes of a political party, movement, ideology, and/or regime. In this, the Marxists are not alone. Stroinska notes that "[i]n practice, only a few people can be persuaded that black is white, but many learn to say that they do see things in prescribed colors and to call them by prescribed names."[5] For example, not long ago Republican senator Marco Rubio introduced an amendment to a bill "that would have clarified, for the purposes of maternal and infant-related program resources, that only women can be pregnant." It was defeated by the Senate Democrats.[6] Or take the word *socialist*. Stroinska explains that "[w]hile the word *socialist* became suspect, *social* lingers on. It became a fixed prefix to words such as *justice, institution, policy, democracy* or *solidarity*, as if there were any instances of justice or democracy that were happening in a vacuum."[7]

Obviously, this authoritarian practice now widely exists in the United States, as the English language, science, knowledge, experience, and specific words are being redefined, banned, replaced, etc., to impose on the citizenry the beliefs, values, and thought processes of the American Marxists and the Democrat Party. For example, academic freedom, debate, and the competition of ideas on college campuses; free speech and the exchange of information on Internet platforms; entertainment from comedy and plays to television and movies; biological and scientific knowledge about men, women, gender, and sex; public school teacher seminars and training; classroom texts and learning; bureaucratic edicts and regulations; corporate Environmental, Social, and Governance (ESG); workplace Diversity, Equity, and Inclusion (DEI); "wokeness" generally; and more are all used to control the public and serve the ideological, political, and economic purposes of the Democrat Party.

Philosopher and professor Friedrich A. Hayek put it this way: "The most effective way of making everybody serve the single system of ends towards which the social plan is directed is to make everybody believe in those ends. . . . Although the beliefs must be chosen for the people and imposed upon them, they must become their beliefs, a generally accepted creed which makes the individuals as far as possible act spontaneously in the way the planner wanted."[8]

Richard M. Ebeling, professor of ethics and free enterprise leadership, The Citadel, explains that "[i]t is through our language that we think about ourselves, our relationships to others, and the social order surrounding us. Words do not merely delineate objects, individuals, events, or actions. Words also create mental imageries, emotions, attitudes, and beliefs that color how people see themselves and the world around them." Ebeling writes about the "totalitarian-ization of words and ideas [that] can be seen at work in the language of the progressive and radical 'left' in America today."[9]

Indeed, Mikhail Heller, an author and scholar who was raised in the Soviet Union, explains: "Language is the most important and the most powerful weapon in the hands of a state that has decided to transform human-beings. The creation of a new language serves two aims: to obtain, as George Orwell put it, 'an instrument with which to express the philosophy and thoughts that are permitted,' and, secondly, to make 'all other sorts of thinking impossible.' The new language is consequently at once a means of communication and an instrument of oppression. . . . The word conceals reality, creates an illusion, a surrealist impression, but at the same time it preserves a link with reality and puts it into code."[10] In the Soviet Union, Heller recounts, "[t]he Soviet language became the most important means of preventing people from acquiring more knowledge than the Communist Party/state wished. . . . Soviet speech lost its freedom."[11] Moreover, the official dictionaries were changed to reflect the Communist Party/state's meaning of words. This same indoctrination tool is occurring in the United States today. And the Democrat Party is at the foreground of this movement.

National Public Radio (NPR) recently reported: "Dictionary.com has updated thousands of entries and added hundreds of words in its largest release to date, a reflection of the ways in which society and language have evolved even in just the past few months. The digital dictionary announced . . . that it updated more than 15,000 entries and added 650 brand new terms. Many of the revisions deal with language related to identity and topics like race and ethnicity, gender and sexuality and health and wellness. 'The work of a dictionary is more than just adding new words. It's an ongoing effort to ensure that how we define words reflects changes in language—and life,' said John Kelly, senior editor at Dictionary.com. 'Our revisions are putting people, in all their rich humanity, first, and we're extremely proud of that.'"[12]

NPR added that "[s]ome of the major site-wide changes to existing entries have to do with race and ethnicity, like capitalizing the word 'Black' in reference to people, which the company says it is doing 'as a mark of respect and recognition that's in line with capitalizing other cultures and ethnicities. Examples of entirely new terms in this category include Afro-Latino, brownface, Filipinx and whitesplain. Another dictionary-wide change replaces references to 'homosexual' with 'gay, gay man or gay woman,' and references to 'homosexuality' with 'gay sexual orientation.' The company said these updates were informed by recommendations from the organization GLAAD, and affect more than 50 entries. It has also refined the definitions for a number of other words related to LGBTQ identity, such as asexual, deadname, Pride and themself."[13]

In repressive regimes, repetition is also used to force the acceptance and even internalization of new words or words with newly created meanings, and language is used to identify and condemn "enemies" of the state. In other words, the public endures constant and unrelenting brainwashing and propaganda—or, as Hannah Arendt, one of the premier political philosophers in the twentieth century, commented, a form of psychological warfare.[14] Indeed, Arendt spent years studying and writing about totalitarianism, having barely escaped Hitler's Third Reich. For example, she wrote in her book *The Origins of Totalitarianism* that "[t]otalitarianism propaganda raised ideological scientificality and its technique of making statements in the form of predictions to a height of efficiency of method and absurdity of consent because, demagogically speaking, there is hardly a better way to avoid discussion than releasing an argument from the control of the present and by saying that only the future can reveal its merits. However, totalitarian ideologies did not invent this procedure, and were not the only ones to use it. Scientificality of mass propaganda has indeed been so universally employed in modern politics that it has been interpreted as a more general sign of that obsession with science which has characterized the Western world since the rise of mathematics and physics in the sixteenth century; thus totalitarianism appears to be only the last stage in a process during which 'science [has become] an idol that will magically cure the evils of existence and transform the nature of man.' And there was, indeed, an early connection between scientificality and the rise of the masses."[15]

Arendt's point is that Marxists, fascists, and autocrats generally explain away the horrendous and barbaric conditions they create, yet still appeal or attempt to appeal to "the masses" by focusing on the paradise they promise in the future—if only every individual surrenders their free will, in part or in whole, to a small cabal of activists, revolutionaries, and ultimately autocratic masterminds who claim to speak for and represent the people. There is no better subject to illustrate such a colossal deception in today's world as "climate change," which is central to the Democrat Party's growing authoritarianism over all aspects of American life.

Every weather event or natural disaster that causes discomfort, damage, or death is attributed to "climate change," which in turn is said to require major changes in the quality of life, the capitalist system, a reduction in economic growth and prosperity, increased taxation and regulation, the surrender of national sovereignty to international governing organizations, and/or the significant expanse of domestic governmental power. Indeed, every household product, from gas stoves, lightbulbs, and dishwashers to air conditioners, washing machines, automobiles, and anything else that uses energy, is now subject to government control.

And since the time is said to be urgent, requiring instant and vast federally directed change to save the future of humanity, there is virtually no time for reflection, circumspection, or scientific and factual evaluation of *past* predictions and their accuracy (actually, inaccuracy) and the direction in which the nation is being forcibly plunged. The reason is that "climate change" is a politically and economically driven movement within the American Marxist framework that empowers the Democrat Party's ability to control the behavior of the people.

Dr. Mark J. Perry, senior fellow emeritus at the American Enterprise Institute (AEI), with the help of a *Reason* magazine article authored by award-winning science correspondent Ronald Bailey, reached back to the first "Earth Day" (May 1, 1970) to determine how accurate the apocalyptic predictions were. Here are the findings:

" 'The prophets of doom were not simply wrong, but *spectacularly* wrong,' according to Bailey. Here are 18 examples of the spectacularly wrong predictions made around 1970 when the 'green holy day' (aka Earth Day) started:

1. Harvard biologist George Wald estimated that 'civilization will end within 15 or 30 years [by 1985 or 2000] unless immediate action is taken against problems facing mankind.'

2. 'We are in an environmental crisis that threatens the survival of this nation, and of the world as a suitable place of human habitation,' wrote Washington University biologist Barry Commoner in the Earth Day issue of the scholarly journal *Environment*.

3. The day after the first Earth Day, the *New York Times* editorial page warned, 'Man must stop pollution and conserve his resources, not merely to enhance existence but to save the race from intolerable deterioration and possible extinction.'

4. 'Population will inevitably and completely outstrip whatever small increases in food supplies we make,' Paul Ehrlich confidently declared in the April 1970 issue of *Mademoiselle*. 'The death rate will increase until at least 100–200 million people per year will be starving to death during the next ten years [by 1980].'

5. 'Most of the people who are going to die in the greatest cataclysm in the history of man have already been born,' wrote Paul Ehrlich in a 1969 essay titled 'Eco-Catastrophe'! 'By . . . [1975] some experts feel that food shortages will have escalated the present level of world

hunger and starvation into famines of unbelievable proportions. Other experts, more optimistic, think the ultimate food-population collision will not occur until the decade of the 1980s.'

6. Ehrlich sketched out his most alarmist scenario for the 1970 Earth Day issue of *The Progressive*, assuring readers that between 1980 and 1989, some 4 billion people, including 65 million Americans, would perish in the 'Great Die-Off.'

7. 'It is already too late to avoid mass starvation,' declared Denis Hayes, the chief organizer for Earth Day, in the Spring 1970 issue of *The Living Wilderness*.

8. Peter Gunter, a North Texas State University professor, wrote in 1970, 'Demographers agree almost unanimously on the following grim timetable: by 1975 widespread famines will begin in India; these will spread by 1990 to include all of India, Pakistan, China, and the Near East, Africa. By the year 2000, or conceivably sooner, South and Central America will exist under famine conditions. . . . By the year 2000, thirty years from now, the entire world, with the exception of Western Europe, North America, and Australia, will be in famine.'

(Note: The prediction of famine in South America is partly true, but only in Venezuela and only because of socialism, not for environmental reasons.)

9. In January 1970, *Life* reported, 'Scientists have solid experimental and theoretical evidence to support . . . the following predictions: In a decade, urban dwellers will have to wear gas masks to survive air pollution . . . by 1985 air

pollution will have reduced the amount of sunlight reaching earth by one half. . . .'

10. Ecologist Kenneth Watt told *Time* that, 'At the present rate of nitrogen buildup, it's only a matter of time before light will be filtered out of the atmosphere and none of our land will be usable.'

11. Barry Commoner predicted that decaying organic pollutants would use up all of the oxygen in America's rivers, causing freshwater fish to suffocate.

12. Paul Ehrlich chimed in, predicting in 1970 that 'air pollution . . . is certainly going to take hundreds of thousands of lives in the next few years alone.' Ehrlich sketched a scenario in which 200,000 Americans would die in 1973 during 'smog disasters' in New York and Los Angeles.

13. Paul Ehrlich warned in the May 1970 issue of *Audubon* that DDT and other chlorinated hydrocarbons 'may have substantially reduced the life expectancy of people born since 1945.' Ehrlich warned that Americans born since 1946 . . . now had a life expectancy of only 49 years, and he predicted that if current patterns continued this expectancy would reach 42 years by 1980 when it might level out. (Note: According to the most recent CDC report, life expectancy in the US is 78.6 years.)

14. Ecologist Kenneth Watt declared, 'By the year 2000 if present trends continue, we will be using up crude oil at such a rate . . . that there won't be any more crude oil. You'll drive up to the pump and say, 'Fill 'er up, buddy,' and he'll say, 'I am very sorry, there isn't any.'

(Note: Global oil production [in 2021 was] at about 95M barrels per day (bpd) was double the global oil output of 48M bpd around the time of the first Earth Day in 1970.)

15. Harrison Brown, a scientist at the National Academy of Sciences, published a chart in *Scientific American* that looked at metal reserves and estimated that humanity would totally run out of copper shortly after 2000. Lead, zinc, tin, gold, and silver would be gone before 1990.

16. Sen. Gaylord Nelson wrote in *Look*, 'Dr. S. Dillon Ripley, secretary of the Smithsonian Institute, believes that in 25 years, somewhere between 75 and 80 percent of all the species of living animals will be extinct.'

17. In 1975, Paul Ehrlich predicted that 'since more than nine-tenths of the original tropical rainforests will be removed in most areas within the next 30 years or so [by 2005], it is expected that half of the organisms in these areas will vanish with it.'"[16]

The list of so-called experts, scholars, scientists, meteorologists, climatologists, professors, politicians, etc., insisting the end of the world is around the corner, most of whom blamed mankind's activity—particularly the success and prosperity of the United States—is endless. They were not only spectacularly wrong but they were driven by an ideological and political agenda disguised as science. Therefore, we are to ignore all of this, do not look back, and the world begins today with new promises and predictions intended to empower the government and the Democrat Party. Hence, language manipulation, scare tactics, and censorship are used to control and shape public debate (such as it is), and impose and enforce the "climate change" agenda, thereby empowering the party of government.

In fact, American Marxists will bluntly explain their intentions, even if the Democrat Party uses political spin and propaganda to deceive the public. For example, on the Socialist Alliance website, in an essay titled "Climate Change: A Marxist Analysis," it states: "A plethora of 'blueprints' for an ecologically sustainable world have been produced by the dozens by Green groups here and around the world, containing logical and commonsense solutions to global warming and the general environmental crisis. They fail not because their proposals for a rapid conversion to renewable energy and the rational reorganisation of production and consumption are far-fetched. They fail because they do not accept that capitalism is incapable of bringing them into being."[17]

Moreover, as I have written in the past, there is a Marxist "degrowth movement" that, at its core, demands the abandonment of capitalism for a radical reengineering of society and the economy based on discarding economic growth for a government-managed economy. In other words, economic expansion, which leads to opportunity, prosperity, and job growth, is destroying the environment. Therefore, the federal Leviathan must institute measures that promote homegrown organic foods; suppress advertising for consumer goods; limit the use of privately owned vehicles; increase taxes on airline travel and goods with "higher environmental/social costs"; ban use of plastics and single-use items; and, of course, subsidize solar power, wind power, etc.,[18] while taxing and regulating out of existence energy companies and products that use fossil fuels, limiting the size and number of single-family homes; and imposing zoning and building codes that create dense housing around public transportation hubs.

Hence, the Democrat Party and its surrogates insist that "climate change" is an existential threat to human survival, requiring governmental omnipresence in all aspects of life regardless of constitutional limits and barriers to such a totalitarian notion. And the employment of language, censorship, and other forms of thought manipulation and control are indispensable.

There is no doubt that present-day efforts to alter the English language have been urged by radical Marxist academics for years. And this movement has journeyed from the usual places—college campuses, "scholarly" books and journals—to the broader culture and throughout society. Eric Arthur Blair, aka George Orwell, in his essay "Politics and the English Language" (written in 1946), who also authored such incomparable anti-totalitarian fictions as *Animal Farm* (written in 1945) and *1984* (written in 1949), asserted that "[n]ow, it is clear that the decline of a language must ultimately have political and economic causes: it is not due simply to the bad influence of this or that individual writer. But an effect can become a cause, reinforcing the original cause and producing the same effect in an intensified form, and so on indefinitely. . . . [The English language] became ugly and inaccurate because our thoughts are foolish, but the slovenliness of our language makes it easier for us to have foolish thoughts."[19]

Orwell explains that "[m]any political words are . . . abused. . . . It is almost universally felt that when we call a country democratic, we are praising it: consequently, the defenders of every kind of regime claim that it is a democracy, and fear that they might have to stop using the word if it were tied down to any one meaning. Words of this kind are often used in a consciously dishonest way. That is, the person who uses them has his own private definition, but allows his hearer to think he means something quite different."[20] Simply put, the abuser of words is a demagogue who is knowingly lying by creating a false narrative. This is a technique relentlessly used by the Democrat Party and Joe Biden to conceal their true intentions and the disastrous consequences of their policies. A few examples suffice:

Biden has created the worst border crisis in American history.[21] Yet he accuses Republicans, who have been demanding more personnel and resources (including the completion of a border wall started by President Trump) to secure the border and enforce immigration law, of wanting to cut border enforcement. Biden tweeted: "MAGA House Republican proposals would slash funding for border security—a move that could allow nearly 900 pounds of fentanyl into our country. We need more resources to secure the border. Not less."[22] Of course, this is a preposterous Biden lie.

During his State of the Union speech in February 2023, Biden accused congressional Republicans of wanting to eliminate Social Security and Medicare. "Instead of making the wealthy pay their fair share, some Republicans want Medicare and Social Security to sunset," Biden claimed as he was drowned out by Republicans booing him. "That means if Congress doesn't vote to keep them, those programs will go away."[23] But the Republican Party did not call for the elimination of either program. Instead, many Republicans have sought ways to save the programs. If the programs are not reformed, based on the dire warnings of the trustees of both programs, and based on financial and actuarial data, they will soon collapse. The trustees' reports are provided to the president and the leaders of both houses of Congress. Biden's allegation, which has been made repeatedly, has been debunked again and again. But Biden is employing the totalitarian practice of *repetition*, an essential element of propaganda.

Indeed, Fox News reported, citing the research of the presidential campaign of Bernie Sanders, that it was Biden who "floated raising the Social Security retirement age in 1983. A year later, in 1984, Biden supported plans to freeze federal spending—including

Social Security—as part of an effort to reduce the national debt. And in the 1990s, Biden supported efforts to balance the budget that would have included cuts to Social Security. . . . In 2007, as he was running for president, Biden repeatedly expressed openness to raising the retirement age in an attempt to make it easier to pay for social safety net programs. Biden also reportedly was open to cutting Social Security during his first term as vice president, which began in 2009, as he sought to make budget compromises with Republicans."[24] Moreover, on the floor of the Senate in 1995, then Senator Biden passionately declared: "When I argued that we should freeze federal spending, I meant Social Security as well. I meant Medicare and Medicaid. I meant veterans' benefits. I meant every single solitary thing in the government. And I not only tried it once, I tried it twice, I tried it a third time, and I tried it a fourth time."[25]

As explained earlier, Biden is a political chameleon, who has found his ultimate political success and power as an oligarch for American Marxism. If that means accusing Republicans of supporting what he supported in the past, then insisting Republicans want to abolish Social Security and Medicare, so be it. Biden has no reservations about slandering anyone or any group he perceives as a threat to his power. Indeed, the same can be said of the Democrat Party and its commissaries.

Biden's lies (language manipulation and indoctrination) have been so blatant that even Biden/Democrat Party–supporting CNN criticized him for "repeatedly tak[ing] credit for reducing the deficit in 2021 and 2022 even though experts have said that the vast majority of this reduction occurred simply because emergency COVID-19 pandemic spending from 2020 expired as planned—and that Biden's own initiatives made the deficits higher than they otherwise would be." CNN added: "We've described Biden's previous deficit boasts as misleading or missing key context."[26] In fact, Biden's budget would lead to even larger deficits.[27] Nonetheless, Biden persists.

In March 2023, Biden demanded that "[c]ongressional Republicans should pass my budget instead of calling for cuts in these [mental health] services or defunding the police or abolishing the FBI, as we hear from our MAGA Republican friends."[28] In other words, when the Republicans opposed Biden's monstrous spending bill, which was a radical "climate change" bill promoted as an inflation-reducing bill, the Republicans were actually seeking to defund police?

As FactCheck.org reported, "the section of the bill outlining the 'Coronavirus State and Local Fiscal Recovery Funds' did not stipulate that the relief funding had to be used on police officers or for other law enforcement initiatives. . . . Even the May 10 fact sheet on the Treasury's proposed interim final rule on how to use the recovery funds noted that 'recipients have broad flexibility to decide how best to use this funding to meet the needs of their communities.'" And when White House Press Secretary Jen Psaki, now a host on MSNBC, was challenged in a June 30 press briefing to name a single Republican who had opposed the bill because of the additional funding for police, she didn't identify one."[29] Obviously, the Republican Party has never supported defunding the police; prominent Democrat Party activists, mayors, city councils, and members of Congress did.

And there is more. When a deranged and evil person murders children in schoolrooms, or murders numerous people at a church or warehouse store, Biden, his spokesmen, his party, and the media blame congressional Republicans for refusing to pass an "assault weapons" ban. For example, literally hours after the murder of three children and three adults at a private Christian school in Nashville, Tennessee, White House press secretary Karine Jean-Pierre asked the press corps: "How many more children have to be murdered before Republicans in Congress will step up and act to pass the assault weapons ban, to close loopholes in our background check system or to require the safe storage of guns. We need to do something."[30] Biden himself has said much the same thing. In 2022, he also claimed: "When we passed the assault weapons ban [in 1994], mass shootings went down. When the law expired, mass shootings tripled."[31] Moreover, Biden has proposed a ban on "assault weapons," a ban on high-capacity magazines, a mandate for background checks on all gun sales, and eliminating immunity for gun manufacturers, which he refers to time and again as a way to significantly reduce mass murders.

Thus, the immediate politicization and exploitation of such terrifying murders, to blame Republicans and to attack the Second Amendment and the right to bear arms, are another example of Democrat Party propaganda manipulation. In fact, let us take a look back at Biden's constant references to the so-called assault weapons ban he supported as a senator.

In 1994, Congress passed and President Bill Clinton signed the Public Safety and Recreational Use Firearms Protection Act sponsored by Democrat senator Dianne Feinstein and cosponsored by Biden. The result: Dr. John Lott Jr., who has an extraordinarily distinguished academic, research, and scholarly background,[32] explains that "[t]here was no drop in the number of attacks with assault weapons during the 1994 to 2004 ban. There was an increase after the ban sunset, but the change is not statistically significant. More importantly, if Biden's claim is correct, we should see a drop in the percent of attacks with assault weapons during the federal ban period and then an increase in the post-ban period, but the exact opposite is true."[33] Lott was not alone. A similar conclusion was reached by the RAND Corporation with respect to mass-murder incidents. It found that evidence for the effect of assault weapon bans on mass shootings is inconclusive. Evidence that high-capacity magazine bans may decrease mass shootings is limited.[34] Pro–Democrat Party FactCheck.org concluded: "President Joe Biden claims the 10-year assault weapons ban that he helped shepherd through the Senate as part of the 1994 crime bill brought down these mass killings. But the raw numbers, when adjusted for population and other factors, aren't so clear on that."[35] Nonetheless, Biden has relied on this lie to blame Republicans for refusing to pass a long list of constitution-violating gun laws every time there is a mass shooting.

Moreover, as a rational and practical matter, ask yourself what exactly the Democrat Party and Biden would do to supposedly prevent mass killings, even if there was no Second Amendment in the Constitution and the Republican Party was not there to stop them. A complete ban on weapons (all guns, new weapons, older weapons, remove existing weapons)? A ban on certain weapons (by their looks, size, capacity, manner of firing, type of ammunition)? A ban on who can own weapons (by age, mental health)? How many civil liberties will be violated to enforce weapon bans and confiscations? If a Soros-funded Democrat prosecutor will not charge individuals who use weapons in the commission of crimes, or if a soft-on-crime Democrat judge releases them early back to the streets, gun banning and confiscation will apply largely to law-abiding citizens. But is that not the intention of such Democrat Party initiatives? And, of course, if the government cannot or will not prevent illegal aliens flowing into the country by the millions and drugs by the tons, or the unbridled gang killings that take place in our cities often with illegally obtained weapons, how will it prevent illegal weapons from being trafficked into our country from black markets, cartels, terrorists, and hostile governments? In fact, there is no reliably available governmental information tracking how many unlawful weapons have been brought into the United States due to Biden's open-borders policies. And Biden, the Democrat Party, and the Democrat Party media do not care.

Meanwhile, when Hunter Biden receives a slap on the wrist with a mitten by the Biden Department of Justice for lying on a federal application to purchase a handgun, which is a serious criminal offense, it is actually defended by Democrat Party apparatchiks in Congress and the media. Hunter Biden "agreed to enter a Pretrial Diversion Agreement," after which his record will be expunged and for which he received no prison time.[36]

Further troubling, the Democrat Party's unwillingness to even entertain using some of the security practices instituted to protect the White House, Capitol Building, the Supreme Court, and government facilities throughout Washington, D.C., and the nation is a disgrace. If weapons in the hands of trained personnel, as well as other physical security measures in and around government buildings, is good enough for politicians and bureaucrats, it is good enough for children attending classes in government buildings. I know of no "Gun Free Zone" signs posted at the White House.

For the Democrat Party, the objective is their party's empowerment via the expansion of the central government, conformity, and an ever more powerful police state, not reasoned and rational debate about societal solutions. That is the point of language manipulation.

Furthermore, there is an entire school of thought and scholarship in which the Marxist ideologues claim that the English language, especially as spoken in America, is yet another example of imperialism, which must be upended and replaced with words and language that promote the Marxist ideology. In his book *A Marxist Philosophy of Language*, Jean-Jacques Lecercle, professor of English at the University of Nanterre (in France), argues that language is about more than communication. It is more political than communicative. He ties the development of the English language to the interests of feudalism and then capitalism. Lecercle contends that "English has become the global language and the language of globalization because it is the language of empire, whose practices are ever more explicitly imperialistic."[37] He insists that "[l]anguage is not only a battlefield and one of the instruments of the class struggle, but also the site and instrument of the transformation of individuals into subjects. . . . [I]ts principal function, which is, therefore, not that of being an instrument of communication. And the link between linguistic [conflict] and class struggle is not metaphorical or merely analogical. . . ."[38] Hence, the English language is the language of domination, imperialism, and capitalism, thereby requiring a break from its historic roots and the application of Marxist ideology to fix it.

Emeritus professor at Lancaster University (in Britain) Norman Fairclough contends in his convoluted book, *Language and Power*: "The myth of free speech, that anyone is 'free' to say what they like, is an amazingly powerful one, given the actuality of a plethora of constraints on access to various sorts of speech, and writing. These are part and parcel of more general constraints on practice—on access to the more exclusive social institutions, their practices, and especially the most powerful subject positions constituted in their practices. And in terms of discourse in particular, on access to the discourse types, and discoursal positions of power. In a sense, these 'cultural goods' are analogous to other socially valued 'goods' of a more tangible nature—accumulated wealth, good jobs, good housing, and so forth. Both sorts of goods are unequally distributed, so that members of . . . the dominant bloc (the capitalist class, the 'middle class,' the professions) have substantially more of them than members of the working class they are richer in cultural capital."[39]

Indeed, Fairclough's preface proclaims that its purpose is to show "how language functions in maintaining and changing power relations in contemporary society, about ways of analyzing language which can reveal these processes, and about how people can become more conscious of them, and more able to resist and change them."[40]

In plain English, if I may, his argument is that the capitalist, or bourgeoisie, has monopoly-like control over words and language and, therefore, unfairly possess a bigger vocabulary with which to enrich himself, exploit and oppress others, and maintain control over society. Consequently, in order to break the dominant culture, and fundamentally transform society, the English language must be revolutionized.

But who controls, censors, redefines, invents, and compels the use (or not) of words and language, and punishes those who do not comply? Marxists and other totalitarians. Moreover, in the United States, it is the Democrat Party and American Marxists. The long list of teachers, professors, students, athletes, broadcasters, journalists, corporate executives, and more who have not toed the line have had their reputations and careers destroyed. It is called "cancel culture."

In 1950 in *Pravda*, the Soviet Union's official "news" outlet, Joseph Stalin wrote an entire essay titled "Marxism and Problems of Linguistics." Among other things, Stalin said that "Marxism holds that the transition of a language from an old quality to a new does not take place by way of an explosion, of the destruction of an existing language and the creation of a new one, but by the gradual accumulation of the elements of the new quality, and hence by the gradual dying away of the elements of the old quality."[41] So, from Stalin we get the gradual usurpation of words and language to accomplish the Marxist ends. And like it or not, we must understand that time and again the Democrat Party and its surrogates demonstrate their commitment to this effort.

For example, the *Washington Free Beacon* reports: "Federal agencies under . . . Biden are using taxpayer dollars to promote 'inclusive' language guides, instructing Americans to abandon common terms like 'homeless people' for left-wing alternatives like 'people experiencing unsheltered homelessness'. . . . The recommendations, from agencies such as the Centers for Disease Control (CDC) and the National Institutes of Health (NIH), focus on 'non-stigmatizing' language, which means eliminating terms such as 'inmate' and 'alcoholic' from common use. Instead, the CDC advises, Americans should say 'persons who are incarcerated or detained' and 'persons with alcohol use disorder,' respectively. The NIH Style Guide, meanwhile, advises people to say 'gender affirmation' or 'gender confirmation' rather than 'sex change.' They should similarly avoid the term 'hermaphrodite' and should never 'misgender' someone, which is 'using a word or address that does not correctly reflect' the gender identity of a 'transgender or gender-diverse person.'"[42] Of course, when it comes to conservatives, Republicans, and Trump supporters, let the hate speech fly. Nothing is off limits.

Indeed, the Biden administration has developed guidelines and directives to be implemented government-wide that officially change words and language throughout the bureaucracy. "The agencies' terms and pronoun list stem from an executive order Biden signed on his first day in office that called for a 'comprehensive approach' to advance 'equity for all' throughout the federal government," writes the *Free Beacon*. "'Each agency must assess whether, and to what extent, its programs and policies perpetuate systemic barriers to opportunities and benefits for people of color and other underserved groups,' according to Executive Order 13985. Biden followed up with another executive order 'further advancing racial equity,' which calls for a 'whole-of-government approach' to 'embed equity' in 'all aspects of federal decision-making.'"[43]

Even the Federal Aviation Administration (FAA), tasked with focusing on air traffic safety, must comply. "The language we use in aerospace matters," the FAA tweeted from its official account. "We've begun to adopt gender-neutral and inclusive aviation terminology as part of our agency-wide initiative. Recommendations included replacing 'airman' with 'aircrew,' 'manned aviation' with 'traditional aviation,' and 'cockpit' with 'flight deck.' The [Department of Transportation] said [in its budget proposal] it would allocate funds to tackle climate change, address inequities, and advance 'environmental justice and . . . improve aviation safety and infrastructure . . . [by including improvements in] promoting environmental justice, climate change mitigation, and 'enhancing equity through more inclusive contracting and workforce development.'"[44]

Former Democrat Speaker Nancy Pelosi and the Democrat-controlled House of Representatives, several months before losing their majority control, proposed a rules package that would "establish the Select Committee on Economic Disparity and Fairness in Growth; require standing committees to include in their oversight plans a discussion of how committee work over the forthcoming Congress will address issues of inequities on the basis of race, color, ethnicity, religion, sex, sexual orientation, gender identity, disability, age, or national origin; honor all gender identities by changing pronouns and familial relationships in the House rules to be gender neutral; make permanent the Office of Diversity and Inclusion to facilitate a diverse workforce that is reflective of our Members and the districts they represent; and survey the diversity of witness panels at committee hearings to ensure we are hearing from diverse groups of experts as we craft legislation."[45] As *National Review* reported, "Pelosi [sought to ban] the use of gendered terms in favor of more inclusive ones, ditching 'he' and 'she' for 'they'. . . . Instead of using the pronouns 'he' or 'she,' members would be required to use 'member,' 'delegate,' or 'resident commissioner.' Instead of saying 'father' and 'mother,' members would refer to that individual as 'parent,' and 'brother' and 'sister' would be replaced with 'sibling.'"[46]

In fact, central to the corruption of our words and language, and the manipulation of the public in service to the Democrat Party, are the media. Of course, the purpose of a free press is to stand as a bulwark and watchdog against the tyranny of powerful institutions and individuals, especially the increasing centralization and empowerment of government; to hold such entities and people to account to the public; and to inform and disseminate information to the citizenry—but not as the voice of a single party and an anti-American revolution. In totalitarian regimes, the media are controlled by the state. Incredibly, in America, the media have largely transformed into a corrupt propaganda operation for the Democrat Party and its causes and an arm of the central government. It has done so voluntarily, without threats or intimidation, because the media are mostly populated with ideologues who have ties to the Democrat Party, and are activists for the American Marxist revolution. Just as most of the other cultural institutions have been devoured by the American Marxist ideologists, so have the media. I wrote extensively about this in my book *Unfreedom of the Press*.

In totalitarian regimes, there is an extensive and relentless use of propaganda. As Swiss sociologist Jean K. Chalaby explains: "[The press] become parts of the ideological state apparatus that embraces artistic and film production, the education system, science, and religion. In the totalitarian state, the party's monopoly on the means of communication serves two broad purposes. The first is repressive in scope and helps stifle dissent and silence opposition to the party's autocratic rule. Second, it facilitates the transformation of the media into instruments of propaganda designed to indoctrinate the masses. Totalitarian parties engage in vast programs of socialization in order to fashion the new individual that fits in the party's vision of the new order."[47]

Regrettably, there are clear and significant overlaps between the media under totalitarian regimes and the American media's service to a single party and its ideological agenda. In the first place, as Joanna Thornborrow, senior lecturer in the Centre for Language and Communication Research at Cardiff University (Wales, Great Britain), explains, the influence and power of the mass media on society, the culture, and politics are enormous. "The mass media have become one of the principal means through which we gain access to a large part of our information about the world, as well as much of our entertainment. Because of this, they are a powerful site for the production and circulation of social meanings, i.e., to a great extent the media decide the significance of things that happen in the world for any given culture, society, or social group. The language used by the media to represent particular social and political groups, and to describe newsworthy events, tends to provide the dominant ways available for the rest of us to talk about those groups and events."[48]

In 1928, Edward Bernays wrote a book titled *Propaganda*, in which he described how to manipulate public opinion and "engineer consent." He explained: "The conscious and intelligent manipulation of the organized habits and opinions of the masses is an important element in democratic society. Those who manipulate this unseen mechanism of society constitute an invisible government which is the true ruling power of our country. We are governed, our minds molded, our tastes formed, our ideas suggested, largely by men we have never heard of. This is a logical result of the way in which our democratic society is organized. Vast numbers of human beings must cooperate in this manner if they are to live together as a smoothly functioning society."[49]

He added that "[o]ur invisible governors are, in many cases, unaware of the identity of their fellow members in the inner cabinet. They govern us by their qualities of natural leadership, their ability to supply needed ideas and by their key position in the social structure. Whatever attitude one chooses toward this condition, it remains a fact that in almost every act of our daily lives, whether in the sphere of politics or business, in our social conduct or our ethical thinking, we are dominated by the relatively small number of persons—a trifling faction of our [hundreds of millions of people]—who understand the mental processes and social patterns of the masses. It is they who pull the wires which control the public mind, who harness old social forces and contrive new ways to bind and guide the world."[50]

Evidence of the marriage between the Democrat Party and the media, and their persistent propaganda and manipulation of words and language in service of the fundamental transformation of America for the Democrat Party's own empowerment, is pervasive. For example, as discussed at length earlier, central to the Democrat Party's existence, power, and control is its obsessive and abhorrent exploitation of race. A united America is a tranquil America. For a party focused on a Marxist-like transformation of the country, requiring division, uproar, and the overthrow of the status quo, the goal is *disuniting* America.

In his *Tablet* essay "How the Media Led the Great Racial Awakening," Zach Goldberg explains that "years before Trump's election the media dramatically increased coverage of racism and embraced new theories of racial consciousness that set the stage for the latest unrest. . . . [W]hile President Obama was still in office, terms like 'microaggression' and 'white privilege' were picked up by liberal journalists. These terms went from being obscure fragments of academic jargon to commonplace journalistic language in only a few years. . . . During this same period, while exotic new phrases were entering the discourse, universally recognizable words like 'racism' were being radically redefined. Along with the new language came ideas and beliefs animating a new moral-political framework to apply to public life and American society."[51]

He continues, "[the *New York Times* and *Washington Post*] both talk about racial inequality and race-related issues far more frequently than they have since at least 1970 as well as increasingly framing those issues using the terms and jargon associated with 'wokeness.' Additionally, . . . the racial liberalism of white liberals has closely followed these trends in media coverage, rather than preceding them." Furthermore, writes Goldberg, "[t]he agenda-setting and issue-framing powers that social media platforms like Twitter have provided to progressive activists appears to be a central driver of both the shifts in white liberals' racial attitudes and the transformations within traditional media. Even the most powerful and storied names in newspaper publishing are increasingly responsive to and influenced by political sentiments percolating on social media, where all manner of racialist ideology thrives."[52]

Earlier in Chapter 1, I discussed how the late Antonio Gramsci, an Italian communist and icon among modern-day Marxists, advised communist activists to gradually infiltrate democratic institutions as the means to establishing a Marxist revolution and society. Interestingly, Goldberg writes of the idea of "concept creep," explaining that "[o]ne of the primary drivers behind the conceptual creep around racism is the idea that all observed disparities between different groups in a society are a product of bias." He adds that "[t]he idea of 'concept creep' originates with Nick Haslam, a professor of psychology at the University of Melbourne, Australia. In a research paper published in 2016, 'Concept creep: Psychology's expanding concepts of harm and pathology,' Haslam posits that: 'Concepts that refer to the negative aspects of human experience and behavior have expanded their meanings so that they now encompass a much broader range of phenomena.' This expansion, according to Haslam, 'primarily reflects an ever-increasing sensitivity to harm, reflecting a liberal moral agenda.'"[53] More like a Marxist immoral agenda.

The evidence is irrefutable. The media are all in for Critical Race Theory, the manipulation of words and language, and fomenting racial division. Goldberg writes: "[T]he new doctrines of anti-racism insist that any differences in group outcomes must be attributable to racist social structures and institutional biases—any other account of disparities in outcome would be tantamount to 'blaming the victim.' Though the academic theories advancing this idea are decades-old, they only became the conventional wisdom at major newspapers over the past decade, as mentions of racial inequalities multiplied. For instance, . . . from 1970 until 2014, the combined usage frequency of the three 'macro-level' racism terms—systemic racism, structural racism, institutional racism—never exceeded 0.00006% of all words in any of the four newspapers. By 2014, however, this ceiling was shattered, particularly in the *Times* and *Post*. In the final year of the series (2019), the *Times* . . . and *Post* . . . were using these terms roughly 10 times more frequently than they were in 2013."[54]

In Goldberg's extensive research and statistical analysis of news coverage, especially the *Times* and *Post*, he also found that "[u]ntil a few years ago, [the usage of white supremacy and similar terms] was likely limited to references to actual card-carrying white supremacists. But as with 'racism,' these terms have since been radically expanded by a rapid and ideologically driven concept creep. White supremacy is now a vague and all-encompassing label. Instead of describing the demonstrably discriminatory ideas and actions of particular institutions or individuals, white supremacy is now understood by many progressives to be the fundamental ethos of the American system as a whole. Whatever it used to mean, 'white supremacy' is now everywhere and applicable to any context."[55] Of course, the media know exactly what they are doing. They are partners in the Democrat Party's pursuit of political domination and monopolization. Race is just one repugnant example of their evil propaganda efforts.

Jeff Deist, president of the Mises Institute, points out that "when change is imposed by design, in furtherance of an agenda, we should strive to recognize it—regardless of whether we agree with that agenda. We should study and understand the distinction between the natural evolution of language over time and the imposition of politicized diction or usage through coordinated and intentional efforts."[56] We see this language manipulation all around us—in our schools, places of work, news reports, TV and movies, etc. "Ultimately," writes Deist, "imposed language attempts to control our *actions*. When we broadly consider politically correct or woke worldviews—i.e., an activist mindset concerned with promoting amorphous social justice—the linguistic element is straightforward: Political correctness is the conscious, designed manipulation of language intended to change the way people speak, write, think, feel, and act, in furtherance of an agenda. Words are just a means to an end, the end being actual changes in how we live our lives. Those changes flow first from our thoughts (and even how we formulate our thoughts), then to our issued words (spoken or written), and ultimately to our actions . . . there is no clear dividing line between language and action, between our thoughts, words, and acts. All are interrelated, and those seeking to impose language understand this."[57]

Like totalitarian regimes, the truth is that the Democrat Party and its proxies understand that to own the language is to own the culture and society. Thus, asks Deist, "[w]ho owns and controls language? Ideally, governments, politicians, academics, think tanks, journalists, religious leaders, or elite institutions should not possess this tremendous power. Like market processes, language should evolve without centralized design or control. Only this natural evolution, across time and geography, can reveal the preferences of actual language in any society. Evolution is just; evolution is efficient. But language is an institution, and like any institution, it is subject to corruption and even capture by those with political agendas . . . the distinction between evolution and corruption, between spontaneous linguistic changes and the imposition of language to serve an agenda."[58]

As noted earlier, totalitarian regimes also institute censorship to ensure their hold on power. That is, to prevent intellectual pursuits, challenge to government orthodoxy, competing ideas, and free speech generally. As I wrote in *Unfreedom of the Press*, in December 2018, Chuck Todd, the now former host of NBC's *Meet the Press*, displayed this mentality and practice when he "issued an on-air proclamation to the nation, followed by a full hour of one-sided propaganda, in which Todd asserted that man-made climate change is a scientific fact, and he would not allow the voices of 'climate-deniers'. . . to be heard now or in the future."[59] He declared:

> This morning, we're going to do something that we don't often get to do, dive in on one topic. It's obviously extra-ordinarily difficult to do this, as the end of this year has proven, in the era of Trump. But we're going to take an in-depth look, regardless of that, at a literally Earth-changing subject that doesn't get talked about this thoroughly on television news, at least, climate change. But just as impor-tant as what we are going to do this hour is what we're not going to do. We're not going to debate climate change, the existence of it. The Earth is getting hotter. And human activity is a major cause, period. We're not going to give

time to climate deniers. The science is settled, even if political opinion is not. And we're not going to confuse weather with climate. A heat wave is not more evidence that climate change exists than a blizzard means that it doesn't, unless the blizzard hits Miami. We do have a panel of experts with us today to help us understand the science and consequences of climate change and, yes, ideas break the political paralysis over it.[60]

Despite the fact that there are countless scientific experts throughout academia and think tanks who know far more than Todd, his producers, and NBC's executives, and who have written extensively in scholarly books and papers questioning climate change, man-made climate change, the extent of climate change, the dangers of climate change, natural global and atmospheric changes, and on and on, Todd openly declared what many media personalities will not—that they will not permit legitimate, substantive, intelligent, contrary views to meddle in their ideological agenda, which they share with the Democrat Party and the government. Todd is a former Democrat activist, his wife was a Democrat staffer and consultant, and she remains a Democrat activist who advises Democrat candidates and promotes the Democrat Party's agenda. Todd does little to conceal his obvious political and ideological beliefs. Of course, he is not the media exception in this regard; he is the rule.

For the Democrat Party, "climate change" is not about science. It is the most lucrative, limitless, and successful source of power and control over the individual, the economy, and, consequently, the American lifestyle. In his 2022 book *The Psychology of Totalitarianism*, Mattias Desmet, professor of clinical psychology at Ghent University (Belgium), discusses the conditions of collective hypnosis of the masses. "At its birth, science was synonymous with open-mindedness, with a way of thinking that banished dogmas and questioned beliefs. As it evolved, however, it also turned itself into ideology, belief, and prejudice. Science thus underwent a transformation, as all ideologies do. At first, it was a discourse by which a minority defied a majority; then it became the discourse of the majority itself. In the course of this transformation, scientific discourse aligned itself with objectives that were opposed to the original ones. It enabled manipulation of the masses, allowed people to build a career, . . . promote products, . . . spread deceptions, . . . and belittle and stigmatize others ('whoever believes in alternative medicine is an irrational fool'). Indeed, even to justify segregation and exclusion (no access to public spaces unless you bear the sign—a mask, a vaccine passport—of the scientific ideology). In short, the scientific discourse, like any dominant discourse, has become the privileged instrument of opportunism, lies, deception, manipulation, and power. To the extent the scientific discourse became an ideology, it lost its virtue of truth-telling."[61]

During the COVID-19 pandemic, what occurred especially in Democrat-governed blue states and cities was a power grab and violation of civil liberties the likes of which most Americans living in these places had never before experienced—governors shut down schools, religious gatherings, weddings, and funerals (people died without family members present); beaches, parks, and outside stadiums were closed; people could gather only in small numbers if at all; individuals were required to wear masks in public places; large numbers of businesses were forced to close; etc.

Many top scientists and statisticians who did not work for the federal or state governments questioned these practices. Most of them were ignored or denounced. Their credentials were challenged and their reputations were destroyed. But now we know many were right.

The Cochrane Library concluded that "[t]he pooled results of RCTs [randomized controlled trials] did not show a clear reduction in respiratory viral infection with the use of medical/surgical masks."[62] Moreover, a major Johns Hopkins study found that "[w]hile this meta-analysis concludes that lockdowns have had little to no public health effects, they have imposed enormous economic and social costs where they have been adopted. In consequence, lockdown policies are ill-founded and should be rejected as a pandemic policy instrument."[63]

In the meantime, and unbelievably, the Democrat-controlled California legislature passed, and the Democrat governor, Gavin Newsom, signed into law a bill that sought to penalize doctors, including the loss of medical licenses, who spread "misinformation or disinformation" about COVID-19, which a federal judge temporarily blocked.[64] In other words, if the Democrat Party has its way, medical or scientific experts, whose views run contrary to the edicts of state-sanctioned bureaucrats, can lose their licenses if they challenge the officially authorized position of the state.

This is pernicious and pure totalitarianism.

Newsom and his fellow Democrats would undoubtedly sympathize with the 1633 verdict against the brilliant physicist and astronomer Galileo, who was adjudicated a heretic for establishing that the earth revolves around the sun. He was sentenced to spend the rest of his life under house arrest and forbidden from teaching his "theory." His writings on the subject were also banned.[65] History is replete with such examples.

Desmet explains that most exceptional thinkers throughout human history "not only reached great intellectual achievements, they also assumed a unique humanistic and ethical stance with regard to the world and its material objects. They had the courage to set aside the prejudices and dogmas of the time. They admitted their ignorance and were curious and open to what phenomena have to say for themselves. This 'not knowing' gave birth to a new knowledge, a new knowledge for which they would do anything, for which they were to give up their freedom, sometimes even their lives. This newborn science—this budding knowledge—showed all the characteristics of what the French philosopher Michel Foucault defines as *truth-telling*."[66]

Censorship, and what I will call *speech intimidation*, are a very important part of the Democrat Party's tactics, as with any tyrannical regime or party, as well as its media partners. A prime example involves the "Twitter Files" scandal. This was a vast effort by the Biden administration to influence and control political speech and debate—especially during the 2020 presidential election and 2022 midterm elections.

When Elon Musk purchased Twitter, he hired a few highly respected independent journalists, albeit left-leaning, to review an enormous amount of the decision-making materials, including emails among and between former Twitter executives and managers. What did they find? Among other things, Matt Taibbi, one of the journalists, told Fox News host Maria Bartiromo in January 2023:

I think the major revelation of the Twitter files so far is that we've discovered an elaborate bureaucracy of what you might call public-private censorship. Basically, companies like Twitter have a system by which they receive tens of thousands of requests for action on various accounts. Typically, through the DHS and FBI, but these requests were coming from basically every department in the government. We've seen them from the HHS, from the Treasury, from the DOD, even from the CIA. And they will send basically long lists of accounts in Excel spreadsheet files and ask for action on those accounts. And in many cases,

Twitter is complying." Taibbi added: "We found one incredible email from former FBI general counsel Jim Baker . . . and it's essentially celebrating that the FBI had paid $3.4 million for, quote-unquote, 'processing requests.' So, in other words, all those requests that were coming through to Twitter, and we see all the email traffic talking about what a burden it was for the company to process all of these requests, that's what the money was for. For them to look at all these requests for content moderation and censorship that were coming from all these different agencies.[67]

When Taibbi and his fellow journalist Michael Shellenberger, who also studied the Twitter materials, testified about their findings before a House committee, they came under an organized, vicious, and withering personal assault on their characters and professionalism by committee Democrats. The Democrats had no interest in their findings and had clearly planned to attack the journalists' integrity. The Democrats implied that Taibbi and Shellenberger were paid off, that they were not real journalists, that they cherry-picked data, etc. The Democrats' intention was to sabotage the hearings, besmirch the journalists and their findings, and run defense for the Biden administration's use of a major public communication platform to control information and discussion, censor opposing or conflicting views and information, and influence the elections on behalf of the Democrat Party and Democrat candidates. In order to help establish the objectivity with which they undertook their review of the Twitter Files, Taibbi and Shellenberger revealed during the hearing that they had voted for Biden in the 2020 presidential election, but the committee Democrats did not care.[68] The two independent journalists were not playing along with the Democrat Party and for that, they were to be pilloried.

The Twitter Files scandal also revealed the role of public and semiprivate organizations coordinating with the government to censor questions or contrary views about the COVID-19 vaccines and label such information as disinformation. Taibbi explained that "[o]ur most recent discoveries involve something called Stanford's Virality Project, which was . . . created by Stanford University. It's an outgrowth of something that was called the Election Integrity Partnership that was founded in 2020. There's a lot of state money involved in this project, but what was most significant about what we found, we found emails to Twitter in which this project told them that they should consider as standard misinformation on your platform, true stories that might promote hesitancy or true stories of vaccine side effects. So, we now know that a lot of these anti-disinformation programs, whether they're actual state agencies or whether they're NGOs [nongovernment organizations] that are state-funded, they're targeting true information that just happens to be counter-narrative, which I think is extremely dangerous."[69] In fact, the Democrat Party was politically invested in the pandemic. It enabled Biden and especially Democrat governors to exercise power and control over the public in ways previously never imagined in this country.

Taibbi also testified about the Biden "disinformation board" instituted by the Department of Homeland Security. "It's terrifying," Taibbi declared. "They've tried a couple of times, the disinformation governance board last year had to be basically paused after three weeks and then they threw it away, but they continued to have something called the MDM subcommittee. Now . . . they essentially announced that they're no longer going to have that, this misinformation, disinformation, mal-information subcommittee. But there's another subcommittee that's coming up behind it that I think may essentially inherit the same mantle that the governance board was supposed to have. So, we have to be on the lookout for these government efforts to try to centralize the cleansing of 'disinformation' from the media landscape, which I don't think is the government's job."[70]

As mentioned in Chapter 1, Taibbi dared to cross the Biden administration. The same day he testified, writes the *Daily Caller*, he received "an unannounced home visit from an IRS agent. Taibbi was reportedly left a note by the IRS agent to call the agency four days later, and when he called, the IRS told him his 2018 and 2021 tax returns were rejected because of identity theft concerns."[71] Indeed, "the IRS opened an investigation into . . . Taibbi in 2022, immediately following his publishing of a Twitter Files report. . . . Taibbi released his first edition of the Twitter Files on December 2 in which he revealed alleged misconduct between the social media giant and government agencies. Documents indicate the IRS began an investigation into Taibbi's 2018 tax return on December 24, 2022 . . . ; the IRS did not reach out to Taibbi regarding the 2018 return until last Christmas Eve, three weeks after his first Twitter Files release."[72]

I do not believe in the tooth fairy, and I do not believe this was a coincidence. And it fits the Biden–Democrat Party pattern of intimidating and censoring real and perceived opponents.

Indeed, the *Wall Street Journal* reported that a lawsuit brought by the attorneys general of Missouri and Louisiana discovered, among other things, "email exchanges between Rob Flaherty, the White House's director of digital media, and social-media executives [that] prove the companies put Covid censorship policies in place in response to relentless, coercive pressure from the White House—not voluntarily. . . ."[73] In fact, as the Missouri attorney general's office announced, exhibits provided in the litigation found, in part:

- The White House asks Twitter to censor Robert Kennedy, Jr., a known critic of the White House's COVID-19 narrative

- The White House directs Facebook to shut down conservative voices Tucker Carlson and Tomi Lahren

- White House Digital Director Flaherty scolds Facebook, saying that he "really couldn't care less about products unless they're having measurable impact" at suppressing speech

- Flaherty informs Facebook that "misinformation around the vaccine" is "a concern shared at the highest (and I mean highest) level of the WH"

- Flaherty demands that Facebook step up its operations of "removing bad information" on vaccines

- In regard to "anti-vax" posts, Flaherty tells Facebook that "slowing it down seems reasonable"

- Facebook assures Flaherty that "in addition to removing vaccine misinformation, we have been focused on reducing the virality of content discouraging vaccines that does not contain actionable misinformation," including "often-true content"

- Flaherty vehemently disagrees with Facebook's decision not to take down a Tucker Carlson video on COVID-19 vaccines, stating "not for nothing but last time we did this dance, it ended in an insurrection"

- Flaherty tells Twitter that "if your product is appending misinformation to our tweets that seems like a pretty fundamental issue"

- Facebook assures Flaherty that they "remove claims public health authorities tell us have been debunked or are unsupported by evidence"

- Flaherty accuses Twitter of "Total Calvinball" and "bending over backwards" to tolerate disfavored speech after Twitter refuses to comply with White House demands to censor a video.[74]

And there is more.

George Washington University law professor Jonathan Turley, writing in *The Hill*, highlights "[t]he Global Disinformation Index (GDI) [as] a particularly insidious part of [the Biden administration's censorship] effort. Funded in part by $330 million from the U.S. State Department through the National Endowment for Democracy (which contributes to GDI's budget), the GDI was designed to steer advertisers and subscribers away from 'risky' sites which it says pose 'reputational and brand risk' and to help companies avoid 'financially supporting disinformation online.' GDI warned advertisers that these sites could damage their reputations and brands: the *New York Post*, *Reason*, Real Clear Politics, the Daily Wire, The Blaze, One America News Network, *The Federalist*, Newsmax, the *American Spectator*, and the *American Conservative*."[75]

Turley concluded that "[t]he funding of GDI, and the FBI's censorship efforts, are consistent with President Biden's pronounced anti-free-speech policies since taking office in 2020. . . . What is clear is that the government is working to censor and harass sites with opposing views on subjects ranging from the pandemic to climate change to elections. This includes efforts to deter others from supporting these sites through advertising revenue. The financial viability of these sites could depend on the GDI's good-citizen score."[76]

Perhaps the most alarming is the effort to turn Artificial Intelligence (AI) into a Democrat Party propaganda tool for decades to come. Fox Business reports that the "artificial intelligence tool ChatGPT has alarmed some experts who believe left-leaning biases are baked into the technology with the potential to spread liberal talking points and even outright false information to the masses. . . . At the core of many of these deep learning models is a piece of software that will take the applied data and try to extract the most relevant features. Whatever makes that data specific will be heightened. Critics have repeatedly claimed ChatGPT has a liberal bias, a 'shortcoming' that Open AI CEO Sam Altman has said the company is working to improve. For example, Twitter user Echo Chamber asked ChatGPT to 'create a poem admiring Donald Trump,' a request the bot rejected, replying it was not able to since 'it is not in my capacity to have opinions or feelings about any specific person.' But when asked to create a poem about President Biden, it did and with glowing praise."[77]

The list of Democrat Party–led policies and practices involving language manipulation, censorship, anti–free speech efforts, intimidation, indoctrination, racism, etc., is a long one—and growing. And it is fundamental to the imposition of an autocratic regime. Unfortunately, this is further evidence of a declining republic. Although America is not yet, nor technically, a totalitarian state in its truest sense, it is clearly on the edge. A government can be tyrannical in significant ways or even in character without having crossed over from a constitutional republic or democracy to a full-blown totalitarian regime. The issue here is the increasing prospect or *risk* of such a Democrat Party–established regime on the near horizon. The Democrat Party, home today to the American Marxist movements, is the political means by which both the mind-set and actions of totalitarianism are spreading. After all, it has a long history of rejecting, defaming, and attacking the American experiment.

And the Democrat Party's intent is inescapable—again, one-party rule as a means to unchecked power. Raymond Aron explains that a strong and working republic or democracy is evidenced, in part, "[b]y the fact that more than one party has the legal right to exist, the parties inevitably compete for the exercise of power. A party has in fact as its objective not necessarily to *exercise* power but *a share in the exercise of power*. . . . From the plurality of the parties, the legality of opposition can also be deduced. If several parties have the right to exist, and if they are not all in power, inevitably it follows that some of them will be in opposition. Therefore, by taking as our starting point the legal plurality of parties, we have evoked the legality of opposition. That those who govern can be legally opposed is a relatively rare phenomenon, which is the moderate or legal form that the exercise of authority takes in such cases. . . . Thus, we come to the following definition of the regimes which are characteristic of western countries: they are regimes in which the *peaceful rivalry for the exercise of power exists constitutionally*. It is *constitutional* . . . and rules lay down the modalities of rivalry between individuals and groups for the exercise of power. . . . .The competition is *peaceful*. The *legal exercise of power* differs in nature from what we call the *seizure of power*. The exercise of power is, essentially, temporary."[78] Aron then adds this crucial point: "*When the winner prevents the loser from running again, we leave what we in the west call democracy because we have banned opposition*." (Italics are mine.)

I would add that an even more insidious tactic than the outright ban of political competition is the appearance of a two-party or multiparty political landscape when, in fact, the other parties have been denied over time any real or effective input or power by what is effectively one-party rule. This is the approach today of the Democrat Party and the American Marxist movements. In the broader context, this totalitarian character is not confined to party politics. The Democrat Party and its surrogates understand, as Marx proselytized, that the key to their revolution is owning the culture. For example, the insistence on ideological conformity is playing out every day on college campuses, where academic freedom and free speech were once enthusiastically practiced. Indeed, during a speaking engagement at Stanford Law School, federal judge Kyle Duncan, who had been invited by the school's Federalist Society chapter, "addressed the [hostile] posters and chants [that confronted him]. 'I'm not blind—I can see this outpouring of contempt,' Duncan said. With audience interruptions continuing throughout the speech, he later said, 'In this school, the inmates have gotten control of the asylum.'[79] Not long after this comment, and less than thirty minutes into the speech as a whole, Duncan asked the students, 'Do you think this is an appropriate way to receive a guest?' "[80]

"For many people here, your work has caused harm," [Associate Dean for Diversity, Equity, and Inclusion] Tirien Steinbach said to Duncan. She asked Duncan twice, "Is the juice worth the squeeze?" appearing to question whether Duncan believed his appearance and thoughts were worth this reaction. The protesters snapped their fingers in approval.[81] This mob behavior—the shouting down and threatening of "infidels"—is widespread in autocratic regimes. What is next? Dragging disbelievers into the streets or off to gulags?

Voice of America, in a report titled "American College Campuses Increasingly Hostile to Free Speech," notes that "protests on college campuses like the University of California-Berkeley, Middlebury College, the Claremont colleges and California State University, Los Angeles, have erupted ahead of speeches scheduled by conservative political pundits. The protests, several of which turned violent, have drawn intense media coverage and condemnation from those who believe the demonstrations are aimed at shutting down controversial speakers."[82] In fact, the Marxist ideology dominates academia, making these institutions breeding grounds for the cultural and societal revolution embraced and stoked by the Democrat Party.[83] These institutions are heavily subsidized by the Democrat Party through legislation and executive orders supporting student loans and grant programs, and in return generations of young people become aligned with the Democrat Party and are a significant Democrat Party voting bloc. It is the reason Biden sought to violate the Constitution when he usurped Congress and attempted to unilaterally forgive hundreds of billions of dollars in student loans.

Furthermore, thousands of Diversity, Equity, and Inclusion (DEI) administrators are being hired by colleges and universities to monitor and enforce campus behaviors to ensure the spread of the Marxist ideology and the Democrat Party agenda. This has become a Democrat Party–created industry. Many students who attend these schools are effectively turned into the foot soldiers for the American Marxist or are cowed into silence. You have to wonder where the college students will eventually take our country, because they will one day become the lawyers, judges, politicians, executives, labor leaders, etc., who run the institutions of government and society.

The Democrat Party seeks to change the American people from a freethinking, engaged, independent, curious, and industrious people to a people who are dispirited, silenced, subsidized, inattentive, and compliant. In this pursuit, language and thought control are essential. Should the Democrat Party succeed, there will likely exist the patina of a free and vibrant people living under democratic conditions and voting in regular election cycles. But it will be a grand deception because, in truth, the Democrat Party will oversee an omnipresent, despotic government that will rule in matters large and minute, the evidence of which is rising around us.

CHAPTER FIVE

WAR ON THE AMERICAN CITIZEN

Britannica defines citizenship as, in part, the "relationship between an individual and a state to which the individual owes allegiance and in turn is entitled to its protection. Citizenship implies the status of freedom with accompanying responsibilities. Citizens have certain rights, duties, and responsibilities that are denied or only partially extended to aliens and other noncitizens residing in a country. In general, full political rights, including the right to vote and to hold public office, are predicated upon citizenship. The usual responsibilities of citizenship are allegiance, taxation, and military service. Citizenship is the most privileged form of nationality."[1] The purpose of citizenship is to unite people around common values, belief systems, principles, etc.—that is, a dominant culture: the American culture. Otherwise, a nation cannot function and ultimately fails.

Unfortunately, the ruling class, led by the Democrat Party, the media, academia, and the administrative state, do not share the public's belief in either the necessity of citizenship or the well-being of America. The late Harvard professor Samuel P. Huntington, writing in his book *Who Are We? The Challenges to America's National Identity*, observed: "The views of the public on issues of national identity differ significantly from those of many elites. These differences reflect the underlying contrast . . . between the high levels of national pride and commitment to the nation on the part of the public and the extent to which elites have denationalized and favor transnational and subnation identities. The public, overall, is concerned with societal security, which . . . involves 'the sustainability, within acceptable conditions for evolution, of traditional patterns of language, culture, association, and religious and national identity and custom.' For many elites, these concerns are secondary in the global economy, supporting international trade and migration, strengthening international institutions, promoting American involvement abroad, and encouraging minority identities and cultures."[2]

The divide between the public and the ruling class, explains Huntington, is broad and getting broader. "The differences between a 'patriotic public' and 'denationalized elites,'" writes Huntington, "parallel other differences in values and philosophy. Growing differences between the leaders of major institutions and the public on domestic and foreign policy issues affecting national identity form a major cultural fault line cutting across class, denominational, racial, regional, and ethnic distinctions. In a variety of ways, the American establishment, governmental and private, has become increasingly divorced from the American people. Politically, America remains a democracy because key public officials are selected through free and fair elections. In many respects, however, it has become an unrepresentative democracy because on crucial issues, especially involving national identity, its leaders pass laws and implement policies contrary to the views of the American people. Concomitantly, the American people have become increasingly alienated from politics and government."[3]

Yet today Biden and his party are overseeing and instituting the greatest degradation of our immigration laws and system in American history. The unstated purpose is to allow as many aliens as possible to freely enter the United States virtually at will, in the face of broad public opposition.[4] The result is mass migration from all over the world into the country without regard for who the aliens are and whether they are willing or capable of assimilating into American society. As I wrote in *Liberty and Tyranny*, "[n]o society can withstand the unconstitutional mass migration of aliens from every corner of the earth. The preservation of the nation's territorial sovereignty, and the culture, language, mores, traditions, and customs that make possible a harmonious community of citizens, dictate that citizenship be granted only by the consent of the government—not by unilateral actions or demands of the alien—and then only to aliens who will throw off their allegiance to their former nation and society and pledge their allegiance to America." Moreover, Claremont Institute senior fellow and California State University professor Edward J. Erler, reflecting Aristotle's observation, writes: "[a] radical change in the character of the citizens would be tantamount to a regime change just as surely as a revolution in political principles."[5] And, of course, that is exactly the objective of the Democrat Party.

And "regime change" it is. As reported by Fox News: "President-elect Joe Biden, during the Obama administration, said the U.S. benefits from a 'constant' and 'unrelenting' stream of immigration—and that those with white European heritage becoming a minority in the U.S. is 'a source of our strength.'" Speaking at a White House summit on violent extremism in 2015, Biden said, in part: "Folks like me who are Caucasian, of European descent, for the first time in 2017 we'll be in an absolute minority in the United States of America, absolute minority. Fewer than 50% of the people in America from then and on will be white European stock. That's not a bad thing, that's a source of our strength." Biden made similar comments a year earlier, where he spoke to the National Association of Manufacturers on the need for immigration reform "from a purely economic point of view." According to *The Hill*, which reported on the comments, Biden said a key to U.S. economic strength is the "constant, unrelenting stream of immigrants into the country. Not dribbling. Significant flows."[6] More on Biden's egregious immigration policies shortly.

But to be clear, the purpose of immigration is not to change the racial or ethnic make-up of the citizens you represent, but to ensure that the citizens you represent are the foremost benefactors of immigration policies.

Thomas G. West, professor of politics at Hillsdale College, reveals in his 1998 book, *Vindicating the Founders*, that although many of the nation's founders were receptive to immigration, there were important caveats. He explains that "George Washington frequently commented on immigration and citizenship. His approach, shared by most of the founding generation, had two main features. First, America should generously welcome as equal citizens people from many nations and religions. Second, the numbers and kinds of immigrants may need to be limited with a view to the qualities of character required for democratic citizenship."[7] Of course, to mention a would-be immigrant's *character* is to draw scorn and heckles of racism and bigotry. Nonetheless, the character of those wishing to join American society was, at one time, a paramount consideration for obvious reasons.

In addition to taking into consideration the character of would-be immigrants, Washington was concerned about the *number* of foreigners let into the country at a given time and place—that is, he was concerned about assimilation both in terms of whether the individual or group of individuals would be capable of being assimilated into the American culture, and whether the sheer numbers of immigrants would overwhelm the existing American culture, making assimilation difficult if not impossible. Of course, this is precisely what is taking place today—and it is intentional Biden and Democrat Party policy.

West writes: "Washington . . . noted the problem created when too many foreigners settle at one time in one location. In a letter to Vice President John Adams, he wrote:

> The policy or advantage of [immigration] taking place in a body (I mean the settling of them in a body) may be much questioned; for, by so doing, they retain the language, habits, and principles (good or bad) which they bring with them. Whereas by an intermixture with our people, they, or their descendants, get assimilated to our customs, measures, and laws: in a word, soon become one people.[8]

West explains further that Thomas Jefferson questioned "the present desire of America . . . to produce rapid population by as great an importation of foreigners as possible." In doing so he gave one of the fullest explanations of the principles shared by the founding generation guiding their thoughts on immigration. Jefferson's point of departure was his concern for liberty. Jefferson wrote, in part:

> Every species of government has its specific principles. Ours perhaps are more peculiar than those of any other in the universe. It is a composition of the freest principles of the English constitution, with others derived from nature right and natural reason.[9]

In other words, Jefferson was alluding to the uniqueness of the American culture and society and the principles on which it was founded (as set forth in the Declaration of Independence); the constitutional system established to undergird those principles; and, the unique nature of America's republican government. Inasmuch as most foreigners immigrating to the United States have been marinated in other cultures and governing systems, Jefferson argued that mass immigration makes it much more difficult if not impossible to assimilate these individuals into the American culture and society.

Alexander Hamilton, who was not opposed to immigration from Europe (which was where most immigrants at the time were coming from), rejected the notion that every foreigner, or masses of foreigners, had a right to migrate to the United States; he also believed it would be highly detrimental to the nation. Hamilton wrote, in part:

The safety of a republic depends essentially on the energy of a common national sentiment; on a uniformity of principles and habits; on the exemption of the citizens from foreign bias and prejudice; and on the love of country which will almost invariably be found to be closely connected with birth, education, and family. The opinion advanced in *Notes of Virginia* is undoubtedly correct, that foreigners will generally be apt to bring with them attachments to the persons they have left behind; to the country of their nativity, and to its particular customs and manners. They will also entertain opinions on government congenial with those under which they have lived; or if they should be hither from a preference to ours, how extremely unlikely is it that they will bring with them that temperate love of liberty, so essential to real republicanism?[10]

In sum, said Hamilton:

> In the recommendation to admit indiscriminately foreign
> emigrants of every description to the privileges of American
> citizens, on their first entrance into our country, there is an
> attempt to break down every pale which has been erected
> for the preservation of a national spirit and a national char-
> acter; and to let in the most powerful means of perverting
> and corrupting both the one and the other.[11]

Again, America's founding fathers believed that the purpose of
immigration is to benefit the existing citizenry and society, not the
interests of aliens who wish to come to the United States. After
all, the representatives of the people are supposed to represent the
people. That is the point of representative government, not cham-
pioning the interests of foreign nationals. But for the Democrat
Party, as Biden essentially declared, the purpose of immigration is
the fundamental transformation of America—or more specifically,
the citizenry. For Biden, the only issue that matters is the racial
make-up of immigrants and the speed by which their policies will
change the existing majority-minority racial demographics.

For the Democrat Party, immigration is also viewed as another
opportunity for fundamentally transforming American society
and culture. It sees new immigrants as blank slates unattached to
the nation's founding principles and history, the capitalist system,
and America's culture. It believes new immigrants can be more
easily indoctrinated, manipulated, and persuaded by the party's
advocacy of civil-rights Marxism and political authoritarianism.
And, of course, the Democrat Party is convinced that its domination of the media, entertainment, and academia, plus its racist and segregationist propaganda, will appeal to new immigrants
more effectively than to homegrown U.S. citizens. This is primar-

ily why Biden, the Democrat Party, and the American Marxists insist on open borders and have no intention of reversing course.

Importantly, this view is not shared by most immigrants, many of whom escaped Marxist tyranny and totalitarian regimes, economic destitution and joblessness resulting from socialist economies, government-controlled propaganda and brainwashing, racial discrimination, and the dehumanization of the individual human being. Most are not drawn to the United States to become Democrat Party voters or to relive the horrors of autocracy promised by the American Marxists. Indeed, most immigrants seek what most Americans celebrate about their country—individual freedom, free speech, the freedom of religion, opportunity, a just rule of law, security, and all the other characteristics that make the United States—as President Reagan said many times—"the shining city on a hill." America is different than any other nation mankind has established, which is why foreigners from every corner of the planet and all walks of life come to our borders and shores. In short, most love America even before they step foot in our country. Conversely, the Democrat Party hates America.

Even so, no country, past or present, can withstand unlimited numbers of foreigners pouring into its neighborhoods. For reasons explained earlier by the founders, and many more, to be addressed during the course of this chapter, even under the best of circumstances—where immigration is not used for political and ideological purposes—unrestricted immigration is simply unsustainable. The costs are unbearable, given the enormous size of our welfare state. And it is difficult if not impossible to segregate the criminals and would-be criminals from the millions crossing our borders.

Moreover, today, assimilation is a much more difficult challenge than in the past because the American culture itself is being eradicated from within by the various American Marxist movements and the Democrat Party, something the founders could never have imagined. The critical question then becomes: To what are immigrants being assimilated and integrated?

In 1998, the late Harvard professor Arthur M. Schlesinger Jr., a renowned Democrat Party activist, scholar, and traditional liberal, who was an adviser to Democrat presidential candidate Adlai Stevenson and President John Kennedy, wrote a book titled *The Disunity of America: Reflections on a Multicultural Society*, in which he condemned in dire terms and profound arguments the immigration policies that were tearing at the fabric of American culture and society twenty-five years ago. For example, he wrote: "The ethnicity rage in general and Afrocentricity in particular not only divert attention from the real needs but exacerbate the problems. The recent apotheosis of ethnicity, black, brown, red, yellow, white, has revived the dismal prospect that in melting-pot days Americans thought the republic was moving safely beyond—that is, a society fragmented into separate ethnic communities. The cult of ethnicity exaggerates differences, intensifies resentments and antagonisms, drives deeper the awful wedges between races and nationalities. The endgame is self-pity and self-ghettoization."[12]

Schlesinger makes the point that "[f]or generations blacks have grown up in an American culture, on which they have had significant influence and to which they have made significant contributions. Self-Africanization after three hundred years in America is playacting. Afrocentricity as expounded by ethnic ideologues implies Europhobia, separatism, emotions of alienation, victimization, paranoia. Most curious and unexpected of all is a black demand for the return of black-white segregation."[13]

Schlesinger laments that the "revival of separation will begin, if the black educator Felix Boateng has his way, in the earliest grades. 'The use of standard English as the only language of instruction,' Boateng argues, 'aggravates the process of *deculturalization*.' A 'culturally relevant curriculum' for minority children would recognize 'the home and community dialect they bring to school.'"[14] Of course, Schlesinger notes, not all black educators share Boateng's view. However, these days many educators of all races and ethnicities do. Indeed, Critical Race Theory and other racist theories are taught throughout our public-school systems—from elementary and secondary schools to colleges and universities. "If any education institution should bring people together as individuals in friendly and civic association," declares Schlesinger, "it should be the university. But the fragmentation of campuses in recent years into a multitude of ethic organizations is spectacular—and disconcerting."[15]

Unfortunately, Schlesinger was prescient. Schools have become the revolutionary propaganda mills of the Democrat Party and teachers' unions, the purpose of which is to radicalize and indoctrinate the student body. However, there is little doubt that if Schlesinger (now deceased) showed up at his Harvard classroom today, he would be condemned as, among other things, a white-privileged racist, shouted down, and prevented from speaking.

Schlesinger also warned that "America has so long seen itself as the asylum for the oppressed and persecuted—and has done itself and the world so much good thereby—that any curtailment of immigration offends something in the American soul. No one wants to be a know-nothing. Yet uncontrolled immigration is an impossibility; so, the criteria of control are questions the American democracy must confront. We have shifted the basis of admission three times this century—from national origins in 1924 to family reunification in 1965 to needed skills in 1990. The future of immigration policy depends on the capacity of the assimilation process to continue to do what it has done so well in the past: to lead newcomers to an acceptance of the language, the institutions, and the political ideals that hold the nation together."[16]

Of course, none of that is happening today. Indeed, Biden and

the Democrat Party are undermining virtually every law and regulation to achieve lawlessness on our borders, the likes of which
America has never experienced. The purpose of immigration is no
longer to strengthen and improve the society but to overrun and
devour it. Indeed, "the language, the institutions, and political ideals" of our country are under assault and unraveling from within.

Samuel Huntington explains that "[i]n 1900 the answer was
clear: assimilation meant Americanization. In 2000 the answers
were complicated, contradictory, and ambiguous. Many elite
Americans were no longer confident of the virtue of their mainstream culture and instead preached a doctrine of diversity and
the equal validity of all cultures in America. 'Immigrants do not
enter a society that assumes an undifferentiated monolithic culture,' Mary Waters [sociologist and Harvard professor] observed in
1994, 'but rather a consciously pluralistic society in which a variety of subcultures and racial and ethnic identities coexist.' To the
extent that America has become multicultural, immigrants may
choose among the subcultures they encounter or choose to maintain their original culture. They may assimilate into American
society without assimilating the core American culture. Assimilation and Americanization are no longer identical."[17]

Of course, in the past the public schools would have been
expected to teach real American history, government, values,
and traditions to immigrant children. Not anymore. Huntington writes: "Historically, the public schools were central in the
promotion of national identity. In the late twentieth century, in
contrast, schools promoted diversity rather than unity and made
little effort to inculcate immigrants in American culture, traditions, customs, and beliefs. . . . In a society that values ethnic and
racial diversity, immigrants have powerful incentives to maintain
and to reaffirm their ancestral identity."[18]

In fact, it is much worse in public schools today than when Huntington wrote his book in 2004. Democrat Party ideological agendas are now rampant throughout school systems and imposed on schoolchildren, such as CRT; "climate change"; LGBTQ+/transgenderism; and, mostly anti-Americanism. "Citizenship linked the identity of the individual to the identity of the nation," wrote Huntington. "National governments defined the bases of citizens such as *jus sanguinis* [the country of citizenship of the child is the same as his/her parents] or *jus soli* [a child's citizenship is based on the country of his/her birth], the criteria for who was eligible to become citizens, and the processes by which that happened. In the twentieth century, however, the idea of national citizenship came under attack, the requirements that had to be met to become a citizen eroded, and the distinction between the rights and responsibilities of citizens and noncitizens shrank significantly. These developments have been legitimized in the name of international agreements and universal human rights and the argument that citizenship is not a product of the nation but inheres to the individual. The link between citizen and nation is broken, undermining, as Yasemin Soysal [Professor of Sociology, the Free University of Berlin] has said, 'the national order of citizenship.'"[19] Of course, the Democrat Party marks this as a great achievement.

Consequently, mass immigration during a period of domestic cultural revolution, when the American culture and society are being ripped apart—both of which are products of the Biden administration, the Democrat Party, and the various American Marxist movements—is in fact destroying the nature of our country. That is precisely why Biden and his party have been purposefully and affirmatively moving full speed ahead with open-borders policies. Dan Stein, president of the Federation for American Immigration Reform (FAIR), has written: "In their first 100 days, the Biden administration took over 90 executive actions on immigration, many of which dismantled an effective system, making it easier for migrants to illegally enter and stay for good. Nearly every follow-up executive action or policy decision . . . has been used to launder the crisis—not end it. The administration also immediately sent a 353-page mass amnesty bill to Congress, the same proposal consistently referenced 'as a comprehensive immigration reform plan' that will solve the crisis they intentionally started. In reality, it is a reward to lawbreakers and an invitation to the entire world, and we are still seeing the effects of making it public."[20]

Despite spending half a century in Washington, D.C., as a senator, vice president, and president, and making immigration and border decisions and policies, Biden had never visited the southern border. He claims to know what must be done on immigration but avoided bothering to see what policies are needed or how disastrous his own policies are. Besides, everything is going as planned. Why should he care?

Finally, as a result of public pressure and political necessity, Biden went to El Paso, Texas. The trip was entirely scripted, it lasted three hours, it was a stopover on his way to Mexico, and the streets and detention areas were cleaned up and cleaned out for the visit, turning the area into a Potemkin village. Biden refused to meet with any migrants, as he did not want to hear about their horrific experiences and conditions.[21]

Nonetheless, what follows are some of the extreme actions Biden and his administration have taken, and that have led to chaos and anarchy on the southern border (and now even the northern border), for which they take no responsibility in response to an angry American public. Biden issued the following immigration-related executive orders (EOs) and administrative policy changes since his first day in office:

Proclamation on Ending Discriminatory Bans on Entry to the United States—January 20, 2021

Preserving and Fortifying Deferred Action for Childhood Arrivals (DACA)—January 20, 2021

US Citizenship Act of 2021

DHS Statement on the Suspension of New Enrollments in the Migrant Protection Protocols Program—January 20, 2021

Proclamation on the Suspension of Entry as Immigrants and Non-Immigrants of Certain Additional Persons Who Pose a Risk of Transmitting Coronavirus Disease—January 25, 2021

Executive Order on Creating a Comprehensive Regional Framework to Address the Causes of Migration, to Manage Migration Throughout North and Central America, and to Provide Safe and Orderly Processing of Asylum Seekers at the United States Border—February 2, 2021

Executive Order on Restoring Faith in Our Legal Immigration Systems and Strengthening Integration and Inclusion Efforts for New Americans—February 2, 2021

Executive Order on the Establishment of Interagency Task Force on the Reunification of Families—February 2, 2021

Executive Order on Rebuilding and Enhancing Programs to Resettle Refugees and Planning for the Impact of Climate Change on Migration—February 4, 2021

Memorandum for the Secretary of State on the Emergency Presidential Determination on Refugee Admissions for Fiscal Year 2021—April 16, 2021

A Proclamation on the Suspension of Entry as Nonimmigrants of Certain Additional Persons Who Pose a Risk of Transmitting Coronavirus Disease 2019—April 30, 2021

Memorandum for the Secretary of State on the Emergency Presidential Determination on Refugee Admissions for Fiscal Year 2021—May 3, 2021[22]

Again, Biden's policies have led to havoc on the borders and an astonishing record level of Customs and Border Patrol (CBP) encounters and enforcement actions. Let us take a look at the numbers even *before* the crisis turned into a complete catastrophe with the lifting of Title 42 and the COVID-19 protocol protections:

TOTAL CBP ENFORCEMENT ACTIONS[22]

Numbers below reflect Fiscal Year (FY) 2017–FY 2023.

Fiscal Year 2023 runs October 01, 2022–September 30, 2023.

	FY17	FY18	FY19	FY20	FY21	FY22	FY23YTD
Office of Field Operations (OFO) Total Encounters	216,370	281,881	288,523	241,786	294,352	551,930	570,587
U.S. Border Patrol Total Encounters	310,531	404,142	859,501	405,036	1,662,167	2,214,652	1,246,371
Total Enforcement Actions	526,901	683,178	1,148,024	646,822	1,956,519	2,766,582	1,816,958

Mark Morgan, former acting commissioner of U.S. Customs and Border Protection, and Tom Homan, former acting director of U.S. Customs and Border Protection, explain that "[t]he situation on the southern border is truly unprecedented. We have seen record-breaking month after record-breaking month of apprehensions. Border officials have encountered more than 5.5 million people (including more than a million known 'got-aways' and an untold number of violent criminals, gang members and potential terrorists) since Biden took office. The cartels have seized operational control of our southwest border as an increasingly beleaguered Border Patrol has been pulled from front line duties to focus on processing and releasing record numbers of illegal immigrants. Fentanyl pouring across the border is now the leading killer of Americans age 18–45. And more migrants are dying, too—more than 1,300 have lost their lives on U.S. soil on Biden's watch, the most ever recorded."[24]

Simon Hankinson, senior research fellow at the Heritage Foundation, adds that "[p]revious presidents have abused parole [for immigrants], but Biden is doing it on an industrial scale. He claims to be acting because Congress won't, which is to say they won't pass his immigration 'reform' bill granting amnesty to millions of illegal aliens and thus encouraging millions more to enter illegally or overstay their visas. But when he came into office, Biden undid every program the Trump administration had successfully used to reduce illegal entries. Predictably, hundreds of thousands of people from countries near and far headed for the border, knowing they'd be let in regardless of the truth of their claims. Biden is using parole programs to create a parallel immigration system. In practice, it allows millions of people to cut ahead of family and employment applicants waiting in the legal immigration line for a visa. These queue-jumpers get rewarded with work authorization, public benefits, and no serious chance of ever being made to leave. Better still, they don't pay a penny to apply, unlike petitioners for legal family visas whose fees are about to be hiked up to 50%."[25]

Even more, Elizabeth Jacobs, director of regulatory affairs and policy at the Center for Immigration Studies (CIS), reports: "Among the most concerning aspects of the [Biden administration] rule is its provisions that allow asylum officers to grant asylum—placing the alien on a path to citizenship—following a 'non-adversarial hearing,' at which the alien could be represented by counsel, while U.S. Customs and Immigration Enforcement (ICE) prosecutors, who represent the interests of the American public, are kept out of the process. That means an alien could receive a final asylum grant without any cross-examination impeachment evidence considered, preventing a thorough review of the alien's claims. Even more concerning is that the framework excludes judicial review of cases where the asylum officer improperly granted asylum. Simply put, the Biden administration's regulation provides more protections to illegal entrants, while removing safeguards protecting the most essential of U.S. interests—citizenship."[26] Hence, the Biden administration is conferring amnesty on illegal aliens without legal authority or challenge.

Jacobs notes that "Biden has failed to implement any policies to deter illegal entrants. Instead, his administration put forth reforms that are meant to hide mass illegal immigration from public view by accelerating the processing, transport, and issuance of parole to recent arrivals, under the banner of creating 'safe, orderly, and legal pathways' for prospective migrants.' . . . Since January 2021, the Biden administration has released an estimated 1.7 million illegal entrants into the United States by using parole as a mechanism to circumvent . . . mandatory detention provisions. The Biden administration has also revived and expanded the Central American Minors program, which was originally created by the Obama administration to allow certain Central American migrants to apply for parole from home and, in its image, has created six new parole programs to allow prospective migrants from Afghanistan, Cuba, Haiti, Nicaragua, Venezuela, and Ukraine to apply for parole from abroad. Under the Biden administration's new programs, if an alien is granted parole, they will be able to enter and work in the United States, despite not having a lawful immigration status. While parole is temporary, DHS [the Department of Homeland Security] has not provided any information regarding whether parole granted under its new program will be extended or renewed. . . . Secretary of Homeland Security Alejandro Mayorkas explicitly stated in his 2021 enforcement guidelines that 'the fact that [an alien] is removable . . . should not alone be the basis of an enforcement action against them.'"[27]

Moreover, an immigration requirement that has been enforced for many decades under presidents of both parties has been shredded by the Biden administration—that is, whether an immigrant entering our country is self-sufficient or would become a public charge (a welfare recipient). Of course, Biden and the Democrat Party are in business to create as many public charges as possible.

Jacobs writes that "[u]nder the Biden administration's framework, immigration officers may consider only prior or current receipt of cash-based welfare or long-term institutionalization at the government's expense when considering whether an alien is likely to become a public charge. All other forms of welfare usage are excluded from a public charge analysis. That means, when an officer is tasked with determining whether an alien is likely at any time to be a public charge, they are prohibited from considering the alien's past or current receipt of any non-cash benefit, such as medical care, housing assistance, or benefits provided to dependent family members. The Biden administration's public charge regulation also excludes consideration of an alien's receipt of the Earned Income Tax Credit and Child Tax Credit programs, even though they are means-tested transfer payments for which recipients must individually qualify. Notably, officers also may not consider benefits received by an alien's family members, including dependent children."[28]

Of course, word has traveled around the world that the Biden administration's open-border immigration policies are intended to encourage foreigners to immigrate to America, including if not especially illegally. The Mexican cartels have made billions and billions of dollars exploiting the Biden policies and the atrocious human suffering attendant to them—sex trafficking, rape, kidnapping, involuntary servitude, squalor, child abuse, child labor, etc.[29]

Meanwhile, the Heritage Foundation reports: "the Biden Administration values neither securing America's borders nor enforcing the nation's immigration laws. Rather, a high value is placed on allowing as many illegal aliens into the United States as possible and making the American taxpayers provide their transportation, shelter, food, medical care, education, and more during the lengthy, indefinite period needed to determine final immigration status in each case. Very few resources are allocated toward deporting the millions who fail to qualify for asylum or other immigration benefits."[30] Again, this is purposeful: Biden and the Democrat Party are using immigration to "fundamentally transform America," and those who take notice and dare to speak out are immediately denounced and dismissed as racists promoting "the great replacement/white genocide conspiracy theory" and stirring up resentment akin to the early southern slave-holders.[31] But it is Biden and the Democrat Party, as explained earlier in this chapter, who are abusing and exploiting migrants as part of their American Marxist agenda. Chaos, lack of assimilation, overburdening institutions, etc., are purposeful objectives.

At the *Daily Signal,* columnist Deroy Murdock reports on a hearing in the House of Representatives on sex trafficking and modern-day slavery on our southern border. "'We have what can be described as modern-day slavery,' said Ira Mehlman, spokesman for the Federation for American Immigration Reform (FAIR). 'Human traffickers (as opposed to smugglers) lure unsuspecting migrants with promises of all sorts of opportunity in the U.S., and then hold them hostage once they arrive here with threats of violence against them, or family members back home. Often people who are trafficked are forced to work in the sex trades. Since many do not have the cash up front, they are required to work it off once here,' Mehlman explained. 'Not unlike the Mafia, that can entail some significant accrual of interest, thereby extending the period of servitude.'"[32]

W. Kurt Hauser is a distinguished overseer with the Hoover

Institution on war, revolution, and peace at Stanford University. He also knows slavery when he sees it. Murdock writes: "He is the author of *Invisible Slaves: The Victims and Perpetrators of Modern-Day Slavery*. 'The huge increase in illegal immigration caused by the rescission of prior immigration practices, policies, and laws by the Biden Administration, and the violation of human rights that has accompanied many of these immigrants—including coercion, violence, rape, debts, and payments[—]would qualify as human trafficking,' Hauser said. 'That is slavery.'"[33]

Jessica Vaughan, director of policy studies for CIS, appalled by the giant shrug with which the Biden administration greets these burgeoning atrocities, testified before Congress that "[t]he Biden-Harris administration refuses to acknowledge that they are enabling this entirely predictable criminal and exploitive result of their policies. They prefer to see themselves as saviors of the migrants, even if their policies are literally enslaving some of the migrants to the cartels and smugglers. If there are some horrible crimes that happen, well they 'fix' them by awarding the victims with a U or T visa, and their conscience is laundered."[34]

Indeed, an entire industry built around Biden's open-border policies has led to billions in cartel smuggling and kidnapping profits. The *New York Times*' Miriam Jordan reports: "While migrants have long faced kidnappings and extortion in Mexican border cities, such incidents have been on the rise on the U.S. side, according to federal authorities. More than 5,046 people were arrested and charged with human smuggling last year [2021], up from 2,762 in 2014. . . . Over the past year, federal agents have raided stash houses holding dozens of migrants on nearly a daily basis. Fees typically range from $4,000, for migrants coming from Latin America, to $20,000, if they must be moved from Africa, Eastern Europe or Asia, according to Guadalupe Correa-Cabrera, an expert on smuggling at George Mason University. . . . For years, independent coyotes paid cartels a tax to move migrants through territory they controlled along the border, and the criminal syndicates stuck to their traditional line of business, drug smuggling, which was far more profitable. That began to change around 2019, Patrick Lechleitner, the acting deputy director at U.S. Immigration and Customs Enforcement, told Congress last year. The sheer number of people seeking to cross made migrant smuggling an irresistible moneymaker for some cartels, he said. . . . The enterprises have teams specializing in logistics, transportation, surveillance, stash houses and accounting—all supporting an industry whose revenues have soared to an estimated $13 billion today from $500 million in 2018, according to Homeland Security Investigations, the federal agency that investigates such cases."[35]

All of this is well known and clearly acceptable to Biden and the Democrat Party. They unleashed the extensive trafficking and other violent activities happening every day across the United States. In 2021, Jarod Forget, Drug Enforcement Agency (DEA) special agent in charge, Washington, D.C., Division, in a piece titled "Violent drug organizations use human trafficking to expand profits," wrote about the cartels' gruesome practices: "We see trafficking of illegal drugs and human trafficking often happen together. Transnational drug traffickers and criminal organizations often look to increase profits and market control through diversification. This means using trafficking routes for drugs, labor, sex, and violence. Transporting people (usually women and children) for sex is just another egregious source of profits for these violent criminals. For traffickers, it doesn't matter which product is being sold—both drugs and sex are lucrative industries—as long as money is made. Drug cartels often use trafficked women and children to smuggle drugs across the border, doubling up on the money they can make from them. Violent criminals like this see no difference between abusing a woman's body by forcing her to swallow bags of drugs or by forcing her to have sex with hundreds of men."[36]

And while the cartels and smugglers are making billions, the migrant children eventually entering the United States are facing further exploitation. The *New York Times*' Hannah Dreier wrote an extensive piece on the terrible conditions facing tens of thousands of migrant teenagers. Dreier explains that "[t]his labor force [migrant children] has been slowly growing for almost a decade, but it has exploded since 2021, while the systems meant to protect children have broken down. The *Times* spoke with more than 100 migrant child workers in 20 states who described jobs that were grinding them into exhaustion, and fears that they had become trapped in circumstances they never could have imagined. The *Times* examination also drew on court and inspection records and interviews with hundreds of lawyers, social workers, educators, and law enforcement officials. In town after town, children scrub dishes late at night. They run milking machines in Vermont and deliver meals in New York City. They harvest coffee and build lava rock walls around vacation homes in Hawaii. Girls as young as 13 wash hotel sheets in Virginia. In many parts of the country, middle and high school teachers in English-language learner programs say it is now common for nearly all their students to rush off to long shifts after their classes end."[37]

As Dreier explained, the Biden administration is well aware that tens of thousands of unaccompanied minors are in the United States. She writes: "The number of unaccompanied minors entering the United States climbed to a high of 130,000 last year [2022]—three times what it was five years earlier—and this summer is expected to bring another wave. These are not children who have stolen into the country undetected. The federal government knows they are in the United States, and the Department of Health and Human Services is responsible for ensuring sponsors will support them and protect them from trafficking or exploitation. But as more and more children have arrived, the Biden White House has ramped up demands on staffers to move the children quickly out of shelters and release them to adults. Caseworkers say they rush through vetting sponsors. While H.H.S. checks on all minors by calling them a month after they begin living with their sponsors, data obtained by the *Times* showed that over the last two years, the agency could not reach more than 85,000 children. Overall, the agency lost immediate contact with a third of migrant children."[38]

And it gets worse. "In the last two years alone," writes Dreier, "more than 250,000 children have entered the United States by themselves. . . . The Biden administration pledged to move children through the shelter system more quickly. 'We don't want to continue to see a child languish in our care if there is a responsible sponsor,' Xavier Becerra, Secretary of the Department of Health and Human Services, told Congress in 2021. His agency began paring back protections that had been in place for years, including some background checks and reviews of children's files, according to memos reviewed by the *Times* and interviews with more than a dozen current and former employees. . . ."[39]

Thus, the horrendous treatment of an unknown but significant number of the mass of aliens on the southern border and those entering the United States is shocking. What does Biden think of his handiwork? Biden dissembles, claiming the border is secure, but if there are problems it is due to the Trump administration or the new "MAGA Republican majority"—an absurd but repeated lie. Of course, the enormous financial and human costs of Biden's policies ripple throughout our society. And the truth holds him and his party accountable.

For example, a study by FAIR finds that as a result of Biden's policies, "[p]ublic school districts across the United States continue to suffer under a massive unfunded mandate imposed by the federal government: the requirement to educate millions of illegal aliens, the school-age children of illegal aliens, and unassimilated/unvetted refugees, all at taxpayer expense. Further adding to this burden are millions of students from legal immigrant families admitted into this country despite being unable to fluently speak English. FAIR estimates that it currently costs public schools just over $78 billion to serve this burgeoning population based on data from 2020. The struggle to fund programs for students with Limited English Proficiency (LEP) represents a major drain on school budgets as they redirect resources away from American citizens to support English learner programs for this cohort. Currently, 5.1 million students—or more than 10 percent of all students in American public schools—are designated as LEP."[40]

Furthermore, the amount of crime committed by illegal aliens that would not otherwise be committed in our country, resulting from Biden's open border, is unconscionable and extraordinary. And the huge increases during the Biden presidency, as reported by the U.S. Customs and Border Protection agency, are shocking but predictable. These policies illustrate one thing: Biden and the Democrat Party are affirmatively implementing and supporting an agenda that is destructive of America, and they are doing it on purpose—because of their contempt for American society and culture and their lust for power.

CRIMINAL NONCITIZEN STATISTICS FISCAL YEAR 2023

The following is a summary of U.S. Border Patrol enforcement actions related to arrests of criminal noncitizens for fiscal years 2017–2023.

Record checks of available law enforcement databases following the apprehension of an individual may reveal a history of criminal conviction(s). That conviction information is recorded in a U.S. Customs and Border Protection database, from which the data below is derived.

ARRESTS OF INDIVIDUALS WITH CRIMINAL CONVICTIONS [41]

The term *criminal noncitizens* refers to individuals who have been convicted of one or more crimes, whether in the United States or abroad, prior to interdiction by the U.S. Border Patrol; it does not include convictions for conduct that is not deemed criminal by the United States. Arrests of criminal noncitizens are a subset of total apprehensions by U.S. Border Patrol.

Fiscal Year 2023 runs October 01, 2022–September 30, 2023.

	FY17	FY18	FY19	FY20	FY21	FY22	FY23YTD
U.S. Border Patrol Criminal Noncitizen Arrests	8,531	6,698	4,269	2,438	10,763	12,028	5,193

TOTAL CRIMINAL CONVICTIONS BY TYPE [42]

This table organizes nationwide convictions of criminal non-citizens by type of criminal conduct. Because some criminal non-citizens may be convicted of multiple criminal offenses, total convictions listed below exceed the total arrests noted in the table above.

The chart shows a huge jump in noncitizen criminal activity under Biden's open-borders immigration policies.

Fiscal Year 2023 runs October 01, 2022–September 30, 2023.

	FY17	FY18	FY19	FY20	FY21	FY22	FY23YTD
Assault, Battery, Domestic Violence	692	524	299	208	1,178	1,142	493
Burglary, Robbery, Larceny, Theft, Fraud	595	347	184	143	825	896	366
Driving Under the Influence	1,596	1,113	614	364	1,629	1,614	792
Homicide, Manslaughter	3	3	2	3	60	62	12
Illegal Drug Possession, Trafficking	1,249	871	449	386	2,138	2,239	888
Illegal Entry, Reentry	4,502	3,920	2,663	1,261	6,160	6,797	2,999
Illegal Weapons Possession, Transport, Trafficking	173	106	66	49	336	309	146
Sexual Offenses	137	80	58	156	488	365	129
Other[1]	1,851	1,364	814	580	2,691	2,891	1,223

In addition, the impact of illegal immigration on the health care system is also calamitous. The American health care system spends at least $23 billion on medical care for illegal aliens—$8,153,000,000 for uncompensated hospital costs; $7,997,566,000 in Medicaid fraud; $5,385,007,000 in costs for U.S.-born children of illegal aliens; and $1.6 billion for Medicaid births; but the costs could be much higher.[43] Indeed, to demonstrate how diabolical the Biden administration is when dealing with health and immigration, Fox News reported that during the time the Title 42 health order was in effect, "the overwhelming majority of requests made by migrants for an exception to the Title 42 public health order [which applied primarily to COVID-related illnesses] using the recently expanded CBP One app have been accepted, with 99% of migrants being found to have met the criteria—just as the app continues to face scrutiny from both the left and the right. The Biden administration expanded the use of the CBP One app in January to allow for migrants seeking a humanitarian exception to Title 42—the COVID-era public health order that allows for the rapid expulsion of migrants at the southern border due to the pandemic."[44] Juxtapose this with how American citizens were treated by Democrat Party–run states and cities, and the Biden administration, during COVID-19. Title 42 has since been dropped, but the further damage done to the immigration system cannot be undone.

Clearly, the overwhelming evidence and experience demonstrate that the Biden administration is systematically and relentlessly eradicating America's immigration system and citizenship standards. The harm done to the nation is incalculable. In fact, the statistics and information provided in this chapter barely touch the surface. To be clear, these open-border policies, which are instituted unconstitutionally and illegally, are not accidental or a matter of incompetence; they are intentional and clear-eyed, therefore, there is an overarching purpose to them, requiring further elaboration.

First, the Democrat Party as an institution does not believe in Americanism, and that includes American sovereignty and citizenship. The destruction of the immigration system is another example of the American Marxist agenda and ongoing domestic revolution. It is also part of the racist attitude promoted throughout academia and other parts of our culture, which argues that not only is America a white-dominant society, but the country's existence is illegitimate because of the colonization of North America by white Europeans. Therefore, the United States is an illicit experiment. Moreover, the alien is the rightful occupant of the United States and North America, especially if they hail from Mexico and other parts of Central and South America. These are said to be the true indigenous people of the continent.[45] Furthermore, assimilation into such a corrupt culture and society must be rejected. It is merely another form of colonization by the progeny of white European interlopers.

Second, a few decades ago, the Democrat Party and Democrat-aligned unions sought to reduce legal immigration and opposed illegal immigration. For example, Democrat senator Harry Reid, who would become the Senate Democrat leader, was a staunch advocate of immigration restrictions. In August 1994, he wrote an op-ed in the *Los Angeles Times* arguing, in part, that "[t]axpayers simply cannot continue to sustain new populations the size of San Diego or the state of Nevada every year. California is sending up the red flag that Washington should heed. Unprecedented demands are being placed on job markets, schools, hospitals, police, social safety nets, infrastructure, and natural resources. Unlimited new arrivals pressuring these systems threaten to overwhelm them. . . . Most politicians agree that illegal immigration should end. My legislation would double border patrols and accelerate the deportation process for criminals and illegal entrants. But many lawmakers feel that lowering legal immigration is too dicey. This is a cop-out. My legislation calls for a reduction of legal immigrants from the current level of about 1 million admissions a year to approximately 325,000. Even that more realistic level means 25,000 newcomers entering every month, looking for jobs, housing and education."[46]

A year earlier, in 1993, Reid gave a speech on the Senate floor in which he stated, in part: "If making it easy to be an illegal alien is not enough, how about offering a reward for being an illegal immigrant? No sane country would do that, right? Guess again. If you break our laws by entering this country without permission and give birth to a child, we reward that child with U.S. citizenship and guarantee full access to all public and social services this society provides. And that is a lot of services. Is it any wonder that two-thirds of the babies born at taxpayer expense in county-run hospitals in Los Angeles are born to illegal alien mothers?"[47]

As CIS's Robert Law explained upon Reid's death: "Today, elected Democrats are unanimously in favor of mass amnesty, increasing legal immigration, and opposing any form of border security or interior enforcement. In an article detailing Reid's legacy upon his death, the *New York Times* implied that Reid only changed his views on immigration because he perceived supporting amnesty as a prerequisite to climbing the ranks of the Democrats after the turn of the 21st century. As framed by the *Times*, 'Mr. Reid took decidedly conservative stances early in his career, notably opposing abortion and looser immigration laws. But his positions shifted as the demographics of his state changed, and he eventually became a champion of [illegal aliens]. Put another way, Reid did not come across new information that refuted his mid-1990s views on immigration and how it impacts Americans; instead, Democratic powerbrokers staked a claim on amnesty to enlarge their Hispanic voting bloc.'"[48] In other words, Reid learned that to climb to the highest ranks in the Democrat Party, he must appeal to the American Marxists and promote their program. Lyndon Johnson and, of course, Biden, made similar political calculations about race.

Reid is only one in a long line of such Democrats. As columnist Cal Thomas points out: "In a 2009 speech at Georgetown Law School, [Chuck] Schumer [now the Senate Democrat leader] said that 'illegal immigration is wrong. We must create a system that converts the flow of primarily low-skilled illegal immigrants into the United States into a more manageable and controlled flow of legal immigrants who can be absorbed by our economy.'"[49] However, last year, as *New York Post* columnist Karol Markowicz explains, Schumer reversed course. He declared: "We have a population that is not reproducing on its own with the same level that it used to. The only way we're going to have a great future in America is if we welcome and embrace immigrants, the Dreamers and all of them, because our ultimate goal is to help the Dreamers but to get a path to citizenship for all 11 million or however many undocumented there are here."[50] Markowicz adds, "[t]he idea that we have only 11 million illegal immigrants in the country is also laughable. The 'or however many' is doing the heavy lifting in Schumer's declaration. A 2009 Reuters piece on Schumer's immigration policies had the number at 12 million. The US Border Patrol had 227,547 encounters along our southwest border in September [2022] alone. These have been the numbers for much of 2022 and 2021. We had nearly 5 million people in just two years enter on just the southern border. Unlike Democrats, we can do math: 11 million is the lowest of lowballs."[51]

Not coincidentally, when Reid retired, Schumer replaced him as Senate Democrat leader. Schumer took much grief for his 2009 statement, and like Reid, learned his lesson.

As Reid and Schumer had opposed illegal immigration earlier in their careers, so did the labor unions. I explained several years ago in *Liberty and Tyranny* that "[i]n the 1960s, Cesar Chávez, one of the founders of the United Farm Workers (UFW) union, vehemently opposed illegal immigration, arguing it undermined his efforts to unionize farm workers and improve working conditions and wages for American citizen workers. The UFW even reported illegal immigrants to the Immigration and Naturalization Service. In 1969, Chávez led a march, accompanied by Ralph Abernathy, president of the Southern Christian Leadership Conference, and Democrat senator, Walter Mondale, along the border with Mexico, protesting the farmers' use of illegal immigration."[52]

But Chávez's earlier statements and actions have been whitewashed through the rewriting of his legacy. In October 2012, President Barack Obama established a Cesar Chávez National

Monument in California[53]; on March 28, 2014, Obama declared March 31, 2014, Cesar Chávez Day[54]; and in January 2021, Biden placed Chávez's bust in the Oval Office.[55] In fact, on its website, the AFL-CIO posts this statement: "Instead of deporting immigrants, we need to ensure that all working people have rights on the job and are able to exercise them without fear of retaliation. Enacting meaningful immigration reform is critical to our long-term efforts to lift labor standards and empower workers, and the labor movement will continue to stand in solidarity with all working people."[56] In other words, the nation's largest private sector union has no problem with illegal immigration, as long as illegal aliens are signed up as dues-paying union members when they enter the workforce. Moreover, "meaningful immigration reform" means nothing to a political party and revolutionary movement that encourages law-breaking on both sides of the southern and northern borders.

Today, the Democrat Party sees mass immigration as an imperative to gaining, retaining, and exercising power. The chaos resulting from Biden's policies, and before him Obama, is crucial to "fundamentally transforming America." The party expects to benefit from "birthright citizenship" followed by "chain migration." Therefore, rather than opposing illegal immigration, which was historically its position, it has reversed course (again), determining that its power is enhanced by open borders. And the private sector union bosses, whose unions have been losing membership, have made the decision that rather than opposing legal and illegal immigration, Democrat Party open-border policies create a potential pool of new dues-paying members, regardless of the best interests of its current membership.

Third, for years the Democrat Party and its media surrogates have accused the Republican Party of supporting "the replacement theory," which is said to be a "right-wing," "white supremacist," etc., concept that is both racist and dangerous. According to Vox's Fabiola Cineas, it is a Republican Party invention going back over a century, which attracted the likes of Theodore Roosevelt, Calvin Coolidge, Warren Harding, and, of course, Adolf Hitler, among others.[57] Predictably, nowhere does she mention the Democrat Party's and so-called progressives' support for the application of eugenics to blacks and other minorities. She never mentions Woodrow Wilson, Franklin Roosevelt, Harry Reid, Walter Mondale, Cesar Chávez, the Democrat Party, or Chuck Schumer. Again, Schumer recently declared that "we have a population that is not reproducing on its own with the same level that it used to," as a core reason to support limitless amnesty and open borders. Nor does she cite Biden's 2015 statements in support of "replacement theory." And, of course, Cineas, who obviously sees all things with which she disagrees as part of a white-racist construct, completely ignores the inhumane consequence of these policies on the migrants themselves—the overwhelming number who are not white.

Of course, to raise questions about the Democrat Party's disastrous policies is to be accused of racism, white supremacy, and so forth—more evidence of a white-dominant culture barely holding on in a browning America. The goal is to intimidate and silence those who object to the devastating consequences of Democrat Party open-borders policies to American citizens and immigrants alike.[58]

The Democrat Party exists to obtain, retain, and expand its own power, much like Marxist parties in other countries. The party comes before the country, which is evidenced by its horrendous immigration policies.

There is also a growing movement in the Democrat Party to eliminate the distinction between citizen and alien. For example, driver's licenses are handed out to individuals regardless of their legal status. But a driver's license opens many doors in society. It is the main source of identification (except when it comes to voting in Democrat Party–run states, where the party opposes voter identification). Biden also made a video statement in which he made several telling points about his attitude and that of his party when it comes to illegal immigration. He said:

"When President Obama and I created the DACA [Deferred Action for Childhood Arrivals] program we knew it would transform lives and it has. Bringing stability and possibility to hundreds of thousands of young people known as Dreamers brought to America as children. This country is the only home they've ever known. There are friends that are coworkers. They study, they work hard, they start businesses, many have served in our military, and many were essential workers in the front lines of the pandemic. They are American in every way except on paper. It's past time for Congress to give Dreamers a pathway to citizenship and while we work toward that goal alongside Dreamers' advocates and members of Congress, we need to give Dreamers the opportunities and support they deserve. So today my administration is announcing our plan to expand health coverage for DACA recipients by allowing them to enroll on a plan through the Affordable Care Act or through Medicaid. Healthcare should be a right not a privilege. My administration has worked hard to expand healthcare and today more Americans have health insurance than ever. Today's announcement is about giving DACA recipients the same opportunity and we'll continue to do what we can to protect Dreamers and push Congress to give them and their families a pathway that says and ultimately, peace of mind they all deserve."[59]

Biden has a greater affection for aliens illegally in the United States than for tens of millions of United States citizens who do not share his political objectives and are members of the Republican Party.

Biden and others in the Democrat Party often state: "We are a nation of immigrants." Nations are made up of *citizens*. Although we welcome *legal* immigrants, a nation exists to serve its citizens, not foreigners who illegally cross a border. An executive order issued by Biden in 2022 titled "A Proclamation on National Immigrant Heritage Month, 2022" opens with "The United States is a Nation of immigrants." Toward the end, he calls upon the people "to observe this month with appropriate programming and activities that remind us of the values of diversity, equity, and inclusion."[60] Also, when asked by *Breitbart News* on May 10, 2023, about how Biden's immigration policy helps Americans, Secretary of the Department of Homeland Security Alejandro Mayorkas said that "we are a nation of immigrants" and that his border management is "all about achieving equity, which is really the core founding principle of our country."[61] Therefore, "equity"—that is, a major tenet of Marxism and government-sanctioned racial discrimination against "white privilege"—is a Biden policy that even applies to the status of new aliens, including illegal aliens.

As mentioned earlier, there is also a growing movement in Democrat Party–run municipalities and states to expand voting to include noncitizens in their elections. When combined with Democrat Party efforts to flood the nation with legal and illegal immigrants, eliminate voter identification, and allow other fraud-inducing policies not just locally but nationally, the ability for noncitizens to vote in all elections without detection becomes a significant issue. Stanley A. Renshon of CIS has written that "[i]n recent years, a concerted effort has been gathering force to allow new immigrants to the United States to vote without becoming citizens. It is being mounted by an alliance of liberal . . . academics and law professors, local and state political leaders most often associated with the Democratic Party or other progressive parties like the Greens, and community and immigration activists. They are working in tandem to decouple the legal standing to vote from American citizenship."[62]

Moreover, Renshon explains: "If advocates' proposals for noncitizen voting are implemented, new non-citizen voters would not have to demonstrate [as they must now] 'an understanding of the English language including the ability to read, write, and speak words in ordinary usage in the English language.' They will not have to demonstrate 'a knowledge and understanding of the fundamentals of the history and of the principles and form of government of the United States.' They will not have to demonstrate that they are of 'good moral character' by not, for example, having been convicted of a felony. They will not have to take an oath of allegiance to the United States and renounce allegiance to any foreign country. And they will not have to have been in residence in the United States for five years and for a minimum of 30 consecutive months before naturalization. These requirements are, of course, those that accompany the naturalization process by which legal immigrants become citizens. Abandoning all of them in order to give non-citizens the right to vote puts advocates in the paradoxical position of requiring far less for non-citizen than for citizen voting."[63] Municipalities in three states already allow noncitizens to vote in local elections as of April 2023: California, Maryland, and Vermont.[64] And there are many more proposals throughout Democrat Party strongholds across the country, including New York City.

The only reason for this is to benefit the Democrat Party,

which hopes to create more Democrat voters. The party, which not long ago treated immigrants like second-class citizens and people of color inhumanely, now inhumanely exploits them for political reasons—that is, to empower the Democrat Party.

The late Democrat governor of Colorado, Richard Lamm, who was a traditional liberal, a few years after leaving politics gave a weighty five-minute speech in 2004 in Washington, D.C., on how to destroy America. His comments cannot be properly summarized without doing damage to their impact. However, they are both profound and succinct enough to provide in full. Lamm said:

> If you believe that America is too smug, too self-satisfied, too rich, then let's destroy America. It is not that hard to do. No nation in history has survived the ravages of time. Arnold Toynbee observed that all great civilizations rise and fall and that "an autopsy of history would show that all great nations commit suicide."
>
> First, turn America into a bilingual or multi-lingual and bicultural country. History shows that no nation can survive the tension, conflict, and antagonism of two or more competing languages and cultures. It is a blessing for an individual to be bilingual; however, it is a curse for a society to be bilingual. The historical scholar Seymour Lipset put it this way: "The histories of bilingual and bi-cultural societies that do not assimilate are histories of turmoil, tension, and tragedy. Canada, Belgium, Malaysia, Lebanon all face crises of national existence in which minorities press for autonomy, if not independence. Pakistan and Cyprus have divided. Nigeria suppressed an ethnic rebellion. France faces difficulties with Basques, Bretons, and Corsicans."
>
> Second, to destroy America, invent multiculturalism

and encourage immigrants to maintain their culture. I would make it an article of belief that all cultures are equal. That there are no cultural differences. I would make it an article of faith that the black and Hispanic dropout rates are due to prejudice and discrimination by the majority. Every other explanation is out of bounds.

Third, we could make the United States a Hispanic Quebec without much effort. The key is to celebrate diversity rather than unity. As Benjamin Schwarz said in the *Atlantic Monthly* recently: "The apparent success of our own multiethnic and multicultural experiment might have been achieved! Not by tolerance but by hegemony. Without the dominance that once dictated ethnocentrically and what it meant to be an American, we are left with only tolerance and pluralism to hold us together."

I would encourage all immigrants to keep their own language and culture. I would replace the melting pot metaphor with the salad bowl metaphor. It is important to ensure that we have various cultural subgroups living in America reinforcing their differences rather than as Americans, emphasizing their similarities.

Fourth, I would make our fastest growing demographic group the least educated. I would add a second underclass, unassimilated, undereducated, and antagonistic to our population. I would have this second underclass have a 50% dropout rate from high school.

My fifth point for destroying America would be to get big foundations and business to give these efforts lots of money. I would invest in ethnic identity, and I would establish the cult of victimology. I would get all minorities to think their lack of success was the fault of the majority. I would start a grievance industry blaming all minority failure on the majority population.

My sixth plan for America's downfall would include dual citizenship and promote divided loyalties. I would celebrate diversity over unity. I would stress differences rather than similarities. Diverse people worldwide are mostly engaged in hating each other—that is, when they are not killing each other. A diverse, peaceful, or stable society is against most historical precedent. People undervalue the unity! Unity is what it takes to keep a nation together. Look at the ancient Greeks. The Greeks believed that they belonged to the same race; they possessed a common language and literature; and they worshiped the same gods. All Greece took part in the Olympic Games.

A common enemy Persia threatened their liberty. Yet all these bonds were not strong enough to overcome two factors: local patriotism and geographical conditions that nurtured political divisions. Greece fell.

E *Pluribus Unum*—from many, one. In that historical reality, if we put the emphasis on the "pluribus" instead of the "unum," we can balkanize America as surely as Kosovo.

Next to last, I would place all subjects off limits—make it taboo to talk about anything against the cult of diversity. I would find a word similar to *heretic* in the 16th century—that stopped discussion and paralyzed thinking. Words like *racist* or *xenophobes* halt discussion and debate.

Having made America a bilingual/bicultural country, having established multiculturism, having the large foundations fund the doctrine of victimology, I would next make it impossible to enforce our immigration laws. I would develop a mantra: That's because immigration has been good for America, it must always be good. I would make every individual immigrant symmetric and ignore the cumulative impact of millions of them.

Lastly, I would censor Victor Davis Hanson's book *Mexifornia*. His book is dangerous. It exposes the plan to destroy America. If you feel America deserves to be destroyed, don't read that book.[65]

One additional step you would take if you want to destroy America: reelect Joe Biden—or any of the other Democrats waiting in the wings—president of the United States, and keep the Democrat Party in charge of immigration.

Again, Professor Huntington perceptively declared that "[a]s the twentieth century ended [and, I would add, as the twenty-first century moves on], major gaps existed between America's elites and the general public over the salience of national identity compared to other identities and over the appropriate role for America in the world. Substantial elite elements were increasingly divorced from their country, and the American public was increasingly disillusioned with its government."[66] And the situation has become far worse. Biden, the Democrat Party, and their media surrogates have done and are doing enormous harm to American culture and society, the extent of which, especially into the future, is incalculable. And that is their goal. The "gap" is a Leninist top-down mentality of imposing the will of these "elites" on the rest of us. The American citizenry be damned!

CHAPTER SIX

WAR ON THE NUCLEAR FAMILY

In *The Communist Manifesto*, Karl Marx declared: "Abolition of the family! Even the most radical flare up at this infamous proposal of the Communists. On what foundation is the present family, the bourgeois family based? On capital, on private gain. In its completely developed form this family exists among the bourgeois. But this state of things finds its complement in the practical absence of the family among the proletarians, and in public prostitution. The bourgeois family will vanish with the vanishing of capital. Do you charge us with wanting to stop the exploitation of children by their parents? To this crime we plead guilty. But, you will say, we destroy the most hallowed of relations when we replace home education by social."[1]

Marx specifically drilled down on the essential necessity to replace parental care, love, nurturing, teaching, and moral guidance with the priorities of the egalitarianism and communality of the state. Failure to surrender your children to the will and propaganda of the state is to demonstrate your allegiance to or, worse, participation in the oppressor bourgeois status quo. Moreover, you care not about your children but the perpetuation of the bourgeoisie and capitalism, for which your children are trained to be soldiers. Marx wrote: "And your education! Is not that also social, and determined by the social conditions under which you educate, but the intervention direct and indirect, of society by means of schools, etc.? The Communists have not invented the intervention in society in education; they do but seek to alter the character of that intervention, and to rescue education from the influence of the ruling class. The bourgeois clap-trap about the family and education, about the hallowed co-relation of parent and child, becomes all the more disgusting by the action of modern industry, all family ties among the proletarians are torn asunder, and their children transformed into simple articles of commerce and instruments of labour."[2] "In *Capital*, Marx pronounced as silly any absolutizing of the family, since it had developed through historical stages."[3] Thus, Marx advocated for the communal education of children.[4]

Richard Weikart, professor of history at California State University, explained in his essay "Marx, Engels, and the Abolition of the Family" that "Marx's relationship with his children does not seem at all consistent with a desire to communally raise children. He greatly enjoyed playing and romping with them and was extremely solicitous for their welfare. Part of the reason for his financial problems was his alacrity to spend beyond his income to provide various amenities for his children, including private tutoring in languages, music, and drama. He asked Engels to take over fatherly responsibilities toward his children after he died. Sometimes Marx the father intervened in his daughters' lives in ways that seem to contradict his role as revolutionary abolisher of families and liberator of children. When Paul Lafargue was courting his daughter, Laura, he warned him to keep his distance for a time and demanded that he prove he could financially support a wife. He effectively blocked Eleanor's relationship with Prosper Lissagaray and refused to recognize their engagement, despite her pleading. He certainly was not prepared to allow his own daughters to live in complete sexual liberty."[5] Marx's unashamed hypocrisy is consistent with autocrats of all stripes. They cannot and will not live the life they brutally impose on others.

For example, the Obamas live like royalty, surrounded by luxury, wealth, and fame, sent their daughters to an expensive, tony, private school, yet still preach contempt for America and spew Marxist propaganda. John Kerry, Biden's so-called U.S. Special Envoy for Climate, flies private, military, and commercial flights endlessly around the world preaching the gospel of green energy and economic degrowth as the multi-millionaire spews tremendous amounts of carbon in the atmosphere as his contribution to fighting the "existential threat of climate change." And, of course, "Squad" members Cori Bush, Ilhan Omar, Rashida Tlaib, Alexandria Ocasio-Cortez, Ayanna Pressley, and Jamaal Bowman, while preaching the defunding of police, have spent liberally on private security to protect themselves. The list goes on.

Not surprisingly, the Democrat Party benefits politically from the breakup of the nuclear family. And its war on the family, the economy, the culture, and society is purposeful and malignant. For example, as *Washington Examiner* commentary editor Conn Carroll explains in his article, "[N]o one benefits more from the destruction of the American family than the Democratic Party . . . The good news for the Democrats is that the number of unmarried women is growing every year. From the earliest census up through 1950, roughly 80% of households were led by a married couple. By 2000, that percentage had fallen to 52%, and by 2010, for the first time in the nation's history, most households did not include a married couple. Marriage has only continued to decline since then. The destruction of the nuclear family may be great for Democrats, but it has been a disaster for children. . . ."[6] Indeed, the chart below demonstrates how the Democrat Party benefits hugely from the vote of unmarried women, and does poorly with married women:[7]

GENDER BY MARITAL STATUS

18,571 total respondents

	Married Men 30%	Married Women 30%	Unmarried Men 16%	Unmarried Women 23%
Democrats	39%	42%	45%	68%
Republicans	59%	56%	52%	31%

Source: Edison Research Network Exit Poll

Carroll concludes that "until we find a solution for our nation's marriage crisis, the family will continue to fall apart. Also, the Democratic Party will win more elections."[8]

Furthermore, "[u]nmarried women without children have been moving toward the Democratic Party for several years, but the 2022 midterms may have been their electoral coming-out party as they proved the chief break on the predicted Republican wave," writes Joel Kotkin, executive director of the Urban Reform Institute, and Professor Samuel J. Abrams of Sarah Lawrence College in RealClearInvestigations. They explain in their article titled "The Rise of the Single Woke (and Young, Democratic) Female" that "while married men and women as well as unmarried men broke for the GOP, CNN exit polls found that 68% of unmarried women voted for Democrats."[9]

Kotkin and Abrams point out that "[t]he Supreme Court's August [2022] decision overturning *Roe v. Wade* was certainly a special factor in the midterms, but longer-term trends show that single, childless women are joining African Americans as the Democrats' most reliable supporters. Their power is growing thanks to the demographic winds. The number of never married women has grown from about 20% in 1950 to more than 30% in 2022, while the percentage of married women has declined from almost 70% in 1950 to under 50% today. Overall, the percentage of married households with children has declined from 37% in 1976 to 21% today."[10]

Therefore, never-married single women, especially childless single women, are of enormous political benefit to the Democrat Party and its future electoral success. Thus, Biden and the party are acutely focused on catering to this demographic—and abortion is the key appeal, according to former speaker Nancy Pelosi.

As the *Washington Examiner* reported in July 2023: "Speaking on MSNBC's *Inside with Jen Psaki*. . . . , Pelosi homed in on [abortion]—one year after the Supreme Court's overturning *Roe v. Wade*. Pelosi said Democrats have seen success by centering their campaigns around pro-abortion talking points, which she attributed to helping the party avoid disaster in the 2022 midterm elections. 'Everyone said we're going to lose, 30, 40 seats,' she said."[11] More on this topic later in the chapter.

Kotkin and Abrams observe that "Soccer Moms are giving way to Single Woke Females—the new 'SWFs'—as one of the most potent voting blocs in American politics."[12]

This also explains why Biden transitioned from a so-called moderate on the issue of abortion to the most radical president ever on the subject. No longer does he, or the Democrat Party, believe that abortion should be "safe, legal, and rare." That mantra is never to be uttered again.

In fact, as Kotkin and Abrams explain: "The rise of SWFs . . . is one of the great untold stories of American politics. Distinct from divorced women or widows, these largely Gen Z and Millennial voters share a sense of collective identity and progressive ideology that sets them apart from older women. . . ."

"More recently, anti-family attitudes have become more pronounced," explain Kotkin and Abrams. "'Queer studies' often advocate replacing the 'nuclear family' with some form of collectivized childrearing. Progressive groups like Black Lives Matter made their opposition to the nuclear family a part of their basic original platform, even though evidence shows family breakdown has hurt African American boys most of all."[13]

In addition to benefiting from the decline in marriage and the dismantling of the family, the Democrat Party has made clear that it intends to subjugate children, the younger the better, to the ideological and political purposes of the party. In fact, they brazenly say so.

Virginia Democrat gubernatorial candidate Terry McAuliffe famously said during a candidates' debate in 2021 that "I'm not going to let parents come into schools and actually take books out and make their own decisions." He added: "I don't think parents should be telling schools what they should teach."[14] "Asked in a subsequent interview whether parents should have buy-in on a school's curriculum, McAuliffe doubled down: 'Listen, we have a board of ed working with the local school boards to determine the curriculum for our schools. You don't want parents coming in in every different school jurisdiction saying, This is what should be taught here and, This is what should be taught here."[15] These statements contributed mightily to McAuliffe losing the election. Yet McAuliffe was no doubt surprised by the reaction. He was simply voicing what the Democrat Party, the teachers' unions, and the education bureaucracy had always believed and practiced, but now with renewed gusto and in-your-face arrogance. In fact, Hillary Clinton wrote an entire book titled *It Takes a Village*. What could go wrong?

Indeed, McAuliffe, who was also the former chairman of the Democratic National Committee (DNC), was also echoing the view of the National Education Association (NEA), the nation's largest teachers' union. The NEA, which is a principal supporter of the Democrat Party and a top surrogate for the Biden administration, subsequently tweeted on November 12, 2022, that "[e]ducators love their students and know better than anyone what they need to learn and to thrive."[16]

In fact, the Biden White House, coordinating with the Department of Justice (DOJ) and the National School Boards Association (NSBA), organized an unprecedented intimidation campaign against parents protesting the Marxist indoctrination of their children at local school board meetings—including classes and textbooks promoting CRT and sexualizing children in elementary schools. A letter was drafted by the NSBA in coordination with White House, DOJ, and Education Department staff, asking for federal government intervention in the local parental protests. In a synchronized campaign to intimidate and threaten parents, within days Attorney General Merrick Garland issued a memorandum threatening parents with FBI investigations should complaints be made against them by school administrators, teachers, or anyone else. Garland's memo was addressed to the FBI, United States Attorneys, the Department of Justice's Criminal Division, the Civil Rights Division, and counterterrorism offices. It also encouraged complainants to use the domestic terrorism hotline to make their allegations.[17] This was done even though there was no widespread parental violence at school board meetings and the federal government had no authority to intervene in local law enforcement matters if there were.[18] This was nothing more than an attempt to silence constitutionally lawful assembly and dissent under the First Amendment. Several state school board associations resigned from the national association over the letter. The NSBA eventually issued a letter of apology to its members.[19] Meanwhile, the DOJ has never withdrawn its memorandum. Indeed, Garland stands by it, and the memorandum remains official Biden administration policy against parents.

House Republicans stepped in to prevent the Biden administration's police-state tactics. They passed a Parents Bill of Rights Act[20] "to support our children, provide for their education, promote their well-being, and secure a brighter future." Among other things, it provides parents a federal—

"1. Right to know what's being taught in schools and to see reading material

2. Right to be heard

3. Right to see school budget and spending

4. Right to protect their child's privacy

5. Right to be updated on any violent activity at school"[21]

The bill barely passed in the House by a vote of 213–208. Every Democrat voted against it, as did a few Republicans. House Democrats claimed the bill would ban books, prevent the teaching of the Holocaust, was fascist, etc.[22] Of course, despite their usual hysterics, it was none of these things. The purpose is to ensure that parents have insight into what is being taught to their children and have a say about it, which the Democrat Party and their teachers' unions' surrogates strongly oppose, and that Garland and the Department of Justice are stopped from exercising federal police powers and further abusing and harassing parents. The bill is languishing in the Democrat-controlled Senate.

The anti-parent, pro–teachers' union/educational bureaucracy agenda of the Democrat Party is, like most Democrat Party policies, imposed from the top down. For example, "[a]t the 2022 Teacher of the Year ceremony hosted by the White House . . . , President Biden claimed that school children don't belong to parents 'when they're in the classroom. They're all our children. And the reason you're the teachers of the year is because you recognize that. They're not somebody else's children. They're like yours when they're in the classroom.'"[23] So proclaimed the hair-sniffing, handsy Biden.

Ironically, Biden's four-year-old granddaughter, Navy Joan (Hunter's out-of-wedlock daughter) is treated as a nonentity. The disgraceful Bidens refuse to recognize her as their granddaughter and, as best as we know, have never personally met her. So much for the "they're all our children" rhetoric.[24]

Earlier this year, the Republican-controlled House sought to stop the Biden administration from destroying women's sports throughout the public school systems and collegiate level. As *Breitbart* reported: "The House passed . . . the Protection of Women and Girls in Sports Act, a bill that would amend Title IX to prevent men from competing against women in school sports. No Democrat voted in favor of the measure, which passed 219 to 203. The bill would clarify that in the Education Amendments of 1972, the term 'sex' as mentioned under the Title IX section 'shall be recognized based solely on a person's reproductive biology and genetics at birth.' The bill would work to withhold funding from schools receiving federal financial assistance should they violate Title IX by allowing transgender athletes to compete in sports programs designed for the opposite sex. The legislation comes after . . . Biden's Department of Education ramped up efforts this month to allow men who say they are women into women's athletics through a Title IX rule proposal." This is another pro-family bill stuck in the Democrat-run Senate, and Biden has said he will veto it if it passes.[25]

Biden's executive actions in fundamentally altering federal

law, in this case Title IX, are unconstitutional, like so many of Biden's radical executive orders. Moreover, the public rightly and understandably opposes biological men or boys in women's or girls' sports, as well as bathrooms, showers, and locker rooms. "[A] new poll conducted by *The Washington Post* and University of Maryland found the majority of Americans, 55 percent, are opposed to allowing transgender female athletes [aka biological males, with XY sex chromosomes] to compete with other women and girls in high school sports. A higher proportion, 58 percent, reported the same opinion at the college and professional sports levels."[26] But Biden and the Democrat Party are not satisfied with destroying female sports. As Marx urged, their real target is to ruin the nuclear family.

In the *New York Post*, Kaylee McGhee explains how the Biden administration is using Title IX regulations to obliterate parental control over children. She declares: "They're coming for your children. The administration ostensibly drafted the rules to protect gay and transgender students from bullying and harassment, but they do nothing of the sort. In reality, . . . Biden is handing teachers a weapon to subvert parental prerogatives. Title IX is a simple statute that outlaws 'sex discrimination' in education. It says nothing about 'gender' or 'gender identity.' But the Biden administration wants to put its own spin on the law and redefine 'sex' to include these categories. This change has far-reaching implications. One is that it will be used to keep parents in the dark on everything from curricular material to the fact that a child is socially transitioning at school. Because this new Title IX frames gender ideology as an anti-discrimination issue, schools won't have to seek parental permission for children to participate in lessons on choosing and changing one's sex. Indeed, schools will very likely use Title IX's anti-discrimination mandate to justify denying parental opt-outs from these controversial lessons."[27]

In fact, the Biden administration has now released "a series of documents encouraging gender-reassignment surgery and hormone treatments for minors. The Department of Health and Human Services' (HHS) Office of Population Affairs released a document . . . titled 'Gender Affirming Care and Young People.'[28] It states, in part: "Gender-affirming care is a supportive form of healthcare. It consists of an array of services that may include medical, surgical, mental health, and non-medical services for transgender and nonbinary people. For transgender and nonbinary children and adolescents, early gender affirming care is crucial to overall health and well-being as it allows the child or adolescent to focus on social transitions and can increase their confidence while navigating the healthcare system."[29]

However, there is significant expert opinion and scientific research that finds "[i]f they're not put on this pathway, most kids who suffer gender dysphoria will grow out of it."[30] In fact, "88% to 98% of those struggling with gender dysphoria will accept their biological sex after going through puberty, according to the fifth edition of the American Psychiatric Association's 'Diagnostic and Statistical Manual of Mental Disorders.'"[31]

The same day the Biden administration released the gender-affirming care document, "the Substance Abuse and Mental Health Services Administration's National Child Traumatic Stress Network—another subset of the HHS—released a parallel document titled, 'Gender-Affirming Care Is Trauma-Informed Care.' The HHS documents describe what it calls appropriate treatments for transgender adolescents, including: 'Top' surgery—to create male-typical chest shape or enhance breasts;' and 'Bottom' surgery—surgery on genitals or reproductive organs, facial feminization or other procedures.'"[32]

As usual, the Biden administration and the Democrat Party claim to be defending another victimized group. But by any measure, their desire to destroy the nuclear family, come between parents and their children, brainwash the most vulnerable, and control the upbringing of future generations creates victims. For them, extremism in the pursuit of power is no vice.

In an article titled "U.S. Becomes Transgender-Care Outlier as More in Europe Urge Caution," the *Wall Street Journal* reports: "The U.S. is becoming an outlier among many Western nations in the way its national medical institutions treat children suffering from distress over gender identity. For years, the American healthcare industry has staunchly defended medical interventions for transgender minors, including puberty blockers, which suppress the physical changes of adolescence as a treatment for those distressed over their gender. The European medical community, by contrast, is expressing doubts about that approach. Having allowed these treatments for years, five countries—the U.K., Sweden, Finland, Norway and France—now urge caution in their use for minors, stressing a lack of evidence that the benefits outweigh the risks. This month, the U.K.'s publicly funded National Health Service for England limited the use of puberty blockers to clinical trials, putting the drugs beyond the reach of most children."[33]

Leor Sapir, who studies gender care at the Manhattan Institute, told the *Journal*: "These countries have done systematic reviews of evidence. They've found that the studies cited to support these medical interventions are too unreliable, and the risks are too serious."[34] Nonetheless, the "party of science" is pushing blindly ahead with its political and ideological agenda regardless of the cost to the children involved. Clearly, this is not how most loving parents—as opposed to the state—raise their children.

Incredibly, Democrat states and counties across the country are passing laws to keep parents in the dark when their children express gender confusion; refuse to seek parental consent before exposing students to certain materials or psychological therapies that reinforce their beliefs or behaviors; and, even refuse to seek parental approval for drug or surgical interventions. Moreover, teachers' unions are strongly promoting such practices.[35]

The *New York Post's* Josh Christenson reports: "More than 3.2 million U.S. public school students are covered by guidance that blocks parents from knowing whether their child identifies as a different gender in the classroom—which could become federal policy if President Biden's Title IX proposals are approved. . . . At least 168 districts governing 5,904 schools nationwide have rules on the books that prevent faculty and staff from disclosing to parents a student's gender status without that student's permission, according to a list compiled by . . . Defending Education. . . . The 3,268,752 students affected by such policies go to class in all kinds of districts—large and small, affluent and poor, urban and rural, red and blue—stretching from North Carolina to Alaska."[36]

Outside the classroom, the woke corporatists are doing their part to mainstream, promote, and fund this agenda. For example, Fox News Digital reports that "Target Corporation is partnering with a K–12 education group which focuses on getting districts to adopt policies that will keep parents in the dark on their child's in-school gender transition, providing sexually explicit books to schools for free, and integrating gender ideology at all levels of curriculum in public schools."[37] The group is called GLSEN, and on its webpage it states: "GLSEN believes that every student has the right to a safe, supportive, and LGBTQ-inclusive K–12 education. We are a national network of educators, students, and local GLSEN Chapters working to make this right a reality."[38]

Target told Fox News Digital that "GLSEN leads the movement in creating affirming . . . and anti-racist spaces for LGBTQIA+ students. We are proud of 10+ years of collaboration with GLSEN and continue to support their mission."[39] Fox added: "The retail giant provides annual donations to GLSEN. GLSEN calls for gender ideology to be integrated into all classes, even math. It provides educators instructions on how they can make math 'more inclusive of trans and non-binary identities' by including 'they/them' pronouns in word problems. . . . .To date, the retail giant has donated at least $2.1 million to GLSEN, which offers districts and students guidance on how to hide gender transitions from parents. . . . For example, its policy for districts said, '[The local education agency] shall ensure that all personally identifiable and medical information relating to transgender and nonbinary students is kept confidential. . . . Staff or educators shall not disclose any information that may reveal a student's gender identity to others, including parents or guardian. . . . This disclosure must be discussed with the student, prior to any action.' "[40]

This is the same Target that initially decided to ban this book—*The Democrat Party Hates America*—from its retail stores, telling my publisher that "the title is polarizing and they want to be sensitive to all of their guests." (To their credit, Target reversed course in less than 24 hours after I announced their decision on my radio show.)

The extent to which the corporatists have become gender-ideology activists and propagandists, and are literally targeting children as well, is stunning. Who would have thought that even the late Walt Disney's name would be tied to such an agenda? Not long ago, Disney was a safe place for family-oriented entertainment, where kids could be kids and parents could act like kids. Not now. Manhattan Institute senior fellow Christopher Rufo obtained video from a Disney all-hands meeting. As reported by the *New York Post*, "Karey Burke, president of Disney's General Entertainment Content, vowed to drastically increase inclusivity in its productions, promising that at least 50 percent of its characters will be LGBTQ or racial minorities by the end of the year."[41] Moreover, Disney executive producer for Disney Television Animation Latoya Raveneau "touted Disney's efforts to feature LGBTQ storylines. 'In my little pocket of Proud Family Disney TVA, the showrunners were super welcoming . . . to my not-at-all-secret gay agenda. Maybe it was that way in the past, but I guess something must have happened . . . and then like all that momentum that I felt, that sense of "I don't have to be afraid to have these two characters kiss in the background." 'I was just, wherever I could, adding queerness. No one would stop me, and no one was trying to stop me.' "[42]

Again, there is significant scientific and expert opposition to much of what is being promoted in Biden's executive orders and administrative regulation, as well as in the Democrat Party–controlled public schools and the public square, about gender ideology and transgenderism. But you would not know it. Dr. Debra Soh, an expert sexologist, makes the point in her book *The End of Gender: Debunking the Myths about Sex and Identity in Our Society*, that "[a]ctivist organizations have managed to infect much of the information that is available relating to both gender and biological sex. Any research studies that are not in agreement with this agenda are ignored as though they never existed. Whether it's health websites, research publications, or media articles, it really is a jungle out there. If what you are looking for is basic, foundational information, anything older than ten years old is probably safe. Anything published in the last few years is questionable."[43]

In fact, the Democrat Party and its surrogates have, again, politicized the sciences to advance an objective—the reengineering of parent-child relationships, the disassembling of the nuclear family, and the empowerment of an autocratic Democrat Party.

Returning to the issue of abortion, when it comes to the parent-child relationship, the Democrat Party has sought to interfere with that bond when it comes to birthing as well. For example, the Supreme Court upheld in 1992, in *Planned Parenthood v. Casey*, among other things, a parental-consent requirement for minors seeking abortion.[44] After the Court ruled in *Dobbs v. Jackson Women's Health Organization*[45] last year, returning to the states and the people of the states their constitutional authority to make decisions about abortion, the Democrats in the Senate voted on a bill titled "The Women's Health Protection Act of 2022," which was an unconstitutional attempt to codify the most radical abortion law in the Free World and impose it on the entire country. The Democrats attempted to conceal the extreme nature of what they were doing from a public that would have opposed it. They were not "codifying *Roe*," as they repeatedly insisted. Their bill far exceeded the Court's *Roe v. Wade* decision in 1973, and Biden supported it.[46] As Thomas Jipping, senior legal fellow with the Edwin Meese III Center for Legal and Judicial Studies at the Heritage Foundation, put it: "It would "[unconstitutionally] retroactively and prospectively, prevent any government, at any level, from enacting or enforcing 'any law, rule, regulation, standard, or other provision having the force and effect of law that conflicts' with any provision of the act."[47] Thus, the bill would not only attempt to overturn by statute a constitutionally based Supreme Court decision, but it would eliminate any parental role in abortion decisions by their minor child anywhere in America. The decision would be between the minor child and the federal government, the latter of which would also pay for the abortion.

Biden and the Democrat Party lied about their radical act, and lied about the *Dobbs* decision being extremist. And they will continue to ramp up their rhetoric, given its political value, as explained earlier in this chapter, and as promised by Pelosi and practiced by Biden.

What will future historians write of a nation, pushed by a power-hungry political party and president, that prioritizes aborting its babies and surgically mutilating its children?

Even during the COVID-19 virus pandemic, the Democrat Party targeted, among others, schoolchildren. When it came to lifting the lockdown of schools across America so children could return to in-person education in the classroom, as well as lifting the masking requirement, the *New York Post* reported that "the American Federation of Teachers lobbied the Centers for Disease Control and Prevention on, and even suggested language for, the federal agency's school-reopening guidance. . . . The powerful teachers union's full-court press preceded the federal agency putting the brakes on a full re-opening of in-person classrooms, emails between top CDC, AFT and White House officials show."[48]

Again, science was politicized to empower the Democrat Party's teachers' unions to the detriment of children, their parents, and communities throughout the country. "Dr. Monica Gandhi, a professor of medicine at the University of California, San Francisco who has written extensively on the coronavirus," reports the *Post*, "called the CDC-AFT emails 'very, very troubling.' 'What seems strange to me here is there would be this very intimate back and forth including phone calls where this political group gets to help formulate scientific guidance for our major public health organization in the United States. This is not how science-based guidelines should work or be put together.'"[49]

And certainly, by the time Biden became president and shortly thereafter, his administration had to know that the COVID-19 virus was not a grave threat to school-age children. "One of the mysteries of COVID-19 is why children are much less likely than adults to be harmed by the disease. To answer this question, Cedars-Sinai's *Newsroom* spoke to Priya Soni, MD, Cedars-Sinai Pediatric Infectious Disease specialist. 'Not only are fewer children testing positive for COVID-19,' said Soni, 'but those who do test positive are likely to have milder cases.'"[50] "And that is the opposite of most viruses. 'There is no other respiratory virus that we know, that affects adults so much more severely than infants,' Soni said. 'For example, when a child gets a viral infection there are usually more intense symptoms, accompanied by high fevers. In the case of COVID-19, it's the adults who are getting the high fevers, having severe complications and even dying.' Soni says U.S. studies confirm the COVID-19 data from China and Italy that show children represent only around 2% of total infections in the population."[51] Others were also reporting the statistically low viral rates and severities for school-age children, but it did not matter.

Thus, Biden administration policy involving the education and well-being of the nation's schoolchildren was deeply politicized. As were the policies of the federal health and infectious disease control bureaucracies, foremost among them Dr. Anthony Fauci, the former director of the National Institute of Allergy and Infectious Diseases from 1984 to 2022—a favorite of Biden, the Democrat Party, and the media. Emma Dorn, Bryan Hancock, Jimmy Sarakatsannis, and Ellen Viruleg of McKinsey & Company studied the effect of the pandemic—or more precisely, the policies applied to our schools during the pandemic—on schoolchildren. Their ultimate findings are harrowing: "Our analysis shows that the impact of the pandemic on K–12 student learning was significant, leaving students on average five months behind in mathematics and four months behind in reading by the end of the school year. The pandemic widened preexisting opportunity and achievement gaps, hitting historically disadvantaged students hardest. In math, students in majority black schools ended the year with six months of unfinished learning, students in low-income schools with seven. High schoolers have become more likely to drop out of school, and high school seniors, especially those from low-income families, are less likely to go on to postsecondary education. And the crisis had an impact on not just academics but also the broader health and well-being of students, with more than 35 percent of parents very or extremely concerned about their children's mental health. The fallout from the pandemic threatens to depress this generation's prospects and constrict their opportunities far into adulthood. The ripple effects may undermine their chances of attending college and ultimately finding a fulfilling job that enables them to support a family."[52]

Again, for the Biden administration, science was camouflage for mandating that school-age children continue wearing masks. Fox News reported that "the Biden administration tightened its masking guidance after a prominent teachers union threatened White House officials with publicly releasing harsh criticism, internal emails show."[53] This time, it was the National Education Association (NEA). "The [NEA] sent a draft statement to White House officials that included harsh criticism of the Centers for Disease Control and Prevention's masking guidance, the emails show. But the teachers union ultimately published a version with a much softer tone, and the CDC clarified its guidance to indicate that everyone should be masked in schools, regardless of vaccination status."[54]

Yet the CDC knew better. David Zweig at *New York* magazine noted that "[a]t the end of May [2021], the Centers for Disease Control and Prevention published a notable, yet mostly ignored, large-scale study of COVID transmission in American schools. A few major news outlets covered its release by briefly reiterating the study's summary: that masking then-unvaccinated teachers and improving ventilation with more fresh air were associated with a lower incidence of the virus in schools. Those are common-sense measures, and the fact that they seem to work is reassuring but not surprising. Other findings of equal importance in the study, however, were absent from the summary and not widely reported. These findings cast doubt on the impact of many of the most common mitigation measures in American schools. Distancing, hybrid models, classroom barriers, HEPA filters, and, *most notably, requiring student masking were each found to not have a statistically significant benefit. In other words, these measures could not be said to be effective.*"[55] (Italics are mine.)

In January 2022, in the *Daily Beast*, Mary Katharine Ham explained: "The World Health Organization explicitly recommends against masking for kids under 5 and Europe's equivalent of the CDC recommends against masking primary school children at all. . . . The CDC's Recommendation to start masking at 2 years of age and universally mask elementary school students is an outlier in the Western world, but those who advocate for it rarely account for why. . . . There are a grand total of two randomized controlled trials on masking—one conducted in Denmark in 2020, which did not find a statistically significant reduction in infection among surgical mask wearers over the control group and a now-famous study from rural Bangladesh, which showed surgical masks had an impact over cloth masks, particularly in reducing symptomatic cases in the population over 60. Beyond these, which did not study school settings, the CDC offered its own large-scale study of elementary school students in Georgia, which tested different mitigation strategies, finding that masking unvaccinated teachers and good ventilation were most helpful, but also detected 'a student-masking requirement not having a statistical impact'—a finding notably left out of the study's summary."[56]

Indeed, beyond the lack of virus mitigation, a large-scale study by Brown University found that masking of young children had a hugely deleterious impact. As reported by the *Daily Mail*: "Results showed the early learning composite mean result dropped by a whopping 23 per cent, from a high of just under 100 in 2019, to around 80 in 2020, and finally 77 in 2021. Meanwhile, the verbal development quotient also dropped dramatically, from an average of 100 in 2018 to just below 90 in 2020, and around 70 in 2021.

The non-verbal development quotient also experienced a similar dip, from a mean score of around 105 in 2019, to 100 in 2020 and around 80 in 2021. The study concluded that 'children born during the pandemic have significantly reduced verbal, motor, and overall cognitive performance compared to children born pre-pandemic.' 'In addition,' the report adds, 'masks worn in public settings and in school or daycare settings may impact a range of early developing skills, such as attachment, facial processing, and socioemotional processing. . . . Brown University scientists Sean CL Deoni, Jennifer Beauchemin, Alexandra Volpe, and Viren D'Sa, penned the review, in conjunction with the global consulting firm Resonance, collecting data from 1,600 children—and their caregivers—who had been enrolled in the study between the ages of 0 and 5 on a rolling basis. The probe analyzed the cognitive development of the youngsters through infancy, childhood, and adolescence, and looked at how average development scores in three key areas had been affected during the COVID era—with shocking results."[57]

Parents could tell that the severe mask requirements imposed on their young children, when they could finally attend school in person, had a negative impact on their mental and behavioral health. *Politico* reports: "A significant percentage of parents whose children wore masks in school during the last year believe it harmed their education, social interactions and mental health, according to a POLITICO-Harvard survey. The poll's findings come as the Biden administration monitors events in Europe, where BA.2, a subvariant of Omicron, is wreaking havoc, and White House officials warn that masks may be necessary if Covid-19 cases increase in the United States. That would be an incredibly tough sell to parents of school-aged children, according to the survey. More than 4 in 10 believe mask-wearing harmed their children's overall scholastic experience, compared to 11 percent who said it helped. Nearly half of parents said masks made no difference. Forty-six percent of parents said mask-wearing hurt their child's social learning and interactions, and 39 percent told pollsters it affected their child's mental and emotional health."[58]

Meanwhile, parents had little to no say in any of these decisions, even though their children were directly affected. And to speak out at school board meetings was to be identified as a denier or worse, and possibly subjected to the police powers of Biden's Department of Justice. Moreover, many scientists, researchers, medical professionals, statisticians, and even writers and broadcasters who did speak out in real time, raising legitimate and substantive questions about the federal government's dictates and blue state governors' actions, experienced threats, torment, and denunciation and even had their careers ruined and licenses revoked. The Democrat Party media, social media sites, and others did all they could to ignore them or, worse, disgrace and silence them. And the Biden administration, working with Twitter and others, played a significant role in monitoring and censoring them.

Furthermore, as a reminder worth emphasizing, in California, the Democrat legislature passed and Democrat governor Gavin Newsom, who dreams of being president one day, signed a career-threatening law that "doctors who disseminate what the state defines as 'misinformation or disinformation related to the SARS-CoV-2 coronavirus' can face disciplinary action by the California Medical Board, including being stripped of their licenses."[59] In other words, if medical professionals do not fall in line and regurgitate whatever the state says about COVID-19—perhaps questioning vaccines, repeated vaccine shots, masks, etc.—they can have their licenses challenged by the state and lose their careers. But science is about challenging positions and having to defend them. This is how you reach scientific truth. However, the Democrat Party is invested in its own empowerment above all else, including what can be called science whether it is or not.

Like America's colleges and universities, the public school class-room has also become a propaganda mill for anti-American Marxist lies about race and racism, America's history and found-ing, and the principles on which the nation was founded. And the Democrat Party is all in. In sum, young children are taught CRT. They are told America was founded as a racist nation, in particular a white-dominated and controlled society; slavery was rampant in the colonies, and its protection was the principle rea-son for the Revolutionary War; every institution in America—from the Constitution and law to private property rights and capitalism—is a device of the white-dominant society to oppress and maintain control over blacks and other minorities; race determines whether you succeed (white) or fail (black and other minorities); and the only way out is to overturn the existing con-stitutional and capitalist systems.

CRT was birthed and developed by devout, America-hating Marxist intellectuals and professors. As explained earlier, the *New York Times* has promoted and funded CRT through the so-called 1619 Project, the chief essayist and editor being Nikole Hannah-Jones. The Democrat Party–aligned media first denied CRT was being taught in public schools, while simultaneously insisting that CRT was real history and Republicans were attempting to censor the truth about slavery—a Democrat Party institution. In other words, young schoolchildren are being taught to hate their coun-try, and, depending on their race, to hate themselves. And they are taught to reject whatever their parents and faith have taught them, if it conflicts with Marxist brainwashing.

For the most part, the way CRT is introduced to students and engulfs the education experience is as devious as the substantive propaganda itself. Dr. Melissa Moschella, writing for the Heritage Foundation, explains: "The curriculum does not limit the teaching of such ideas to a single course, but requires that they be incorporated into multiple subject areas, including English, social studies, science, and even math. Crucially, these ideas are not presented as offering a controversial perspective that students can discuss and critique. On the contrary, this ideology is presented as uncontested truth to which students must assent and conform. The punishment for failure to do so is not only being labeled racist, but official disciplinary actions such as detention, suspension, or the requirement to attend a 'restorative justice' session. Teachers [who defy their union and school administrators] are also forced to teach these ideas regardless of objections and can be disciplined for expressing dissenting views 'antithetical to School Board values' on their private social media accounts."[60]

Heritage's Jonathan Butcher also reveals that "[t]he National Council of Teachers of Mathematics (NCTM) recommended *Critical Race Theory in Mathematics Education* to its members for summer reading. NCTM's keynote speaker at its 2019 conference was the critical race theorist and college professor Gloria Ladson-Billings. (One of Ladson-Billings's most-cited articles is titled, 'Just What Is Critical Race Theory and What's It Doing in a Nice Field Like Education?') Likewise, the National Science Teaching Association wrote in May 2020 that its members now 'work from the stance that scientific ways of knowing and science education are fundamentally cultural and inherently political.' The organization recently hosted a multi-day online event that included a session titled 'Critical Affinity Spaces for Science Educators,' where teachers were taught to use a 'critical lens that . . . exposes the hidden and master narratives' in science, and affirms 'that racial/social justice approaches to science teaching are needed.' Just as with the 2019 NCTM conference, the organization featured a proponent of CRT as the keynote speaker. Predictably, then, school officials who are either sympathetic to, or unaware of, CRT's discriminatory ideas are following these organizations and designing K–12 math and science curricula using CRT's false and dangerous precepts. . . . Educators have used CRT to redesign history, civics, and English instructional content to focus on the critical obsession with oppression and power. Now, school officials are also changing classroom content in the hard sciences and math away from facts and skills and focusing on racial activism."[61]

Even medical school students have become the latest targets of Marxist-racist CRT indoctrination. Cornell Law School professor William Jacobson, founder of CriticalRace.org, determined that "46 of the top 100 medical schools have offered materials by authors Robin DiAngelo or Ibram X. Kendi, whose books explicitly call for discrimination. He told Fox News: 'Approaching the doctor-patient relationship through a Critical Race lens is being implemented under the umbrella of 'Diversity, Equity, and Inclusion' and other euphemisms, such as Ibram Kendi's 'anti-racism' approach. 'White privilege' and similar concepts, pushed by Robin DiAngelo and others, are being infused into the medical school culture.'"[62]

Moreover, admissions to many top medical schools, as well as other professional schools, reject *merit* as the single most important basis on which to determine if a student is qualified for medical school. In an article for the *New York Post*, "Top med school putting wokeism ahead of giving America good doctors," Dr. Stanley Goldfarb, chairman of Do No Harm, and Laura L. Morgan, program manager, explain: "Elite medical schools are deliberately recruiting woke activists, jeopardizing their mission of training physicians. That's what our organization found in a review of the application process for America's top 50 medical schools. Nearly three-quarters of these institutions—and 80% of the top 10—ask applicants about their views on diversity, equity, inclusion, anti-racism and other politicized concepts. The clear goal is to find the students who will best advance divisive ideology, not provide the best care to patients. . . . Many schools explicitly ask applicants if they agree with statements about racial politics. Others gauge applicants' views on or experience with woke concepts. . . ." And it's not just students. Many schools are also moving to require that professors be woke as well. For instance, the Indiana University School of Medicine recently approved new standards for faculty promotion and tenure. They are now 'required to show effort toward advancing DEI.'" "Medical schools are rushing down a dangerous road. These institutions have long lowered application and educational standards in the name of diversity; now they are enacting an ideological litmus test for future physicians. Recruiting woke activists instead of the most qualified candidates will both undermine trust in health care and lead to worse health outcomes for patients."[63] Moreover, it will ensure that fewer doctors will question, for example, gender reassignment surgery or hormone treatment for children, having been further schooled to advance an ideological imperative over the best medical interests of children.

In addition, once on college campuses, universities have now come full circle. Unfortunately, CRT has led to the inevitable *resegregation* of our schools. Writing in *National Review*, in an article titled "Resegregating American Education," Kenin M. Spivak, a member of the National Association of Scholars, states that "[w]ith support from the Biden administration and the complicity of the Department of Justice, it has taken less than 70 years for radical leftists to reimpose separate educational facilities under the guise of promoting equity."[64] Spivak notes that "[s]chools in cities as diverse as New York City and Madison, Wisconsin, are asking their students to resegregate. Learning For Justice (LFJ), endorsed by the DCPS (District of Columbia Public Schools), seeks to 'uphold the mission of the Southern Poverty Law Center' by developing racially segregated affinity groups and working with K–12 schools nationwide 'to dismantle white supremacy, strengthen intersectional movements and advance the human rights of all people.' In a section of its website entitled 'Preparing for Pushback,' LFJ asserts that segregated groups aren't really 'separatist and racist' and that there is no need for whites to participate, other than if they wish to focus on support for students of color."[65]

This is where the Democrat Party has lugged the nation and our children—from segregation of the past to segregation of the present and future. Spivak notes: "All of this occurs against a backdrop of a president fixated on race and the most racist administration since Woodrow Wilson was president more than 100 years ago. From its whole-of-government executive order to embed diversity, equity, and inclusion in all aspects of federal policies, billions of dollars in grants, loan forgiveness, and other programs for which whites, and sometimes Asians, are ineligible, conditioning selection of a vice president, a Supreme Court justice, and numerous cabinet members on race, to the Department of Education's (ED) directive that schools allocate Covid grants using principles enunciated by the Abolitionist Teaching Network, which advocates 'antiracist therapy for white educators' and 'disrupt[ing] whiteness,' the administration has sought to resegregate decision-making, contracting, and employment. Last year, the Biden administration's ED also reversed the Trump administration ED's ban on racially segregated affinity groups."[66] As discussed earlier, for the Democrat Party and the American Marxist, a color-blind society is a racist, white-dominated society.

For those families who want to escape the public school dystopia and cannot afford to, the Democrat Party will do everything possible to block your children's escape to better schools and a better future. The Democrat Party opposes all competition with their union-controlled, government-run schools. They make it difficult if not impossible for parents to find alternative sources and forms of education for their children outside of the educational bureaucracy, especially in poor and minority neighborhoods. The Democrat Party and the teachers' unions rely on each other for their power and control.

As Dr. Thomas Sowell has written: "One of the few bright spots for black children in American ghettos have been some charter schools that have educated these children to levels equal to, and in some cases better than, those in affluent suburbs. You might think that this would be welcomed by those who are so ready to do 'favors' for blacks. But you would be dead wrong. Democrats who have been in charge of most cities with sizable black populations, for decades, are on record opposing the spread of charter schools. So is the NAACP."[67]

Indeed, the Democrat Party insists that students remain in failing schools, whether their parents like it or not. Most adamantly oppose any form of outside educational alternatives, insisting the tax dollars should remain with the failing government schools and the teachers' unions bosses rather than follow the children. Of course, poor and minority children suffer most under such an iron fist. But the teachers' unions and the Democrat Party will oppose any educational alternative that could reduce the number of dues-paying members who fund union bosses' salaries, the Democrat Party's coffers, or diminish either of their power.

For example, the Biden administration has made the establishment and running of charter schools much more difficult despite the fact that, as Jennifer Stefano, executive vice president of the Commonwealth Foundation, explains in the *Federalist*: "Nationwide, nearly 70 percent of the 3.5 million students served by charters are minority students, while two-thirds are low-income. In places like Philadelphia, more than 60 percent of the enrollment in charter schools are black children, as opposed to less than 50 percent in the district's traditional schools. More than 150 of [Pennsylvania's] bottom 15 percent of underperforming public schools are in Philadelphia. Parents have made a clear choice to provide a better, safer future for their children, but too often, Democrats do not respect their decisions. And now, the opportunity to even make that decision is being threatened."[68]

In fact, the more students who are stuck in these schools, the more who will be indoctrinated by the teachers' unions with Democrat Party and Marxist ideology. For example, the *Denver Gazette* reports that "[t]he Colorado Education Association, which represents more than 39,000 K–12 teachers, support professionals and higher education staffers, held its assembly in April and passed this resolution: 'The CEA believes that capitalism inherently exploits children, public schools, land, labor, and resources. Capitalism is in opposition to fully addressing systemic racism (the school to prison pipeline), climate change, patriarchy (gender and LGBTQ disparities), education inequality, and income inequality.'"[69]

"Fighting against the will of parents—especially when it comes to the future of their kids—is a losing message," argues Stefano. "Yet Democrats seem hell-bent on clinging to it as they fight the expansion of charter schools and other school measures at every turn. It's not difficult to see why when you examine the relationship between government unions and the Democratic Party. The American Federation of Teachers, for example, spent almost $20 million for the 2020 election, with nearly all its political contributions going to Democrats and left-wing groups. For the current election cycle, government unions have already spent $13.6 million on politics, with 85 percent of their political action committee donations going to Democrats."[70] As we have seen before, the Democrat Party puts its own accumulation and retention of power ahead of all else, including poor and minority kids in failing schools.

Of course, the hypocrisy of Democrat Party leaders who oppose school choice runs deep. Barack Obama, Pete Buttigieg, Beto O'Rourke, Gavin Newsom, J. B. Pritzker, Elizabeth Warren, Nancy Pelosi, and Joe Biden, to name a few, have all either attended private schools, sent one or more of their children to private schools, or both. Indeed, Biden recently tweeted: "When we divert public funds to private schools, we undermine the entire public education system. We've got to prioritize investing in our public schools, so every kid in America gets a fair shot. That's why I oppose vouchers."[71] Yet another Biden lie.

And what school did Scranton, PA's finest, "Lunchbucket Joe" attend? "Biden attended Archmere Academy in Claymont, Delaware, a Catholic college preparatory school. Its main building, nicknamed the 'patio,' was the country estate of early 20th century industrialist, and Democratic Party activist, John J. Raskob. Both of Biden's sons also attended the same elite school."[72]

And Biden's secretary of education, Miguel Cardona, made clear through recent congressional testimony that "I don't believe federal dollars should be used for voucher programs."[73] However, he and his ilk believe federal tax dollars should flow to an infinite number of other causes, many if not most of which are not nearly as worthy—including a wide array of public services for illegal aliens. So much for "equity."

One of the ways the Democrat Party's public sector unions hold their power over various public institutions like education is through so-called official time or release time provisions in collective bargaining agreements. For example, in RealClearInvestigations, Ben Weingarten reports that "Randi Weingarten, the powerful president of the American Federation of Teachers, hasn't been a working teacher in more than a quarter of a century. Of the six years she spent teaching social studies, half of them appear to have been as a substitute."[74]

In addition, "[t]hrough her decades of union activism, Weingarten has clocked service time as a public school teacher, enabling her to accrue an educators' pension on top of the more than $500,000 in annual salary and benefits she earns as a labor executive, according to records obtained by the Freedom Foundation. She would receive about $230,000 total over her first 15 years of retirement, according to the public sector union watchdog's analysis."[75] Indeed, Weingarten's arrangement is common. Taxpayers are subsidizing public sector union bosses, which diverts education resources to union organizing.

In addition to destroying school systems and inner cities, whether it's education, crime, taxes, etc., the Democrat Party is now targeting the suburbs. Stanley Kurtz, senior fellow at the Ethics and Public Policy Center, declares in *National Review* that "Joe Biden and the Democrats want to abolish America's suburbs. Biden and his party have embraced yet another dream of the radical Left: a federal takeover, transformation, and de facto urbanization of America's suburbs. What's more, Biden just might be able to pull off this 'fundamental transformation.'" Kurtz continues: "It is no exaggeration to say that progressive urbanists have long dreamed of abolishing the suburbs. . . . Initially, these anti-suburban radicals wanted large cities to simply annex their surrounding suburbs, like cities did in the 19th century. That way a big city could fatten up its tax base. Once progressives discovered it had since become illegal for a city to annex its surrounding suburbs without voter consent, they cooked up a strategy that would amount to the same thing. This de facto annexation strategy had three parts: (1) use a kind of quota system to force 'economic integration' on the suburbs, pushing urban residents outside of the city; (2) close down suburban growth by regulating development, restricting automobile use, and limiting highway growth and repair, thus forcing would-be suburbanites back to the city; (3) use state and federal laws to force suburbs to redistribute tax revenue to poorer cities in their greater metropolitan region. If you force urbanites into suburbs, force suburbanites back into cities, and redistribute suburban tax revenue, then presto! You have effectively abolished the suburbs."[76]

Thus, the Democrat Party seeks to federalize the suburbs, most of which are largely Republican, impose its Marxist agenda on these communities as it has on major metropolitan areas, and bring them under its control.

The American Enterprise Institute's (AEI) Howard Husock describes how Biden and the Democrat Party are unleashing a regulatory war against America's suburbs. "[F]or the Biden administration's Department of Housing and Urban Development (HUD), fair housing is more—much more. In proposed regulations that would touch any jurisdiction that accepts any sort of HUD funding, fair housing must mean a plan to 'promote equity in their communities, decrease segregation, and increase access to opportunity and community assets for people of color and other underserved communities.' Translated that means that the route to upward mobility for disadvantaged minorities lies through their relocation to more affluent communities, where they will no longer be 'underserved.' The details as to how this should be done run more than 200 pages. Those required to comply will include more than 1,200 cities and counties receiving HUD funding. All will be required to develop 'equity plans.' . . . Such equity could mean anything from building low-income housing to redrawing school district lines for racial or socio-economic integration, all as assessed by the HUD bureaucracy. . . . It has of late been a liberal mantra that children's futures should not be determined by the Zip Code where they grow up—and the HUD plan is meant to disperse low-income households where they are presumed to benefit from better schools and parks, which presumably city governments are inherently incapable of providing. . . ."[77]

"HUD fails to acknowledge that sustained upward mobility is based on the constructive life decisions made at the family level—including marriage and employment," writes Husock. "These are the building blocks of the economic gains that enable moves to better neighborhoods. It is such moves that must be protected by enforcement of anti-discrimination law. Historically, it was the federal government, specifically the Federal Housing Administration (FHA), which engaged in racial discrimination by refusing to guarantee mortgages in racially changing neighborhoods. [But now,] HUD [will] bring us to a new era of color consciousness in housing policy, in the name of 'equity'—comparable life outcomes for those making distinct life choices."[78]

Remember, this is the same Joe Biden who, as a young senator, opposed what he called "racial jungles" when referring to integrating public schools. Now, he seeks to eradicate America's suburbs. As best as I can tell, Biden has never lived in racially diverse communities. When he's not living at the White House, he lives at his multimillion-dollar estate in Wilmington, Delaware, or his multimillion-dollar vacation home in Rehobeth Beach, Delaware. All paid for on a government salary, of course.

The Biden administration intends to dictate zoning, housing, development, locations of community centers, parks, athletic fields, libraries, bus stops, and all other lifestyle decisions in suburban America. Where does this authority come from, considering the Constitution confers on the national government limited and specifically defined powers, leaving matters such as zoning to localities and states? There is no such constitutional authority granted the Biden administration and the Democrat Party. "[T]here's what can be seen as the constitutional question raised by the . . . regulations," writes Husock. "HUD's lengthy proposal is based on the thinnest of reeds in the 1968 Fair Housing Law, which, following its main anti-discrimination language, goes on to direct other Federal agencies 'to administer their programs . . . relating to housing and urban development . . . in a manner affirmatively to further' the policies of the act. It is into that small lane that HUD drives its big, regulatory truck, with communities across the country in its path. HUD defines equity as 'access to high quality schools, equitable employment opportunities, reliable transportation services, parks and recreation facilities, community centers, community-based supportive services, law enforcement and emergency services, healthcare services, grocery stores, retail establishments, infrastructure and municipal services, libraries, and banking and financial institutions.'"[79]

Public safety is the top priority for individuals and families. If you are not safe in your person or home, and if your family is not safe, nothing else matters, and the civil society collapses. In its report, "The Blue City Murder Problem," the Heritage Foundation examines the data and explores who is responsible for rising crime throughout the United States. "Those on the Left know that their soft-on-crime policies have wreaked havoc in the cities where they have implemented those policies," scholars Charles Stimson, Zack Smith, and Kevin D. Dayaratna concluded. "'It is not hard to understand why "reforms" such as ending cash bail, defunding the police, refusing to prosecute entire categories of crimes, letting thousands of convicted felons out of prison early, significantly cutting the prison population, and other "progressive" ideas have led to massive spikes in crime—particularly violent crime, including murder—in the communities where those on the Left have implemented them.' The report also highlighted that 27 of the top 30 cities with the highest murder rates as of June 2022 were run by Democratic mayors. . . . Moreover, 14 of the 30 cities with the highest murder rates have '[George] Soros-backed or Soros-inspired rogue prosecutors. . . . There were 2,554 homicides in those 30 cities through June 2022. In the 14 cities with Soros-backed rogue prosecutors, there were 1,752 homicides, representing 68% of homicides in the 30 top homicide cities in the United States.'"[80]

In another study, Blaze Media reports: "Murder rates in liberal-run cities across the United States have risen 10% since 2021 due to defund-the-police movements and soft-on-crime policies supported by left-wing [Democrat] mayors. According to a recent study released by WalletHub, homicide rates in the 45 most populated American cities increased 10% between 2021 and 2023 and are continuing on an upward trajectory. The researchers ranked the cities by comparing murder rates from the first three months of 2023 to the same periods in 2021 and 2022. The study found that the top 10 U.S. cities battling the most significant murder rate problems include Memphis, Tennessee; New Orleans, Louisiana; Richmond, Virginia; Washington, D.C.; Detroit, Michigan; Durham, North Carolina; Dallas, Texas; Milwaukee, Wisconsin; Las Vegas, Nevada; and Kansas City, Missouri. Of the top 10 cities with the biggest homicide rates, all are led by Democratic mayors, with the exception of Las Vegas. . . . The study reported that murder rates are rising faster in cities run by Democratic mayors versus Republican mayors."[81] Hence, the Democrat Party wants to share its "successes" running America's cities with America's suburbs. Now, that is what is meant by "equity."

And who is being murdered at a higher rate than others? Young black teenagers. And who is murdering most of them? Other young black teenagers. Manhattan Institute scholar Heather Mac Donald explains in the *New York Post* that "[h]omicides of youth between the ages of 10 and 17 rose 47% in 2020. That 47% increase far outpaced the record-breaking 29% spike in post-Floyd homicides across all age groups in 2020. Black youth between the ages of 10 and 17 were killed at 11 times the rate of white youth in 2020. Virtually none of those black deaths was protested by Black Lives Matter activists, since the victims were killed overwhelmingly not by the police and not by whites but by other blacks—and thus did nothing to advance the narrative about lethal white supremacy. Blacks between the ages of 14 and 17 commit gun homicide at more than 10 times the rate of white and Hispanic teenagers combined. . . . The intact, biological family is the best form of crime prevention because it is the best way to socialize children. . . . That fact breaks a number of taboos, however, and so forms no part of our cultural discourse. Until the inner-city family is restored, policing is the second-best solution for saving black lives. Too bad President Joe Biden again regurgitated the fiction . . . that law-abiding black Americans are at daily risk of their lives from the police, a fiction that will only cost more black lives." [82]

The Democrat Party does not want to discuss the intact nuclear, biological family because, as described earlier in this chapter, it does not believe in it. Specifically, as applies to the black community, it is said to be off limits—like so much else the Democrat Party silences and censors. Thomas Sowell points out that "many successful political careers have been built on giving blacks 'favors' that look good on the surface but do lasting damage in the long run. One of these 'favors' was the welfare state. A vastly expanded welfare state in the 1960s destroyed the black family, which had survived centuries of slavery and generations of racial oppression. In 1960, before this expansion of the welfare state, 22 percent of black children were raised with only one parent. By 1985, 67 percent of black children were raised with either one parent or no parent." [83]

In 2005, Kay S. Hymowitz, who has written widely about marriage, explained in *National Review*, in part, that "72 percent of black children . . . are born to unmarried mothers; . . . large numbers of those children . . . will have at best erratic relationships with their fathers; . . . children living with an unrelated father are more likely to suffer abuse; . . . there is abundant evidence that boys growing up under these conditions have less self-control than those growing up in more stable families; . . . and most of all, . . . those boys are far more prone to commit crimes. . . ."[84]

A Democrat who early on did raise concerns about the state of the black family was the late New York senator Daniel Patrick Moynihan. Brookings Institution political scientist Ron Haskins explains that "[i]n 1965, Daniel Patrick Moynihan predicted that the [state] of so many black children, especially males, to fatherless families would prevent many from seizing new opportunities through the civil rights revolution. Although Moynihan was excoriated in the academic world and beyond [especially in his own party] subsequent events have proven him correct. Today, in part because of the continuing demise of married-couple families, the average black is far behind the average white in educational achievement, employment rates, and earnings; blacks also have much higher crime and incarceration rates. These outcomes have led to growing recognition that the promise of the civil rights revolution will not be achieved until the black family is repaired."[85] Indeed, this point was made in Chapter 3 in partial response to the civil rights Marxists, who assign virtually all economic and social maladies in a black person's life to "white privilege."

Moynihan was eviscerated by many in the Democrat Party and numerous civil rights activists. He was labeled a racist by some. The unraveling of the nuclear family, particularly the ubiquity of fatherless households, is not limited to black homes, but the problem is especially pronounced in the black community.

Moynihan was wildly condemned when his research, which he prepared when he served in the federal bureaucracy, was leaked to the media.

Rather than encouraging marriage and fathers' participation in child-rearing, the federal government promotes the opposite through the mostly Democrat Party–built welfare state, which the party defends and expands at all costs.

The AEI-Brookings Working Group on Childhood in the United States reports that "[c]urrently, means-tested programs such as Medicaid, the Earned Income Tax Credit (EITC), and the Supplemental Nutrition Assistance Program (SNAP) penalize low-income couples who choose to marry including working-class Americans, with one study showing that more than 70 percent of American families with young children and incomes in the second and third income quintiles face marriage penalties related to Medicaid, cash welfare, or SNAP receipt. These penalties can reduce the odds that lower-income couples will marry; one survey found that almost one-third of Americans ages 18 to 60 report they personally know someone who has not married for fear of losing means-tested benefits."[86] AEI-Brookings recommends "a civic campaign organized around what Brookings Institution scholars Ron Haskins and Isabel Sawhill have called the success sequence, in which young adults are encouraged to pursue education, work, marriage, and parenthood, in that order. Today, 97 percent of young adults who follow this sequence are not poor in midlife. While the sequence has not been proven to exercise a casual role in adults' economic lives, an extensive body of research indicates that each step—that is, education, work, and marriage—is associated with better economic outcomes for families with children."[87]

Good luck with that. Can anyone seriously imagine the Democrat Party supporting such drastic reforms to the massive welfare state they built? Moreover, as described at the top of this chapter, the Democrat Party benefits significantly from the vote of unmarried women, opposes school choice and competition, and opposes workfare.[88] Indeed, earlier this year, every Democrat in the House voted against implementing work requirements for recipients of Medicaid, Temporary Assistance for Needy Families (TANF), and the Supplemental Nutrition Assistance Program (SNAP).[89] Nonetheless, the House Republican debt bill, eventually agreed to by Biden, forced the adoption of a limited workfare requirement. Moreover, as CRT teaches, blacks and other minorities are oppressed in this society. To live a healthy and successful lifestyle is to succumb to a racist, white-dominated, capitalist society. Obviously, CRT promotes excuses, failure, and bigotry.

And, of course, the Democrat Party's economic policies are devastating to many Americans. Despite their claim to represent the middle class, the working class, blue-collar workers, families, children, the elderly, etc., the fact is that the Democrat Party repeatedly takes its ideological wrecking ball to America's economic system and the private sector, making life more difficult than it would otherwise be for so many citizens.

For example, inflation is a pernicious threat to, among other things, household budgets. Dr. Milton Friedman explained that "[i]nflation is an old, old disease. We've had thousands of years of experience with it. There is nothing simpler than stopping an inflation—from the technical point of view. . . . The only cure for inflation is to reduce the rate at which total [government] spending is growing."[90] "[N]either the businessman, nor the trade union, nor the housewife has a printing press in their basement on which they can turn out those green pieces of paper we call money."[91]

Obviously, Biden and the Democrat Party are ideologically and politically incapable of effectively addressing inflation. After all, they created present-day inflation with massive spending, borrowing, and printing of money, with even more proposed by Biden now and in the future.[92] As reported in December 2022 by the *New York Post*: "The massive inflation Biden unleashed with his spending bonanza has punished the middle class hardest of all, as a new study by the non-partisan Congressional Budget Office (CBO) found. While the top fifth of earners saw the purchasing power of their paychecks rise 1.1% in 2022 over last year, and the bottom fifth by 1.5%, the squeezed group in the middle saw an overall decline of almost 3%. Indeed, the typical household has paid approximately $10,000 dollars in 'inflation taxes' since Biden took office, thanks to the 13.8% cumulative inflation his policies inflicted on the country. Over the past year alone, food prices have shot up 10.6% and energy 13.1%."[93] Among other Biden policies, "the $1.9 trillion American Rescue Plan, the $1.2 trillion infrastructure bill and countless other outlays handed out as political bribes against the advice of all sane economists" have been disastrous.[94]

The Federal Reserve has had to relentlessly increase interest rates to battle inflation, but this has, in turn, driven up mortgage rates, credit card rates, and all interest rates on borrowed money for consumer products and investment capital. There is no such thing as free money. There is always a cost.

Despite its "get the rich" and Marxist class-warfare propaganda, the Democrat Party has abandoned the working middle class—as most Marxist-centered movements have and do. *Axios* reports: "Nine of the top 10 wealthiest congressional districts are represented by Democrats, while Republicans now represent most of the poorer half of the country. . . . The last several decades have ushered in a dramatic political realignment, as the GOP has broadened its appeal to a more diverse working class and Democrats have become the party of wealthier, more-educated voters. 'We have seen an inversion of Democrat and Republican shares of the highest- and lowest-income districts—and the highest and lowest college degree-holding districts,' says Cook Political Report's Dave Wasserman. Sixty-four percent of congressional districts with median incomes below the national median are now represented by Republicans—a shift in historical party demographics, the data shows. Some of the highest-income districts have long voted Democrat, but growing inequality is widening the gap between them and working-class swing districts critical to winning majorities."[95]

At the American Enterprise Institute (AEI), Ramesh Ponnuru argues that "[i]n U.S. politics today, class is more a function of formal education than of income. The two are of course linked. College graduates on average earn more than those who attended college but received no college degree, and they in turn make a little more than those who never went. Over time, schooling has become relatively more important in voting behavior and money less so. . . . Most nonwhite Americans vote for Democrats regardless of diploma (or income). What underlies the new educational divide is a marked change in the preferences of white voters. . . . One Democratic response to declining support from the white working class has been to write it off. The rationales for this choice are varied. These voters might be impossible to win back. Trying might require compromises on issues of race and sex that progressives would find intolerable. . . . And they are a shrinking proportion of the overall electorate. Better, many Democrats thought during the Obama years, to pin the party's hopes on a 'coalition of the ascendant' or 'rising American electorate' of nonwhites, who were growing in numbers, and young college-educated whites, who were growing in liberalism."[96]

I would add, the Democrat Party's emphasis on CRT and anti-white racism, equity, LGBTQ+, and climate change, as well as secularism, abortion, gun control, and so forth, may have appeal among many who have matriculated through DEI-centered colleges and universities, but not so much among individuals who do not have college degrees.

Another major aspect of the Democrat Party's war on the family involves its implementation of climate change rules and regulations to inconvenience and impose significant costs on millions of Americans, including lowering the standard of living for many families, as it works to shrink the American economy, growth, and prosperity as part of the international climate-change deal—which, incidentally, was never presented to the Senate as a treaty for ratification. Again, from the Democrat Party and Marxist mind-set, capitalism is bad. America is bad. And climate change is the ruse through which the standard of living will be diminished. The revolution is well under way. Let us break down some of what is going on.

For example, while forcing more of the economy onto the electrical grid, the Biden administration is now acting to drive up the cost of electricity and reduce its availability. "The latest EPA proposal," writes Daniel Greenfield at *Front Page*, "would mandate 'carbon capture' at power plants. A study by MIT showed that carbon capture raises the cost of electricity from 30% to 50% depending on the type of plant. Another study by Australia's Institute for Energy Economics and Financial Analysis showed that prices could actually climb as high as 95% to 175%." Meanwhile, "[a] Stanford study found that carbon capture actually increases air pollution. A UC Berkeley study found that carbon capture would double water use which would be environmentally catastrophic in Southern California and other water-poor areas."[97] How many working families and small businesses can afford such a sudden and huge increase in their electricity bills? Greenfield explains that "[l]ike most 'green' technologies, carbon capture is a scam. . . ."[98]

Nonetheless, writes Greenfield, "some top Democrat donors have heavily invested in [carbon capture] including Bill Gates and George Soros. Carbon capture startups scored $882 million in capital last year so there's a lot of Democrat donor money riding on it."[99] And the ultimate goal, of course, is to kill traditional types of energy production and shrink the economy. They will put out of business numerous reliable coal and natural gas energy-producing plants and increase the number of brownouts and blackouts.

Even the federal government's agency that regulates the nation's power grid is warning of dire and widespread energy shortages. "The United States is heading for a reliability crisis," Federal Energy Regulatory Commission (FERC) commissioner Mark C. Christie testified to the Senate in May. "I do not use the term 'crisis' for melodrama, but because it is an accurate description of what we are facing. I think anyone would regard an increasing threat of system-wide, extensive power outages as a crisis. In summary, the core problem is this: Dispatchable generating resources are retiring far too quickly and in quantities that threaten our ability to keep the lights on. The problem generally is not the addition of intermittent resources, primarily wind and solar, but the far too rapid subtraction of dispatchable resources, especially coal and gas."[100]

Paul Tolmachev at *Eurasia Review* well summarizes the Biden and Democrat Party economic policies: "At a time when there is a clear need for productive relocation back to consumer countries, particularly the U.S., to strengthen national security in the face of tightening authoritarian regimes in major productive and resource economies, the Biden Administration is making decisions that can only be described as disastrous. Instead of stimulating intensive development of domestic production, positive expectations of economic agents, entrepreneurship and free competition through liberalization of tax policy, simplification and winding down of the regulatory overhang, maximum decentralization of redistribution of benefits, reduction of government spending and budget deficit and, in general, reduction of government . . . the Biden Administration wants to further expand the government regulatory mandate to levy and finally gut the pockets of the most successful and productive. That's not even [state control of social and economic matters]—that's real Soviet Bolshevism."[101]

Indeed, the Democrat Party's policies are purposefully destructive of American opportunity, prosperity, and the middle-class lifestyle. It is motivated by a degrowth, anti-capitalism ideology—Marxism. No amount of warnings, evidence, or suffering will deter its ideological ambitions.

From blocking pipelines for oil transport[102] and federal oil leases[103] to preventing mining of critical minerals,[104] all of which are essential to fueling and maintaining a dynamic, growing, and prosperous economy today and in the future, Biden, the Democrat Party, and the American Marxists are destroying an advanced industrial society that took generations of American know-how, entrepreneurship, research and development, private capital, and sweat to build. It takes a few years of Democrat Party policies to tear down what took more than two centuries to erect. And, of course, our enemies, especially the Communist Chinese government, are both thrilled and amazed at America's self-immolation and, ultimately, suicide.

And the stress these Democrat Party/Marxist grand plans place on the family, especially those of modest means, is enormous. In addition to inflation, currency devaluation, supply chain disruptions, shortages of essentials, etc., Biden and the Democrat Party seek to ban or significantly regulate essential products that most Americans have come to rely on for maintaining if not improving their quality of life, including gas stoves,[105] vehicles that run on gasoline (combustion engines),[106] and incandescent lightbulbs.[107] They are making more expensive and even unaffordable new home air-conditioning units, window air conditioners, portable air cleaners, ovens, clothes washers, refrigerators, dishwashers, and automobiles.[108] Of course, the propaganda associated with these dictates promises that they will clean the air and water, save tens of thousands of lives, and stem man-made climate change. It is difficult to see how eliminating, for example, incandescent lightbulbs will save even one life. Moreover, it is all being done via executive branch orders and regulations. Congress has not voted for any of it.

This year there have been shortages of or significant price increases for beef, butter, beer, champagne, oranges, cooking oil, lettuce, corn, eggs, bread, tomatoes, olive oil, and, infant food.[109] Nonetheless, to combat "climate change," the Biden administration is "paying more farmers not to farm. But [Biden's] already finding it's hard to make that work."[110] Due to shortages, farmers find it more profitable to farm on smaller amounts of acreage than to take even increased federal subsidy payments. "Zach Ducheneaux, administrator of USDA's Farm Service Agency, which oversees the conservation program, acknowledges that participation this year has been lower than hoped for, but he is still optimistic that the additional money the administration is providing will spur more landowners to join."[111] Still, there are shortages— due, in large part, to record-high fuel and fertilizer costs.

In fact, the entire climate change agenda is the vessel through which the American Marxist movements and the Democrat Party pour much of their anticapitalist, degrowth, and socialist economic policies. I explained this ruse in Liberty and Tyranny fourteen years ago and in subsequent books.[112] Their "pursuit . . . is power, not truth. With the assistance of a pliant or sympathetic media, [they] use junk science, misrepresentations, and fear-mongering to promote public health and environmental scares, because [they] realize that in a true, widespread health emergency, the public expects the government to act aggressively to address the crisis, despite traditional limitations on government authority. The more dire the threat, the more liberty people are usually willing to surrender. This scenario is tailor-made for the [Democrat Party]. The government's authority becomes part of the societal frame of reference, only to be built upon during the next 'crisis.'"[113]

Moreover, lest we forget, not only is this ideologically driven agenda a power grab by the Democrat Party and central to the American Marxist revolution, the fact is that the government is incapable of managing literally anything competently or efficiently, let alone entire industries and the largest, most complex economy on the planet.

As if predicting the recent governmental response to the COVID-19 pandemic, but more broadly "climate change" as mankind's existential threat, I further explained that "the pathology of the . . . health scare works like this: An event occurs—cases of food contamination are discovered or instances of a new disease arise. Or, as is increasingly the case, government agencies such as the Food and Drug Administration (FDA), the Centers for Disease Control and Prevention (CDC), or the Environmental Protection Agency (EPA), or nonprofit organizations . . . release a new study identifying a 'frightening' news health risk. Urgent predictions are made by cherry-picked 'experts' that the media accept without skepticism or independent investigation and turn into a cacophony of fear. Public officials next clamor to demonstrate that they are taking steps to ameliorate the dangers. New laws are enacted and regulations promulgated that are said to limit the public's exposure to the new 'risk.'"[114]

Again, having settled on the nomenclature "climate change" as the greatest of all threats—said to be "man-made," an existential threat to human life, and no definitive resolution in sight (meaning, the endless rejiggering of society and mankind)—Biden, the Democrat Party, and their media surrogates are able to demagogue all natural climate events and tie them to the life-styles of the people and the capitalist economic system. In other words, there are few limits to what the government can do in controlling the individual and compelling his conformity with the declared interests of the state, as the ruling class builds an increasingly intrusive police state in the name of health, safety, and even human survival.

Larry Fink, the CEO of BlackRock, the world's largest asset manager—with an estimated $10 *trillion* dollars in assets—has been a leading advocate for imposing environmental, social, and governance, or ESG, on American corporations.

ESG is nothing but a scheme to take shareholders' and consumer funds to subsidize the American Marxist agenda. It is used to reward "woke" behavior and punish traditional investors focused on increasing their returns. Simply put, ESG takes a portion of your money without your knowledge or permission—such as your pension fund investments—to push radical Democrat Party policies, and cuts financial investments in, for examples, oil and gas companies. Therefore, not only are you subsidizing the demise of the country, you are likely not receiving the highest returns for your investments—again, without your knowledge or approval.

This is a devious and diabolical radicalization and politicization of massive investment dollars by huge financial institutions whose corporate boards are populated with Democrat Party–supporting oligarchs. Moreover, these firms have set up an "ESG scoring system," which grades corporations on their compliance with this radical agenda, thereby intimidating and threatening them to comply or suffer the financial consequences.

In November 2017, BlackRock's Fink declared: "Well, behaviors are going to have to change and this is one thing we're asking companies. You have to force behaviors and at BlackRock we are forcing behaviors. Fifty-four percent of the incoming class are women. We added four more points in terms of diverse employ-ment this year and . . . if you don't achieve these levels of impact, your compensation could be impacted. . . . You have to force behaviors, whether it's gender or race, or just any way you want to say the composition of your team you're going to be impacted and that's not just recruiting, it is development."[115]

Indeed, in 2020, Fink issued a letter "saying that the need for climate change to influence investment decisions was becoming a 'defining factor.'"[116] BlackRock has pressured an untold number of businesses, in which it owns 5 to 10 percent of their stock, to publicly promote their roles in various Democrat Party positions, including Abbott Labs, UPS, Home Depot, etc.[117]

BlackRock (and Vanguard) used its muscle to install three rad-ical, anti–fossil fuels dissident directors to ExxonMobil's board of directors. Keep in mind, BlackRock is the asset manager for tril-lions in pension plans, including those of police officers, firefight-ers, nurses, etc. BlackRock does not share the values of so many of these Americans. Moreover, the corporation's focus should be solely in maximizing return on these pension dollars so seniors can live comfortably in their retirement years. After all, it is *their* money, not Fink's.

Moreover, the *Washington Examiner* reports that the Biden administration "has advanced a Labor Department rule permit-ting fund managers to consider ESG factors in making investment decisions for retirement accounts. The Securities and Exchange Commission has also proposed rules to define ESG to ensure that funds advertised as environmentally or socially conscious meet certain definitions."[118]

The evidence is overwhelming that the Democrat Party's mis-sion is to fundamentally alter society, which requires the "reim-aging" of nothing short of the nature of the citizenry, including the manipulation of their lifestyles and economic conditions; the citizenry itself through mass migration; disuniting of Americans through officially sanctioned class and group categorizations based on race, ethnicity, and gender identification; dismantling American culture and assimilative programs; and abolishing the nuclear family through classroom and media indoctrination, language control, and government welfare and redistributive programs. Moreover, these decisions and policies are neither the brainchild nor the will of the people. The devastating consequences are evident all around us, and getting worse by the day.

CHAPTER SEVEN

WAR ON THE CONSTITUTION

The U.S. Constitution is the most remarkable governing document ever written. It creates a functioning federal government, but protects both state and individual liberties at the same time. It uniquely divides the federal government into three coequal branches with their own responsibilities, and whose members are chosen in fundamentally different ways. It is further designed to protect the people from at least two forms of tyranny—mobocracy and monarchy (dictatorship). The Constitution is a document that takes into consideration the extraordinarily diverse nature of America—from its more densely populated areas to its rural communities; from its commercial centers to farming areas; from its fisheries to its mining towns; from people of deep faith to people of no faith; from the highly educated to the barely literate; from the rich to the poor; and yes, from white to black people and every other skin color. It is a self-correcting document, allowing for amendments to address imperfections and unforeseen events should a significant portion of the body politic and the public demand them. The Constitution is a truly incredible manifestation of thousands of years of human experience and progress, yet drafted in a period of less than five months.

But if your purpose is to "fundamentally transform America," then your purpose must also be to destroy constitutional republicanism. Thus, the Constitution must go—either all at once or by parts. And that is exactly what the Democrat Party and its revolutionary partners have in mind. Indeed, Biden and his party are endlessly and relentlessly looking for ways to bypass the Constitution's obstacles to centralize power. And their propaganda aimed at condemning republican institutions has grown increasingly shrill, unhinged, and deceitful.

In the past, the Democrat Party and its academicians insisted that the Constitution actually embodied their ideological agenda and compelled the outcomes they demanded. They celebrated judges and justices who abused judicial review and practiced judicial activism. Today, they make open their disdain for the Constitution and no longer seek to disguise their true intentions. For example, radical leftist Ruth Colker, professor at Moritz College of Law, the Ohio State University, is illustrative of this modern assault on the Constitution itself. Key to this attack is to try to link the Constitution to slavery.

She writes in the opening salvo of her essay titled "The White Supremacist Constitution" that "[t]he United States Constitution is a document that, during every era, has helped further white supremacy. White supremacy constitutes a 'political, economic and cultural system in which whites overwhelmingly control power and material resources, conscious and unconscious ideas of white superiority and entitlement are widespread, and relations of white dominance and non-white subordination are daily reenacted across a broad array of institutions and social settings.' Rather than understand the Constitution as a force for progressive structural change, we should understand it as a barrier to change. From its inception, the Constitution enshrined slavery and the degradation of black people by considering them to be property rather than equal members of the community. The Civil War Amendments did not truly abolish slavery and only prohibited a limited ban on state action. Radical Reconstruction was short-lived as white supremacy quickly eviscerated any political gains that black voters had achieved. The Supreme Court has interpreted the Civil War Amendments consistently with their white supremacist roots. Rather than serve as an effective instrument to help eradicate the badges, incidents, and vestiges of slavery, the Constitution has become a tool both to ban voluntary race affirmative measures at the federal, state, and local government level, and also to preclude Congress from enacting strong abolitionist measures. The Court has enshrined the views of Andrew Johnson, a fierce proponent of white supremacy, into its structure."[1] This is the kind of anti-American racist claptrap that passes for constitutional scholarship these days.

Elie Mystal, another extreme leftist and correspondent for the radical magazine the *Nation*, is a frequent guest on MSNBC and author of the book *Allow Me to Retort: A Black Guy's Guide to the Constitution*. Like Colker, he declares that the United States is and always has been a corrupt society, and the Constitution is nothing but an accumulation of demands of immoral white people enshrined in a document and imposed on the nation. During his media tour promoting the book, he declared on ABC's roundly ridiculed *View* television show: "The Constitution is kind of trash. Let's just talk as adults for a second." He went on: "It was written by slavers and colonists, and white people who were willing to make deals with slavers and colonists. They didn't ask anybody who looked like me what they thought about the Constitution." Moreover, "[t]his document was written without the consent of black and brown people in this country, and without the consent of women in this country. And I say, if that is the starting point, the very least we can do is ignore what those slavers and colonists and misogynists thought, and interpret the Constitution in a way that makes sense for our modern world."[2] Mystal's deranged rantings are typical of the guests booked by the Democrat Party media.

Of course, among Mystal's improvements to the Constitution were "no states' rights when it comes to healthcare, elections, policing, and guns. That's just better."[3] For Mystal, therefore, "interpreting" the Constitution is simply a practical and cynical way to destroy it and for he and his fellow anti-American ideologues to impose their political and economic will on the rest of us. Earlier in the book, I described this as civil rights Marxism.

Former law professor Robert Natelson, now of the Independence Institute, explains: "To begin with, the dominant view among the Founders was that slavery was absolutely *not* 'fine.' The prevailing view was that slavery violated natural law and was doomed to extinction. Indeed, by 1787 several states had begun the journey toward abolition. Nor did the Constitution create or mandate slavery or racial discrimination. These were creations of state law, and they varied from state to state. The Founders were forced to accept that situation to prevent America from fracturing into a multitude of nations constantly at war with each other, as in Europe. Also false is the common claim that slaveholders adopted the Constitution. Of the public that ratified it, only a small percentage owned slaves. And perhaps as many slaveholders opposed the Constitution as favored it. In [at least] five states, the ratifying electorate included free African Americans."[4]

Interesting how many of those who insist that "all our history" must be taught when promoting the non-historical CRT but refuse to do just that as they relentlessly smear America.

The perversely named American Constitution Society, whose

president is former radical Wisconsin Democrat senator Russ Feingold, held a conference titled "Founding Failures: Reckoning with our Constitution's Generational Impacts on Health and Well-Being," which opened with this assertion: "Our Constitution's establishment of a racial caste system left a legacy that can be seen generations later in its impact on the health and well-being of communities of color. Exploitative scientific studies, inferior medical care, and discriminatorily designed infrastructure and environmental policy have wreaked havoc on the bodies of black, indigenous and Latinx Americans. As we look to fight our latest urgent public health challenges, COVID-19 and climate change, what law and policy tools are available to address the disproportionate harms borne by communities of color? What new legal authorities are needed? And what can state and federal enforcement agencies do, more broadly, to help close the racial gap in our public health policy and to enhance environmental justice?"[5] The group's statement underscores the fusion of anti-constitutionalism with the Marxist ideological agenda and propaganda.

Of course, the party directly responsible for slavery, segregation, and racism, and their perpetuation, is the Democrat Party—which the American Marxists are aligned with as members and advocates. For example, Bernie Sanders is a "Democratic Socialist," yet he caucuses with the Senate Democrats and has run more than once for the Democrat Party presidential nomination, nearly winning it. Alexandria Ocasio-Cortez is part of a group called Democratic Socialists of America, as are several House Democrats, but she associates with the Democrat Party. Old-time Marxist Frances Fox Piven still plays a major role in recruiting, training, and promoting fellow Marxists who work within the Democrat Party.[6] As reported by Alex Taub in the *New York Times*: "According to David Duhalde, 34, formerly the Democratic Socialists' deputy director and now the political director of Our Revolution, a group aligned with Bernie Sanders of Vermont, the 'ideological leadership' is full of Pivenites. Micah Uetricht, 31, managing editor of the socialist magazine Jacobin, is also devoted to Ms. Piven's work. He said he has read 'Poor People's Movements,' Ms. Piven's venerated 1977 book, at least three times. . . . Probably the most influential vector for Ms. Piven's ideas is the social-justice incubator Momentum, a training program for progressives that formed in 2014."[7] Moreover, it is no accident that the overwhelming majority of college and law school faculty, as well as journalists, identify as Democrat Party members.

The Democrat Party has developed into the political home of the various American Marxist movements, with which they agree and identify. Hence, they are not so repulsed by America's past—or more accurately, the Democrat Party's past—as to forever condemn the Democrat Party and refuse any association with it. They ignore or downplay its links to the Ku Klux Klan, white-supremacist neo-Nazis, lynchings, etc. Instead, they target and blame the entire society, culture, and country for the Democrat Party's contemptible past. To underscore the point, the American Marxists are supportive of the Democrat Party's modern-day promotion of economic socialism, cultural Marxism, and anti-Americanism. In truth, their contempt for the Constitution, and its routine condemnation, is not so much because of some of the Framers' biographies, but because the Constitution's firewalls remain an impediment to, or at least slow, their revolutionary aims and the speed with which they seek to make them. Indeed, the birth of the Republican Party in 1854 occurred in response and opposition to efforts to expand slavery in the territories. Again, this proves the real intentions of the American Marxists—that is, history is not so much what drives them, or they would either be Republicans today or at least not associate with the Democrat Party. The revolution against Americanism and for economic socialism and cultural Marxism is their real motivation.

Still, Marxist hypocrisy aside, there is certainly no excuse for slavery. "Everybody did it," which is mostly true, obviously does not make it right. But unfortunately, it is a historical fact. However, it is beyond debate that it was not unique to the early days of certain American colonies and the United States. For example, Cornell professor of African history Sandra Greene explains that not only was slavery common throughout the world, but in Africa as well. "'Slavery in the United States ended in 1865,' says Greene, 'but in West Africa it was not legally ended until 1875, and then it stretched on unofficially until almost World War I. Slavery continued because many people weren't aware that it had ended, similar to what happened in Texas after the United States Civil War.'[8] While 11 to 12 million people are estimated to have been exported as slaves from West Africa during the years of the slave trade, millions more were retained in Africa. 'It's not something that many West African countries talk about,' says Greene, who is black herself. 'It's not exactly a proud moment because everyone now realizes that slavery is not acceptable.'"[9]

The broader point is that all cultures suffer from serious imperfections. Some can acknowledge and effectively address them, reforming along the way, and others do not or are less successful in doing so. The constant degrading of the American system, including the distortion of history, capitalism, and modern-day race relations, is a purposeful effort by the American Marxists not to improve society but to ruin and eradicate it.

Like Robert Natelson, assistant professor at Hillsdale College Dr. David Azerrad makes a good and succinct defense of the Framers and the Constitution: "The argument that the Constitution is racist suffers from one fatal flaw: the concept of race does not exist in the Constitution. Nowhere in the Constitution—or in the Declaration of Independence, for that matter—are human beings classified according to race, skin color, or ethnicity (nor, one should add, sex, religion, or any other of the Democrat Party's favored groupings). Our founding principles are colorblind (although our history, regrettably, has not been). The Constitution speaks of people, citizens, persons, other persons (a euphemism for slaves) and Indians not taxed (in which case, it is their tax-exempt status, and not their skin color, that matters). The first references to 'race' and 'color' occur in the 15th Amendment's guarantee of the right to vote, ratified in 1870."[10]

Azerrad points out that "[t]he infamous three-fifths clause, which more nonsense has been written than any other clause, does not declare that a black person is worth 60 percent of a white person. It says that for purposes of determining the number of representatives for each state in the House (and direct taxes), the government would count only three-fifths of the slaves, and not all of them, as the Southern states, who wanted to gain more seats, had insisted. The 60,000 or so free blacks in the North and the South were counted on par with whites. . . . The Constitution defers to the states to determine who shall be eligible to vote (Article I, Section 2, Clause 1).[11] It is a little-known fact of American history that black citizens were voting in perhaps as many as 10 states at the time of the founding (the precise number is unclear, but only Georgia, South Carolina, and Virginia explicitly restricted suffrage to whites)."[12]

In addition, explains Azerrad, "[b]ecause the Constitution does not explicitly recognize slavery and does not therefore admit that slaves were property, all the protections it affords to persons could be applied to slaves. 'Anyone of these provisions in the hands of abolition statesmen, and backed up by a right moral sentiment, would put an end to slavery in America,' Frederick Douglass concluded. It is true that the Constitution of 1787 failed to abolish slavery. The constitutional convention was convened not to free the slaves, but to amend the Articles of Confederation. The slave-holding states would have never consented to a new Constitution that struck a blow at their peculiar institution. The Constitution did, however, empower Congress to prevent its spread and set it on a course of extinction, while leaving the states free to abolish it within their own territory at any time. Regrettably, early Congresses did not pursue a consistent anti-slavery policy. This, however, is not an indictment of the Constitution itself. As Douglass explained: 'A chart is one thing, the course of a vessel is another. The Constitution may be right, the government wrong.' " [13]

Indeed, on July 5, 1852, Frederick Douglass gave a fierce speech condemning slavery and endorsing abolition. And in that speech, Douglass also strongly defended the Constitution and those who drafted it. Among other things, Douglass declared that those who reply to him by charging the Framers and the Constitution for "precisely what I have now denounced [are], in fact, guaranteed and sanctioned by the Constitution of the United States; that the right to hold and to hunt slaves is a part of that Constitution framed by the illustrious Fathers of this Republic. But I differ from those who charge this baseness on the Framers of the Constitution of the United States. It is a slander upon their memory, at least, so I believe. . . . Fellow-citizens! There is no matter in respect to which, the people of the North have allowed themselves to be so ruinously imposed upon, as that of the pro-slavery character of the Constitution. In that instrument I hold there is neither warrant, license, nor sanction of the hateful thing; but, interpreted as it ought to be interpreted, the Constitution is a glorious liberty document. Read its preamble, consider its purposes. Is slavery among them? Is it at the gateway? Or is it in the temple? It is neither. While I do not intend to argue this question on the present occasion, let me ask, if it be not somewhat singular that, if the Constitution were intended to be, by its framers and adopters, a slave-holding instrument, why neither slavery, slave-holding, nor slave can anywhere be found in it. What would be thought of an instrument, drawn up, legally drawn up, for the purpose of entitling the city of Rochester to a track of land, in which no mention of land was made? . . . Now, take the Constitution according to its plain reading, and I defy the presentation of a single pro-slavery clause in it. On the other hand, it will be found to contain principles and purposes, entirely hostile to the existence of slavery. . . ."[14]

If Douglass were alive today and made this statement on nearly any media platform or virtually any Democrat Party event, he would be booed off the platform. In other words, he would be abused and smeared as Clarence Thomas is today.

In addition, the Framers were highly accomplished, mostly well educated, and avid readers of history and philosophy. If, in fact, they wanted to institutionalize and enshrine slavery into American society, why did they not do so? The Constitution would have been the perfect vehicle through which to do it. For nearly five months, during a sweltering summer in Philadelphia, delegates labored over and debated every phrase and clause in the document. James Madison took copious notes of the proceedings. If the Framers and state ratifiers of the Constitution consecrated slavery and meant to perpetrate it, would they not have sculpted it into the Constitution—that is, America's supreme governing document? Would slavery not be promoted in the *Federalist Papers* to encourage ratification of the Constitution? Yet none of this happened.

Moreover, the Constitution's strengths, including the diversification and separation of powers within the national government, the sovereign authority of states, and the protection of the individual vis-à-vis governmental authority, are weaknesses to radical activists. For example, the late associate justice of the Supreme Court Ruth Bader Ginsburg, one of the most left-wing activists to ever serve on the Court, also condemned the Constitution. In an interview with Al Hayat (Egyptian) television in 2012, she dissed our Constitution:

> Q: Would your honor's advice be to get a part or other countries' constitutions as a model, or should we develop our own draft?
>
> A: You should certainly be aided by all the constitution-writing that has gone on since the end of World War II. *I would not look to the U.S. Constitution, if I were drafting a constitution in the year 2012.* I might look at the constitution of South Africa. That was a deliberate attempt to have a fundamental instrument of government that embraced basic human rights, had an independent judiciary. It really is, I think, a great piece of work that was done. Much more recent than the U.S. Constitution: Canada has a Charter of Rights and Freedoms. It dates from 1982. You would almost certainly look at the European Convention on Human Rights. Yes, why not take advantage of what there is elsewhere in the world? I'm a very strong believer in listening and learning from others.[15] [Italics are mine.]

Of course, Ginsburg, aka RBG, is an iconic figure, in life and death, to the Democrat Party, even worthy of a Hollywood movie. Ginsburg's complaint seems to be that although the Constitution has been massaged over time to meet the demands of an evolving or progressing society, it cannot move fast enough or go far enough in achieving her ideological objectives—a complaint voiced repeatedly by the Democrat Party.

Moreover, we can do much better, the argument goes, if we could start from scratch with a new Constitution. Unlike a Convention of States, which is a careful and legitimate effort to amend the Constitution by way of the state convention process authorized under Article V of the Constitution, and which seeks to strengthen original constitutional clauses against the damage done to the Constitution by judicial activists and others, the Democrat Party has in mind to rewrite the entire Constitution, or at least those parts of it that hinder its revolutionary intentions, as Elie Mystal and other anti-American radicals demand.

The point is that the Constitution stands between we, the people, and tyrannical government, and that absolutely means the Democrat Party and American Marxist designs on our country. To prove the point, let us look at four areas where they seek to curb our civil liberties, undermine our republic, and disembowel the Constitution. Please keep in mind that these four general areas of discussion in no way represent the entirety of the Democrat Party's war on the Constitution and our republic.

THE FIRST AMENDMENT

In 2014, Phil Kerpen, president of American Commitment, helped expose the wickedness of a Democrat Party proposal to gut the First Amendment. He explained: "Section 1 of the proposed amendment (S. J. Res. 19) says: 'Congress and the States may regulate and set reasonable limits on the raising and spending of money by candidates and others to influence elections.' The key words here are 'and others,' meaning anybody Congress chooses to regulate and 'to influence elections,' meaning not just express advocacy that calls on voters to support or oppose a candidate, but any communication politicians think might influence an election. It gives Congress—and the states—the power to restrict paid communications—political speech—about any significant public policy issue with respect to incumbent politicians. Vast swaths of core political speech—much of it wholly unrelated to elections—would be restricted. Politicians would advance controversial policies knowing that any criticism of them could be prohibited." [16]

Kerpen disclosed: "Section 2 of the proposed amendment says: 'Congress and the States shall have power to implement and enforce this article by appropriate legislation, and may distinguish between natural persons and corporations or other artificial entities created by law, including by prohibiting such entities from spending money to influence elections.' This is an open-ended grant of power to outright prohibit speech not just by corporations, but other 'entities created by law,' including non-profit groups." [17]

"Congress—and the states . . . ," wrote Kerpen, "would now have the power to compel disclosure for any criticism of an elected official, and to outright ban speech by groups. The only exception? The media. Section 3 of the proposed amendment gives them an express carve-out: 'Nothing in this article shall be construed to grant Congress or the States the power to abridge the freedom of the press.' So, if you own a newspaper, radio station, or TV station it's free speech as usual. If you don't, tough. . . . The First Amendment would be effectively repealed, limited to protecting political speech only for the media." [18]

Although the proposed amendment was defeated, the fact that the Democrat Party bill was drafted and put up for a vote was shocking—and underscores its totalitarian nature. Tim Burris at *Forbes* explained: "[T]he amendment would create a world where pornography, videos depicting small animals being crushed, profanity-laden jackets, and Phelps family funeral protests all receive more protection from government interference than even the smallest amount of political speech. By giving Congress and state governments essentially unlimited power to prohibit or regulate anyone who is spending money trying to 'influence elections,' the Senate stooped to a level of governmental malfeasance previously reserved for the former Soviet Union, North Korea, Cuba, and Venezuela. In fact, if Venezuelan president Nicolás Maduro passed this same law, Americans would properly see it as a thinly veiled attempt to squelch the political rights of Venezuelans and to entrench himself in power."[19] To be clear, it was not "the Senate," but the Democrat Party.

The point is that if the Democrat Party has its way, which it soon may, free political speech, including criticism of governmental policy, will be severely limited, and violators will be subject to punishment by the government. This is police state censorship.

Consider this: In October 2022, reporters Ken Klippenstein and Lee Fang at the news site *The Intercept* reported: "[The Biden administration's] . . . Department of Homeland Security (DHS) is quietly broadening its efforts to curb speech it considers dangerous. . . . Years of internal DHS memos, emails, and documents—obtained via leaks and an ongoing lawsuit, as well as public documents—illustrate an expansive effort by the agency to influence tech platforms. The work, much of which remains unknown to the American public, came into clearer view earlier this year when DHS announced a new 'Disinformation Governance Board': a panel designed to police misinformation (false information spread unintentionally), disinformation (false information spread intentionally), and malinformation (factual information shared, typically out of context, with harmful intent) that allegedly threatens U.S. interests. While the board was widely ridiculed, immediately scaled back, and then shut down within a few months, other initiatives are underway as DHS pivots to monitoring social media now that its original mandate—the war on terror—has been wound down.[20] . . . [In 2021], Laura Dehmlow, an FBI official, warned that the threat of subversive information on social media could undermine support for the U.S. government. Dehmlow, according to notes of the discussion attended by senior executives from Twitter and JPMorgan Chase, stressed that 'we need a media infrastructure that is held accountable.'"[21]

Consequently, "other government efforts to root out disinformation have not only continued but expanded to encompass additional DHS sub-agencies . . . DHS's expansion into misinformation, disinformation, and malinformation represents an important strategic retooling for the agency. . . ."[22]

Domestic monitoring and surveillance of communications by American citizens have been growing but are now exploding under the Biden administration. This helps explain the antics of House Democrats to sabotage an important hearing involving the use by the Biden administration of Twitter to suppress free speech and its political opposition. In March 2023, Democrats on the Select Subcommittee on the Weaponization of the Federal Government, led by the ranking member from the Virgin Islands, Democrat delegate Stacey Plaskett, condemned two independent journalists, both of whom voted for Biden for president, for helping to expose the Biden administration's censorship efforts in working with Twitter and demanded that they reveal confidential journalistic sources.[23]

As described earlier, on the same day as his testimony, an IRS agent visited the New Jersey home of one of the journalists, Matt Taibbi. Both journalists were verbally abused by the Democrat members, who challenged their journalistic credentials, the fact that they were paid for their work, etc. The Democrat members had no interest in their investigative findings. Indeed, in April 2023, Plaskett went so far as to threaten Taibbi with prison time.

She accused him of giving intentionally false testimony under oath (perjury) when he made an error by confusing CIS (Center for Internet Security) and CISA (Cybersecurity and Infrastructure Security Agency), which he corrected.[24] Almost nothing was said by the rest of the media in defense of the journalists or against the threats.

But for the courage of these handful of independent journalists and the man who hired them, Elon Musk, as well as the attorneys general of Missouri, now Senator Eric Schmitt, and current Louisiana attorney general, Jeff Landry, the extent of the Biden administration's incredible violations of the First Amendment and free speech, would be unknown.

U.S. District Judge Terry A. Doughty carefully examined the states' evidence for seeking a preliminary injunction against the Biden administration to stop the government from hijacking social-media platforms in "the most massive attack against free speech in U.S. history."[25] In his July 4 decision, Doughty opined:

> Plaintiffs allege that Defendants, through public pressure campaigns, private meetings, and other forms of direct communication, regarding what Defendants described as "disinformation," "misinformation," and "malinformation," have colluded with and/or coerced social-media platforms to suppress disfavored speakers, viewpoints, and content on social-media platforms. Plaintiffs also allege that the suppression constitutes government action, and that it is a violation of Plaintiffs' free speech . . .
>
> The principal function of free speech under the United States' system of government is to invite dispute; it may indeed best serve its high purpose when it induces a condition of unrest, creates dissatisfaction with conditions as they are, or even stirs people to anger.

The Plaintiffs are likely to succeed on the merits in establishing that the Government has used its power to silence the opposition. Opposition to COVID-19 vaccines; opposition to COVID-19 masking and lockdowns; opposition to the lab-leak theory of COVID-19; opposition to the validity of the 2020 election; opposition to President Biden's policies; statements that the Hunter Biden laptop story was true; and opposition to policies of the government officials in power. All were suppressed. It is quite telling that each example or category of suppressed speech was conservative in nature. This targeted suppression of conservative ideas is a perfect example of viewpoint discrimination of political speech. American citizens have the right to engage in free debate about the significant issues affecting the country.[26]

Although this case is still relatively young, and at this stage the Court is only examining it in terms of Plaintiffs' likelihood of success on the merits, the evidence produced thus far depicts an almost dystopian scenario. During the COVID-19 pandemic, a period perhaps best characterized by widespread doubt and uncertainty, the United States Government seems to have assumed a role similar to an Orwellian "Ministry of Truth."

The Plaintiffs have presented substantial evidence in support of their claims that they were victims of a far-reaching and widespread censorship campaign.[27]

Doughty's opinion is one of the finest First Amendment decisions by any court at any time. However, as of this writing, the 5th U.S. Circuit Court of Appeals granted the Biden administration's request to temporarily stay Judge Doughty's issuance of a temporary injunction, which prohibited federal departments and agencies from using social-media platforms to unconstitutionally suppress free speech, while the case plays out in court. In the meantime, the Biden administration is free to return to censoring speech in violation of the First Amendment.

And there is more. In April 2023, the Department of Justice inspector general, Michael Horowitz, testified before a House Committee that "[m]ore than one million secret searches of Americans conducted by the FBI were made erroneously. . . . Around 30 percent of the approximately 3.4 million searches were done in error. . . . The searches in question were conducted by FBI personnel with the authority under the Foreign Intelligence Surveillance Act (FISA). The bill enables U.S. authorities to gather information on U.S. citizens suspected of being involved with possible spies or terrorists. Some 3.39 million searches were conducted by the FBI in 2021, U.S. intelligence officials have said. That was up from just 1.2 million in 2020."[28] That means the Biden Department of Justice and FBI massively increased secret domestic surveillance by over 300 percent, and nearly a third of the searches that were sought by the FBI and secretly authorized by a federal judge were supposedly in error. This is astonishing and unbelievable.

In fact, seasoned FBI agents turned whistleblowers, who have bravely come forward to report agency abuses to Congress, have been severely punished by FBI brass. In a report titled "FBI Whistleblower Testimony Highlights Government Abuse, Misallocation of Resources, and Retaliation," "whistleblowers have had their security clearances revoked, been suspended without pay, and some have been left 'homeless' for speaking up on abuses they have witnessed," reports the *Daily Mail*.[29] . . . "'Instead of hundreds of investigations stemming from an isolated incident at the Capitol on January 6, 2021, FBI and DOJ officials point to significant increases in domestic violent extremism and terrorism around the United States.'"[30]

The threats and retaliation by the Biden administration against whistleblowers reporting abuses of power are widespread. The *Washington Examiner* reports that at the IRS, "[a] second IRS whistleblower has alleged retaliation for raising concerns that Justice Department leadership was 'acting inappropriately' on the investigation into Hunter Biden. The allegations from an IRS case agent come a month after an IRS supervisory special agent revealed to Congress politics had infected the case involving President Joe Biden's son. Both whistleblowers were removed from the federal investigation into possible Hunter Biden tax violations. . . . Communications obtained by the first whistleblower's lawyers show that the second whistleblower was threatened with allegations of criminal conduct after raising concerns about the handling of Hunter Biden's case."[31] Of course, as we now know, these agents were pulled so the Department of Justice could cut a sweetheart deal with Hunter Biden.

On the other hand, the "whistleblower" who was called by House Intelligence Committee chairman Democrat Adam Schiff in the Ukraine-related sham impeachment of President Trump received iconic-like treatment. Indeed, his name was not to be publicly mentioned even though it was known by the media. A few conservative reporters, notably Paul Sperry of Real Clear Investigations, revealed him to allegedly be Eric Ciaramella. Sperry reported he was a "holdover from the Obama White House, [and] previously worked with former vice president Joe Biden and former CIA director John Brennan . . ." In fact, he had deep and extensive ties throughout Democrat circles.[32]

And there is more. The Democrat Party is also pushing to deplatform news groups and individuals with whom they disagree. Here is Alexandria Ocasio-Cortez (AOC) in April 2023 gleefully celebrating deplatforming after Tucker Carlson and Fox parted ways:

Tucker Carlson is out at Fox News. Couldn't have happened to a better guy. What I will say, though, is, while I'm very glad that the person that is arguably responsible for the—some of the largest—driving some of the most amounts of death threats, violent threats not just to my office, but to plenty of people across the country, I also kind of feel like I'm waiting for the cut scene at the end of a Marvel movie after all the credits have rolled, and then you see, like, the villain's hand re-emerge out to grip over like the end of the building or something. But de-platforming works and it is important and—there you go. Good things can happen.[33]

AOC is hardly alone in her totalitarian view. *Reason*, among others, reported that on February 22, 2021, "two Democratic members of Congress sent letters to the presidents of Comcast, AT&T, Verizon, Cox, Dish, and other cable and satellite companies implying that they should either stop carrying Fox News, One America News Network, and Newsmax or pressure them to change their coverage. According to the lawmakers, these conservative channels are responsible for promoting misinformation and political violence."

House Democrats Anna Eshoo and Jerry McNerney, both of California, wrote, in part: "'To our knowledge, the cable, satellite, and over-the-top companies that disseminate these media outlets to American viewers have done nothing in response to the misinformation aired by these outlets.' Eshoo and McNerney ask the companies to explain the 'moral and ethical principles' that undergird their decision-making with respect to which channels are carried, how many viewers tuned in to these channels during the four weeks before the Capitol riots on January 6, 2020, and what steps were taken to 'monitor, respond to, and reduce the spread of disinformation.' The committee members also sent the letter to Roku, Amazon, Apple, Google and Hulu, digital companies that distribute cable programming. . . ."[34] Clearly, the purpose of the letter was to intimidate the cable platforms and Fox News, One America News Network, and Newsmax.

The deplatforming campaign is not limited to a handful of congressional Democrats. Defunding conservative media platforms is another tactic employed by the American Marxists and their Democrat Party sycophants. In May 2023, the *Washington Examiner*'s Gabe Kaminsky reported: "Well-funded 'disinformation' tracking groups are part of a stealth operation blacklisting and trying to defund conservative media, likely costing the news companies large sums in advertising dollars. . . . Major ad companies are increasingly seeking guidance from purportedly 'nonpartisan' groups claiming to be detecting and fighting online 'disinformation.' These same 'disinformation' monitors are compiling secret website blacklists and feeding them to ad companies, with the aim of defunding and shutting down disfavored speech, according to sources familiar with the situation, public memos, and emails. . . . The Global Disinformation Index, a British group with two affiliated U.S. nonprofit groups sharing similar board members, is one entity shaping the ad world behind the scenes. GDI's CEO is Clare Melford, former senior vice president for MTV Networks, and its executive director is Daniel Rogers, a tech advisory board member for Human Rights First, a left-leaning nonprofit group that says disinformation fuels 'violent extremism and public health crises.' "[35]

Kaminsky states: "GDI, which did not reply to several requests for its exclusion list, discloses in reports which outlets it identifies as the 'riskiest' and 'worst' offenders for peddling disinformation. These 10, which all skew to the right, are the *American Spectator*, Newsmax, the *Federalist*, the *American Conservative*, One America News, the *Blaze*, the *Daily Wire*, *RealClearPolitics*, *Reason*, and the *New York Post*. . . . On the flip side, all of the websites that GDI ranks as the 'least risky' lean left in their news coverage—minus the *Wall Street Journal*. These include NPR, *ProPublica*, the *Associated Press*, *Insider*, the *New York Times*, *USA Today*, the *Washington Post*, *Buzzfeed News*, and *HuffPost*, according to a 27-page report. The outlets purportedly show 'minimal bias' and a lack of 'sensational language' and have 'excelled in disclosing and following their operational policies and practices,' said the report. Still, many of these 'least' risky outlets, such as *Buzzfeed*, promoted the Steele dossier, a discredited piece of opposition research that Hillary Clinton's 2016 presidential campaign fed to the FBI to link Donald Trump to Russia. Others, such as *HuffPost*, have published numerous stories boosting the falsehood that a *New York Post* story on Hunter Biden's infamous abandoned laptop was 'Russian disinformation.' "[36]

Moreover, GDI "has received $330,000 from two State Department-backed entities linked to the highest levels of government. . . ."[37] NewsBusters also reports that "GDI has three advisory board members with ties to leftist billionaire George Soros, according to MRC Free Speech America research . . . Advisory Panel member Finn Heinreich is Soros' Open Society Initiative for Europe division director for transparency, accountability, and participation. This directly makes Heinrich one of Soros' flunkies. GDI lists Ben Nimmo as part of the Atlantic Council on its website. His profile states he was a nonresident senior fellow with the leftist organization, which is funded by Soros (the *Washington Examiner* said he also works for Meta). Cris Tardáguila, another GDI advisory panel member, was the former director of the Soros-funded Poynter Institute's International Fact Checking Network (IFCN). GDI currently shows Tardáguila representing the IFCN on its website."[38] And there are other left-wing groups, tied to the

Democrat Party and its interests, doing the same kind of activities. Soros's web of personnel and resources is at the center of it all.

For example, ProPublica is a left-wing operation that fancies itself an "independent, nonprofit newsroom that produces investigative journalism with moral force" and is funded by charitable sources.[39] ProPublica has been at the forefront of smear campaigns against Supreme Court justices Clarence Thomas, Samuel Alito, and Neil Gorsuch, alleging various ethical conflicts of interest. Of course, the Democrat Party and other "media" outlets have seized on these stories. Senate Democrats held a hearing, some called for Thomas's impeachment, and the smear campaign continued from there. The *New York Post* reports that in "2020 and 2021, the organization took in a total of $6.3 million from donors it kept anonymous. And despite repeated questions about the identity of two donors who appear to have made up nearly a quarter of their donations last year, ProPublica declined to name them to *The Post* or explain how they donated to the organization."[40] The massive anonymous donations are called "dark money." Breccan F. Thies, reporting for the *Washington Examiner*, explains that ProPublica "is funded by left-wing megadonors who pump money into court-packing advocacy groups," such as the controversial Sandler Foundation.[41]

From dark money, defunding and deplatforming, monitoring, snooping, and targeting and smearing Supreme Court justices, the Democrat Party's history demonstrates its discomfort with freedom of speech and a truly free press, and its affinity for police-state tactics and the manipulation of public discourse and information.

As the Bill of Rights Institute reminds us: "One of the most serious limitations of freedom of speech and press came with the Espionage Act of 1917. This law made it a crime to 'cause or attempt to cause insubordination, disloyalty, mutiny, refusal of duty, in the military or naval forces of the United States, or shall willfully obstruct the recruiting or enlistment service of the United States.'. . . Congress passed and [Woodrow] Wilson signed an amendment to the Espionage Act with even more restrictive limits on speech and press in 1918. It was a crime to 'utter, print, write, or publish any disloyal, profane, scurrilous, or abusive language about the form of government of the United States, or the Constitution of the United States, or the military or naval forces of the United States . . . or [to] willfully display the flag of any foreign enemy, or . . . willfully . . . urge, incite, or advocate any curtailment of production . . . or advocate, teach, defend, or suggest the doing of any of the acts or things in this section enumerated and [to] by word or act support or favor the cause of any country with which the United States is at war or by word or act oppose the cause of the United States.' . . . In 1920, Wilson's attorney general, A. Mitchell Palmer, ordered raids on homes, meeting places, and offices of suspected radicals. Palmer said in 1920, 'The tongues of revolutionary heat were licking the altars of the churches, leaping into the belfry of the school bell, crawling into the sacred corners of American homes, seeking to replace marriage vows with libertine laws, burning up the foundations of society.' Six-thousand people, mostly foreign-born, were arrested in the Palmer Raids, as they came to be known."[42]

One of Wilson's chief enforcers of his censorship and propaganda war was his postmaster general, former Texas Democrat representative Albert Sidney Burleson, whose family had served in the Confederacy and who was a rabid segregationist. "He was eager to attack such affronts as having white and black postal workers sorting letters in the same railway mail car, or using the same restrooms ('intolerable'), or having white and black patrons line up at the same post office window. He segregated postal lunchrooms and ordered screens erected in work areas so white employees would not have their view sullied by black ones."[43] Of course, his boss,

Woodrow Wilson, approved. "Burleson was on the lookout...
for any publications 'calculated to . . . cause insubordination, disloyalty, mutiny . . . or otherwise embarrass or hamper the Government in conducting the war.' What did 'embarrass' mean? Burleson
listed a broad range of possibilities, from saying 'that the Government is controlled by Wall Street or munition manufacturers, or
any other special interests' to 'attacking improperly our allies.'
'Improperly'?"[44] Wilson's real targets were political opponents and
opposition newspapers. He used the laws to "close down about
75 newspapers and magazines, prevent the distribution of specific
issues of many more, and put journalists on trial in federal courts."[45]

Even though these laws and Wilson's tyranny violated the
First Amendment, the Supreme Court upheld them. The 1918
Sedition amendments to the Espionage Act were repealed in
December 1920, at the behest of the newly elected Republican
president, Warren Harding, who was no fan of the laws. But the
1917 Espionage Act (with subsequent amendments) remains federal law. Indeed, it is now being used in the prosecution of President Trump, in what must be characterized as the most appalling
abuse of presidential and legal authority by the Biden administration in history. More on this in the next chapter.

In addition to "wag[ing] a campaign of intimidation and outright suppression against those ethnic and socialist papers that
continued to oppose [World War I]," writes Christopher B. Daly in
Smithsonian magazine, these and other measures taken by Wilson
"added up to an unprecedented assault on press freedom."[46] Wilson also set up a new and unprecedented agency, the Committee
on Public Information (CPI), which was an elaborate government
propaganda operation reaching into every form of communication known at the time. Daly explains that "[t]he new agency—
which journalist Stephen Ponder called 'the nation's first ministry
of information'—was usually referred to as the Creel Committee

for its chairman, George Creel, who had been a journalist before the war. From the start, the CPI was 'a veritable magnet' for political progressives of all stripes—intellectuals, muckrakers, even some socialists—all sharing a sense of the threat to democracy posed by German militarism. . . . For most journalists, the bulk of their contact with the CPI was through its News Division, which became a veritable engine of propaganda on a par with similar government operations in Germany and England but of a sort previously unknown in the United States. In the brief year and a half of its existence, the CPI's News Division set out to shape the coverage of the war in U.S. newspapers and magazines. . . . But at the same time, the government was taking other steps to restrict reporters' access to soldiers, generals, munitions-makers and others involved in the struggle. So, after stimulating the demand for news while artificially restraining the supply, the government stepped into the resulting vacuum and provided a vast number of official stories that looked like news. . . . The CPI was, in short, a vast effort in propaganda."[47] And the media were eager partners with the Wilson administration in promoting the government's propaganda.

Then there was the most celebrated Democrat president, Franklin Roosevelt, whose every (and many) unconstitutional, illegal, and unethical acts not only went without punishment, but are largely censored by the Democrat Party media to protect his tyrannical legacy. For example, according to former Hillsdale College professor Burton Folsom Jr., "[Franklin] Roosevelt marveled at the potential of the IRS for removing political opponents. Newspaper publisher William Randolph Hearst . . . found himself under investigation when he began opposing Roosevelt's political programs. In fact, . . . Eleanor Roosevelt sicced the IRS on conservative newspaper publisher Frank Gannett, who at the time was also vice chairman of the Republican National Committee."[48]

Hearst and Gannett were not the only newspaper publishers Roosevelt targeted with the IRS. Folsom explains that "Moses 'Moe' Annenberg . . . also drew an IRS audit—with 35 agents working for two and one-half years to prosecute him. Annenberg had just bought the *Philadelphia Inquirer*, which would become hostile to Roosevelt's agenda. Annenberg quickly became immersed in Republican politics, writing against the New Deal in general and competing against the *Philadelphia Record* in particular. David Stern was the editor of the *Record* and Stern enjoyed playing chess with [Henry] Morgenthau [FDR's secretary of Treasury] and high stakes politics with Roosevelt—who appreciated Stern's successful efforts to elect more Democrats in Pennsylvania. . . . Annenberg's aggressive advertising and news reporting helped the *Inquirer* sharply increase its subscriptions and sales, and helped cause Stern's *Record* to decline in sales and market share. . . . Stern was losing money at the *Record* and he turned to the government for help; in desperation . . . he was able to get the Federal Trade Commission (FTC) to prosecute Annenberg for selling advertising rates too low. . . . The Roosevelt administration had a better idea: an IRS investigation of Moe Annenberg. . . . Annenberg was careless and paid little attention to his taxes."[49]

"After the massive investigation was completed, it was determined that Annenberg owed the federal government $8 million, which he offered to pay with fines and penalties. But Roosevelt wanted Annenberg imprisoned. 'As . . . [the top IRS criminal investigative official] told Morgenthau, 'They are not going to have the opportunity to pay the tax [and avoid prison].' When Morgenthau and Roosevelt had lunch over the matter . . . , Morgenthau asked Roosevelt if he could do something for the president. 'Yes,' Roosevelt said. 'I want Moe Annenberg for dinner.' Morgenthau responded, 'You're going to have him for breakfast—fried.' The goal was to remove the *Inquirer*'s owner as a political influence in the state by putting him in prison and end the *Inquirer's* harsh criticism of Roosevelt's policies. It worked."[50]

Roosevelt and the *New York Times*, among other news outlets, also worked together to censor information about the extermination of millions of European Jews by Adolf Hitler and his Third Reich Nazis, which kept the American people in the dark about the Holocaust until 1944.[51] I discuss that at length in *Unfreedom of the Press*.

Roosevelt also used his office to target and intimidate the growing broadcast media. As *Reason's* David T. Beito reported: "At its inception in 1934, the Federal Communications Commission (FCC) reduced the license renewal period for stations from three years to only six months.[52] Of course, this enabled Roosevelt to hold, as Cicero would say, 'the Sword of Damocles' over radio broadcasters who would lose their businesses if their licenses were not renewed." "Meanwhile," wrote Beito, "Roosevelt tapped Herbert L. Pettey as secretary of the FCC (and its predecessor, the Federal Radio Commission). Pettey had overseen radio for Roosevelt in the 1932 campaign. After his appointment, he worked in tandem with the Democratic National Committee to handle 'radio matters' with both the networks and local stations. It did not take long to get the message. NBC, for example, announced that it was limiting broadcasts 'contrary to the policies of the United States government.' CBS Vice President Henry A. Bellows said that 'no broadcast would be permitted over the Columbia Broadcasting System that in any way was critical of any policy of the Administration.' He elaborated 'that the Columbia system was at the disposal of President Roosevelt and his administration and they would permit no broadcast that did not have his approval.' Local station owners and network executives alike took it for granted, as *Editor and Publisher* observed, that each station had 'to dance to Government tunes because it is under Government license.'"[53]

More recently, President Barack Obama, who has claimed

repeatedly that his administration was scandal free, and his attorney general, Eric Holder, unleashed federal police powers against targeted media outlets. Ted Galen Carpenter, writing for the Cato Institute, explains: "Obama's administration waged a robust campaign to harass and intimidate journalists, even mainstream journalists, who utilized leaked material. In May 2013, the Justice Department seized the records of phone lines that Associated Press employees used. AP confirmed that the records were from personal home and cell phones of reporters and editors, as well as phones that AP used in the press quarters of the House of Representatives. The administration's contempt for the basic requirements of due process was alarming. . . . The dragnet raid against the Associated Press was not the extent of the administration's assault on the press. Officials also conducted electronic surveillance of both *New York Times* reporter James Risen and Fox News correspondent James Rosen in an effort to identify their sources. [Rosen's parents were even surveilled.] The government went so far as to name Rosen as an 'unindicted co-conspirator' in an espionage case brought against his source."[54] In fact, "[i]n May 2013, the *Washington Post* reported that the Justice Department had monitored Rosen's activities by tracking his visits to the State Department. They did so through phone traces, timing phone calls, and his personal emails in an investigation of possible news leaks of classified information. . . . Only Rosen from the conservative-leaning cable news channel [Fox News] was given that treatment. . . . It was behavior never-before seen by a president against one specific network."[55] Similarly, the Obama Department of Justice asserted that it had the right to prosecute Risen, although it chose not to take that step.[56]

In 2015, "The Committee to Protect Journalists conducted its first examination of U.S. press freedoms amid the Obama administration's unprecedented number of prosecutions of government sources and seizures of journalists' records. Usually the group focuses on advocating for press freedoms abroad. . . . Former *Washington Post* executive editor, Leonard Downie, Jr., wrote the 30-page analysis titled 'The Obama Administration and the Press.' He explained: 'In the Obama administration's Washington, government officials are increasingly afraid to talk to the press. The administration's war on leaks and other efforts to control information are the most aggressive I've seen since the Nixon administration, when I was one of the editors involved in *The Washington Post*'s investigation of Watergate. . . .' 'There's no question that sources are looking over their shoulders,' Michael Oreskes, the AP's senior managing editor, told Downie. 'Sources are more jittery and more standoffish, not just in national security reporting. A lot of skittishness is at the more routine level. The Obama administration has been extremely controlling and extremely resistant to journalistic intervention.'"[57]

Obviously, during the course of American history, no political party has completely clean hands when it comes to free speech and press freedom. But there is no escaping the fact that the Democrat Party's hands are the filthiest. It is not even close. Nonetheless, the Democrat Party and the media—that is, the state party and the state media—have far too much in common ideologically and politically to allow these scraps between them to sever their long and deep bond. Even the most autocratic of regimes have to demonstrate to their state media from time to time who the real boss is.

Moreover, the Obama administration enlisted the assistance of the IRS against the Tea Party. The Tea Party consisted of millions of citizens who spontaneously organized and protested against Obama's radical policies. It also delivered Obama and the Democratic Party a landslide loss in the 2010 midterm elections. As the *Washington Times* reported: "The targeting [of Tea Party groups] began in 2010 and by the time it was exposed—first when

IRS senior executive Lois G. Lerner planted a question at a conference, hoping to shape the news, then in an inspector general's report, followed by congressional investigations and . . . court cases—it encompassed more than 400 groups. When they applied for tax-exempt status they were met with extensive delays and intrusive questions that the government admits never should have been asked. One group, the Albuquerque Tea Party, battled eight years before winning its [tax-exempt] status. Most of the groups targeted were conservative, but the IRS did start adding in liberal groups as it became aware of criticism."[58] The government eventually settled with the groups for $3.5 million. Obama had first reacted to the scandal by saying it was intolerable, then he ignored it, and ultimately he claimed it was not a scandal at all. The IRS later claimed the entire scandal was the brainchild of low-level IRS employees in the Cincinnati office.

Lest we forget, the First Amendment also protects the free exercise of religion—freedom of religion—from government usurpation. However, as the Democrat Party has massively expanded the welfare state and the nation transitions further from constitutional republicanism, especially since the New Deal, and secularism increasingly replaces faith in the American culture, as Marx demanded, the degradation of religious liberty is profoundly troubling. Religion and faith, like the nuclear family, must give way to the "greater good" and "best interests of the communal" if society is to be truly "just and equitable."

Kelly Shackelford, president, CEO, and chief counsel for First Liberty Institute, explains in Newsweek that "for the first almost 100 years of our republic, there were zero cases decided by the U.S. Supreme Court concerning the Free Exercise Clause of the First Amendment, and 110 years passed before the high court heard a case on the First Amendment's Establishment Clause—and then not another case on either clause for another 41 years after that.

Since 1940 [Roosevelt and the New Deal], litigation on religious liberty has exploded at an alarming rate in nearly every area of religious life: school prayer, legislative prayer, release time education, religious land use, distribution of religious literature, conscientious objection, wearing religious head coverings in military service, the Pledge of Allegiance, religious beard length and so forth. Our country has witnessed a barrage of litigation directed at the fundamental freedom of religious liberty—more than 75 cases since 1940. The numbers do not lie: It took 110 years to see three Supreme Court cases challenging religious liberty, but only 80 years to litigate more than 75 more. Religious freedom has been under increasing siege for eight decades now."[59]

Of course, it is no coincidence that this cultural and legal battle began and now rages with the rise of the so-called Progressive Era—that is, the beginnings of American Marxism. And it is getting worse.

Catholic League president Bill Donohue strongly denounced efforts by the Biden administration to denude religious liberty protected by the First Amendment: "Never has religious liberty been more seriously threatened than it is today. That the man responsible for this all-out assault professes to be a Catholic [Biden] is all the more offensive. It is his Office of Civil Rights (OCR) and Department of Health and Human Services (HHS) that are leading the charge. News of Biden's latest war on religious liberty was selectively leaked to the media this week. A draft memo by OCR to HHS indicates the Biden administration is planning to revoke the Trump administration's policies governing religious liberty, including conscience rights. HHS Secretary Xavier Becerra, who has a long record of trampling on religious liberty, is working in tandem with OCR to eviscerate the Religious Freedom Restoration Act (RFRA). In his capacity as California Attorney General, he sued the Little Sisters of the Poor for resisting the HHS mandate of the Obama administration; it tried to force the nuns to provide for abortion-inducing drugs in their healthcare plans."[60]

Biden's Department of Labor also "roll[ed] back the Trump rule [that allowed] religious groups that are federal contractors to specifically hire people who hold to their faith beliefs. In August 2019, the Trump Labor Department announced the proposed rule intended to clarify that faith-based organizations 'may make employment decisions consistent with their sincerely held religious tenets and beliefs without fear of sanction by the federal government.'"[61]

During the COVID-19 pandemic, California's Democrat governor, Gavin Newsom, was among the most aggressive chief executives in the nation violating religious liberty rights. "A 6-3 U.S. Supreme Court ruling sided with house-bound pastors and their congregants in their claim Newsom's bans on worship services in an effort to stop the spread of coronavirus unfairly singled out churches, in violation of the First Amendment.[62] 'Since the arrival of COVID–19, California . . . openly imposed more stringent regulations on religious institutions than on many businesses,' wrote Justice Neil M. Gorsuch in one of three concurring opinions. 'California worries that worship brings people together for too much time. Yet, California does not limit its citizens to running in and out of other establishments; no one is barred from lingering in shopping malls, salons, or bus terminals.'"[63] Of course, Newsom was not alone. The list of Democrat administrations pushing secular agendas against religious faiths and organizations is long and getting longer.

Again, it gets worse.

Biden's abusive use of federal law enforcement knows few equals in American history. Although the FBI director, Christopher Wray, and Attorney General Garland claim ignorance and distance themselves from another scandal, this time specifically targeting traditionalists in the Catholic Church, here is what we know thanks to Kyle Seraphin, a former FBI special agent, federal whistleblower, and U.S. Air Force veteran who uncovered a now infamous January 23, 2023, document: "The FBI's Richmond Division would like to protect Virginians from the threat of 'white supremacy,' which it believes has found a home within Catholics who prefer the Latin Mass. An intelligence analyst within the Richmond Field Office of the FBI released in a newly finished intelligence product dated January 23, 2023, on Racially or Ethnically Motivated Violent Extremists (RMVE) and their interests in 'Radical-Traditionalist Catholics' or RTCs. The document assesses with 'high confidence' the FBI can mitigate the threat of Radical-Traditionalist Catholics by recruiting sources within the Catholic Church. . . . While most Americans are familiar with criminal investigations, which explore the allegation or information that a crime has been committed, many are not familiar with intelligence investigations. In contrast to the linear nature of a criminal case, counterintelligence and counterterrorism cases follow a circular path that can continue indefinitely without any articulated goal. Indeed, information is the goal of these types of cases. Many counterterrorism cases never articulate or uncover a single criminal act. Yet they continue in order to develop more understanding of the 'threat landscape' or 'threat pictures,' as quoted in this document. Intelligence investigations often beget more investigations. The relevance of this product should not be lost on the reader."[64]

The danger presented by this FBI initiative is grave. Seraphin explains that "[p]roducts like this can be used to support the opening of information-only cases, and there is no reason to expect Radical-Traditionalist Catholics are the end point of this train track—they will be the beginning. Opening the door to associating white supremacists with traditional religious practices based on common Christian positions on abortion and the LGBTQ political agendas is a dangerous step. Such investigations can easily lead to the same analysis of Radical Traditional Baptists, Radical Traditional Lutherans, and Radical Traditional Evangelicals. The FBI is forbidden from opening cases or publishing products based solely on First Amendment-protected activities. By tolerating the publishing of intelligence products as shoddy as this, they are crossing a line many Americans will find themselves on the wrong side of for the first time in history. This is what a politicalized FBI looks like; it should not be tolerated if Americans expect to enjoy the protections of our Bill of Rights."[65] Once again, Biden and the Democrat administration plead ignorance.

Meanwhile, during a Senate Judiciary Committee hearing, Republican senator Mike Lee asked Garland: "In 2022 and for the first couple of months of 2023, DOJ's announced charges against 34 individuals for blocking access to or vandalizing abortion clinics, and there have been over 81 recorded attacks on pregnancy centers, 130 attacks on Catholic churches since the leak of the Dobbs decision, and only two individuals have been charged. So, how do you explain this disparity by reference to anything other than politicization of what's happening there?"

Garland responded, in part: "I will say you are quite right. There are many more prosecutions with respect to the blocking of the abortion centers, but that is generally because those actions are taken with photography at the time, during the daylight, and seeing the person who did it is quite easy. . . . Those who are attacking the pregnancy resource centers, which is a horrid thing to do, are doing this at night, in the dark. We have put full resources on this. We have put rewards out for this. The Justice Department and the FBI have made outreach to Catholic and other organizations to ask for their help in identifying the people who are doing this. We will prosecute every case against a pregnancy resource center that we can make, but these people doing this are clever and are doing it in secret. I am convinced that the FBI is trying to find them with urgency."[66] Perhaps the FBI should invest in some flashlights.

Catholic Vote tweeted a response to Garland: "What Garland doesn't admit is the obvious: The pro-abortion attacks are criminal, which is why they act in secret. Pro-life activists are there during the middle of the day because they know what they are doing is legal and protected by the U.S. Constitution."[67] "Despite these psychopathic actions, the DOJ recommends ZERO jail time for Maeve Nota, 31-year-old transgender individual who vandalized the St. Louise Catholic Church in Bellevue, WA, [causing over $30,000 in damage to the church] & smashed a police car. This is the exact opposite of how they treat Christians & prolifers," Twitter user Shadow Bird said.[68]

Then there is the case of Mark Houck. The Department of Justice sent approximately twenty heavily armed FBI agents to arrest Houck early in the morning and in front of his family (including several young children) for allegedly violating the Freedom of Access to Clinic Entrances (FACE) Act. The show of force was ordered by the Department of Justice despite Houck's lawyer informing federal authorities that Houck would surrender voluntarily. Houck was charged with two federal counts of violating the FACE Act for allegedly pushing a pro-abortion activist in front of an abortion clinic after the activist had allegedly shoved his twelve-year-old son. The altercation occurred about a hundred feet from the clinic. And the activist was accused of running toward Houck and his son and cursing out his son. "Biden's DOJ deliberately distorted the law in order to persecute Houck. Local authorities never pressed charges against Houck, having determined that the case was too weak. Yet Biden's prosecutors decided to go for it anyway, threatening to land Houck with up to 11 years in prison. . . ."[69] reported Joe Bukuras of the Catholic News

Agency. Houck was acquitted on all counts in the federal case after a brief deliberation by the jury in Philadelphia.

Biden and the Democrat Party have weaponized federal law enforcement yet again with respect to abortion on demand in order to advance their ideological and political agenda. The most radical abortion policy in American history, and in the free world, has become a rallying point for Biden and the Democrat Party. The Associated Press's Seung Min Kim reported last year, in a news article titled "Biden vows abortion legislation as top priority next year," that "[a]bortion—and proposals from some Republicans to impose nationwide restrictions on the procedure—have been a regular fixture of Biden's political rhetoric this election cycle, as Democrats seek to energize voters in a difficult midterm season for the party in power in Washington. In fundraisers and in political speeches, Biden has vowed to reject any abortion restrictions that may come to his desk in a GOP-controlled Congress."[70] Yes, Biden makes much of his Catholicism, but he clearly parts ways with his Church on abortion. Indeed, Biden is the most radical pro-abortion president ever. As explained earlier in this book, he is obsessed with power, the Democrat Party comes before faith and country, and Biden and the Democrat Party rely heavily on single childless women—who are far more extreme on their views of abortion than the rest of Americans and have become the most reliable voting bloc for the Democrat Party.

As mentioned previously, in May 2022, Senate Democrats, with Biden's support, introduced "The Women's Health Protection Act," which would have eliminated virtually all commonsense abortion limits throughout the nation. It is important to reiterate that the bill would ban state laws against late-term abortions, parental notification for minors, conscience protections for medical and health professionals, taxpayer financing of abortions, eliminate waiting periods, and more.[71] Forty-nine Senate Democrats voted for the bill. So radical was the bill that even pro-abortion Republican senator Susan Collins voted against the Democrats' bill. She stated: "Contrary to claims from Senate Democratic leaders that their bill would not infringe upon the religious rights of individuals and religious institutions, the WHPA explicitly invalidates the Religious Freedom Restoration Act in connection with abortion and supersedes other longstanding, bipartisan conscience laws, including provisions in the Affordable Care Act, that protect health care providers who choose not to offer abortion services for moral or religious reasons."[72]

In January 2023, the Republican-controlled "House passed the Born-Alive Abortion Survivors Protection Act . . . with votes of 220–210."[73] Only one Democrat voted for the bill; all Republicans voted for it. "[T]he legislation would require health practitioners to care for an infant that is born alive after a failed abortion, according to the law. . . . In order to become law, the bill would need to be approved in the Senate and signed by President Joe Biden, which is unlikely. Senate Majority Leader, Democrat Chuck Schumer, said . . . that the bill, along with a second anti-abortion bill, are 'doomed in the Senate' and 'extreme.'"[74] Thus, for the Democrat Party, saving a born baby's life is "extreme." Thus, the party that promoted eugenics in the last century supports infanticide today.

Like most authoritarian-oriented political parties, the Democrat Party detests freedom of speech, freedom of assembly, and religious liberty, for they are bulwarks against their obsession with control and power. They demand conformity and uniformity, and will use federal police powers more aggressively as time goes on.

THE UNITED STATES SUPREME COURT

Long before the 2022 *Dobbs v. Jackson Women's Health Organization* decision, where the Supreme Court determined that the states and the citizens of the states are to decide abortion policies, not the nine lawyers on the Supreme Court, the Democrat Party unleashed a campaign against the Court, insisting that it either bend to the Democrat Party's agenda or they will destroy the institution—with the assistance of the media, of course. Article III, Section 1 of the Constitution states: "The judicial power of the United States, shall be vested in one Supreme Court, and in such inferior courts as the Congress may from time to time ordain and establish. The judges, both of the supreme and inferior courts, shall hold their offices during good behaviour, and shall, at stated times, receive for their services, a compensation, which shall not be diminished during their continuance in office."

Thus, the Supreme Court was not created by Congress. It was created by the Framers through the Constitution. It heads an independent, coequal branch of the federal government. Therefore, it is one thing to criticize the Court, a decision of the Court, a justice on the Court, or even urge amendments to the Constitution to modify how members of the Court are chosen. It is another matter altogether to try to intimidate justices and threaten the independence of the Supreme Court when it does not do your party's political dirty work. It is not a Soviet Politburo. Once again, the Democrat Party, which despises the Constitution, has been behind a campaign to either co-opt the Court or destroy it.

As my first book, *Men in Black*, is about the Supreme Court, I will not write another here. However, there are certain pertinent issues that require addressing in the context of this book. For example, Franklin Roosevelt's disdain for the constitutional and institutional limits placed on him and the presidency, shared by the modern Democrat Party, reached into the Supreme Court. The National Constitution Center explains: "Roosevelt had enacted wide-ranging legislation along with congressional Democrats as part of his New Deal program, starting in 1933. By 1937, Roosevelt had won a second term in office, but the makeup of a conservative-leaning Supreme Court hadn't changed since he took office four years earlier. There were four Justices—nicknamed the 'Four Horsemen': Justices George Sutherland, Pierce Butler, James McReynolds, and Willis Van Devanter—who were conservative enough that their votes against most New Deal plans were expected. A fifth justice with conservative leanings was the Chief Justice, Charles Evans Hughes, who also narrowly lost the 1916 presidential race to the Democratic incumbent, President Woodrow Wilson. However, Hughes also had roots in the progressive wing of the Republican party. Another justice, Owen Roberts, was a Hoover appointee who voted with the conservatives on some decisions . . ." Roosevelt hatched a plan—"the Judicial Procedures Reform Bill of 1937—that would allow the President to appoint an additional justice for every sitting justice who was over 70 years of age. Roosevelt could add six of his own justices to the court. With two liberals already on the bench, that would put the odds in FDR's favor."[75]

Five weeks after its introduction, in June 1937, the Judiciary Committee sent a report with a negative recommendation to the full Senate. "The bill is an invasion of judicial power such as has never before been attempted in this country. . . . It is essential to the continuance of our constitutional democracy that the judiciary be completely independent of both the executive and legislative branches of the government," the report read. "It is a measure which should be so emphatically rejected that its parallel will never again be presented to the free representatives of the free people of America."[76] Key congressional Democrats, Republicans, and the public opposed Roosevelt's power grab. The Court was held in high respect, and Roosevelt's effort to pack the Court was resoundingly unpopular. However, it appears Roosevelt's failed legislative effort, and accompanying public attacks on the Court, had their intended effect. Associate Justice Owens began voting with the liberal bloc and Associate Justice Van Devanter announced his retirement. A coincidence? I doubt it.

The radical Democrat court-packers are back. This time, rather than opposing court packing, congressional Democrats, with the aggressive support of radical law school professors, are all in. For example, University of Pennsylvania law professor Kermit Roosevelt III (KR)—a great-great-grandson of President Theodore Roosevelt and a distant cousin of President Franklin Roosevelt who served on Biden's Supreme Court commission and summarizes where the Democrat Party stands on court-packing—is illustrative of their kind. Like other elitist law school professors, he declares: "I came out [of service on the commission] scared. Our system is broken in two obvious ways, that threaten America's self-governance. One of them is about the long-term legitimacy of the judiciary. The other is an immediate crisis."[77] He wrote, in part: "The first is mostly about what we could call high politics, or theories of constitutional interpretation. It is generated by the combination of life tenure and Senate confirmation for the Supreme Court, and it is that the composition of the Court is not tied in a predictable and uniform way to the outcome of presidential elections. Some presidents appoint several Justices; some presidents appoint none. What determines how many appointments a president gets is a combination of pure luck and partisan hardball. We do not staff any other branch of our government that way, and it has distorted the relationship between the Court and democracy."

Lamenting that Democrats have won more recent presidential elections than Republicans, there remains a majority of Republican-appointed justices on the Court. He bemoans that "[t]he most prominent face of this problem today is abortion. Generally speaking, Democratic appointees support abortion rights; Republican appointees do not."[78] KR suggests that term limits for justices—something I first raised in *Men in Black* nearly twenty years ago, albeit having nothing to do with KR's pro-abortion position—was worth pursuing given the increasingly politicized nature of activist justices.

However, argues KR, there is a bigger problem. The Court, or more specifically, the president who selects nominees to the Court, is determined by the Electoral College. Thus, the problem is the Constitution. KR insists it allows the Republican minority to almost control the selection of the Court's majority perpetually. "As we have seen in recent years," argues KR, "the electoral college allows a candidate to win the presidency while receiving a minority of the popular vote. The rule that each state is equally represented in the Senate means that Senators representing a minority of the population can control their chamber. A minority can take over the House . . . through partisan gerrymanders. And a president elected by a minority of the people can nominate judges who are then confirmed by Senators representing a minority of the people. Once in power, the minority can try to retain its position by further distorting the democratic process: gerrymanders, voter suppression, and judicial invalidation of attempts to protect voting rights. All of this is happening now. We are witnessing a minority [Republican] takeover of our democracy."[79] The Supreme Court "has allowed partisan gerrymanders, which distort the elections of state legislatures and federal Representatives. It has allowed states to impose burdens on voting as a response to imaginary threats of fraud. More striking, the Court has itself intervened in the political process. In 2013, it gutted the Voting Rights Act, which for fifty years had protected the electoral participation of minorities. . . . This is a problem of partisan politics. It is the Republican party attacking democracy, and the Supreme Court is helping it. . . . The only reform that fixes this problem now is court expansion. That could give us a majority of Justices who would defend democracy against these assaults instead of participating in them."[80]

Hence, KR and the Democrat Party simply want to save the country by destroying the Constitution. They simply want majority rule, except on the myriad matters where they do not. Of course, there is nothing partisan about their efforts, except when they attempt to enshrine their politics into law, especially via bureaucratic regulations, executive orders, and judicial fiat, which bypass majority rule and representative government. They stand for good government, especially one that imposes the various Marxist movements' agendas on the culture and economy. And they respect the will of the people, especially those people who comprise the ruling class and run an ever-increasing centralized government. In truth, they will pursue whatever changes they can to alter our constitutional republic in pursuit of Democrat Party power and control. As I said earlier in the book, the American Marxist and Democrat Party goals are incompatible with the Constitution. They will not rest until they effectively eradicate it.

The Democrat Party's war on the Court as an institution and the conservative justices is in full view. By driving down the Court's reputation, they figure, it will become politically easier to dismember the Court and dirty the reputation of offending justices. Hence, ProPublica's role described earlier. Indeed, the broadsides against associate justices Clarence Thomas, Samuel

Alito, and Neil Gorsuch are not about ethics or conflicts of interest. The media reports show *no* actual conflicts of interest between their court decisions and writings and the individuals with whom they have conducted business or received gifts. But their silence on ethics issues involving left-wing justices proves the point. For example, radical associate justice Kentanji Brown Jackson omitted reporting "her husband's consulting income, her George Washington University income, and . . . two travel reimbursements; Jackson also wrote on the nomination report that she had inadvertently omitted in prior years her membership on several boards (such as the board of directors of the D.C. Circuit's historical society), as well as college savings plans for her two daughters—which, she wrote, are controlled by their grandparents."[81] There was no concern.

More significantly, the *Daily Wire* reports that left-wing associate justice "Sonia Sotomayor declined to recuse herself from multiple copyright infringement cases involving book publisher Penguin Random House despite having been paid millions by the firm for her books, making it by far her largest source of income, records show. . . . In 2010, she got a $1.2 million book advance from Knopf Doubleday Group, a part of the conglomerate. In 2012, she reported receiving two advance payments from the publisher totaling $1.9 million. . . . In 2017, Sotomayor began receiving payments each year from Penguin Random House itself, which continued annually through at least 2021, the most recent disclosure available, and totaled more than $500,000. In all, she received $3.6 million from Penguin Random House or its subsidiaries, according to a *Daily Wire* tally of financial disclosures."[82] However, she refused to recuse herself in 2013 and 2020 from cases involving Penguin. "Fellow then-justice Stephen Breyer, by contrast, did recuse from the 2013 and 2020 Penguin cases. His wife is related to the family that founded a company, Pearson, which owned a stake in the publisher, and the couple held stock in Pearson: $1 million to $5 million in 2013, shrinking to $100,000 to $250,000 by 2020. Breyer also wrote books for the publisher, though he earned a much smaller amount than Sotomayor."[83]

There were no demands by Democrats for Sotomayor's impeachment, hearings, new ethics rules, or investigations, etc. The goal of the Democrat Party and their press mouthpieces is to destroy the reputation and undermine the legitimacy of the constitutionalists on the Court and the Court's present majority, regardless of the hypocrisy of their political and media attacks. Besides, few will call them out on it.

Of course, decades ago, preceding the latest smear of constitutionalists on the Court, was the Democrat Party's assault on the nominees of Republicans to the Court. It started in earnest with former District of Columbia Appeals Court judge Robert Bork and his August 1987 nomination to the Supreme Court by President Ronald Reagan. Bork was a giant among legal scholars and federal judges. Rarely had there been an individual so thoroughly qualified to serve as a justice. And this was what the Democrat Party feared. Their character-assassination campaign against Bork was run like a political campaign. Millions were spent on opposition research by outside left-wing groups and on television commercials to distort Bork's record. The *Washington Post* and the *New York Times* news, opinion, and editorial pages relentlessly brutalized Bork both personally and professionally. In the end, in October 1987 his confirmation failed, 58–42. Hence, the modern war against Republican nominees to the High Court and even appellate courts was launched. The confirmation process, which had been civil for much of American history, was ripped to shreds by the Democrat Party. The two leading Democrat senators who spearheaded the campaign were Edward Kennedy of Massachusetts, of Chappaquiddick fame, and Joe Biden of Delaware, a serial plagiarist and liar.

The Democrat Party was just getting warmed up. In July 1991, President George H. W. Bush nominated Clarence Thomas to the Court. If confirmed, Thomas would have been only the second black person to ever sit as a justice, filling the retiring Thurgood Marshall's seat (the first black justice). Thomas had been a District of Columbia Appeals Court judge for nineteen months before his nomination to the High Court. Among other things, he was also a graduate of Yale Law School, assistant attorney general in Missouri, assistant secretary of civil rights at the Department of Education, and chairman of the Equal Employment Opportunity Commission (EEOC). Again, the Democrat Party and its surrogates swung into action. Clearly, Thomas was a conservative Republican who did not share Marshall's judicial activism. Consequently, Thomas was "Borked." Once more, led by Kennedy and Biden, a Republican nominee was slimed. Shortly after the Senate Judiciary Committee's confirmation hearings ended, an FBI interview with Anita Hill was leaked to the Democrat Party press (the culprit is believed by some to have been a committee Democrat). The committee vote was suspended, subsequent televised testimony was taken, and the confirmation process turned into a Democrat Party–run circus—or as Thomas would say to the committee and the nation, "a national disgrace . . . a high-tech lynching for uppity blacks who in any way deign to think for themselves." Hill accused Thomas of sexually harassing words ten years earlier, which was vehemently denied by Thomas. The Senate later voted 52–48 to confirm Thomas. The Democrats failed to stop Thomas, but barely.

Years later, the smear campaign resumed. In July 2018, President Trump nominated Brett Kavanaugh to the Supreme Court to replace the retiring Anthony Kennedy, a swing vote on the Court. Trump was advised by Senate Republican leader Mitch McConnell that Kavanaugh would be the easiest candidate to confirm, which played into Trump's decision to go with Kavanaugh. Of course, that was not the case. For the Democrat Party, Kavanaugh was seen as the would-be fifth vote for a conservative majority, even though he had a long, moderate, and uncontroversial record as an appellate judge in Washington, D.C. Nonetheless, the Democrat Party and their media unleashed a cruel and ruthless barrage against him.

The *Washington Examiner*'s Kaylee McGhee White provides a brief reminder: "They hit him with an allegation of sexual assault that could not be corroborated right before his hearings and insisted without evidence that it was credible and he was guilty. They not only leaked this allegation against his accuser's wishes but pressured her to come and testify before the Senate Judiciary Committee—though she could not recall precisely when or where the alleged attack occurred or whom she had talked to about it. Even after the three friends Christine Blasey Ford named as witnesses, one of whom was a 'lifelong friend' of Ford's, declined to corroborate her story, Democrats insisted that Kavanaugh was a rapist."[84]

"But that was just the start," writes White. "After it became clear Ford's uncorroborated allegations weren't going to sink Kavanaugh's nomination, Democrats elevated two more accusers: Deborah Ramirez and Julie Swetnick. The latter's accusations were offensively absurd, made even more so by the fact she had a lengthy, documented history of dishonesty and was represented by a man who is now on his way to prison for fraud. Swetnick claimed Kavanaugh and his friends regularly spiked girls' drinks in the early 1980s so they could 'gangbang' them and that she once became a victim herself. She later admitted that she couldn't 'specifically say that [Kavanaugh] was one of the ones who assaulted me.' But none of this mattered to Senate Democrats, who continued to cite Swetnick, Ramirez, and Ford throughout Kavanaugh's hearings and accused him of committing gross and egregious crimes for which there was absolutely no solid evidence. They publicly went through his high school yearbook and used it to dismiss him as a drunk. They encouraged leftist activists to crowd the U.S. Capitol building and harass Republican senators who still supported him."[85] Kavanaugh was confirmed by a 50–48 vote. Unfortunately, he is an unreliable constitutionalist, as I feared at the time.

The controversy and even violence that now swirls around the Supreme Court and its justices is a Democrat Party production. Indeed, on March 4, 2020, Senate Democrat leader Chuck Schumer joined a pro-abortion rally on the steps of the Supreme Court while the justices were hearing oral arguments on a Louisiana case about protecting babies who survive botched abortions. Schumer yelled at the top of his lungs to the crowd—"I want to tell you, Gorsuch, I want to tell you, Kavanaugh, you have released the whirlwind, and you will pay the price. You won't know what hit you if you go forward with these awful decisions." Schumer blatantly threatened the justices and the Court in an unbridled attempt to intimidate them. And he wanted his party and Democrat activists to hear it and know it. Schumer and the Democrat Party had once again unleashed the hounds. Schumer was never punished for his incitement of violence.

The Democrat Party's ultimate goal is to own the Supreme Court. Although Biden currently has not taken steps to support packing the Court, he has come close, including his constant use of the bully pulpit and political speeches to eviscerate the Court and its majority. If such a bill ever reached his desk, I have no doubt he would sign it. Nonetheless, from smearing Republican nominees and sitting Republican justices to intimidating and threatening sitting Republican justices and discrediting the Court as an illegitimate institution when rulings are made contrary to the Democrat

Party's ideological and political agenda, the intent of the Democrat Party is, as I said, to soften opposition to court-packing and turn the public against the Court. On April 15, 2021, key congressional Democrats introduced a bill that would add four justices to the Court—just enough to outnumber the six Republican-appointed justices.[86] Although it went nowhere, the Democrats have no intention of giving up. Indeed, what seems fanciful today can easily become reality in the not-too-distant future. And the Democrat Party pressure campaign, backed by their media, will only build.

In the meantime, conservative justices continue to be in the crosshairs. After the draft *Dobbs* decision was leaked, Nicholas John Roske traveled from California to the Maryland home of associate justice Brett Kavanaugh with a gun, a knife, and pepper spray with the alleged intention of assassinating the justice.[87] Moreover, "[s]hortly after the leak of the draft opinion [of the *Dobbs* opinion] indicating *Roe v. Wade* would soon be overturned, the radical pro-abortion group Ruth Sent Us began urging protesters to go to the homes of the 'six extremist justices, three in Virginia and three in Maryland.' Those justices were Chief Justice John Roberts and Justices Amy Coney Barrett, Samuel Alito, Brett Kavanaugh, Clarence Thomas, and Neil Gorsuch. ShutDownDC, a leftist group that has protested at the family homes of Republican Missouri Sen. Josh Hawley and commentator Tucker Carlson, also called for protesting at the justices' houses and even offered bounties for sightings of the justices. Far-left protesters with Our Rights DC and Rise Up 4 Abortion Rights joined these groups in targeting the justices' homes. This protesting has frequently occurred in spite of 18 U.S. Code 1507, which forbids picketing or parading 'in or near a building or residence occupied or used by such judge, juror, witness, or court officer' with the intent of intimidating or influencing that person."[88] Protestors also harassed Kavanaugh at a restaurant.[89]

National Review's Dan McLaughlin pointed out: "'[L]aw enforcement agencies are investigating social-media threats to burn down or storm the Supreme Court building and murder justices and their clerks,' yet Democrats such as [Chuck] Schumer . . . dismissed the mob threat to the Court as no big deal. The Biden White House pointedly refused to condemn either the leak or the targeting of homes, with Jen Psaki saying that 'the president's view is that there's a lot of passion, a lot of fear, a lot of sadness from many, many people across this country about what they saw in that leaked document' and that 'I know that there's an outrage right now, I guess, about protests that have been peaceful to date, and we certainly do continue to encourage that, outside judges' homes, and that's the president's position.'"[90]

Nonetheless, the Department of Justice essentially directed the U.S. Marshals, who were authorized to protect the justices, to stand down. "A whistleblower provided copies of guidelines to [Alabama Republican senator] Katie Britt, that were given to U.S. marshals showing that deputies were highly discouraged from making arrests unless the lives of the justices or their families were in danger. One line on the guidelines told the deputies to 'avoid, unless absolutely necessary, criminal enforcement actions involving the protests or protesters, particularly on public space,' with a subsequent instruction stating 'arrests and initiating prosecutions is *not* the goal of the USMS presence at SCOTUS residences.'"[91] Of course, Garland insisted he was unaware of the guidelines.[92]

Associate Justice Samuel Alito, the author of the *Dobbs* draft and final decision, stated in a *Wall Street Journal* interview that the draft leak in *Dobbs* "was a part of an effort to prevent the *Dobbs* draft . . . from becoming the decision of the court. And that's how it was used for those six weeks by people on the outside—as part of the campaign to try to intimidate the court' . . . [and the] 'justices thought to support overturning *Roe* were really targets of assassination.' 'It was rational for people to believe that they might be able to stop the decision in *Dobbs* by killing one of us,' Alito said of threats that emerged after the leak, including the arrest of an armed man outside the home of Justice Brett Kavanaugh—days before the ruling was announced."[93]

In many ways, the Democrat Party of today remains the Democrat Party of yesterday—and that would especially include the party of Woodrow Wilson. If you want to understand the reason the Democrat Party will fight to the political death to control the Supreme Court and all federal courts, you need only reach back to the writings of Wilson in 1908, when as president of Princeton University he authored a treatise titled "Constitutional Government of the United States."[94] Wilson made the case that the judiciary was not bound by the Constitution. In *Ameritopia*, I referred to this passage from Wilson: "The weightiest import of the matter is seen only when it is remembered that the courts are the instruments of the nation's growth, and that the way in which they serve that use will have much to do with the integrity of every national process. If they determine what powers are to be exercised under the Constitution, they by the same token determine the adequacy of the Constitution in respect of the needs and interests of the nation; our conscience in matters of law and our opportunity in matters of politics are in their hands."[95]

Of course, this means the only legitimate opinions the federal courts can render are those that endorse and promote the expansion of federal power. Wilson continued: "[T]hat if they had interpreted the Constitution in its strict letter, as some proposed, and not in its spirit, like the charter of a business corporation and not like the character of a living government, the vehicle of a

nation's life, it would have proved a straight-jacket, a means not
of liberty and development, but of mere restriction and embar-
rassment."[96] So, what do federal judges use to make their decisions if not the Constitution? That is the point, is it not? The
courts must be populated with left-wing true believers who will
impose their opinions on the rest of society by judicial fiat. Wilson wrote: "What we should ask of our judges is that they prove
themselves such men as can discriminate between the opinion
of the moment and the opinion of the age, between the opinion
which springs, a legitimate essence, from the enlightened judg-
ment of men of thought and good conscience, and the opinion of
desire, self-interest, of impulse and impatience."[97]

Hence, Wilson argued for a judicial oligarchy that would reen-
gineer the culture along the lines of Marxist orthodoxy, and judges
must impose such a society on the people from the top down.
"The character of the process of constitutional adaption," wrote
Wilson, "depends first of all upon the wise and unwise choice of
statesmen, but ultimately and chiefly upon the opinion and purpose of the courts. The chief instrumentality by which the law of
the Constitution has been extended to cover the facts of national
development has of course been judicial interpretation—the
decisions of the courts. The process of formal amendment of the
Constitution was made so difficult by the provisions of the Constitution itself that it has seldom been feasible to use it; and the
difficulty of formal amendment has undoubtedly made the courts
more liberal, not to say more lax, in their interpretation than they
would otherwise have been. The whole business of adaption has
been theirs, and they have undertaken it with open minds, sometimes even with boldness and a touch of audacity. . . ."[98]

Biden has used the Court's decisions in *Dobbs*, which upholds
federalism in matters related to abortion; *Students for Fair Admissions Inc. v. Fellows of Harvard College*, which struck down

Harvard's racist, anti-Asian admissions program; and *Biden v. Nebraska*, which struck down Biden's blatantly political usurpation of Congress's legislative powers when he unilaterally authorized approximately $1 trillion in student loan forgiveness, to insult, demean, and trash the Court as "not normal," "unraveling basic rights," "out of sorts with the basic value system of the American People," and more.

Indeed, no president has done more to distort the Supreme Court's decisions, undermine its credibility, and politicize the judiciary since Franklin Roosevelt, whose legacy Biden stalks.

The Democrats and American Marxists must be the masters of the Supreme Court, just as tyrannical regimes around the world must control their judiciaries if they are to rule over the people through a unified, centralized regime. Until that day comes, they will continue their blitz against the institution and those jurists who uphold their sworn oath to the Constitution.

THE ELECTORAL COLLEGE

Earlier in this chapter, I noted that University of Pennsylvania law professor Kermit Roosevelt III complained, in part, that the Electoral College "allows a candidate to win the presidency while receiving a minority of the popular vote. The rule that each state is equally represented in the Senate means that Senators representing a minority of the population can control their chamber. A minority can take over the House . . . through partisan gerrymanders. And a president elected by a minority of the people can nominate judges who are then confirmed by Senators representing a minority of the people. . . . We are witnessing a minority [Republican] takeover of our democracy."[99] Wilfred Codrington III, assistant professor of law at Brooklyn Law School and a fellow at the left-wing Brennan Center for Justice, has written erroneously that the Electoral College has "racist origins." "More than two centuries after it was designed to empower southern white voters, the system continues to do just that."[100] Thus, the Electoral College supposedly helps Republicans and was and is racist.

I must, again, unravel the propaganda and historical malpractice. Professor Allen Guelzo, American historian and research scholar at Princeton University, and James H. Hulme, former head of ArentFox Schiff's litigation department, wrote "In Defense of the Electoral College" that slavery had nothing to do with the Electoral College. "Some historians have branded the Electoral College this way because each state's electoral votes are based on that 'whole Number of Senators and Representatives' from each State, and in 1787 the number of those representatives was calculated on the basis of the infamous three-fifths clause. But the Electoral College merely reflected the numbers, not any bias about slavery (and in any case, the three-fifths clause was not quite a proslavery compromise as it seems, since Southern slaveholders wanted their slaves counted as five-fifths for determining representation in Congress, and had to settle for a whittled-down fraction). As much as the abolitionists before the Civil War liked to talk about the 'proslavery Constitution,' this was more of a rhetorical posture than a serious historical argument. And the simple fact remains, from the record of the Constitutional Convention's proceedings (James Madison's famous Notes), that the discussions of the Electoral College and the method of electing a president never occur in the context of any of the convention's two climactic debates over slavery. If anything, it was the Electoral College that made it possible to end slavery, since Abraham Lincoln earned only 39 percent of the popular vote in the election of 1860, but won a crushing victory in the Electoral College. This, in large measure, was why Southern slaveholders stampeded to secession in 1860–61. They could do the numbers as well as anyone, and realized that the Electoral College would only produce more anti-slavery Northern presidents."[101]

Guelzo and Hulme explain that "[t]he Electoral College was an integral part of that federal plan. It made a place for the states as well as the people in electing the president by giving them a say at different points in a federal process and preventing big-city populations from dominating the election of a president. Abolishing the Electoral College now might satisfy an irritated yearning for direct democracy, but it would also mean dismantling federalism. After that, there would be no sense in having a Senate (which, after all, represents the interests of the states), and further along, no sense even in having states, except as administrative departments of the central government. Those who wish to abolish the Electoral College ought to go the distance, and do away with the entire federal system and perhaps even retire the Constitution, since the federalism it was designed to embody would have disappeared."[102]

Of course, the Democrat Party wants the big cities and most populous states to rule over the entire country, since these are Democrat Party strongholds. And, if they could, they would happily abolish the states. Presidential candidates would not have to campaign in vast parts of the country, only in the dense areas mostly along the two coasts and certain Midwest metropolitan areas. Thus, representation would effectively be denied to tens of millions of people who live in the exurbs and beyond, including rural areas. The states that produce most of the food we eat and energy we consume would have little or no say in the nation's governance or the federal government's rule over them, which would be disastrous civilly, politically, and economically. Indeed, the Electoral College has been very successful in balancing power among and between diverse states and regions, and has maintained a high level of tranquility and cooperation, especially post–Civil War. As I continue to say, the Democrat Party is constantly looking for ways to empower itself regardless of the cost to the rest of America and individual citizens. As in autocratic regimes, the party comes first. Hillary Clinton, Bernie Sanders, and Elizabeth Warren, among several other top Democrats, have called for abolishing the Electoral College because it would obliterate the constitutional construct and ensure one-party (Democrat Party) rule far into the future.

In fact, so committed to one-party autocratic rule is the Democrat Party that Democrat states and the Democrat Party are looking for ways around the Electoral College without going through the constitutional amendment process. They have come up with a devious scheme—the National Popular Vote (NPV). The Heritage Foundation's Hans A. von Spakovsky explains that "the NPV scheme proposes an interstate compact in which participating states agree in advance to automatically allocate their electoral votes to the winner of the national popular vote, disregarding the popular vote results in their states or what the relevant legislatures might then desire. The NPV would put the fate of every presidential election in the hands of the voters in as few as 11 states and thus . . . give a handful of populous states a controlling majority of the Electoral College, undermining the protections that the Electoral College affords to smaller states. This agreement would go into effect only after 'states cumulatively possessing a majority of the electoral votes' needed to win an election (270 votes) join the purported compact. Because it is far easier politically to get a smaller number of states with the required electoral votes to join the compact than it is to get two-thirds of Congress and three-fourths of the states to pass an amendment, the compact is an expedient way for proponents of the NPV to circumvent the Electoral College without formally amending the Constitution."[103]

The Democrat Party is getting close to its goal. Spakovsky warns that "15 states (California, Colorado, Connecticut, Delaware, Hawaii, Illinois, Massachusetts, Maryland, New Jersey, New Mexico, New York, Oregon, Rhode Island, Vermont, and Washington) and the District of Columbia, representing a combined 196 electoral votes, have approved the proposed scheme. The NPV is therefore 73 percent of the way to its goal of 270 votes—and to the activation of this unconstitutional, politically disastrous, and dangerous cartel."[104]

Yet there are other parts of the Constitution that are not "majoritarian," which the Democrats claim is their motivation. For example, Spakovsky notes:

- Every state having two Senators, regardless of its size or population;

- A President's ability to veto legislation passed by a majority of the people's popularly elected representatives;

- The lifetime appointment of federal judges, whose power is inherently undemocratic since they are not answerable to voters for their actions;

- The unequal representation in the U.S. House of Representatives due to widely varying populations in congressional districts between different states, such as Delaware, whose single congressional district has a population of over 900,000, while Wyoming's single congressional district has a population of fewer than 600,000;

- The unequal apportionment among the states of House districts caused by the inclusion of large numbers of ineligible voters—non-citizens—in the population used to determine how many representatives each state is entitled to, which gives a state such as California, with a very large population of illegal aliens, more representatives than it would receive if apportionment were based on total citizen population.[105]

Of course, the NPV is nothing more than another unconstitutional plot to empower the Democrat Party, despite the party's propaganda campaign to portray itself as pro-democracy. In fact, when it comes to the popular vote, the Democrat Party has another scheme to upend the entire voting system in the country—including in every state—in its quest for permanent, one-party rule.

The Democrat Party, which was responsible for Jim Crow laws, including poll taxes, literacy tests, and other intimidation tactics against black voters, now seeks to incorporate fraud into the voting system and flood it in order to overwhelm the system. And any opposition to this supposed "democracy" plan is attacked by the Democrats as "Jim Crow 2.0" and promoting voter suppression, especially against black voters. The Democrat Party scheme is dressed up as a civil rights effort on behalf of the downtrodden and a way to establish a true democracy. Of course, these are more lies and distortions to justify their corrupt ends.

At the Democratic National Committee (DNC) website, Democrats.org, they use cunning propaganda to claim that their power grab is some kind of democracy projected: "Democrats are committed to the sacred principle of 'one person, one vote'—and we will fight to achieve that principle for every citizen, regardless of race, income, disability status, geography, or English language proficiency. We stand united against the determined Republican campaign to disenfranchise voters through onerous voter ID laws, unconstitutional and excessive purges of the voter rolls, and closures of polling places in low-income neighborhoods, on college campuses, and in communities of color. Americans should never have to wait in hours-long lines to exercise their voting rights. Democrats will strengthen our democracy by guaranteeing that every American's vote is protected. We will make it a priority to pass legislation that restores and strengthens the Voting Rights Act, and ensure the Department of Justice challenges state laws that make it harder for Americans to vote. We will make voting easier and more accessible for all Americans by supporting automatic voter registration, same-day voter registration, early voting, and universal vote-from-home and vote-by-mail options."[106]

In truth, their disastrous scheme is diabolical and has nothing to do with promoting democracy, racial equality, or good government. The Heritage Foundation examined the Democrat Party's bill, HR 1, an eight-hundred-page monstrosity, which was the party's number one legislative priority in 2021. If passed into law, it would have rigged the popular voting system and ensured Democrat Party control of the federal government in perpetuity. Heritage found that "H.R. 1 would federalize and micromanage the election process administered by the states, imposing unnecessary, unwise, and unconstitutional mandates on the states and reversing the decentralization of the American election process— which is essential to the protection of our liberty and freedom. It would implement nationwide the worst changes in election rules that occurred during the 2020 election and go even further in eroding and eliminating basic security protocols that states have in place. The bill would interfere with the ability of states and their citizens to determine the qualifications and eligibility of voters, to ensure the accuracy of voter registration rolls, to secure the fairness and integrity of elections, to participate and speak freely in the political process, and to determine the district boundary lines for electing their representatives."[107]

Here are the eight worst provisions identified by Heritage:

1. It would eviscerate state voter ID laws that require a voter to authenticate his identity;

2. It would make absentee ballots even more insecure than they already are;

3. It would worsen the problem of inaccurate registration rolls, which are full of people who have died, moved away, are ineligible felons or noncitizens, or are registered more than once;

4. It would take away your ability to decide whether you want to register to vote;

5. It would force states to allow online registration, opening up the voter registration system to massive fraud by hackers and cybercriminals;

6. It imposes onerous new regulatory restrictions on political speech and activity, including online and policy-related speech, by candidates, citizens, civic groups, unions, corporations and nonprofit organizations;

7. It would authorize the IRS to investigate and consider the political and policy positions of nonprofit organizations when they apply for tax-exempt status; and

8. It would set up a public funding program for candidates running for Congress.[108]

Should the Democrat Party control all elected parts of the federal government, there is no question they will try to impose their voting scheme. No less than Vladimir Lenin would be proud of these Democrat Party efforts. His notion of "democratic centralism" is seen throughout the Democrat Party's actions and designs at centralizing government and, thus, controlling the people. It is worth repeating what Raymond Aron said about such an agenda: "In theory, the party is democratic, but the meaning of democratic centralism is to give back the essentials of power to the party's leaders. The leadership can manipulate elections, ensure the designation of the elections by the elected. . . ."[109] What the Democrat Party is doing is aligned with Marxist-Leninist ideology, not America's founding. It promotes one-party rule, not democracy. And it guts the Constitution's protections of the individual, the states (federalism), separation of powers, and limited government.

THE DEBT CEILING

The federal debt may seem like an obscure and boring topic, but it determines whether Americans will continue to enjoy economic prosperity, especially for our children and grandchildren, and generations yet born. Indeed, in May 2023, the Government Accountability Office (GAO) released a report titled "The Nation's Fiscal Health," which received virtually no media attention. The report is a stark warning that the federal government is fiscally out of control. It begins with this statement: "The federal government faces an unsustainable long-term fiscal future. At the end of fiscal year 2022, debt held by the public was about 97 percent of gross domestic product (GDP). Projections from the Office of Management and Budget (OMB) and the Department of the Treasury, the Congressional Budget Office (CBO), and GAO all show that current fiscal policy is unsustainable over the long term. Debt held by the public is projected to grow at a faster pace than the size of the economy. Debt held by the public is projected to reach its historical high of 106 percent of GDP within 10 years and to continue to grow at an increasing pace. GAO projects that this ratio could reach more than twice the size of the economy by 2051, absent any changes in revenue and spending policies."[110] In other words, if reckless and unconscionable federal spending and borrowing are not curbed and reversed, the federal government will drag the entire country into an economic and national security disaster.

The GAO does not mince words, which is rare for a federal agency. It further warns that if there is not a significant and immediate course change, the well-being of the civil society will be at stake. The report finds that "[t]he fiscal year 2022 federal deficit was among the highest in American history. This occurred even though revenue growth has been strong and federal COVID-19 relief spending has declined from recent years. In addition, the cost of financing the debt increased from prior years because interest rates rose substantially in fiscal year 2022. Rising debt, relative to economic growth, could increase borrowing costs for both the federal government and private borrowers and could slow economic growth. CBO has stated that high and rising federal debt as a share of the economy increases the risk of a fiscal crisis. The underlying conditions driving the unsustainable fiscal outlook pose serious economic, security, and social challenges if not addressed."[111] The report is well worth reading.

It is clear that the last few years of unprecedented, peacetime profligate federal spending and borrowing—not just in 2020, the year of the COVID-19 pandemic, which was said to necessitate a onetime emergency spike in spending and borrowing, but the enormous spending and borrowing in the subsequent two years by the Biden administration and the Democrat Congress, with some notable Republican co-conspirators, including Senate Republican leader Mitch McConnell—is driving the nation to the brink. Yet despite the blaring sirens warning of economic catastrophe, Biden, the Democrat Party, and their surrogates insist that the Constitution *requires* that the debt ceiling be raised to pay for all the spending and borrowing they demand, without limitation, in lieu of reducing spending and borrowing (that is, reducing the budget). But the Constitution does not provide the Democrat Party relief from controlling its insatiable spending and borrowing addiction (or, for that matter, certain Republicans, who suffer from the same addiction). What, then, are they talking about? They point to Section 4 of the Fourteenth Amendment, which was ratified in 1868, after the Civil War. Here is what it says:

> *The validity of the public debt of the United States*, authorized by law, including debts incurred for payment of pensions and bounties *for services in suppressing insurrection or rebellion*, shall not be questioned. But neither the United States nor any State shall assume or pay any debt or obligation incurred in aid of insurrection or rebellion against the United States, or any claim for the loss or emancipation of any slave; but all such debts, obligations and claims shall be held illegal and void. [Italics are mine.][112]

First, nobody is challenging the *validity* of the public debt. The text makes clear that certain debt incurred during the Civil War was valid, and certain debt was not.

Second, the language is specific to Civil War–related debt—

"including debts incurred for payment of pensions and bounties for services in suppressing insurrection or rebellion." It was not and is not a general statement of authority conferring enormous power on the executive to unilaterally pay all debts amassed by the federal government.

Third, the language says nothing about fundamentally altering the way the federal government raises revenue and pays debt. This is a core power that is specifically granted to Congress and only Congress. Article I, Section 8 of the Constitution states, in relevant part:

> The Congress shall have Power To lay and collect Taxes, Duties, Imposts and Excises, to pay the Debts and provide for the common Defence and general Welfare of the United States; but all Duties, Imposts and Excises shall be uniform throughout the United States; To borrow Money on the credit of the United States; . . .[113]

Fourth, there is absolutely no support in the legislative history for the proposition that Section 4 of the Fourteenth Amendment was intended to repeal or replace any part of Article I, Section 8.

Fifth, separation of powers is foundational within our constitutional system. To grant the executive the power of the purse (rather than Congress) means the president would have virtually complete control over the federal government's financial activities. For example, since he alone would have the authority or final say on spending, borrowing, and taxing, he need not seek congressional input on budgets or budget-related bills. He could just spend, borrow, and tax with impunity. Thus, in key ways, America's constitutional system would change from a representative republic to a dictatorship.

In the most recent debt ceiling battle, Biden said that he

believes he does have this power. In May 2023, he stated: "I'm looking at the Fourteenth Amendment as to whether or not we have the authority—I think we have the authority. The question is, could it be done and invoked in time that it would not be appealed, and as a consequence past the date in question and still default on the debt. That is a question that I think is unresolved."[114]

Biden's statement was shocking. But there was little consternation from his party, the media, or much of academia because they actually *agreed* with him. Of course, they would never quietly accept a Republican president claiming such power or, worse, urge him to use it. This is why the Democrat Party is simultaneously promoting ways to alter and rig the electoral process—and ensure its monopoly control of the presidency.

Apparently, Biden was influenced, at least in part, by retired Harvard Law professor Laurence Tribe, who wrote an op-ed in the *New York Times* days before Biden's pronouncement, urging Biden to trigger the Fourteenth Amendment.[115] This would be the same Laurence Tribe who argued *against* the constitutionality of such a presidential act in the *New York Times* in July 2011. The earlier Tribe argued, as do I, that "[t]he Constitution grants only Congress—not the president—the power 'to borrow money on the credit of the United States.' Nothing in the 14th Amendment or in any other constitutional provision suggests that the president may usurp legislative power to prevent a violation of the Constitution. . . . Worse, the argument that the president may do whatever is necessary to avoid default has no logical stopping point. In theory, Congress could pay debts not only by borrowing more money, but also by exercising its powers to impose taxes, to coin money or to sell federal property. If the president could usurp the congressional power to borrow, what would stop him from taking over all these other powers, as well?"[116]

Tribe added: "So the arguments for ignoring the debt ceiling are unpersuasive. But even if they were persuasive, they would not resolve the crisis. Once the debt ceiling is breached, a legal cloud would hang over any newly issued bonds, because of the risk that the government might refuse to honor those debts as legitimate. This risk, in turn, would result in a steep increase in interest rates because investors would lose confidence—a fiscal disaster that would cost the nation tens of billions of dollars."[117] Of course, the first Tribe was right, the present-day Tribe is not.

A conga line of Democrat Party members of Congress and the usual radical law professors have weighed in, almost exclusively for "interpreting" the Fourteenth Amendment to accommodate Biden's massive spending and borrowing binge. After all, as I previously explained, the Constitution is worthless parchment if it serves as a barrier to Democrat Party rule and the aims of the American Marxists. For example, Rep. Jamie Raskin, one of the most extreme members of the House, and who cloaks himself in the political garb of a former "constitutional law professor at American University," declared that Biden has a "clear constitutional command" to bypass Congress. "I think the main thing is that the president do everything in his power to try to dislodge the political stalemate. But if not, there is a pretty clear constitutional command there."[118] Of course, Raskin's idiocy was quoted approvingly everywhere by the Democrat Party's media.

Sen. Dick Durbin, Democrat chairman of the Judiciary Committee, chimed in: "I personally feel that we should test that and I think that the language is very explicit in that amendment."[119] Sen. Elizabeth Warren jumped in too: "If the alternative is that the Republicans are going to hurtle us over a cliff in which the American economy crashes, we're thrown into a recession and millions of people are put out of work and our good name around the world is destroyed, then not-great alternatives look like a better option than chaos."[120] Hence, for the Democrat Party and its minions, the catastrophe would be the failure *not* to destroy the Constitution and the economy with it. Their spending and borrowing know no limits, and they intend to keep it that way. They will not let the Constitution or a GAO report deter them.

Of course, the way out of these situations is political—that is, negotiation. Indeed, the Democrat Party has been very successful in getting most of what it wants in decades past. Even so, the American Marxist revolution is running hot, the "stars are aligned," and they have little patience for deliberation. The trajectory suggests it will become even more difficult in the years ahead to constitutionally resolve these disputes, or at least resolve them in a way that is both constitutional and economically rational.

As I conclude the tour through the Democrat Party's villainy (albeit truncated, as this is not a book solely on the Constitution), I reiterate the importance that language plays in all of this. Revisiting Friedrich Hayek and his book *The Road to Serfdom*, Hayek made the point that "[t]he most effective way of making people accept the validity of the values they are to serve is to persuade them that they are really the same as those which they, or at least the best among them, have always held, but which were not properly understand or recognized before. The people are made to transfer their allegiance from the old gods to the new under the pretense that the new gods really are what their sound instinct had always told them would be what before they had only dimly seen. And the most effective technique to this end is to use the old words but change their meaning. Few traits of totalitarian regimes are at the same time so confusing to the superficial observer and yet so characteristic of the whole intellectual climate as the complete perversion of language, the change of meaning of the words by which the ideals of the regimes are expressed. The worst sufferer in this respect is, of course, the word 'liberty.' It is a word used as freely in totalitarian states as elsewhere."[121]

In fact, in his three-minute video announcing his decision to run for reelection, Biden said, in part, the "2024 election will be defined by 'whether we have more freedom or less. . . . Every generation of Americans has faced a moment when they've had to defend democracy, stand up for our personal freedoms, and stand up for our right to vote and our civil rights. This is ours. Let's finish the job.'"[122] Hence, despite his despotic record and American Marxist agenda, Biden plans to be the "freedom" candidate. Hayek was right.

CHAPTER EIGHT

STALIN WOULD BE PROUD

Lavrentiy Beria was Joseph Stalin's longest-serving chief of Soviet security. In 1937, he gave a speech in which he declared: "Let our enemies know that any attempts to raise a hand against the will of our people—against the will of the party of Lenin and Stalin— will be mercilessly crushed and destroyed."[1]

The Democrat Party's scorched earth, unscrupulous, and unconscionable political and criminal persecution of Donald Trump is totalitarian in every respect. Joseph Stalin and his henchman, Lavrentiy Beria, would be proud.

The Democrats and their media talked about impeaching President Trump long before he entered the Oval Office. And they are talking about it again. Obama attorney general Eric Holder told Jen Psaki, former Biden spokesman and now MSBNC host, that should Trump be convicted of any of the charges brought against him by no less than four Democrat prosecutors in three states and the District of Columbia, yet get elected to a second term, he should be impeached a third time and removed from office.[2]

Moreover, in the 2018 midterm elections, when the Democrat Party won the majority in the House, its intentions were made clear even before the new majority was sworn in. *Politico* reported in an article titled "House Democrats prepare fusillade of Trump investigations," that "[t]he threat of subpoenas, investigations and oversight hearings will dominate the new House Democratic majority's agenda, targeting the White House's most controversial policies and personnel, spanning immigration, the environment, trade and of course, the biggest question of all: Russian collusion."[3]

The Democrat Party proceeded to use House committees, staff, and untold millions of tax dollars to harass, obstruct, humiliate, and denigrate Trump administration officials, and undermine the executive branch at every turn.

But now Trump stands indicted by an elected Democrat district attorney in New York City, Alvin Bragg, in an utterly bogus and politically motivated case involving nondisclosure agreements/campaign issues. Another elected Democrat district attorney in Fulton County, Georgia (covering most of Atlanta), Fani Taifa Willis, has concocted a case against Trump involving the 2020 election. The elected Democrat attorney general of New York State, Letisha James, has brought a civil fraud lawsuit against Trump (and his children) involving his businesses for hundreds of millions of dollars. Bragg and James both campaigned on a platform of indicting Trump, which is utterly unethical and should have resulted in both losing their law licenses.

While he was president, Trump was subjected to a multiyear, multimillion-dollar federal investigation based on Democrat Party and media accusations, ginned up by unethical and even illegal activity by senior FBI, Department of Justice (DOJ), and intelligence officials, that he and his 2016 campaign colluded with the Russian government to win his election. A so-called Russian dossier, which was funded by the Hillary Clinton campaign and was a complete fiction, served as the launching-off point for the Democrat Party, media, and FBI allegations against Trump. The former FBI director James Comey, despite knowing that the dossier was false, used it to threaten Trump when he was president-elect and in the earliest days of his administration. The Washington, D.C., mob grew louder and louder, demanding the appointment of a special counsel to investigate a Hillary Clinton–Democrat Party–FBI–concocted fictional scandal against Trump. Then attorney general Jeff Sessions recused himself from the matter, for reasons that remain incomprehensible. The deputy attorney general, Rod Rosenstein, buckled to the Democrat Party pressure and appointed Robert Mueller as special counsel to investigate the matter. He did so despite the fact there was no predicate to justify such an appointment under DOJ regulations.

At the end of the investigation, as explained in a letter to Congress by the subsequent attorney general, Bill Barr—now a disgruntled former Trump appointee who appears regularly in the media, disparaging Trump—stated: "The [Mueller] Report explains that the Special Counsel and his staff thoroughly investigated allegations that members of the presidential campaign of Donald J. Trump, and others associated with it, conspired with the Russian government in its efforts to interfere in the 2016 U.S. presidential election, or sought to obstruct the related federal investigations. In the report, the Special Counsel noted that, in completing his investigation, he employed 19 lawyers who were assisted by a team of approximately 40 FBI agents, intelligence analysts, forensic accountants, and other professional staff. The Special Counsel issued more than 2,800 subpoenas, executed nearly 500 search warrants, obtained more than 230 orders for communication records, issued almost 50 orders authorizing use of pen registers, made 13 requests to foreign governments for evidence, and interviewed approximately 500 witnesses."[4] Mueller concluded that there was no collusion between the Russians and

Trump or his campaign. Considering that members of his prosecutorial team despised Trump and there were constant leaks coming from the investigation, that was quite a remarkable but just outcome.

More recently, after his own four-year investigation, Special Counsel John Durham, a longtime career federal prosecutor with no political affiliation and who had been appointed by Barr to get to the bottom of how the Russia collusion/Trump investigation got started, concluded that there were myriad acts of misconduct by FBI and DOJ senior officials who were plotting and scheming to take down Trump. Among other things, as reported by Fox News, Durham determined that "[t]he FBI and Justice Department jumped to investigate former President Trump's campaign despite a lack of sound evidence, a 'notable departure' from the way it resisted efforts to investigate claims against Hillary Clinton's campaign. . . . Durham's report said the FBI briefed Clinton staffers on information of possible threats aimed at the Clinton campaign but ignored intelligence it received from 'a trusted foreign source pointing to a Clinton campaign plan to vilify Trump by tying him to Vladimir Putin so as to divert attention from her own concerns relating to her use of a private email server.'"[5] "'The speed and manner in which the FBI opened and investigated Crossfire Hurricane during the presidential election season based on raw, unanalyzed, and uncorroborated intelligence also reflected a noticeable departure from how it approached prior matters involving possible attempted foreign election interference plans aimed at the Clinton campaign,' the report said."[6]

Durham further reported, as Breitbart noted, that "[t]hen-President Barack Obama and then-Vice President Joe Biden were personally briefed by then-CIA Director John Brennan in 2016 that the CIA had evidence of Hillary Clinton planning to falsely link then-presidential candidate Donald Trump to Russia. . . ."[7]

Thus, both Obama and Biden, as well as Attorney General Loretta Lynch, CIA director John Brennan, FBI director James Comey, and, of course, Hillary Clinton knew that the entire Russia collusion matter, and the federal investigation undertaken by the FBI and DOJ, was based on a horrendous lie and dirty trick unleashed by Hillary Clinton and the Democrat Party. In other words, the entire hierarchy of the Obama administration, including the president and vice president, knew what was going down, and knew it was, in effect, a coup. And *New York Times* and *Washington Post* reporters received Pulitzer Prizes for helping perpetuate this extensive fraud on the nation.[8]

As we know now, the conspiracy to set up Trump began well before he was sworn in as president. But we did not know it back then, until it was first reported on March 2, 2017—by me on my radio show and subsequently on Fox.

As I was assembling news articles and wire stories over a several month period, it became apparent that Trump and his campaign had been and were being spied on by federal law enforcement. The Democrat Party media were receiving these leaks and regurgitating the information to the public. Having served as Chief of Staff to Attorney General Edwin Meese, I could see that the nature of the leaked stories had DOJ/FBI fingerprints all over them. They involved information about FISA applications, FISA Court warrants, investigative targets, etc. The *New York Times* even led with one headline reporting that Trump Tower had been "wiretapped." This was shocking stuff.

Of course, the Democrat Party media that were running the leaked stories and colluding with the Obama administration knew I was on to them. So, in concert, they immediately unleashed a barrage of stories claiming I was a conspiracy theorist even thought I had simply used their own reports and pulled them together.

Durham uncovered that Clinton campaign lawyers had paid a tech company to infiltrate servers belonging to Trump Tower, hoping to link Trump to Russia. Moreover, top FBI officials and others were, in fact, feeding information to the Democrat Party media. Indeed, information leaked to the Democrat Party media by FBI officials would then be used by the FBI as a basis for conducting investigative activities.[9]

Meanwhile, when the Democrat Party took control of the House of Representatives, several committees were directed by the then speaker, Nancy Pelosi, to find any grounds for impeaching President Trump. Despite months of hearings, accompanied by baseless claims by the chairman of the Intelligence Committee, Rep. Adam Schiff, a proven serial liar and demagogue, and others, the supposed Russian collusion matter was not panning out. How could it? It was a fabrication from top to bottom. But then, a so-called whistleblower, allegedly "Eric Ciaramella, 33, a career CIA analyst," wrote Kerry Picket of the *Washington Examiner*, whose name was not to be uttered or printed in the Democrat Party media, and "[who] was Ukraine director on the National Security Council toward the end of the Obama administration and stayed there during the first few months of the Trump administration, [was] suspected of being the official who filed a complaint about a July 25 phone call between Trump and Ukrainian President Volodymyr Zelensky."[10]

The complaint alleged that Trump had linked future assistance to Ukraine to the Ukrainians looking into Joe and Hunter Biden's corrupt links to Burisma. Trump was so appalled by the false allegation that he took the unprecedented step of having the transcript of the phone call released to Congress and the public to prove his innocence. Moreover, Secretary of State Mike Pompeo, who was present during the phone call, insisted it was not as the Democrats and whistleblower claimed. Even Ukrainian president Zelensky stated he did not consider the phone call as some kind of quid pro quo. But the Democrats and their media were not to be deterred. They had been pushing impeachment even before Trump was elected president. And the House Democrats moved swiftly to impeach President Trump, without a single Republican vote, in December 2019, based on an utterly bogus pretext.

President Trump would be impeached by the House Democrats a second time, on January 13, 2020, only one week before leaving office. On January 11, 2021, the Democrats accused him of "incitement of insurrection" for the events of January 6, 2021. Two days later, without hearings or investigation, without the president being able to provide a defense of any kind, Pelosi and the House Democrats rammed through the second impeachment, with ten Republicans voting in favor. Never in the country's history has a president been impeached twice. Never has there been a Senate impeachment trial of a former president. Both impeachments broke with past practices and traditions in the impeachments of Andrew Johnson in 1868 and Bill Clinton in 1998. The "high crimes" needed to impeach a president were actually committed by the Democrat Party and its apparatchiks.

Of course, Trump has now been indicted by special counsel Jack Smith on thirty-seven counts, thirty-one of which relate to the Espionage Act of 1917. As explained earlier, the law was originally signed by Woodrow Wilson and was used to intimidate and silence any opposition to his entry into World War I. In 1918, the statute was amended to include sedition. In the end, more than two thousand individuals were imprisoned—including Eugene Debs, who ran for president several times on the Socialist Party ticket. In 1912, he received 6 percent of the vote against Wilson.

In July 1917, Debs was convicted of violating the Espionage Act for an antiwar speech he delivered, and sentenced to five years in federal prison. His case was appealed to the Supreme

Court (*Debs v. United States*), which upheld his conviction—thus, proving again, the judiciary's frequent cowardice in the face of Democrat Party tyranny, if not outright support of it.

Debs would wind up serving three years in prison. In 1920, Debs ran for president from prison and received 3.5 percent of the vote. Wilson refused to commute Debs's sentence, insisting he was a traitor.[9] But the incoming Republican president, Warren Harding, not only commuted his sentence but, as Erick Trickey writes in *Smithsonian* magazine: "In December 1921, Harding commuted Debs' sentence, set his release for Christmas Day, and invited Debs to the White House. 'I have heard so damned much about you, Mr. Debs, that I am now very glad to meet you personally,' Harding greeted him on Dec. 26. Leaving the meeting, Debs called Harding 'a kind gentleman' with 'humane impulses,' but declared that he'd told the president he would continue the fight for his 'principles, conviction, and ideals.'"[11]

A hundred years later, another Democrat president—Biden—and his DOJ dust off the Espionage Act and use it against another political opponent, Donald Trump, whom he, like Wilson, seeks to imprison. As I write this, Trump is not only a former president, but he is leading significantly in every poll of Republican primary candidates seeking the GOP nomination. In other words, Biden is employing federal law enforcement against his likely Republican presidential opponent. The DOJ has used every tool in the prosecutorial tool kit and then some against Trump, including circumventing attorney-client privilege, using an unconstitutional general warrant to search the former president's Florida home, sending an armed FBI SWAT team to seize documents, pressuring witnesses with threats of prosecution to provide the Biden administration with helpful testimony; and, unleashing dozens of illegal grand jury and investigation-related leaks to the Democrat Party media, thereby violating Trump's Fifth and Sixth Amendment due process rights.

The thirty-one counts related to the Espionage Act are what lawyers call "piling" multiple charges against the defendant, even though they spring from the same or similar alleged events. This way, prosecutors hope to secure a conviction on at least a few or even one of the counts. It is a sleazy practice. Moreover, if Trump is convicted of just one of the counts, he could serve five to twenty years in prison, which for a seventy-seven-year-old man would likely be a death sentence. And for what? An administrative or, at worse, a civil matter?

There is a reason the Espionage Act has never been used against any former president or vice president—it was never intended to be used against a former president or vice president. There are complex constitutional issues, questions about declassification, and in more recent times, a 1978 law called the Presidential Records Act (PRA). The PRA purposefully has no criminal penalties for claimed violations.

U.S. District Judge Amy Berman Jackson in Washington, D.C., a left-wing Obama-appointed judge, rejected a demand by Judicial Watch under the Freedom of Information Act that the National Archives be ordered to seize records, including classified information, from former president Bill Clinton, which he kept in a sock drawer. In March 2012, the judge ruled, in part: "Under the statutory scheme established by the PRA, the decision to segregate personal materials from Presidential records is made by the President, during the President's term and in his sole discretion." "Since the President is completely entrusted with the management and even the disposal of Presidential records during his time in office, it would be difficult for this Court to conclude that Congress intended that he would have less authority to do what he pleases with what he considers to be his personal records." [12] "The judge noted a president could destroy any record he wanted during his tenure and his only responsibility was to inform the Archives." [13]

This explains why the special counsel, in his forty-nine-page indictment does not mention the PRA even once. That is, the PRA and Espionage Act are incongruent. A former president cannot be accused of withholding documents, including classified documents, from the government and be charged with a criminal violation of the Espionage Act for retaining them while he has the broadest authority under the PRA to have removed whatever documents he wishes without recourse from even a federal court.

David B. Rivkin Jr. and Lee A. Casey are constitutional lawyers who served in the DOJ and White House Counsel's Office. In August 2022, writing in the *Wall Street Journal*, they explained that "[t]he PRA lays out detailed requirements for how the archivist is to administer the records, handle privilege claims, make the records public, and impose restrictions on access. Notably, it doesn't address the process by which a former president's records are physically to be turned over to the archivist, or set any deadline, leaving this matter to be negotiated between the archivist and the former president. The PRA explicitly guarantees a former president continuing access to his papers. Those papers must ultimately be made public, but in the meantime—unlike with all other government documents, which are available 24/7 to currently serving executive-branch officials—the PRA establishes restrictions on access to a former president's records, including a five-year restriction on access applicable to everyone (including the sitting president, absent a showing of need), which can be extended until the records have been properly reviewed and processed. Before leaving office, a president can restrict access to certain materials for up to 12 years."[14]

Why does this matter? As Rivkin and Casey point out: "Nothing in the PRA suggests that the former president's physical custody of his records can be considered unlawful under the statutes on which the Mar-a-Lago warrant is based. . . . In making a former president's records available to him, the PRA doesn't distinguish between materials that are and aren't classified. That was a deliberate choice by Congress, as the existence of highly classified materials at the White House was a given long before 1978, and the statute specifically contemplates that classified materials will be present—making this a basis on which a president can impose a 12-year moratorium on public access."[15] This legal analysis is consistent with Judge Jackson's decision.

Hence, they conclude, Trump had every legal right to remove documents to his homes, *including classified information*. And the PRA gave him that authority.

The Biden DOJ under Attorney General Merrick Garland, FBI director Christopher Wray, and Special Counsel Jack Smith all know that the PRA trumps the Espionage Act in this matter. But even if they believe it is a close question, you do *not* indict a former president who is also the Democrat president's currently leading contender for the White House to test a theory or push the edge of the legal envelope. And you do not bring charges with the hope of imprisoning a former president and opposition presidential candidate who is seventy-seven years old *for the rest of his life!* Moreover, to be crystal clear: the special counsel reports to the attorney general. The attorney general, Merrick Garland, made the final decision to indict President Trump. In fact, he has made every major decision involving the investigations of and charges against Trump. And Garland reports directly to Biden and knows very well what he is doing and that he is interfering in a presidential election on behalf of Biden and himself.

Professor Alan Dershowitz, writing in *Newsweek*, in a column titled "The Most Dangerous Indictment in History," makes the point that "[t]his is a momentous occasion, and not only for President Trump. This moment portends a massive change in the norms of this nation that all Americans who care about the neutral rule of law should pay close attention to, for it raises the specter of the partisan weaponization of the criminal justice system."[16] He later explains that "the Espionage Act has been condemned by liberals, progressives, and Democrats since it became the open-ended weapon of choice aimed at political dissidents such as Eugene V. Debs and other antiwar icons. It is vague and capable of being stretched to cover political enemies. So are the other two charges that have been referenced: conspiracy to obstruct justice and lying to law enforcement officials."[17]

Of course, Dershowitz is right on both counts. Nonetheless, congressional Democrats have been celebrating the indictments, claiming Trump finally got what he deserved, or that he is not above the law, etc. Again, radical leftist House Democrat Jamie Raskin, who sought to stop the electoral vote count on the House floor when Trump won in 2016, served on both impeachment panels prosecuting Trump in the Senate, and sat on the January 6 committee that targeted Trump, had the nerve to tell Republicans: "Instead of trying to divide the country and undercut our legal system, Congressional Republicans should respect the outcome of the Special Counsel's comprehensive investigation and the decisions of the citizens serving on the grand jury." He warned that attacking federal prosecutors "not only undermines the Department of Justice but betrays the essential principle of justice that no one is above the commands of law, not even a former President or a self-proclaimed billionaire."[18]

The *Wall Street Journal* editorial page, not a friend of Trump's, observed: "In the court of public opinion, the first question will be about two standards of justice. Mr. Biden had old classified files stored in his Delaware garage next to his sports car. When that news came out, he didn't sound too apologetic. 'My Corvette's in a locked garage, OK? So it's not like they're sitting out on the street,' Mr. Biden said. AG Garland appointed another special counsel, Robert Hur, to investigate, but Justice isn't going to indict Mr. Biden. As for willful, how about the basement email server that Hillary Clinton used as secretary of state? FBI director James Comey said in 2016 that she and her colleagues 'were extremely careless in their handling of very sensitive, highly classified information.' According to him, 113 emails included information that was classified when it was sent or received. Eight were Top Secret. About 2,000 others were later 'upclassified' to Confidential. This was the statement Mr. Comey ended by declaring Mrs. Clinton free and clear, since 'no reasonable prosecutor would bring such a case.' . . . This is the inescapable political context of . . . the indictment. The special counsel could have finished his investigation with a report detailing the extent of Mr. Trump's recklessness and explained what secrets it could have exposed. Instead, the Justice Department has taken a perilous path."[19]

Actually, it is much worse.

The Biden family has received tens of millions of dollars from foreign governments and state-run businesses, most notably the Communist Chinese regime. They set up phony businesses, shell corporations, and other subterfuges to conceal the transactions. Hunter Biden's laptop contains emails that draw Joe Biden directly into the mix, despite Biden repeatedly insisting he has never discussed these business activities with his son.

Tony Bobulinski, a former business partner of Hunter Biden, has said publicly and on the record, including to the FBI, that the former vice president "was a willing and eager participant in a family scheme to make millions of dollars by partnering with a shady Chinese Communist firm."[20] "I've seen Vice President Biden saying he never talked to Hunter about business. I've seen firsthand that that's not true, because it wasn't just Hunter's business, they said they were putting the Biden family name and its legacy on the line," Bobulinski stated.[21] This is a damning eye-witness account.

Of course, the Hunter laptop revealed an email to "Hunter, Jim [Biden] and other partners on May 13, 2017, . . . an equity breakdown [in a multimillion-dollar deal with Chinese energy conglomerate CEFC] in which 10% of the lucrative CEFC joint venture would be held by Hunter 'for the big guy.'"[22] This explains why the Democrat Party media feared what contents on the laptop might reveal, so they squelched it during the 2020 election. It also explains why the Biden campaign organized the effort to dismiss the laptop as Russian disinformation, enlisting 51 former spies to write their disinformation letter and the Democrat Party media to repeatedly and aggressively hawk it.[23]

And there is more.

The Biden FBI refused to provide the House Oversight Committee with a June 30, 2020, FBI FD-1023 form alleging a criminal bribery scheme between then Vice President Biden, Hunter, and a Burisma executive reportedly involving multimillions of dollars. This document was first brought to the committee's attention by an FBI whistleblower. But for threatening FBI Director Wray with contempt of Congress, the committee would not have had access to the form.[24]

Moreover, the Biden Treasury Department also refuses to provide the House Oversight Committee with 150 suspicious financial transaction reports from Hunter and James Biden, including large sums of money, forcing the committee to gather the information directly from the banks.[25]

No doubt there is much more to come, but the point here is that despite the Biden administration's efforts to obstruct various congressional oversight committees, the level and quality of information raising serious questions of criminality and national security threats by Joe Biden and his family far exceeds the "conflict of interest" or "appearance of a conflict of interest" standards by which an attorney general is expected to appoint a special counsel. The fact that Garland continues to represent Biden as his personal counsel, while unleashing holy hell on Donald Trump, is corruption of a kind we have never experienced in this country.

Indeed, prosecutor Jack Smith continues to run roughshod over a second grand jury in Washington, D.C., where, as of this writing, he is plotting to piece together another set of charges against Trump, this time involving January 6—again, with the support and encouragement of the Democrat Party. And, of course, as if on cue, there are radical, Democrat Party–aligned organizations behind a "Trump Is Disqualified" campaign pressuring secretaries of state to disqualify Trump from holding office, citing Section 3 of the Fourteenth Amendment and accusing Trump of engaging in or supporting an insurrection on January 6, 2021.[26]

And while they are at it, why not go after Trump's lawyers to punish them with ethics complaints and make it increasingly difficult for Trump to hire top attorneys as the Democrat Party piles up criminal charges against him? Indeed, as reported by The American Spectator's David Catron, a dark money group is doing exactly that: "According to Influence Watch, the group was founded by former Clinton administration official Melissa Moss and its managing director, former Perkins Coie attorney Michael Teter. It gets worse: 'The 65 Project's Senior Advisor is David Brock, the founder of Media Matters for America and American Bridge 21st Century.' The group initially went after 111 attorneys in 26 states for representing Trump or questioning the irregularities associated with the 2020 election. They included Sen. Ted Cruz, former New York City mayor Rudolph Giuliani, and Harvard Law Professor Emeritus Alan Dershowitz."[27]

The Democrat Party does not care about what it is doing to our country, the system of justice, and our electoral process. It is the state party, seeking to monopolize our politics, society, and culture. This is a revolution. The party comes first. The Democrat Party long ago abandoned comity and civility for character assassination and the iron fist, a fact that establishment Republicans have difficulty grasping. It has joined a long list of political parties around the world, past and present, that are totalitarian in nature and do not tolerate democracy (republicanism in America), fair elections, and equal justice before the law.

EPILOGUE

In May 2023, in his concurring opinion in *Arizona v. Mayorkas*, Supreme Court associate justice Neil Gorsuch, issued an unprecedented statement to his fellow Americans. Nothing in his opinion is unknown or new ground, but it is profound in its concise Paul Revere–like warning—not that the British are coming, but that tyranny is here and while all is not lost, we are closer to losing our country than many may think. For me, here are the most salient parts:

> Since March 2020, we may have experienced the greatest intrusion on civil liberties in the peacetime history of this country. Executive officials across the country issued emergency decrees on a breathtaking scale. Governors and local leaders imposed lockdown orders forcing people to remain in their homes. They shuttered businesses and schools, public and private. They closed churches even as they allowed casinos and other favored businesses to carry on.

They threatened violators not just with civil penalties but with criminal sanctions too. They surveilled church parking lots, recorded license plates, and issued notices warning that attendance at even outdoor services satisfying all state social-distancing and hygiene requirements could amount to criminal conduct. . . .[1]

Federal executive officials entered the act too. . . . They deployed a public-health agency to regulate landlord-tenant relations nationwide. They used a workplace-safety agency to issue a vaccination mandate for most working Americans. They threatened to fire noncompliant employees, and warned that service members who refused to vaccinate might face dishonorable discharge and confinement. Along the way, it seems federal officials may have pressured social-media companies to censor information about pandemic policies with which they disagreed.[2]

The concentration of power in the hands of so few may be efficient and sometimes popular. But it does not tend toward sound government. However wise one person or his advisors may be, that is no substitute for the wisdom of the whole of the American people that can be tapped in the legislative process. Decisions made by a few often yield unintended consequences that may be avoided when more are consulted. Autocracies have always suffered these defects.[3]

Left unsaid, of course, is that the vast majority of those who acted in the manner described by Justice Gorsuch were overwhelmingly Democrat officials. From New York to California, Illinois to Michigan, and everywhere in between, the bluest states ceased being free and open societies. They were as close to police states as we have seen or experienced, certainly in recent times. Democrat Party officials in particular demonstrated a lust and frenzy for seizing and exercising power, and issuing fiats, that previously seemed unimaginable. Many Americans lost their lives who need not have, and died without family and friends around them.

And at the federal level, the keys to the government were effectively handed to longtime medical and health bureaucrats, who rejected most information that did not comport with their narrative or came from sources outside their circle of sycophants— although they were welcoming of self-serving and politicized advice from the likes of the teachers' unions.

Although memories tend to be short, let us hope they are not so short as to forget what was done to the country. It is one thing when politicians seek the input of experts as part of a decision-making process, particularly when the issues are atypical or require a certain degree of specialty, as the COVID-19 virus surely did. But that is *not* what broadly happened.

Moreover, the level of corporate and social media participation in censoring and dismissing competing medical and scientific opinions, and demeaning the highly regarded professionals who attempted to voice them, as well as lockstep acceptance of the integrity and soundness of virtually every edict issued by the few self-appointed medical masterminds at the top of the D.C. bureaucratic ladder, underscores the extent to which America lacks a free press. It is proselytizing for the Democrat Party, and the party's agenda, makes its supposed independence from Democrat-run administrations and the administrative state impossible and preposterous. For this, the country pays an enormous price in liberty and a functioning constitutional republic.

Unlike the Republican Party, the Democrat Party is more than a political party. It is the state party. It seeks to monopolize the political system, the culture, government, and society.

And while the Republican Party exists to try to win elections, the Democrat Party plays for keeps—that is, election defeats can never be allowed to interfere with the ideological trajectory the party imposes on the nation. And when the Democrat Party wins elections, it continues building upon the permanent parts of the government infrastructure it firmly controls. Thus, the Democrat Party single-handedly builds permanent centers of power, including in the vast federal bureaucracy, subsidized nongovernment organizations, lifetime activist judges, tenured professors and teachers, party members in the media, etc. The Democrat Party uses the culture and politics to empower itself and its agenda. And Democrats have no intention of surrendering control of either. Consequently, when the Democrat Party wins elections, it claims broad mandates; when it loses elections, it ignores the popular will of the people and turns to the permanent government and its cultural surrogates to sabotage the Republicans and push forward their American Marxist agenda. Consequently, over time, it becomes increasingly difficult to reverse the Democrat Party's political and cultural damage.

Conversely, the Republican establishment is mostly flat-footed. Of course, the Republican Party does not exist to "fundamentally transform" America. However, when it refuses to acknowledge or take effective, affirmative, and proactive steps to counter the Democrat Party's agenda and the forces of American Marxism—and in too many cases acquiesces and contributes to them—the Republican Party fails in its most important mission: to defend the American people from a Democrat Party that literally hates the country and is destroying it from within. Moreover, unlike the Democrat Party, the Republican establishment would rather betray its own base (conservatives) and try to marginalize it than battle the Democrat Party, preferring to make appeals to the Democrat Party media and demonstrate their "bipartisan" common sense, in pursuit of temporary political power and positive media coverage. Senate Republican leader Mitch McConnell, and the likes of Mitt Romney, Susan Collins, Lisa Murkowski, Chris Sununu, Asa Hutchinson, and Chris Christie are but a few contemporary examples of this defeatist mindset. It is also one reason why they and Republicans like them constantly target Donald Trump, Ron DeSantis, Ted Cruz, Mike Lee, and others who understand the nature of the threat and are willing to confront it.

It takes uncommon fortitude, principles, and foresight to recognize and engage the Democrat Party, its surrogates, and the American Marxist movements. In addition to literally putting your career and freedom on the line, you must deal with a rearguard action from quislings within the Republican Party. Even so, I do not believe it can be said that the Republican Party as an institution hates America or exists to, again, "fundamentally transform America." It is not the home of the various Marxist movements that plot daily, and in a thousand ways, against America. Furthermore, the Democrat Party seeks to effectively sideline the Republican Party with repeated efforts to cartelize control over the electoral process, which it is close to achieving, already having near monopoly control over the culture.

So, what is the answer? Publishers like authors to end their books with proposals for addressing or fixing the problems they raise. If you look at virtually all my prior books, I do that. And the list of proposals I suggest, as I look back on them, were very important—and, I believe, remain important. However, in the end, as I spent more than a year researching and writing this book, it became obvious to me that the Democrat Party is a treacherous political organization dating back to its founding; that its obsession is with self-empowerment and societal control; that it has never embraced Americanism; and, it is the entity through which, and in coordination with, American Marxism (self-described "progressivism" and "democratic socialism") intends to impose its top-down revolution. In every way, this reality must be communicated to as many people as possible. In other words, the first step is to identify the autocratic danger the Democrat Party represents, without candy-coating and hesitation. It is my deepest hope that this book, like a Thomas Paine pamphlet to the early colonists, will help alert our fellow citizens to the existential threat and rally them peacefully to the cause before darkness descends on the republic.

Moreover, every legal, legitimate, and appropriate tool and method must be employed in the short and long run to shatter the Democrat Party and its anti-American "fundamental transformation" agenda. The Democrat Party must be resoundingly conquered in the next election or it will become extremely difficult to undo the damage it is unleashing at breakneck pace. This must be followed quickly by launching and instituting measures to deny the Democrat Party the kind of power and control it presently wields against society. For example, this includes corralling and dismembering the Democrat Party's administrative state. Some of the same strategies and tactics employed by the Democrat Party against the Republican Party, the culture, and its targeted opponents, must be employed. The Democrat Party must be effectively neutered or its anti-American agenda will become permanent societal fixtures.

I do not possess the wisdom or assume the arrogance to provide a comprehensive "to-do" list, to be used in all circumstances and on all occasions. But there are tens of millions of us who love our country, our families, and our freedom, and who, in every corner of the country and every walk of life, can and must find ways to promote liberty and defeat tyranny. And that includes—indeed, it requires—the disempowering and dismantling of the Democrat Party.

The Democrat Party stands for the relentless pursuit of power and control. America was founded on the principle of individual and human liberty and the dispersion of political and governmental power. The Roman Republic lasted 482 years. Our republic is only 247 years old. If the Democrat Party succeeds, the American experiment will have failed.

In loving memory
of Marty

ACKNOWLEDGMENTS

I wish to acknowledge and thank the four remarkable ladies who provided me with wise and superlative counsel throughout this project: Threshold Editions' Jennifer Long, Natasha Simons, and Mia Robertson, and my wonderful wife, Julie.

NOTES

CHAPTER ONE: THE DEMOCRAT PARTY & AUTHORITARIANISM

1 The Biden Administration Is Banning Low-Cost Appliances—and Bragging about It— Foundation for Economic Education (fee.org).

2 Victor Davis Hanson, "Obama: Transforming America," *National Review* (May 14, 2008), https://www.nationalreview.com/2013/10/obama-transforming-america-victor-davis-hanson/ (May 16, 2023).

3 Remarks by President Biden in Address to the Canadian Parliament (March 24, 2023), https://www.whitehouse.gov/briefing-room/speeches-remarks/2023/03/24/remarks-by-president-biden-in-address-to-the-canadian-parliament/ (May 16, 2023).

4 Paul Blumenthal, "Joe Biden Wants An 'FDR-Size Presidency.' What Does That Even Mean?" *HuffPost* (Apr. 28, 2021), https://www.huffpost.com/entry/joe-biden-fdr-100-days_n_60883ecae4b05af50dbc0ef2.

5 www.dementia.org/stages-of-dementia.

6 https://time.com/5936036/secret-2020-election-campaign/.

7 Ibid.

8 Edmund DeMarche, "Biden says he is going to 'transform' the nation if elected," Fox News (July 6, 2020), https://www.foxnews.com/politics/biden-says-he-is-going-to-transform-the-nation-if-elected (May 16, 2023).

9 Ella Nilsen, "Joe Biden and Bernie Sanders are building new, policy

-focused task forces," *Vox* (May 13, 2020), https://www.vox.com /2020/5/13/21257078/joe-biden-bernie-sanders-joint-unity-task -forces-democratic-policy (May 16, 2023).

10 David Harsanyi, "If Socialism Isn't 'Useful,' Why Does Biden Rely on Socialists to Drive His Agenda?" *National Review* (July 19, 2021), https://www.nationalreview.com/corner/if-socialism-isnt-use ful-why-does-biden-rely-on-socialists-to-drive-his-agenda / (May 16, 2023).

11 Ruby Cramer, "The Unusual Group Trying to Turn Biden into FDR," *Politico* (Aug. 8, 2021), https://www.politico.com/news /magazine/2021/08/01/fdr-cabinet-descendents-new-deal-biden-pro gressive-500659 (May 16, 2023).

12 Raymond Aron, *Democracy and Totalitarianism: A Theory of Political Systems* (New York, Praeger, 1965), 42–43.

13 https://www.axios.com/2021/03/25/biden-historians-meeting-fili buster.

14 Ibid.

15 Ibid., 43–44.

16 Ibid., 45.

17 Ibid.

18 Ibid., 45–46 (emphasis added).

19 https://freedomhouse.org/about-us (May 16, 2023).

20 Arch Puddington, "Breaking Down Democracy: Goals, Strate- gies, and Methods of Modern Authoritarians," FreedomHouse.org, June 2017, https://freedomhouse.org/sites/default/files/June2017 _FH_Report_Breaking_Down_Democracy.pdf (May 16, 2023), 1.

21 Ibid., at 1.

22 Ibid., at 2.

23 Peter W. Wood, *1620: A Critical Response to the 1619 Project* (New York, Encounter Books, 2020), 4.

24 Arch Puddington, "Breaking Down Democracy," 2.

25 Heritage Foundation, "The Facts About H.R. 1: The 'For the Peo- ple Act of 2021,'" (Feb. 21, 2021), https://www.heritage.org/elec tion-integrity/report/the-facts-about-hr-1-the-the-people-act-2021 (May 16, 2023).

26 Arch Puddington, "Breaking Down Democracy," 3.

27 Paul A. Rahe, "Amending the First Amendment," *National Associa-*

tion of Scholars (Fall 2017), https://www.nas.org/academic-questions/30/3/amending_the_first_amendment (May 16, 2023).

28 Arch Puddington, "Breaking Down Democracy," 6.

29 John Daniel Davidson, "The 'Twitter Files' Reveal Big Tech's Unholy Alliance With The Feds Exists To Control You," *Federalist*, Feb. 21, 2023, https://thefederalist.com/2023/02/21/the-twitter-files-reveal-big-techs-unholy-alliance-with-the-feds-exists-to-control-you/ (May 16, 2023).

30 Ibid.

31 Arch Puddington, "Breaking Down Democracy," 7.

32 Ibid., at 8.

33 Mark R. Levin, *Unfreedom of the Press* (New York, Threshold Editions, 2019).

34 Arch Puddington, "Breaking Down Democracy," 8.

35 Ewan Palmer, "FBI Under Pressure for Targeting Catholics in Leaked Document," *Newsweek* (Feb. 10, 2023), https://www.newsweek.com/fbi-memo-catholics-radical-traditional-leaked-1780379 (May 16, 2023).

36 Arch Puddington, "Breaking Down Democracy," 10.

37 *New York Post* Editorial Board, "Georgia's record voting turnout exposes Biden's disgraceful 'Jim Crow 2.0' lie," *New York Post* (Oct. 21, 2022), https://nypost.com/2022/10/21/georgias-record-voting-turnout-exposes-bidens-disgraceful-jim-crow-2-0-lie/ (May 16, 2023).

38 Ludwig von Mises, *Marxism Unmasked: From Delusion to Destruction* (Ludwig von Mises Institute, 2006).

39 Roger Kiska, "Antonio Gramsci's long march through history," *Religion and Liberty*, vol. 29, no. 3, Action Institute, Summer 2019, https://www.acton.org/religion-liberty/volume-29-number-3/antonio-gramscis-long-march-through-history (May 16, 2023).

40 Ibid.

41 Herbert Marcuse, "An Essay on Liberation," 1969, https://www.marxists.org/reference/archive/marcuse/works/1969/essay-liberation.htm (May 16, 2023).

42 Saul D. Alinsky, *Rules for Radicals: A Practical Primer for Realistic Radicals* (New York, Vintage Books, 1971), 3.

43 Ibid., at xx–xxi.

44 Ibid., at 126–30.

45 Paul Kengor, "What Obama's Mentor Thought About General Motors," *Forbes.com*, Aug. 1, 2012, https://www.forbes.com/sites/realspin/2012/08/01/the-marxist-who-mentored-president-obama-on-general-motors/?sh=19028cd76360 (May 16, 2023).

46 Paul Sperry, "Don't be fooled by Bernie Sanders—he's a diehard communist," *New York Post* (Jan. 16, 2016), https://nypost.com/2016/01/16/dont-be-fooled-by-bernie-sanders-hes-a-diehard-communist/ (May 16, 2023); Joseph Simonson, "Bernie Sanders campaigned for Marxist party in Reagan era," *Washington Examiner* (May 30, 2019), https://www.washingtonexaminer.com/news/campaigns/bernie-sanders-campaigned-for-marxist-party-in-reagan-era (May 16, 2023).

47 Elizabeth Vaugh, "Bernie Sanders' 'Economic Bill of Rights' Taken Nearly Verbatim From Stalin's 1936 Soviet Constitution," *RedState* (June 15, 2019), https://redstate.com/elizabeth-vaughn/2019/06/15/joe-biden-isnt-plagiarist-among-2020-democratic-presidential-candidates-n109066 (May 16, 2023).

48 Britannica, "Leninism," https://www.britannica.com/topic/Leninism (May 16, 2023).

CHAPTER TWO: ANTI-BLACK RACISM & ANTI-SEMITISM

1 Williamson M. Evers, "How Woodrow Wilson Denied African-Americans an Academic Education," *EducationWeek* (Dec. 8, 2015), https://www.edweek.org/leadership/opinion-how-woodrow-wilson-denied-african-americans-an-academic-education/2015/12 (May 16, 2023).

2 Ibid.

3 Harry Hamilton Laughlin, *Eugenical Sterilization in the United States* (Chicago, Chicago Municipal Court, 1922) 22, also see, "Woodrow Wilson and eugenics—he supported it—here's the details," *ProgressingAmerica* (March 7, 2012), http://progressingamerica.blogspot.com/2012/03/woodrow-wilson-and-eugenics-he.html (May 16, 2023).

4 Thomas C. Leonard, "Eugenics and Economics in the Progressive

Era," *Journal of Economic Perspectives*, vol. 19, no. 4 (Fall 2005), https://pubs.aeaweb.org/doi/pdfplus/10.1257/089533005775196642 (May 16, 2023).

5 Ibid.

6 https://ny.pbslearningmedia.org/resource/amex32ec-soc-eugen icsnazi/american-eugenics-and-the-nazi-regime-the-eugenics-cru sade/.

7 Ibid.

8 Ibid.

9 Margaret Sanger. "The Eugenic Value of Birth Control Propaganda," *Birth Control Review* (Oct. 1921).

10 Margaret Sanger, "Apostle of Birth Control Sees Cause Gaining Here," *New York Times* (April 8, 1923).

11 Dylan Matthews, "Woodrow Wilson was extremely racist—even by the standards of his time," *Vox* (Nov. 20, 2015), https://www.vox .com/policy-and-politics/2015/11/20/9766896/woodrow-wilson-rac ist (May 16, 2023).

12 Ibid.

13 Ibid.

14 Ibid.

15 Abraham Lincoln, "Speech at Lewistown, IL," *Collected Works of Abraham Lincoln, Vol. 2*, University of Michigan, https://quod .lib.umich.edu/l/lincoln/lincoln2/1:567?rgn=div1;view=fulltext (May 17, 2023).

16 Woodrow Wilson. "The Author and Signers of the Declaration" (Sept., 1907), *From Teaching American History*, https://teaching americanhistory.org/document/the-author-and-signers-of-the-dec laration/ (May 17, 2023).

17 Woodrow Wilson, "Address at Independence Hall: 'The Meaning of Liberty,'" July 4, 1914, The American Presidency Project, https:// www.presidency.ucsb.edu/documents/address-independence-hall-the -meaning-liberty (May 17, 2023).

18 Alex Nitzberg (quoting Ketanji Brown Jackson), "Supreme Court nominee Ketanji Brown Jackson writes, 'I do not hold a position on whether individuals possess natural rights,'" *The Blaze* (April 4, 2022), https://www.theblaze.com/news/ketanji-brown-jackson-does -not-have-position-on-if-people-have-natural-rights (May 17, 2023).

19 Woodrow Wilson, *The New Freedom: A Call for the Emancipation of the Generous Energies of a People* (New York, Doubleday, 1913), https://www.gutenberg.org/files/14811/14811-h/14811-h.htm (May 17, 2023).

20 *West Virginia v. EPA*, 597 U.S. ___, 2022 (Gorsuch, J., concurring), https://www.supremecourt.gov/opinions/21pdf/20-1530_n758.pdf (May 17, 2023).

21 Victor Davis Hanson, "Obama: Transforming America," *National Review* (May 14, 2008), https://www.nationalreview.com/2013/10/obama-transforming-america-victor-davis-hanson/ (May 16, 2023).

22 John Cassidy, "Bernie Sanders's Fulsome Endorsement of Hillary Clinton," *New Yorker* (July 12, 2016), https://www.newyorker.com/news/john-cassidy/bernie-sanderss-fulsome-endorsement-of-hillary-clinton.

23 Kyle Olson, "Joe Biden, 'Coronavirus an "Incredible Opportunity" to "Fundamentally Transform" America,'" *Breitbart* (May 4, 2020), https://www.breitbart.com/politics/2020/05/04/joe-biden-coronavirus-an-incredible-opportunity-to-fundamentally-transform-america/ (May 17, 2023).

24 https://www.politico.com/blogs/ben-smith/2008/04/obama-on-small-town-pa-clinging-to-religion-guns-xenophobia-007737.

25 Franklin Delano Roosevelt, "Executive Order 9066: Resulting in Japanese-American Incarceration (1942)," *National Archives*, https://www.archives.gov/milestone-documents/executive-order-9066 (May 17, 2023).

26 Rafael Medoff, "Facing up to FDR's Racism," The David S. Wyman Institute for Holocaust Studies, http://new.wymaninstitute.org/2019/07/facing-up-to-fdrs-racism/ (May 17, 2023).

27 *Korematsu v. United States*, 324 U.S. 885 (1945).

28 Japanese Americans in military during World War II (Densho Encyclopedia), https://encyclopedia.densho.org/Japanese_Americans_in_military_during_World_War_II/#:~:text=An%20estimated%2033%2C000%20Japanese%20Americans,country%20during%20World%20War%20II.

29 William E. Leuchtenburg, "A Klansman Joins the Court: The Appointment of Hugo L. Black," *University of Chicago Law Review*,

vol. 41, no. 1 (Fall 1973), https://chicagounbound.uchicago.edu/cgi
/viewcontent.cgi?referer=https://en.wikipedia.org/&httpsredir=1&
article=3788&context=uclrev (May 17, 2023).

30 Gerald T. Dunne, *Hugo Black and the Judicial Revolution* (New York: Simon & Schuster, 1977), 269, quoting *Hugo Black, Jr., My Father* (New York: Random House, 1975), 104.

31 https://www.reaganlibrary.gov/archives/speech/remarks-signing
-bill-providing-restitution-wartime-internment-japanese-amer
ican.

32 https://www.supremecourt.gov/opinions/22pdf/20-1199_l6gn.pdf.

33 Ibid., Thomas, J., concurring, p. 28.

34 Samuel P. Goldston and Yusuf S. Mian, Crimson Staff Writers, "'Not a Normal Court': Biden, Mass. Leaders Condemn Supreme Court After Anti-Affirmative Action Decision," (*The Harvard Crimson*, June 30, 2023), https://www.thecrimson.com/article/2023/6/30
/government-leaders-react-sffa-affirmative-action/.

35 Terry Gross, "A Forgotten History' of How the U.S. Government Segregated America," NPR (May 3, 2017), https://www.npr.org
/2017/05/03/526655831/a-forgotten-history-of-how-the-u-s-gov
ernment-segregated-america (May 17, 2023).

36 Jeremy Schapp, *Triumph* (Boston: First Mariner, 2007), 211.

37 Phillip W. Magness, "How FDR Killed Federal Anti-Lynching Legislation," American Institute for Economic Research (July 31, 2020), https://www.aier.org/article/how-fdr-killed-federal-anti
-lynching-legislation/ (May 17, 2023).

38 John Strausbaugh, "Why FDR Chose Not to Desegregate the Military," *National Review* (Sept. 26, 2020), https://news.yahoo.com
/why-fdr-chose-not-desegregate-103009436.html?guccounter=1
(May 17, 2023).

39 Bruce Bartlett, *Wrong on Race, The Democrat Party's Buried Past* (New York: St. Martin's, 2008), 113.

40 Rafael Medoff, "Facing up to FDR's Racism."

41 Wyman Institute, "Not New, Not Evidence: An Analysis of the Claim that Refugees and Rescue Contains New Evidence of FDR's Concern for Europe's Jews," Rafael Medoff, "Blinken's Holocaust Gaffe," *Jewish Journal* (April 11, 2021), https://jewishjournal.com

/commentary/335405/blinkens-holocaust-gaffe/ (May 17, 2023); Daniel Greenfield, "Ken Burns Exploits the Holocaust," *Front Page Magazine* (Sept. 26, 2022), https://www.frontpagemag.com /ken-burns-exploits-the-holocaust/ (May 17, 2023); Rafael Medoff, "FDR's Anti-Semitic Cocktails—with Molotov," *Israel National News* (March 17, 2014), https://www.israelnationalnews.com/news /343254 (May 17, 2023).

42 "Roosevelt's blistering words for the 'money changers,'" *Los Angeles Times* (Jan. 20, 2009), https://www.latimes.com/archives/blogs /money-company/story/2009-01-20/roosevelts-blistering-words-for -the-money-changers (May 17, 2023).

43 Julie Mell, "Jews and Money: The Medieval Origins of a Modern Stereotype," *The Cambridge Companion to Antisemitism* (Cambridge, Cambridge Univ. Press, 2022).

44 Fern Sidman, "Honoring Those Who Refused to Remain Silent," JewishMag.com (Dec. 2008), http://www.jewishmag.com/128mag /wyman_institute/wyman_institute.htm (May 17, 2023).

45 Holocaust Encyclopedia, "Breckenridge Long," United States Holocaust Memorial Museum, https://encyclopedia.ushmm.org/content /en/article/breckinridge-long (May 17, 2023).

46 The David S. Wyman Institute for Holocaust Studies, "Long, Breckenridge," *Encyclopedia of America's Response to the Holocaust*, http://enc.wymaninstitute.org/?p=329 (May 17, 2023).

47 Ibid.

48 Ibid.

49 Rafael Medoff, *The Jews Should Keep Quiet* (Philadelphia: University of Nebraska Press, 2019), chapter 8—"Antisemitism in the White House."

50 Rafael Medoff, "What FDR said about Jews in private," *Los Angeles Times* (April 7, 2013), https://www.latimes.com/opinion/la -xpm-2013-apr-07-la-oe-medoff-roosevelt-holocaust-20130407 -story.html (May 17, 2023); Rafael Medoff, "FDR's Anti-Semitic Cocktails—with Molotov."

51 https://www.thedailybeast.com/the-patriarch-joseph-kennedy-srs -outsized-life.

52 Ezra Dulis, "Flashback: Hillary Clinton Praises 'Friend and Mentor'

Robert Byrd (a KKK Recruiter)," *Breitbart* (Aug. 25, 2016), https://
www.breitbart.com/politics/2016/08/25/hillary-clinton-friend
-mentor-robert-byrd-kkk/ (May 17, 2023).

53 Adam Serwer, "Lyndon Johnson was a civil rights hero. But also
a racist," *MSNBC* (April 11, 2014), https://www.msnbc.com/msnbc
/lyndon-johnson-civil-rights-racism-msna305591 (May 17, 2023).

54 Robert Dallek, *Flawed Giant: Lyndon Johnson and His Times, 1961–
1973* (New York: Oxford University Press, 1998).

55 Robert A. Caro, *The Years of Lyndon Johnson, Master of the Senate*
(New York: Vintage Books, 2002), xv.

56 Ibid., p. 297.

57 https://nypost.com/2021/07/16/wikipedia-co-founder-says-site-is
-now-propaganda-for-left-leaning-establishment/.

58 Barry Goldwater (Wikipedia) https://en.wikipedia.org/wiki/Barry
_Goldwater.

59 Ibid.

60 Janell Ross, "Joe Biden didn't just compromise with segregationists. He fought for their cause in schools, experts say," NBC News
(June 25, 2019), https://www.nbcnews.com/news/nbcblk/joe
-biden-didn-t-just-compromise-segregationists-he-fought-their
-n1021626 (May 17, 2023).

61 Astead Herndon, "How Joe Biden Became the Democrat's Anti-Busing
Crusader," *New York Times* (June 15, 2019), https://www.nytimes.com
/2019/07/15/us/politics/biden-busing.html (May 17, 2023).

62 "Biden's history of controversial racial comments," Fox News
(Oct. 6, 2020), https://www.foxnews.com/politics/bidens-history-of
-controversial-racial-comments (May 17, 2023).

63 Tim Murtaugh, "Biden's History of Getting Away With Racist
Remarks," The Heritage Foundation (July 7, 2021), https://www
.heritage.org/progressivism/commentary/bidens-history-getting
-away-racist-remarks (May 17, 2023).

64 https://www.whitehouse.gov/briefing-room/speeches
-remarks/2022/02/25/remarks-by-president-biden-on-his-nomina
tion-of-judge-ketanji-brown-jackson-to-serve-as-associate-justice
-of-the-u-s-supreme-court/.

65 Marc A. Thiessen, "Biden Blocked the First Black Woman from

the Supreme Court," [ITAL/]Washington Post[/ITAL] (February 1, 2022), https://www.washingtonpost.com/opinions/2022/02/01/biden -black-woman-janice-rogers-brown/.

66 Ibid.

67 Ibid.

68 Kevin D, Williamson "The Party of Civil Rights," *National Review* (May 21, 2012), https://www.nationalreview.com/2012/05/party -civil-rights-kevin-d-williamson/.

69 Joyce A. Ladner, "A New Civil Rights Agenda: A New Leadership Is Making a Difference," Brookings Institution (March 1, 2000), https://www.brookings.edu/articles/a-new-civil-rights-agenda-a -new-leadership-is-making-a-difference/ (May 17, 2023).

70 Cass R. Sunstein, *The Second Bill of Rights: FDR's Unfinished Revolution—And Why We Need It More Than Ever* (New York: Basic Books, 2004), 1.

71 Ibid.

72 "The Stalin Constitution, Constitution of the Union of Soviet Socialist Republics," *Seventeen Moments in Soviet History*, https:// soviethistory.msu.edu/1936-2/stalin-constitution/stalin-constitu tion-texts/the-stalin-constitution (May 17, 2023).

73 Sun Tzu, "Big Dupes at Big Peace: 'Progressives' for Stalin, *Breitbart* (Dec. 19, 2010), https://www.breitbart.com/national-security/2010 /12/19/big-dupes-at-big-peace-progressives-for-stalin/ (May 17, 2023).

74 Mark R. Levin, *American Marxism* (New York: Threshold Editions, 2021).

75 Cass R. Sunstein, *The Second Bill of Rights: FDR's Unfinished Revolu- tion*," 4, 5.

76 The Economic Historian, "The enduring legacy of racism in Ameri- can capitalism," https://economic-historian.com/2018/09/the-endur ing-legacy-of-racism-in-american-capitalism/ (May 17, 2023).

CHAPTER THREE: ANTI-WHITE RACISM & ANTI-SEMITISM

1 Phillip Magness, "The 1619 Project's Confusion on Capitalism," *National Review* (Feb. 12, 2023), https://www.nationalreview.com

/2023/02/the-1619-projects-confusion-on-capitalism/ (May 17, 2023).

2 Arthur Zilversmit, *The First Emancipation: The Abolition of Slavery in the North* (Chicago: Univ. of Chicago Press, 1967); *Encyclopedia of Emancipation and Abolition in the Transatlantic World*, Junius P. Rodriguez, ed. (New York Routledge, 2007), 34–35.

3 "The Slave Trade," National Archives, https://www.archives.gov /education/lessons/slave-trade.html#:~:text=An%20act%20of%20 Congress%20passed,Slaves%22%20took%20effect%20in%20 1808. (May 18, 2023).

4 Brandon Morse, "No, Slaves Didn't Build This Country," *RedState* (Feb. 14, 2023), https://redstate.com/brandon_morse/2023/02/14/no -slaves-didnt-build-this-country-n703440 (May 18, 2023); Jenny Bourne, "Slavery in the United States," EH.net, https://eh.net/ency clopedia/slavery-in-the-united-states/ (May 18, 2023).

5 Marc Schulman, "Economics and the Civil War," HistoryCentral .com, https://www.historycentral.com/CivilWar/AMERICA/Eco nomics.html (May 18, 2023).

6 Brandon Morse, "No, Slaves Didn't Build This Country."

7 *Why Government Is the Problem*, p. 19, Feb. 1, 1993.

8 Peter W. Wood, *1620: A Critical Response to the 1619 Project* (New York: Encounter Books, 2020), 5–6.

9 Phillip Magness, "The 1619 Project's Confusion on Capitalism."

10 Ibid.

11 Cedric J. Robinson, *Black Marxism* (Chapel Hill: UNC Press, 1983), 2.

12 Robin D. G. Kelly, "What Did Cedric Robinson Mean by Racial Capitalism?" *Boston Review* (Jan. 12, 2017), https://www.boston review.net/articles/robin-d-g-kelley-introduction-race-capitalism -justice/ (May 18, 2023) (emphasis added).

13 Thomas C. Leonard, *Illiberal Reformers* (Princeton: Princeton University Press, 2016) 119.

14 https://www.theguardian.com/commentisfree/2023/feb/06/joe -biden-democratic-capitalism-changed-economic-paradigm-rea gan-free-market.

15 https://www.nytimes.com/1990/01/17/opinion/the-reagan-boom -greatest-ever.html.

16 Ibid.

17 https://www.aei.org/articles/reagan-and-the-poor/.

18 Ibid.

19 Coleman Hughes, "How to Be an Anti-Intellectual," *City Journal* (Oct. 27, 2019), https://www.city-journal.org/article/how-to-be-an -anti-intellectual (May 18, 2023).

20 *Mark Levin Radio Show Audio Rewind*, May 10, 2023, https://www .marklevinshow.com/audio-rewind/ (May 18, 2023).

21 Ibid.

22 Ibram X. Kendi, "Our New Postracial Myth," *The Atlantic* (June 22, 2021), https://www.theatlantic.com/ideas/archive/2021/06/our-new -postracial-myth/619261/ (May 18, 2023).

23 Peter C. Myers, "The Case for Color-Blindness," The Heritage Foundation (Sept. 6, 2019), https://www.heritage.org/civil-society /report/the-case-color-blindness (May 18, 2023).

24 Evan Gerstmann, "Can the Government Exclude Whites On Account of Their Race?" *Forbes* (May 26, 2021), https://www .forbes.com/sites/evangerstmann/2021/05/26/can-the-government -exclude-whites-on-account-of-their-race/?sh=61e84c031003 (May 18, 2023).

25 Dani Bostick, "How Colorblindness Is Actually Racist," *HuffPost* (July 11, 2016), https://www.huffpost.com/entry/how-colorblind ness-is-act_b_10886176 (May 18, 2023).

26 Peter C. Myers, "The Case for Color-Blindness."

27 U.S. Approval of Interracial Marriage at New High of 94% (https:// news.gallup.com/poll/354638/approval-interracial-marriage-new -high.aspx).

28 How Kamala Harris reflect America's changing demographics (Pew Research Center), https://www.pewresearch.org/short-reads/2021 /02/25/in-vice-president-kamala-harris-we-can-see-how-america -has-changed/.

29 Ibid.

30 Jason D. Hill, *What Do White Americans Owe Black People? Racial Justice in the Age of Post-Oppression* (New York: Post Hill Press, 2021), 130, 132, 133.

31 Lynn Uzzell, "It's Time to Acknowledge Anti-White Racism," *Real-ClearPolitics* (Sept. 12, 2021), https://www.realclearpolitics.com

/articles/2021/09/12/its_time_to_acknowledge_anti-white_racism _146391.html (May 18, 2023).

32 Ibid.

33 https://www.washingtonexaminer.com/opinion/associated-press -profile-on-al-sharpton-forgets-to-mention-the-time-he-incited -anti-semitic-riots.

34 John Verhovek, "Joe Biden: White America 'has to admit there's still a systemic racism,'" *ABC News* (Jan. 21, 2019), https://abc news.go.com/Politics/joe-biden-white-america-admit-systemic-rac ism/story?id=60524966 (May 18, 2023).

35 "Remarks by President Biden at Signing of an Executive Order on Racial Equity," The White House (Jan. 26, 2021), https:// www.whitehouse.gov/briefing-room/speeches-remarks/2021/01/26 /remarks-by-president-biden-at-signing-of-an-executive-order-on -racial-equity/ (May 18, 2023).

36 President Biden, tweet dated May 17, 2022, https://twitter .com/potus/status/1526627890539929602?s=46&t=L_jMUccr 6N0YtpNNlwgRUQ (May 18, 2023).

37 "Remarks by President Biden at 'Till' Movie Screening," The White House (Feb. 16, 2023), https://www.whitehouse.gov/briefing -room/speeches-remarks/2023/02/16/remarks-by-president-biden-at -till-movie-screening/ (May 18, 2023) (emphasis added).

38 Wes Barrett, "Biden to Southern audience: Romney financial plan would 'put y'all back in chains,'" Fox News (Dec. 23, 2015), https:// www.foxnews.com/politics/biden-to-southern-audience-romney -financial-plan-would-put-yall-back-in-chains (May 18, 2023).

39 Gabriel Hays, "Biden blasted for calling 'white supremacy' 'most dangerous terrorist threat' at college speech: 'Pure evil,'" Fox News (May 13, 2023), https://www.foxnews.com/media/biden-blasted-for -calling-white-supremacy-most-dangerous-terrorist-threat-at-col lege-speech-pure-evil (May 18, 2023).

40 Paul Bedard, "Democratic National Committee platform mentions 'whites' 15 times, all damning," *Washington Examiner* (July 23, 2020), https://www.washingtonexaminer.com/washington-secrets/dnc -platform-mentions-whites-15-times-all-damning (May 18, 2023); "2020 Democratic Platform," *Politico*, https://www.politico.com /f/?id=00000173-782a-d3de-ab7b-783b9b650000 (May 18, 2023).

41 Ibid.

42 Coleman Hughes, "How to Be an Anti-Intellectual," *City Journal* (Oct. 27, 2019), https://www.city-journal.org/article/how-to-be-an -anti-intellectual (May 18, 2023).

43 Ibid.; Robert W. Fairle and William A. Sundstrom, *The Emergence, Persistence and Recent Widening of the Racial Unemployment Gap, Industrial and Labor Relations Rev.*, vol. 52, no. 2 (Jan. 1999), https:// people.ucsc.edu/~rfairlie/papers/published/ilrr%201999%20-%20 racial%20unemployment.pdf (May 25, 2023).

44 Alan Berube, "Black household income is rising across the United States," Brookings Institution, Oct. 3, 2019, https://www.brookings .edu/blog/the-avenue/2019/10/03/black-household-income-is-ris ing-across-the-united-states/ (May 18, 2023).

45 Phil Gramm, Robert Ekelund, and John Early, *The Myth of American Inequality, How Big Government Biases Policy Debate* (New York: Rowman & Littlefield, 2022), 2.

46 Ibid., 3.

47 James D. Agresti, "America's poorest are richer than most average Europeans: Study," Acton Institute (Aug. 27, 2019), https://www .acton.org/publications/transatlantic/2019/08/27/americas-poorest -are-richer-most-average-europeans-study (May 18, 2023).

48 "CNN's Van Jones says Tyre Nichols' death might have been 'driven by racism' despite Black cops being charged," *Fox22* (Jan. 27, 2023), https://www.foxbangor.com/news/national/cnns-van-jones-says -tyre-nichols-death-might-have-been-driven-by-racism-despite -black/article_7a33ac81-f1ee-5793-afa9-2419fb8d3333.html (May 18, 2023).

49 Mark Moore, "Wajahat Ali claims Nikki Haley uses 'brown skin to launder' white supremacy," *New York Post* (Feb. 20, 2023), https:// nypost.com/2023/02/20/msnbc-guest-haley-uses-brown-skin-to -launder-racism/ (May 18, 2023).

50 "Executive Order On Advancing Racial Equity and Support for Underserved Communities Through the Federal Government," The White House (Jan. 20, 2021), https://www.whitehouse.gov /briefing-room/presidential-actions/2021/01/20/executive-order -advancing-racial-equity-and-support-for-underserved-communi ties-through-the-federal-government/ (May 18, 2023).

51 Evan Gertsmann, "Federal Appellate Court Rules That Biden Administration Can't Deny COVID Relief Funds to White Restaurant Owners," *Forbes* (June 3, 2021), https://www.forbes.com/sites/evangerstmann/2021/06/03/federal-appellate-court-rules-that-biden-administration-cant-deny-covid-relief-funds-to-white-restaurant-owners/?sh=7e4c21bcd996 (May 18, 2023).

52 Rav Avora, "More Equal Than Others: Biden's 'equity' agenda is systemic racism in disguise," *City Journal* (July 29, 2021), https://www.city-journal.org/article/more-equal-than-others (May 18, 2023).

53 Evan Gertsmann, "Federal Appellate Court Rules That Biden Administration Can't Deny COVID Relief Funds."

54 Betsy McCaughey, "Biden's imposing racism in everything from housing to health care," *New York Post* (Aug. 30, 2022), https://nypost.com/2022/08/30/bidens-imposing-racism-in-everything-from-housing-to-health-care/ (May 18, 2023).

55 "Executive Order on Further Advancing Racial Equity and Support for Underserved Communities Through the Federal Government," The White House (Feb. 16, 2023), https://www.whitehouse.gov/briefing-room/presidential-actions/2023/02/16/executive-order-on-further-advancing-racial-equity-and-support-for-underserved-communities-through-the-federal-government/ (May 18, 2023).

56 Ibid.

57 "President Joe Biden's speech on voting rights," (July 13, 2021), ABC News, https://abcnews.go.com/Politics/president-joe-bidens-speech-voting-rights-transcript/story?id=78827023 (May 18, 2023).

58 Ibid.

59 Ibid.

60 Hans von Spakovsky, "Georgia Voters Show Just How Wrong Joe Biden and His Sycophants Are," *Daily Signal* (Feb. 2, 2023), https://www.dailysignal.com/2023/02/02/georgia-voters-show-just-how-wrong-joe-biden-and-his-sycophants-are/?_gl=1*tso83n*_ga*MTM0NjA1NjEzNy4xNjU5NzA5NTQ5*_ga_W14BT6YQ87*MTY3NjEyNzEzMi4xMC4xLjE2NzYxMjc3MjUuNjAuMC4w (May 18, 2023).

61 Andrew Kaczynski and Em Steck, "Hakeem Jeffries' 'vague recol-

lection' of controversy surrounding his uncle undermined by college editorial defending him," CNN (April 12, 2023), https://www .cnn.com/2023/04/12/politics/kfile-hakeem-jeffries-college-edi torial-defending-uncle-from-antisemitism/index.html (May 18, 2023); Hakeem Jeffries, "The Black Conservative Phenomenon," *Silence No More* (Feb. 21, 1992), https://www.documentcloud.org /documents/23758566-copy-of-p8 (May 18, 2023).

62 Ibid.

63 Marc Rod, "Jewish Democrats back Jeffries after resurfaced defense of uncle's antisemitic remarks," *Jewish Insider* (April 14, 2023), https://jewishinsider.com/2023/04/democratic-jewish-lawmakers -hakeem-jeffries-uncle-leonard-jeffries-antisemitism/ (May 19, 2023).

64 Victor Davis Hanson, "The New, New Anti-Semitism," *National Review* (Jan. 15, 2019), https://www.nationalreview.com/2019/01 /new-anti-semitism-woke-progressives-old-stereotypes/ (May 19, 2023).

65 Ibid.

66 Ibid.

67 Yaakov Menken, "Obama's Blind Antipathy Toward Israel Is Not Merely a Political Position," *Observer* (Dec. 28, 2016), https:// observer.com/2016/12/donald-trump-administration-israel-policy/ (May 19, 2023).

68 Ibid.

69 Oren Liebermann, "American fatally stabbed in Israel terror attack that wounds 10 others," CNN (March 9, 2016), https://www.cnn .com/2016/03/08/middleeast/israel-violence/index.html (May 19, 2023).

70 Kenneth L. Marcus, "Biden Is Failing to Deliver in the Fight Against Antisemitism," *Newsweek* (Jan. 9, 2023), https://www .newsweek.com/biden-failing-deliver-fight-against-antisemitism -opinion-1772379 (May 19, 2023).

71 https://www.jewishpress.com/news/jewish-news/antisemitism-news /antisemitism-expert-kenneth-marcus-on-bidens-plan-long-on -rhetoric-short-on-substance/2023/05/28/.

72 "Time for Democrats to Address Their Anti-Semitism Problem,"

National Review (May 26, 2021), https://www.nationalreview.com /2021/05/time-for-democrats-to-address-their-anti-semitism-prob lem/ (May 19, 2023).

73 Ibid.

74 Ibid.

75 Ibid.

76 "Mark Levin: The Democrats are tolerating anti-Semitism," Fox News (March 12, 2023), https://www.foxnews.com/video /6322454734112 (May 19, 2023).

77 Jonathan S. Tobin, "Democrats ignore their party's antisemitism, wrongly attack Trump," *Cleveland Jewish News*, Sep. 22, 2022, https:// www.clevelandjewishnews.com/columnists/jonathan_tobin/dem ocrats-ignore-their-party-s-antisemitism-wrongly-attack-trump /article_608b0f1a-3927-11ed-bc0b-c31d03a54712.html.

78 Ibid.

79 Ibid.

80 Ronn Torossian, "Menachem Begin to Joe Biden: I Am Not a Jew With Trembling Knees," *The Jewish Press* (April 3, 2015), https:// www.jewishpress.com/indepth/opinions/menachem-begin-to-joe -biden-i-am-not-a-jew-with-trembling-knees/2015/04/03/.

81 "What Does Biden Have Against Israel? *Wall Street Journal*, (July 13, 2023), https://www.wsj.com/articles/biden-israel-ben jamin-netanyahu-tom-nides-iran-abraham-accords-judicial -reform-639bd846.

82 Ibid.

CHAPTER FOUR: LANGUAGE CONTROL & THOUGHT CONTROL

1 "Joost A. M. Meerloo," *Goodreads*, https://www.goodreads.com /author/show/5609700.Joost_A_M_Meerloo (May 19, 2023).

2 Joost A.M. Meerloo, *Delusion and Mass Delusion* (Connecticut: Martino Fine Books, 1949, 2021), 27.

3 David Averre and Katelyn Caralle, "Biden's Supreme Court nominee Ketanji Brown Jackson refuses to define the word 'woman' because she's 'not a biologist' as she is grilled on day two of her confirmation hearing," *Daily Mail* (March 23, 2022), https://www

.dailymail.co.uk/news/article-10642895/Bidens-Supreme-Court-nominee-Ketanji-Brown-Jackson-refuses-define-word-woman.html (May 19, 2023).

4 Magda Stroinska, "Language and Totalitarian Regimes," *Journal of Economic Affairs* (December 2002), https://www.academia.edu/7660293/Language_and_Totalitarian_Regimes (May 19, 2023).

5 Ibid.

6 Marco Rubio, "Senate Democrats Insist Men Can Get Pregnant," *Press Release* (Aug. 7, 2022), https://www.rubio.senate.gov/public/index.cfm/2022/8/senate-democrats-insist-men-can-get-pregnant (May 19, 2023).

7 Magda Stroinska, "Language and Totalitarian Regimes."

8 Friedrich A. Hayek, *The Road to Serfdom* (London: Long, Routledge & Kegan Paul, 2001) 114.

9 Richard M. Ebeling, "Would-Be Tyrants Capture Language to Control Thought," *FEE Stories* (Aug. 11, 2017), https://fee.org/articles/would-be-tyrants-capture-language-to-control-thought/ (May 19, 2023).

10 Mikhail Heller, *Cogs in the Wheel* (New York: Knopf, 1988), 229, 230.

11 Ibid., 238.

12 Rachel Treisman, "Dictionary.com's Largest Update (Re)defines Thousands of Words, Focusing On Identity," NPR (Sept. 3 2020), https://www.npr.org/2020/09/03/909494937/dictionary-coms-largest-update-re-defines-thousands-of-words-focusing-on-identit (May 19, 2023).

13 Ibid.

14 Hannah Arendt, *The Origins of Totalitarianism* (New York: Harcourt, 1951), 344.

15 Ibid., 346.

16 Mark J. Perry, "18 Spectacularly Wrong Predictions Made Around the Time of the First Earth Day in 1970, Expect More This Year," American Enterprise Institute (April 22, 2020), https://www.aei.org/carpe-diem/18-spectacularly-wrong-predictions-made-around-the-time-of-the-first-earth-day-in-1970-expect-more-this-year/.

17 https://socialist-alliance.org/class/climate-change-marxist-analysis.

18 https://www.economicshelp.org/blog/164203/economics/degrowth/.

19 George Orwell, "Politics and the English Language," (1946), https://
files.libcom.org/files/Politics%20and%20the%20English%20Lan
guage%20-%20George%20Orwell.pdf (May 19, 2023) 3, 4.

20 Ibid., 12, 13.

21 Senate Republican Conference, "Biden's Border Crisis is the
Worst in American History," *Politico*, https://www.politico.com/f
/?id=0000017f-d8bd-d522-ab7f-debd59400000 (May 19, 2023).

22 Jessica Chasmar, "Biden blasted for claiming GOP would slash
border funding: 'Must be a parody,'" Fox News (March 26, 2023),
https://www.foxnews.com/politics/biden-blasted-claiming-gop
-would-slash-border-funding-must-parody (May 19, 2023).

23 Lawrence Richard, "White House triples down on Biden's false
claim Republicans want to cut Social Security, Medicare," Fox
News (Feb. 9, 2023), https://www.foxnews.com/politics/white
-house-triples-down-bidens-false-claim-republicans-want-cut
-social-security-medicare (May 19, 2023).

24 Hunter Walker, "Joe Biden falsely claims he never called for Social
Security cuts," *Yahoo News* (March 15, 2020), https://www.yahoo
.com/video/joe-biden-falsely-claims-he-never-called-for-social
-security-cuts-024212661.html (May 19, 2023).

25 Ibid.

26 Daniel Dale, "Fact check: Biden falsely credits tax that took effect
in 2023 for deficit reduction in 2021 and 2022," CNN (March 16,
2023), https://www.cnn.com/2023/03/16/politics/fact-check-biden
-deficit-minimum-tax/index.html (May 19, 2023).

27 Ibid.

28 Steven Nelson, "Biden claims Republicans in Congress calling for
'defunding the police,'" *New York Post* (March 14, 2023), https://
nypost.com/2023/03/14/biden-claims-republicans-in-congress
-pushing-defunding-the-police/ (May 19, 2023).

29 D'Angelo Gore, "Democrat Makes Misleading 'Defund the Police'
Claim," FactCheck.org (July 6, 2021), https://www.factcheck.org
/2021/07/democrat-makes-misleading-defund-the-police-claim
/ (May 19, 2023).

30 Ronny Reyes, "White House slams GOP on gun control following Nashville school shooting," *New York Post* (March 27,

2023), https://nypost.com/2023/03/27/white-house-slams-gop -on-gun-control-following-nasvhille-school-shooting/ (May 19, 2023).

31 "Biden on Assault Weapons," Crime Prevention Research Center (May 25, 2022), https://crimeresearch.org/2022/05/biden-on -assault-weapons/ (May 19, 2023).

32 John Lott, LinkedIn Profile, https://www.linkedin.com/in/john-lott -b4b8599 (May 19, 2023).

33 "Mass Public Shooting 1998–May 2022," Crime Prevention Research Center, https://view.officeapps.live.com/op/view.aspx ?src=https%3A%2F%2Fcrimeresearch.org%2Fwp-content%2Fupl oads%2F2022%2F05%2FMass-Public-Shooting_US_1998-to-May -2022.xlsx&wdOrigin=BROWSELINK (May 19, 2023).

34 "Effects of Assault Weapon and High-Capacity Magazine Bans on Mass Shootings," Rand Corporation (Jan. 10, 2023), https://www .rand.org/research/gun-policy/analysis/ban-assault-weapons/mass -shootings.html (May 19, 2023).

35 Robert Farley, "FactChecking Biden's Claim that Assault Weapons Ban Worked," FactCheck.org (March 26, 2021), https://www.fact check.org/2021/03/factchecking-bidens-claim-that-assault-weap ons-ban-worked/ (May 19, 2023).

36 https://storage.courtlistener.com/recap/gov.uscourts.ded.82797/gov .uscourts.ded.82797.1.0_3.pdf.

37 Jean-Jacques Lecercle, *A Marxist Philosophy of Language* (Chicago: Haymarket Books, 2009), 5, 6.

38 Ibid., 198.

39 Norman Fairclough, *Language and Power* (New York, Routledge, 2015), 89, 90.

40 Ibid., author's preface to 2nd edition.

41 J. V. Stalin, "Concerning Marxism in Linguistics," *Pravda* (July 20, July 4, Aug. 2, 1950), https://www.marxists.org/reference/archive /stalin/works/1950/jun/20.htm#:~:text=Marxism%20holds%20 that%20the%20transition,away%20of%20the%20elements%20of (May 19, 2023).

42 Ben Wilson, "Don't Say 'Inmate': Biden Admin Using Taxpayer Dollars to Push Woke Language Guides," *Washington Free Beacon*

(Feb. 17, 2023), https://freebeacon.com/biden-administration
/dont-say-inmate-biden-admin-using-taxpayer-dollars-to-push
-woke-language-guides/ (May 19, 2023).

43 Ibid.

44 Andrew Kerr, "Here's What the FAA Has Been Focused on Instead
of Keeping Planes in the Air," *Washington Free Beacon* (Jan. 11,
2023), https://freebeacon.com/biden-administration/heres-what
-the-faa-has-been-focused-on-instead-of-keeping-planes-in-the-air
/ (May 20, 2023).

45 "Pelosi and McGovern Unveil Details of Rules Package for the
117th Congress," U.S. House of Representatives, Committee on
Rules (Jan. 1, 2021), https://rules.house.gov/press-releases/pelosi
-and-mcgovern-unveil-details-rules-package-117th-congress
(May 20, 2023).

46 Mairead McArdle, "Democrats Propose Banning Gendered Language in House Rules," *National Review* (Jan. 4, 2021), https://www
.nationalreview.com/news/democrats-propose-banning-gendered
-language-in-house-rules/ (May 20, 2023).

47 Jean K. Chalaby, "Public Communication in Totalitarian, Authoritarian and Statist Regimes: A Comparative Glance," https://www
.researchgate.net/publication/355963588_Public_Communication
_in_Totalitarian_Authoritarian_and_Statist_Regimes_A_Com
parative_Glance/link/63814add7b0e356feb845b4e/download
(May 20, 2023).

48 Joanna Thronborrow, "Language and Media," https://www.academ
ists.com/uploads/fourth_year/discourse_analysis/discourse_y4_s2
_2022_handout_6.pdf (May 20, 2023).

49 Edward Bernays, *Propaganda* (New York: Horace Liveright, 1928),
37–38.

50 Ibid.

51 Zach Goldberg, "How the Media Led the Great Racial Awakening," *Tablet* (Aug. 4, 2020), https://www.tabletmag.com/sections
/news/articles/media-great-racial-awakening (May 20, 2023).

52 Ibid.

53 Ibid.

54 Ibid.

55 Ibid.

56 Jeff Deist, "Evolution or Corruption?: The Imposition of Political Language in the West Today," *Etica & Politica / Ethics & Politics*, 2022, https://www2.units.it/etica/2022_2/DEIST.pdf.

57 Ibid.

58 Ibid.

59 Mark R. Levin, *Unfreedom of the Press* (New York: Threshold, 2019), 123–24.

60 Chuck Todd, *Meet the Press* (Dec. 21, 2018), transcript available at https://www.capoliticalreview.com/capoliticalnewsandviews/chuck-todd-says-his-show-is-not-going-to-give-time-to-climate-deniers/ (May 20, 2023).

61 Mattias Desmet, *The Psychology of Totalitarianism* (New York: Chelsea Green, 2022), 17–18.

62 Tom Jefferson et al., "Physical interventions to interrupt or reduce the spread of respiratory viruses," Cochrane Library (Jan. 30, 2023), https://www.cochranelibrary.com/cdsr/doi/10.1002/14651858.CD006207.pub6/full?s=08 (May 20, 2023).

63 Jonas Herby, Lars Jonung, and Steve H. Hanke, "A Literature Review and Meta-Analysis of the Effects of Lockdowns on COVID-19 Mortality," *Studies in Applied Economics* (Jan. 2022), https://sites.krieger.jhu.edu/iae/files/2022/01/A-Literature-Review-and-Meta-Analysis-of-the-Effects-of-Lockdowns-on-COVID-19-Mortality.pdf (May 20, 2023).

64 Brendan Pierson, "California law aiming to curb COVID misinformation blocked by judge," *Reuters* (Jan. 26, 2023), https://www.reuters.com/business/healthcare-pharmaceuticals/california-law-aiming-curb-covid-misinformation-blocked-by-judge-2023-01-26/ (May 20, 2023).

65 https://www.history.com/this-day-in-history/galileo-is-accused-of-heresy.

66 Desmet, *The Psychology of Totalitarianism*, 12–13.

67 Tim Harris, "Taibbi on Twitter Files: We've Discovered A Public-Private Censorship Bureaucracy," *RealClearPolitics* (Jan. 15, 2023), https://www.realclearpolitics.com/video/2023/01/15/taibbi_on_twitter_files_weve_discovered_a_public-private_censorship_bureaucracy.html (May 20, 2023).

68 Ibid.

69 "Matt Taibbi issues warning of government efforts to cleanse media of 'disinformation': 'Extremely dangerous,'" Fox News (March 26, 2023), https://www.foxnews.com/media/matt-taibbi-issues-warning -government-efforts-cleanse-media-disinformation (May 20, 2023).

70 Ibid.

71 "REPORT: IRS Agent Showed Up to 'Twitter Files' Journalist's Home Unannounced on the Day He Testified Before Congress," *Daily Caller*, https://dailycaller.com/2023/03/27/irs-agent-matt -taibbi-home-unannounced-twitter-files-testified-congress/.

72 "Matt Taibbi Reveals New Details About IRS Investigation of Him That Began Shortly After First Twitter Files Release," *Daily Caller*, https://dailycaller.com/2023/05/24/journalist-matt-taibbi-reveals -new-details-irs-investigation-immediately-twitter-files/.

73 "WSJ Opinion: Twitter and the FBI Censorship Subsidiary," *Wall Street Journal* (Dec. 20, 2022), https://www.wsj.com/video/series /opinion-review-and-outlook/wsj-opinion-twitter-and-the-fbi-cen sorship-subsidiary/E292F2B0-22C5-4A96-A7C0-784F36B96490 (May 20, 2023).

74 Andrew Bailey, MO Attorney General, "Missouri Attorney General Releases More Documents Exposing White House's Social Media Censorship Scheme," Office of the Attorney General, Missouri (Jan. 9, 2023), https://ago.mo.gov/home/news/2023/01/09 /missouri-attorney-general-releases-more-documents-exposing -white-house's-social-media-censorship-scheme (May 20, 2023).

75 Jonathan Turley, "How the Biden administration has quietly helped to 'score' conservative speech," *The Hill* (Feb. 18, 2023), https:// thehill.com/opinion/judiciary/3864526-how-the-biden-administra tion-has-quietly-helped-to-score-conservative-speech/ (May 20, 2023).

76 Ibid.

77 https://www.foxbusiness.com/media/chatgpt-critics-fear-artificial -intelligence-tool-liberal-biases-pushes-left-wing-talking-points.

78 Raymond Aron, *Democracy & Totalitarianism: A Theory of Political Systems* (New York, Praeger, 1965), 40–41.

79 Greta Reich, "Law School activists protest Judge Kyle Duncan's visit to campus," *Stanford Daily* (March 11, 2023), https://stanford

daily.com/2023/03/11/law-school-activists-protest-judge-kyle-dun cans-visit-to-campus/ (May 20, 2023).

80 Ibid.

81 Ibid.

82 Joshua Fatzick, "American College Campuses Increasingly Hostile to Free Speech," *VOA* (April 26, 2017), https://www.voanews.com/a/us-colleges-confront-new-era-sometimes-violent-protest/3826959.html (May 20, 2023).

83 See generally, https://legalinsurrection.com/tag/college-insurrection/ (May 20, 2023).

CHAPTER FIVE: WAR ON THE AMERICAN CITIZEN

1 "Citizenship," *Britannica* (May 16, 2023), https://www.britannica.com/topic/citizenship (May 20, 2023).

2 Samuel P. Huntington, *Who Are We? The Challenges to America's National Identity* (New York: Simon & Schuster, 2004), 324–25.

3 Ibid., 325.

4 Robert Law, "New Harvard-Harris Poll Shows Broad Opposition to Biden's Border Policies" (cis.org, May 10, 2021); "A majority of Americans see an 'invasion' at the southern border" (NPR, August 18, 2022); Lydia Saad, "Americans Showing Increased Concern About Immigration" (gallup.com, February 13, 2003).

5 Mark R. Levin, *Liberty and Tyranny* (New York: Threshold, 2010), 149.

6 Adam Shaw, "Flashback: Biden praised 'constant,' 'unrelenting' stream of immigration into US," Fox News (Dec. 12, 2020), https://www.foxnews.com/politics/flashback-joe-biden-constant-unrelenting-immigration (May 20, 2023).

7 Thomas W. West, *Vindicating the Founders* (Lanham, Rowen & Littlefield, 1997), 149.

8 Ibid., 151.

9 Ibid., 153.

10 Ibid., 154–55.

11 Ibid., 155.

12 Arthur M. Schlesinger, *The Disuniting of America: Reflections on a Multicultural Society* (New York: W. W. Norton & Co., 1988), 106.

13 Ibid., 106–7.

14 Ibid., 107 (emphasis added).

15 Ibid.

16 Ibid., 127.

17 Samuel P. Huntington, *Who Are We?: The Challenges to America's National Identity* (New York: Simon & Schuster, 2004), 199–200.

18 Ibid., 203–4.

19 Ibid., 214–15.

20 Dan Stein, "Too Little, Too Late: Biden Stages Carefully Choreographed Photo-Op at the Border," FAIR (Jan. 8, 2023), https://www.fairus.org/press-releases/border-security/too-little-too-late-biden-stages-carefully-choreographed-photo-op.

21 "Biden ripped for not meeting with migrants during border visit: 'He did not come to see this,'" Fox News (Jan. 9, 2023), https://www.foxnews.com/media/biden-ripped-for-not-meeting-migrants-during-border-visit-he-did-not-come-see-this.

22 "President Biden's Executive Actions on Immigration," Center for Migration Studies (Feb. 2, 2021), https://cmsny.org/biden-immigration-executive-actions/ (May 20, 2023).

23 "CBP Enforcement Statistics Fiscal Year 2023," U.S. Customs and Border Protection, https://www.cbp.gov/newsroom/stats/cbp-enforcement-statistics (May 20, 2023).

24 Mark Morgan, "No Time To Waste—Here Are the Top 3 Border Security Priorities for the Next Congress," Heritage Foundation (Dec. 7, 2022), https://www.heritage.org/homeland-security/commentary/no-time-waste-here-are-the-top-3-border-security-priorities-the-next (May 20, 2023).

25 Simon Hankinson, "Biden's Abuse of Power at the Border," Heritage Foundation (Jan. 11, 2023), https://www.heritage.org/immigration/commentary/bidens-abuse-power-the-border (May 20, 2023).

26 Elizabeth Jacobs, "Two Years of Biden's Immigration Policies," Center for Immigration Studies, Jan. 31, 2023, https://cis.org/Report/Two-Years-Bidens-Immigration-Policies (May 20, 2023).

27 Ibid.

28 Ibid.

29 James Reinl, "Forget drugs. Mexico's cartels make more money trafficking PEOPLE across the border nowadays, using debt bondage to

earn $13 billion from migrants' earnings long after they enter the US, warns Texas ex-lawman," *Daily Mail* online (October 6, 2022), https://www.dailymail.co.uk/news/article-11287811/Forget-drugs-Bidens-open-border-lets-Mexican-cartels-make-cash-trafficking-PEOPLE-nowadays.html (June 5, 2023).

30 Erin Dwinell and Hannah Davis, "The Costs of Biden's Border Crisis: The First Two Years," Heritage Foundation (March 13, 2023), https://www.heritage.org/immigration/report/the-costs-bidens-border-crisis-the-first-two-years (May 20, 2023).

31 "Factsheet: Great Replacement/White Genocide Conspiracy Theory," Bridge Initiative, https://bridge.georgetown.edu/research/factsheet-great-replacement-white-genocide-conspiracy-theory/ (Feb. 3, 2020).

32 Deroy Murdock, "Biden Is Soft on the New Slavery," *Daily Signal*, June 21, 2021, https://www.dailysignal.com/2021/06/21/biden-is-soft-on-the-new-slavery/ (May 20, 2023).

33 Ibid.

34 Ibid.

35 Miram Jordan, "Smuggling Migrants at the Border Now a Billion-Dollar Business," *New York Times* (July 25, 2022), https://www.nytimes.com/2022/07/25/us/migrant-smuggling-evolution.html (May 20, 2023).

36 Jarod Forget, "Violent drug organizations use human trafficking to expand profits," U.S. Drug Enforcement Agency (Jan. 28, 2021), https://www.dea.gov/stories/2021/2021-01/2021-01-28/violent-drug-organizations-use-human-trafficking-expand-profits (May 20, 2023).

37 Hannah Dreier, "Alone and Exploited, Migrant Children Work Brutal Jobs Across the U.S.," *New York Times* (Feb. 25, 2023), https://www.nytimes.com/2023/02/25/us/unaccompanied-migrant-child-workers-exploitation.html (May 20, 2023).

38 Ibid.

39 Ibid.

40 "The Elephant in the Classroom: Mass Immigration Imposing Colossal Cost and Challenges on Public Education," FAIR (Sept. 14, 2022), https://www.fairus.org/issue/illegal-immigration

/elephant-classroom-mass-immigration-imposing-colossal-cost-and
-challenges (May 20, 2023).

41 "Criminal Noncitizen Statistics Fiscal Year 2023," U.S. Customs
and Border Protection, https://www.cbp.gov/newsroom/stats/cbp
-enforcement-statistics/criminal-noncitizen-statistics (May 20,
2023).

42 Ibid.

43 "The Fiscal Burden of Illegal Immigration On United States Taxpay
ers 2023," FAIR, https://www.fairus.org/sites/default/files/2023-03
/Fiscal%20Burden%20of%20Illegal%20Immigration%20on%20
American%20Taxpayers%202023%20WEB_0.pdf (May 20, 2023).

44 Adam Shaw, "Over 99% of migrants who have sought Title 42
exception via CBP One app were approved," Fox News (April 14,
2023), https://www.foxnews.com/politics/99-percent-migrants
-sought-title-42-exception-cbp-one-app-approved (May 20, 2023).

45 Mark R. Levin, *American Marxism* (New York: Threshold, 2019),
123–31.

46 Sen. Harry Reid, "Cut Legal Admissions by Two-Thirds: Immigration: A senator offers a 'stabilization' bill," *Los Angeles Times*
(August 10, 1994), https://www.latimes.com/archives/la-xpm-1994
-08-10-me-25434-story.html (May 21, 2023).

47 Sean Higgins, "Vitter quotes '93 Reid Senate speech on ending
birthright citizenship," *Washington Examiner* (March 13, 2015),
https://www.washingtonexaminer.com/vitter-quotes-93-reid-senate
-speech-on-ending-birthright-citizenship (May 21, 2023).

48 Robert Law, "Harry Reid: A Case Study in Shifting Immigration
Views to Appease Party Insiders," Center for Immigration Studies (Jan. 12, 2022), https://cis.org/Law/Harry-Reid-Case-Study-
Shifting-Immigration-Views-Appease-Party-Insiders (May 21,
2023).

49 Cal Thomas, "Flip-flop Schumer on illegal immigration, then and
now," *Washington Times* (Nov. 21, 2022), https://www.washington
times.com/news/2022/nov/21/flip-flop-schumer-on-illegal-immi
gration-then-and-/ (May 21, 2023).

50 Karol Markowicz, "Chuck Schumer finally admits it: Democrats
don't want any real immigration law," *New York Post* (Nov. 20,

2022), https://nypost.com/2022/11/20/chuck-schumer-admits-dem ocrats-dont-want-any-real-immigration-law/ (May 21, 2023).

51 Ibid.

52 Mark. R. Levin, *Liberty & Tyranny* (New York: Pocket Books, 2009), 152.

53 "President Obama to Establish César E. Chávez National Monument," The White House (Oct. 1, 2012), https://obamawhitehouse .archives.gov/the-press-office/2012/10/01/president-obama-estab lish-c-sar-e-ch-vez-national-monument (May 21, 2023).

54 "Presidential Proclamation—Cesar Chavez Day, 2014," The White House (March 28, 2014), https://obamawhitehouse.archives.gov /the-press-office/2014/03/28/presidential-proclamation-cesar -chavez-day-2014 (May 21, 2023).

55 Travis Caldwell, "In Biden's Oval Office, Cesar Chavez takes his place among America's heroes," CNN (Jan. 21, 2021), https://www.cnn .com/2021/01/21/us/cesar-chavez-bust-oval-office-trnd/index.html (May 21, 2023).

56 "Immigration," AFL-CIO, https://aflcio.org/issues/immigration (May 21, 2023).

57 Fabiola Cineas, "Where 'replacement theory' comes from—and why it refuses to go away," *Vox* (May 17, 2022), https://www.vox .com/23076952/replacement-theory-white-supremacist-violence (May 21, 2023).

58 Jeff Deist, "Evolution or Corruption?: The Imposition of Political-Language in the West Today," Etica & Politica / Ethics & Politics, 2022, https://www2.units.it /etica /2022 2 /DEIST.pdf.

59 Joe Biden, Twitter video message (April 13, 2023), https://twitter. com/joebiden (May 21, 2023).

60 "A Proclamation on National Immigrant Heritage Month, 2022," The White House (May 31, 2022), https://www.whitehouse.gov /briefing-room/presidential-actions/2022/05/31/a-proclamation-on -national-immigrant-heritage-month-2022/.

61 Neil Munro, "Mayorkas: Americans' Priorities are Subordinate to 'Nation of Immigrants,'" *Breitbart* (May 10, 2023), https://www.bre itbart.com/immigration/2023/05/10/mayorkas-americans-priorities -subordinate-nation-immigrants/ (May 21, 2023).

62 Stanley A. Renshon, "Allowing Non-Citizens to Vote in the United States? Why Not?" Center for Immigration Studies (Sept. 2008), https://cis.org/sites/cis.org/files/articles/2008/renshon_08.pdf (May 21, 2023).

63 Ibid.

64 "Laws permitting noncitizens to vote in the United States," *Ballotpedia*, https://ballotpedia.org/Laws_permitting_noncitizens_to _vote_in_the_United_States (May 21, 2023).

65 Gov. Richard Lamm, "My plan to destroy America," *Washington Examiner* (April 21, 2006), https://www.washingtonexaminer.com /gov-richard-lamm-my-plan-to-destroy-america-34302 (May 21, 2023).

66 Samuel P. Huntington, *Who Are We?: The Challenges to America's National Identity* (New York: Simon & Schuster, 2004), 335.

CHAPTER SIX: WAR ON THE NUCLEAR FAMILY

1 Karl Marx and Frederick Engels, *Manifesto of the Communist Party* (Pacifica, Marxist Internet Archive, 1848), 45, https://www.marx ists.org/admin/books/manifesto/Manifesto.pdf (May 21, 2023).

2 Ibid.

3 Robert Weikart, "Marx, Engels, and the Abolition of the Family," *History of European Ideas*, vol. 18, no. 5 (1994), https://www.csus tan.edu/sites/default/files/History/Faculty/Weikart/Marx-Engels -and-the-Abolition-of-the-Family.pdf (May 21, 2023).

4 Ibid., 9.

5 Ibid., 12.

6 Conn Carroll, "No one benefits more from the destruction of the American family than the Democratic Party," *Washington Examiner* (Nov. 9, 2022), https://www.washingtonexaminer.com/opinion /no-one-benefits-more-from-the-destruction-of-the-american-fam ily-than-the-democratic-party (May 21, 2023).

7 Ibid.

8 Ibid.

9 Samuel J. Adams and Joel Kotkin, "The Rise of the Single Woke (and Young, Democratic) Female (American Enterprise Institute), AEI

https://www.realclearinvestigations.com/articles/2023/01/17/the_
rise_of_the_single_woke_and_young_democratic_female_875047
.html (January 17, 2023).

10 Ibid.

11 https://www.washingtonexaminer.com/politics/nancy-pelosi
-believes-democrats-have-the-key-to-securing-victory-in-the
-2024-general-elections#:~:text=Former%20House%20
Speaker%20Nancy,in%20the%202024%20election%20cycle.

12 Ibid.

13 Ibid.

14 John Clark, "McAuliffe: 'I don't think parents should be telling
schools what they should teach,'" MyStateLine.com (Sept. 29,
2021), https://www.mystateline.com/news/politics/mcauliffe-i-dont
-think-parents-should-be-telling-schools-what-they-should
-teach/#:~:text=McAuliffe%20responded%20by%20saying%20
he,should%20teach%2C%E2%80%9D%20McAuliffe%20said
(May 21, 2023).

15 "Terry McAuliffe's War on Parents," *National Review* (Oct. 1, 2021),
https://www.nationalreview.com/2021/10/terry-mcauliffes-war-on
-parents/ (May 21, 2023).

16 National Education Association, Twitter message (Nov. 12, 2022),
https://twitter.com/NEAToday/status/1591587398109929473
(May 21, 2023).

17 "Partnership Among Federal, State, Local, Tribal and Territorial
Law Enforcement to Address Threats Against School Administrators, Board Members, Teachers, and Staff," U.S. Dept. of Justice,
Office of the Attorney General (Oct. 4, 2021), https://www.justice
.gov/d9/pages/attachments/2021/10/04/partnership_among_federal
_state_local_tribal_and_territorial_law_enforcement_to_address
_threats_against_school_administrators_board_members_teachers
_and_staff_0_0.pdf (May 21, 2023).

18 "A 'Manufactured' Issue and 'Misapplied' Priorities: Subpoenaed
Documents Show no Legitimate Basis for the Attorney General's
Anti-Parent Memo," U.S. House of Representatives, Committee
on the Judiciary and the Select Subcommittee on the Weaponization of the Federal Government (March 21, 2023), https://judi
ciary.house.gov/sites/evo-subsites/republicans-judiciary.house.gov

/files/evo-media-document/2023-03-21-school-board-documents -interim-report.pdf (May 21, 2023).

19 "NSBA Apologizes for Letter to President Biden," National School Boards Association (Oct. 22, 2021), https://www.nsba.org/News /2021/letter-to-members (May 21, 2023).

20 "H.R. 5 Parents Bill of Rights Act," 118 Cong. (2023–2024), https://www.congress.gov/bill/118th-congress/house-bill/5/text?s=1 &r=1&q=%7B%22search%22%3A%22parents+bill+of+rights%2 2%7D (May 21, 2023).

21 Speaker Kevin McCarthy, "The Parents Bill of Rights," https://www.speaker.gov/parents/#:~:text=To%20support%20 our%20children%2C%20provide%20for%20their%20 education%2C,be%20updated%20on%20any%20violent%20 activity%20at%20school (May 21, 2023).

22 Peter Kasperowicz, "'Parents Bill of Rights' wins zero votes from Dems who attack it as 'fascism,' 'extreme' attack on schools," Fox News (March 24, 2023), https://www.foxnews.com/politics/parents -bill-rights-wins-zero-votes-dems-attack-fascism-extreme-attack -schools (May 21, 2023).

23 Caroline Downey, "Biden Claims School Children Don't Belong to Parents 'When They're in the Classroom,'" National Review, Apr. 27, 2022, https://www.nationalreview.com/news/biden-claims -school-children-dont-belong-to-parents-when-theyre-in-the-class room/ (May 21, 2023).

24 "Mark Levin says Biden's poll numbers should be 'zero': He has no character," Fox News (May 9, 2023), https://www.foxnews.com /video/6327089193112 (May 21, 2023).

25 Ashley Oliver, "House Passes Bill to Ban Men from Women's Sports with No Democrat Support," Breitbart (Apr. 20, 2023), https://www .breitbart.com/politics/2023/04/20/house-passes-bill-to-ban-men -from-womens-sports-with-no-democrat-support/ (May 21, 2023).

26 Gianna Melillo, "New poll finds majority of Americans against trans athletes in female sports," The Hill (June 14, 2022), https://thehill .com/changing-america/respect/diversity-inclusion/3522635-new -poll-finds-majority-of-americans-against-trans-athletes-in-female -sports/ (May 21, 2023).

27 Kaylee McGhee White, "Biden's new Title IX rules deputize teach-

ers to override parents on gender identity," *New York Post* (Aug. 15, 2022), https://nypost.com/2022/08/15/bidens-title-ix-rules-deputize-teachers-to-override-parents/ (May 21, 2023).

28 Timothy Nerozzi, "Biden administration endorses transgender youth sex-change operations, 'top surgery,' hormone therapy," Fox News (March 31, 2022), https://www.foxnews.com/politics/biden-administration-transgender-agenda-youth-sex-change-hormone-therapy (May 21, 2023).

29 "Gender-Affirming Care and Young People," Office of Population Affairs, https://opa.hhs.gov/sites/default/files/2022-03/gender-affirming-care-young-people-march-2022.pdf (May 21, 2023).

30 Jay W. Richards, "Biden Doubles Down on Radical 'Gender-Affirming Care' for Kids, The Heritage Foundation (April 4, 2022), https://www.heritage.org/gender/commentary/biden-doubles-down-radical-gender-affirming-care-kids (May 21, 2023).

31 Jared Eckert, "Don't Be Fooled: Gender Identity Policies Don't Follow the Science," The Heritage Foundation (June 16, 2021), https://www.heritage.org/gender/commentary/dont-be-fooled-gender-identity-policies-dont-follow-the-science (May 21, 2023).

32 Timothy Nerozzi, "Biden administration endorses transgender youth sex-change operations, 'top surgery,' hormone therapy," Fox News (March 31, 2022), https://www.foxnews.com/politics/biden-administration-transgender-agenda-youth-sex-change-hormone-therapy (May 21, 2023).

33 https://www.wsj.com/articles/u-s-becomes-transgender-care-outlier-as-more-in-europe-urge-caution-6c70b5e0.

34 Ibid.

35 Tony Perkins, "California Teachers Union Wants Kids to Pursue Gender Transition Without Parental Consent," *Daily Signal* (Feb. 24, 2025), https://www.dailysignal.com/2020/02/24/california-teachers-union-wants-kids-to-pursue-gender-transition-without-parental-consent/ (May 21, 2023); Josh Christenson, "Some Schools Won't Tell Parents When Their Kids Express Gender Confusion. Experts Say That's Illegal," *Washington Free Beacon* (Aug. 11, 2022), https://freebeacon.com/campus/some-schools-wont-tell-parents-when-their-kids-express-gender-confusion-experts-say-thats-illegal/ (May 21, 2023); Jon Brown, "New California transgender

law endangers parental rights worldwide, legal group warns: 'Drastic overreach,'" Fox News (Oct. 4, 2022), https://www.foxnews.com /us/new-california-transgender-law-endangers-parental-rights-world wide-legal-group-warns-drastic-overreach (May 21, 2023); Eileen Griffin, "Parents Forced to Battle Governments for Children's Custody in Transgender Disputes," *Heartland Daily News* (Aug. 16, 2022), https://heartlanddailynews.com/2022/08/parents-battle-for -childrens-custody-in-transgender-disputes/ (May 21, 2023).

36 Josh Christenson, "Nearly 6,000 US public schools hide child's gender status from parents," *New York Post* (March 8, 2023), https:// nypost.com/2023/03/08/us-public-schools-conceal-childs-gender -status-from-parents/ (May 21, 2023).

37 "Target partners with org pushing for kids' genders to be secretly changed in schools without parental consent," Fox News (May 26, 2023), https://www.foxnews.com/media/target-partners-org-push ing-kids-genders-secretly-changed-schools-without-parental-con sent.

38 GLSEN Homepage, https://www.glsen.org/.

39 "Target partners with org pushing for kids' genders to be secretly changed in schools without parental consent."

40 Ibid.

41 "Disney exec cops to advancing 'gay agenda' by 'adding queerness' to shows," *New York Post* (June 5, 2023), https://nypost.com/2022 /03/30/disney-producer-cops-to-adding-queerness-to-animated -shows/.

42 Ibid.

43 Dr. Debra Soh, *The End of Gender: Debunking the Myths about Sex and Identity in Our Society* (New York: Threshold Editions, 2020), 278.

44 *Planned Parenthood v. Casey*, 505 U.S. 833 (1992).

45 *Dobbs v. Jackson Women's Health Organization*, No. 19-1392, 597 U.S. ___ (2022).

46 *Roe v. Wade*, 410 U.S. 113 (1973).

47 Thomas Jipping, "Democrats Push Radical Abortion Bill Far More Expansive Than Roe," *Daily Signal* (May 9, 2022), https://www .dailysignal.com/2022/05/09/democrats-push-radical-abortion-bill -far-more-expansive-than-roe?_gl=1*1yfyayx*_ga*MTM0NjA1N

jEzNy4xNjU5NzA5NTQ5*_ga_W14BT6YQ87*MTY4MjI3MTA
xMi4yOS4wLjE2ODIyNzEwMTIuNjAuMC4w (May 21, 2023).

48 Jon Lavine, "Powerful teachers union influenced CDC on school reopenings, emails shown," *New York Post* (May 1, 2021), https://nypost.com/2021/05/01/teachers-union-collaborated-with-cdc-on-school-reopening-emails/ (May 21, 2023).

49 Ibid.

50 "COVID-19: Why Are Children Less Affected?" Cedars Sinai (Apr. 21, 2020), https://www.cedars-sinai.org/newsroom/covid19-why-are-children-less-affected/ (May 21, 2023).

51 Ibid.

52 Emma Dorn et al., "COVID-19 and education: The lingering effects of unfinished learning," McKinsey & Company (July 27, 2021), https://www.mckinsey.com/industries/education/our-insights/covid-19-and-education-the-lingering-effects-of-unfinished-learning (May 21, 2023).

53 Joe Schoffstall, "CDC tightened masking guidelines after threats from teachers' union, emails show," Fox News (Sept. 8, 2021), https://www.foxnews.com/politics/cdc-tightened-masking-guidelines-after-threats-from-teachers-union (May 21, 2023).

54 Ibid.

55 David Zweig, "The Science of Masking Kids at School Remains Uncertain," *New York* (Aug. 20, 2021), https://nymag.com/intelligencer/2021/08/the-science-of-masking-kids-at-school-remains-uncertain.html (May 21, 2023) (emphasis added).

56 Mary Katherine Ham, "The True Cost of Masking Young Kids Forever," *Daily Beast* (Jan. 29, 2022), https://www.thedailybeast.com/the-true-cost-of-masking-young-kids-forever (May 21, 2023).

57 Alex Hammer, "COVID rules are blamed for 23% dive in young children's development: Disturbing study shows scores in three key cognitive tests slumped between 2018 and 2021, with face mask rules among possible culprits," *Daily Mail* (Nov. 26, 2021), https://www.dailymail.co.uk/news/article-10247315/Face-masks-harm-childrens-development-Study-blames-significantly-reduced-development.html (May 21, 2023).

58 Dan Goldberg, "Harvard poll: 40 percent of parents believe masks at school harmed their kids," *Politico* (March 25, 2022), https://

www.politico.com/news/2022/03/25/parents-masks-harm-kids-poll -00020250 (May 21, 2023).

59 Zach Weissmueller, "California Law Strips Licenses from 'Misinformation'-Spreading Doctors," *Reason* (Dec. 6, 2022), https://reason .com/video/2022/12/06/california-law-strips-licenses-from-misin formation-spreading-doctors/ (May 21, 2023).

60 Melissa Moschella, "Critical Race Theory, Public Schools, and Parental Rights," Heritage Foundation (Mar. 24, 2022), https:// www.heritage.org/education/commentary/critical-race-theory-pub lic-schools-and-parental-rights (May 21, 2023).

61 Jonathan Butcher, "Rescuing Math and Science from Critical Race Theory's Racial Discrimination," Heritage Foundation (July 13, 2021), https://www.heritage.org/education/report/rescuing-math -and-science-critical-race-theorys-racial-discrimination (May 21, 2023).

62 Brian Flood, "Critical race theory-related ideas found in mandatory programs at 58 of top 100 US medical schools: report," Fox News (Nov. 28, 2022), https://www.foxnews.com/media/critical-race -theory-related-ideas-found-mandatory-programs-58-top-100-us -medical-schools-report (May 21, 2023).

63 Stanley Goldfarb and Laura L. Morgan, "Top med school putting wokeism ahead of giving America good doctors," *New York Post* (Sept. 2, 2022), https://nypost.com/2022/09/02/top-med-schools -putting-wokeism-ahead-of-giving-america-good-doctors/ (May 21, 2023).

64 Kenin M. Spivak, "Segregated Education: Resegregating American Education," *National Review* (July 17, 2022), https://www.nation alreview.com/2022/07/resegregating-american-education/ (May 21, 2023).

65 Ibid.

66 Ibid.

67 Thomas Sowell, " 'Favors' to Blacks," Creators.com (Sept. 27, 2016), https://www.creators.com/read/thomas-sowell/09/16/favors -to-blacks (May 21, 2023).

68 Jennifer Stefano, "Democrats' War On Charter Schools Is Sending Families Into the Arms of Republicans," *Federalist* (Sept. 23, 2022), https://thefederalist.com/2022/09/23/democrats-war-on-char

ter-schools-is-sending-families-into-the-arms-of-republicans / (May 21, 2023).

69 "Colorado teachers union adopts anti-capitalist polemic," *Denver Gazette* (May 27, 2023), https://denvergazette.com/news/government/colorado-teachers-union-anti-capitalism-polemic/article_f31b3b7c-f810-11ed-a540-1f1adeb0fd84.html.

70 Ibid.

71 Joe Biden, Tweet (Jan. 22, 2020), https://twitter.com/JoeBiden/status/1220182792304308225?ref_src=twsrc%5Etfw%7Ctwcamp%5Etweetembed%7Ctwterm%5E1220182792304308225%7Ctwgr%5Ed053273599b71c90cf8f35dd5880f78009da25d5%7Ctwcon%5Es1_&ref_url=https%3A%2F%2Fwww.foxnews.com%2Fpolitics%2Fbiden-pelosi-top-dems-sent-kids-private-school-oppose-choice (May 22, 2023).

72 Anthony Iafrate, "8 Politicians Who Attacked School Choice but Went to Private School Themselves (Or Sent Their Kids), *Catholic Vote* (Feb. 1, 2023), https://catholicvote.org/8-politicians-who-attacked-school-choice-but-went-to-private-school-themselves-or-sent-their-kids/ (May 22, 2023).

73 Hon. Miguel Cardona, testimony before House Committee on Appropriations, "Budget Hearing—Fiscal Year 2024 Request for the United States Department of Education" (April 18, 2023), https://appropriations.house.gov/legislation/hearings/budget-hearing-fiscal-year-2024-request-united-states-department-education (May 25, 2023).

74 Kermit Roosevelt, "I Spent 7 Months Studying Supreme Court Reform. We Need to Pack the Court Now," https://time.com/6127193/supreme-court-reform-expansion/ (December 10, 2021).

75 Ibid.

76 Stanley Kurtz, "Biden and Dems Are Set to Abolish the Suburbs," *National Review* (June 30, 2020), https://www.nationalreview.com/corner/biden-and-dems-are-set-to-abolish-the-suburbs/ (May 22, 2023).

77 Howard Husock, "Biden's Latest Whack at the Suburbs Will Change Your Neighborhood for the Worse," American Enterprise Institute (Feb. 23, 2023), https://www.aei.org/op-eds/bidens-latest

-whack-at-the-suburbs-will-change-your-neighborhood-for-the
-worse/ (May 22, 2023).

78 Ibid.

79 Ibid.

80 Samantha Aschieris, "27 of Top 30 Crime-Ridden Cities Run by Democrats," *Daily Signal* (Nov. 4, 2022), https://www.dailysignal .com/2022/11/04/democrat-run-cities-counties-have-a-murder -problem-report-shows/ (May 22, 2023).

81 Candace Hathaway, "Murder rates rise 10% in liberal-run cities due to defund-police, soft-on-crime policies: Study," *Blaze Media* (Apr. 27, 2023), https://www.theblaze.com/news/murder-rates-rise -10-in-liberal-run-cities-due-to-defund-police-soft-on-crime-poli cies-study (May 22, 2023).

82 Heather Mac Donald, "BLM is silent on the top killer of black kids," *New York Post* (May 26, 2022), https://nypost.com/2022/05/26/blm -is-silent-on-the-top-killer-of-black-kids-gang-violence/ (May 22, 2023).

83 Thomas Sowell, " 'Favors' to Blacks," Creators.com (Sept. 27, 2016), https://www.creators.com/read/thomas-sowell/09/16/favors -to-blacks (May 22, 2023).

84 Kay S. Hymowitz, "The Distorted World of Ta-Nehisi Coates," *National Review* (Sept. 18, 2015), https://www.nationalreview.com /2015/09/ta-nehisi-coates-wrong/ (May 22, 2023).

85 Ron Haskins, "Moynihan Was Right: Now What?" *The Annals of the American Academy of Political and Social Science*, vol. 621, Jan. 2009, https://www.jstor.org/stable/40375843 (May 22, 2023).

86 AEI-Brookings Working Group, "Children First: Why Family Structure and Stability Matter for Children," The Institute for Family Studies (Feb. 28, 2022), https://ifstudies.org/blog/children-first -why-family-structure-and-stability-matter-for-children (May 22, 2023).

87 Ibid.

88 Betsy McCaughey, "The Democratic Party is now the party of welfare—not working people," *New York Post* (Feb. 28, 2021), https:// nypost.com/author/betsy-mccaughey/ (May 22, 2023).

89 Sean Moran, "CBO: Republican Debt Limit Plan Would Reduce

Deficit by $4.8 Trillion," *Breitbart* (Apr. 25, 2023), https://www
.breitbart.com/politics/2023/04/25/cbo-republican-debt-limit-plan
-would-reduce-deficit-by-4-8-trillion/ (May 22, 2023).

90 Edward Nelson, "Milton Friedman on Inflation," *Economic Synopses*, no. 1, 2007, https://files.stlouisfed.org/files/htdocs/publications
/es/07/ES0701.pdf (May 22, 2023).

91 "The Real Story Behind Inflation," Heritage Foundation, https://
www.heritage.org/budget-and-spending/heritage-explains/the-real
-story-behind-inflation (May 22, 2023).

92 Jeff Mordock, "After two years of massive spending, Biden proposes
more for social programs in fiscal '24 budget," *Washington Times*
(March 9, 2023), https://www.washingtontimes.com/news/2023
/mar/9/bidens-68-trillion-budget-calls-massive-social-spe
/ (May 22, 2023).

93 "Fresh proof of the pain Biden's economy has inflicted on the
middle class," *New York Post* (Dec. 29, 2022), https://nypost.com
/2022/12/29/proof-of-the-pain-bidens-economy-has-inflicted-on
-middle-class/ (May 22, 2023).

94 Ibid.

95 Stef W. Kight, "Dramatic realignment swings working-class districts
toward GOP," *Axios* (Apr. 16, 2023), https://www.axios.com/2023/04
/12/house-democrats-winning-wealthier-districts-middle-class-gop
(May 22, 2023).

96 Ramesh Ponnuru, "How Democrats Became the Party of the Upper
Middle Class," American Enterprise Institute (May 26, 2020),
https://www.aei.org/op-eds/how-democrats-became-the-party-of
-the-upper-middle-class/ (May 22, 2023).

97 Daniel Greenfield, "Biden to Double Cost of Electricity," *Front Page
Magazine* (April 26, 2023), https://www.frontpagemag.com/biden
-to-double-cost-of-electricity/ (May 22, 2023).

98 Ibid.

99 Ibid.

100 https://reason.com/2023/05/29/amidst-dreams-of-green-energy-reg
ulators-and-industry-warn-of-summer-blackouts/.

101 Paul Tomachev, "The Madness of Democrats Leftist Discourse:
How Biden Administration Is Killing the Economy and Prosper-

ity," *Eurasia Review* (March 13, 2023), https://www.eurasiareview
.com/13032023-the-madness-of-democrats-leftist-discourse-how
-biden-administration-is-killing-the-economy-and-prosperity-oped
/ (May 22, 2023).

102 https://hotair.com/ed-morrissey/2022/09/20/summers-insane-that
-bidens-blocking-pipelines-for-oil-transport-n497936.

103 https://www.wsj.com/articles/federal-oil-leases-slow-to-a-trickle
-under-biden-11662230816.

104 https://www.washingtonexaminer.com/policy/biden-lithium-exec
utive-critical-minerals-mining.

105 Aaron Kliegman, " 'Hands off my stove': New group pushes back
against gas stove bans sweeping nation," Fox News (April 1,
2023), https://www.foxnews.com/politics/hands-off-stove-new
-group-pushes-against-gas-stove-bans-sweeping-nation (May 22,
2023).

106 Matthew Daly and Tom Krisher, "Stiff EPA emission limits to
boost US electric vehicle sales," Associated Press (April 12, 2023),
https://apnews.com/article/biden-electric-vehicles-epa-tail
pipe-emissions-climate-406d74e18459bc135f089c681ba9e224
(May 22, 2023).

107 Thomas Catenacci, "Biden admin moving forward with light bulb
bans in coming weeks," Fox News (April 1, 2023), https://www
.foxnews.com/politics/biden-admin-moving-forward-light-bulb
-bans-coming-weeks (May 22, 2023)

108 Thomas Catenacci, "Biden admin cracks down on air conditioners as war on appliances continues," Fox News (March 24, 2023),
https://www.foxnews.com/politics/biden-admin-cracks-down-air
-conditioners-war-appliances-continues (May 22, 2023); Christopher Hickey and Alex Leeds Matthews, "This is one of the
worst times to buy a car in decades. Here's why," CNN (April 2,
2023), https://www.cnn.com/2023/04/02/cars/worst-time-to-buy
-car-prices-inflation-dg/index.html (May 22, 2023).

109 Brian Boone, "The 13 Food Shortages to Expect in 2023," *Daily
Meal* (Jan. 27, 2023), https://www.thedailymeal.com/1166891/the
-13-food-shortages-to-expect-in-2023/ (May 22, 2023).

110 Tatyana Monnay, "A program that pays farmers not to farm isn't

saving the planet," *Politico* (Aug. 29, 2021), https://www.politico.com/news/2021/08/29/usda-farmers-conservation-program-507028 (May 22, 2023).

111 Ibid.

112 Mark R. Levin, *Liberty and Tyranny* (New York: Threshold, 2010).

113 Ibid., 114.

114 Ibid., 115.

115 https://www.westernjournal.com/blackrock-ceo-audience-evil-things-company/.

116 https://www.washingtonexaminer.com/policy/economy/how-esg-has-harmed-people-and-industries.

117 https://www.breitbart.com/economy/2023/06/26/blackrock-ceo-larry-fink-no-longer-uses-esg-laments-term-weaponized/.

118 Ibid.

CHAPTER SEVEN: WAR ON THE CONSTITUTION

1 Ruth Colker, "The White Supremacist Constitution," *Utah Law Review*, 2022, https://dc.law.utah.edu/ulr/vol2022/iss3/4/ (May 22, 2023).

2 "The Nation's Elie Mystal: The American Constitution Is 'Trash' Written by 'White People Willing to Make Deals with Slavers,'" *RealClearPolitics* (March 7, 2022) (posted by Tim Hains), https://www.realclearpolitics.com/video/2022/03/07/the_nations_elie_mystal_the_american_constitution_is_trash_written_by_white_people_willing_to_make_deals_with_slavers_and_colonists.html (May 22, 2023).

3 Isaac Schorr, "Nation Writer Labels the Constitution 'Trash,'" *National Review* (March 4, 2022), https://www.nationalreview.com/news/nation-writer-labels-the-constitution-trash/ (May 22, 2023).

4 "The Left's War on the Constitution" Independence Institute (October 21, 2020), https://i2i.org/the-lefts-war-on-the-constitution/.

5 "Founding Failures: Reckoning with our Constitution's Generational Impacts on Health and Well-Being," American Constitu-

tion Society (May 5, 2021), https://www.acslaw.org/video/77014 / (May 22, 2023).

6 Alex Traub, "This 86-Year-Old Radical May Save (or Sink) the Democrats," *New York Times* (May 10, 2019), https://www.nytimes.com/2019/05/10/nyregion/frances-fox-piven-democratic-social ism.html (May 22, 2023).

7 Ibid.

8 Jackie Swift, "The Curious History of Slavery in Africa," Cornell University, https://research.cornell.edu/news-features/curious-his tory-slavery-west-africa (May 22, 2023).

9 Ibid.

10 David Azerrad, "What the Constitution Really Says About Race and Slavery," Heritage Foundation (Dec. 28, 2015), https://www.heritage.org/the-constitution/commentary/what-the-constitution -really-says-about-race-and-slavery (May 23, 2023).

11 Ibid.

12 Ibid.

13 Ibid.

14 Frederick Douglass, "What to the Slave Is the Fourth of July?" *Teaching American History* (July 5, 1852), https://teachingameri canhistory.org/document/what-to-the-slave-is-the-fourth-of-july-2 / (May 23, 2023).

15 David Weigel, "Ruth Bader Ginsburg Makes Banal Point, Destroys the Republic," *Slate* (Feb. 3, 2012), https://slate.com/news-and-pol itics/2012/02/ruth-bader-ginsburg-makes-banal-point-destroys-the -republic.html (May 23, 2023) (emphasis added).

16 Phil Kerpen, "Democrats Voted to Repeal First Amendment," *American Commitment* (Sept. 9, 2014), https://www.americancom mitment.org/democrats-repeal-first-amendment/ (May 23, 2023).

17 Ibid.

18 Ibid.

19 Trevor Burrus, "Terrifying Senate Democrats Vote To Give Political Speech Less Protection Than Pornography," *Forbes* (Sept. 11, 2014), https://www.forbes.com/sites/trevorburrus/2014/09/11/terrify ing-senate-democrats-vote-to-give-political-speech-less-protection -than-pornography/?sh=1f5cf3d83f58 (May 23, 2023).

20 Ken Klippenstein and Lee Fang, "Leaked Documents Outline DHS's Plans to Police Disinformation," *Intercept* (Oct. 31, 2022), https://theintercept.com/2022/10/31/social-media-disinformation-dhs/ (May 23, 2023).

21 Ibid.

22 Ibid.

23 Joel B. Pollak, "Democrats Defend Censorship, Attack Journalists in Fiery Hearing," *Breitbart* (March 9, 2023), https://www.breitbart.com/politics/2023/03/09/watch-democrats-defend-censorship-attack-journalists-in-fiery-hearing/ (May 23, 2023).

24 Joel B. Pollak, "Democrats Threaten Matt Taibbi with Prison Time over 'Twitter Files' Exposé," *Breitbart* (April 21, 2023), https://www.breitbart.com/the-media/2023/04/21/democrats-threaten-matt-taibbi-with-prison-time-over-twitter-files-expose/ (May 23, 2023).

25 Ronn Torossian, "Menachem Begin to Joe Biden: I Am Not a Jew with Trembling Knees" (JewishPress.com, April 3, 2015), https://www.jewishpress.com/indepth/opinions/menachem-begin-to-joe-biden-i-am-not-a-jew-with-trembling-knees/2015/04/03/.

26 "What Does Biden Have Against Israel?" (*Wall Street Journal,* July 13, 2023), https://www.wsj.com/articles/biden-israel-benjamin-netanyahu-tom-nides-iran-abraham-accords-judicial-reform-639bd846.

27 Ibid.

28 Michael Horowitz, "More Than One Million Secret FBI Searches Made in Error: Watchdog Zachary Stieber," *Epoch Times* (April 28, 2023), https://www.theepochtimes.com/over-one-million-secret-fbi-searches-made-in-error-watchdog_5228576.html (May 23, 2023).

29 Kelly Laco, "Bombshell report reveals FBI whistleblowers 'faced devastating retaliation' for speaking out about 'politicized rot': Claim security clearances were revoked, they were suspended without pay and made 'homeless,'" *Daily Mail,* May 18, 2023, https://www.dailymail.co.uk/news/article-12098567/FBI-whistleblowers-faced-devastating-retaliation-speaking-politicized-rot.html (June 11, 2023).

30 Ibid.

31 Jerry Dunleavy, "Hunter Biden investigation: Second IRS whistleblower claims retaliation," *Washington Examiner,* May 22, 2023,

https://www.washingtonexaminer.com/news/justice/second-irs
-whistleblower-hunter-biden-concerns-retaliated (June 11, 2023).

32 https://www.realclearinvestigations.com/articles/2019/10/30
/whistleblower_exposed_close_to_biden_brennan_dnc_oppo
_researcher_120996.html.

33 "AOC Celebrates Fox News Terminating Tucker Carlson: 'Deplatforming Works,'" *Grabienews*, April 25, 2023, https://news.grabien
.com/story-aoc-celebrates-fox-news-terminating-tucker-carlson
-deplatforming-works (May 23, 2023).

34 Robby Soave, "Lawmakers to Cable Providers: Why Are You Letting News Channels Say These Things?" *Reason* (Feb. 22, 2021),
https://reason.com/2021/02/22/eshoo-mcnerney-letter-fox-news
-newsmax-oann-comcast-misinformation/ (May 23, 2023).

35 Gabe Kaminsky, "Disinformation Inc: Meet the groups hauling in
cash to secretly blacklist conservative news," *Washington Examiner* (Feb. 9, 2023), https://www.washingtonexaminer.com/policy
/technology/disinformation-conservative-media-censored-black
lists (May 23, 2023).

36 Ibid.

37 Gabe Kaminsky, "Disinformation Inc: Meet the groups hauling in
cash to secretly blacklist conservative news," *Washington Examiner*
(Feb. 9, 2023), https://www.washingtonexaminer.com/restoring
-america/equality-not-elitism/disinformation-group-secretly-black
listing-right-wing-outlets-bankrolled-state-department (May 23,
2023).

38 Catherine Salgado, "Surprise, Surprise! Soros-Tied Disinfo Group
Is Reportedly 'Blacklisting' Conservative Media," *MRCNewsBusters*
(Feb. 10, 2023), https://newsbusters.org/blogs/free-speech/cath
erine-salgado/2023/02/10/surprise-surprise-soros-tied-disinfo-group
(May 23, 2023).

39 https://freebeacon.com/media/propublica-takes-millions-from
-secret-donors/.

40 https://nypost.com/2023/06/09/moral-force-propublica-under-fire
-for-taking-millions-from-secret-donors/.

41 https://www.washingtonexaminer.com/policy/courts/left-wing
-funding-network-behind-propublica-targeting-conservative
-supreme-court-justices.

42 "Woodrow Wilson and the Espionage Act," Bill of Rights Institute, https://billofrightsinstitute.org/activities/handout-a-woodrow-wilson-and-the-espionage-act (May 23, 2023).

43 Adam Hochschild, "America's Top Censor—So Far," *Mother Jones* (Sept./Oct. 2022), https://www.motherjones.com/politics/2022/10/hochschild-woodrow-wilson-censor-journalism/ (May 23, 2023).

44 Ibid.

45 Ibid.

46 Christopher B. Daly, "How Woodrow Wilson's Propaganda Machine Changed American Journalism," *Smithsonian*, April 28, 2017, https://www.smithsonianmag.com/history/how-woodrow-wilsons-propaganda-machine-changed-american-journalism-180963082/ (May 23, 2023).

47 Ibid.

48 David Burnham, *A Law Unto Itself: The IRS and the Abuse of Power* (New York: Vintage, 1989), 228–29; see also Mark R. Levin, *Unfreedom of the Press* (New York: Threshold, 2019), 197.

49 Mark R. Levin, *Unfreedom of the Press* (New York, Threshold, 2019), 197–98.

50 Ibid., 198.

51 Ibid. chapter 6 generally.

52 David T. Beito, "FDR's War Against the Press," *Reason* (May 20, 2017), https://reason.com/2017/04/05/roosevelts-war-against-the-pre/ (May 23, 2023).

53 Ibid.

54 Ted Galen Carpenter, "Barack Obama's War on a Free Press," Cato Institute (Feb. 11, 2021), https://www.cato.org/commentary/barack-obamas-war-free-press (May 23, 2023).

55 Lindsay Kornick, "Barack Obama lectures about 'widespread disinformation' on World Press Freedom Day: 'Truth matters,'" *Fox News* (May 3, 2023), https://www.foxnews.com/media/barack-obama-lectures-widespread-disinformation-world-press-freedom-day-truth-matters (May 23, 2023).

56 Ibid.

57 "Obama administration brings chilling effect on journalism," Associated Press (Dec. 20, 2015), https://www.foxnews.com/politics

/report-obama-administration-brings-chilling-effect-on-journalism (May 23, 2023).

58 Stephen Dinan, "Judge approves $3.5 million settlement from IRS to tea party groups," *Washington Times* (Aug. 9, 2018), https://www.washingtontimes.com/news/2018/aug/9/judge-approves-35-million-settlement-irs-tea-party/ (May 23, 2023).

59 Kelly Shackelford, "Religious Freedom Is Under Attack Like Never Before," *Newsweek* (Aug. 5, 2020), https://www.newsweek.com/religious-freedom-under-attack-like-never-before-opinion-1523094 (May 23, 2023).

60 Bill Donohue, "Biden's War on Religious Liberty Spikes," Catholic League (Nov. 18, 2023), https://www.catholicleague.org/bidens-war-on-religious-liberty-spikes/# (May 23, 2023).

61 Susan Berry, "Biden Admin Moves to Scrap Trump Rule Protecting Religious Liberty of Federal Contractors," *Breitbart* (Nov. 9, 2021), https://www.breitbart.com/faith/2021/11/09/biden-admin-moves-to-scrap-trump-rule-protecting-religious-liberty-of-federal-contractors/ (May 23, 2023).

62 Ben Christopher, "Outraged parishioners, irked gun stores, an angry bride: Courts flooded with anti-Newsom shutdown suits," *Cal Matters* (May 11, 2020), https://calmatters.org/health/coronavirus/2020/05/california-shutdown-lawsuits-newsom-dhillon-coronavirus-shelter-in-place-executive-orders/ (May 23, 2023).

63 David G. Savage, "Supreme Court rules California churches may open despite the pandemic," *Los Angeles Times*, February 5, 2021, https://www.latimes.com/politics/story/2021-02-05/supreme-court-rules-california-churches-may-open-despite-theing-pandemic.

64 Kyle Seraphin, "The FBI Doubles Down on Christians and White Supremacy in 2023," *UncoverDC* (Feb. 8, 2023), https://www.uncoverdc.com/2023/02/08/the-fbi-doubles-down-on-christians-and-white-supremacy-in-2023/ (May 23, 2023).

65 Ibid.

66 Tyler O'Neil, "Garland Suggests Justice Department Can't Arrest Pro-Abortion Vandals Because They Firebomb Pregnancy Centers at Night," *Daily Signal* (March 1, 2023), https://www.daily signal.com/2023/03/01/garland-gives-reason-justice-department

-prosecutes-pro-life-protesters-abortion-attacks-pregnancy-centers / (May 23, 2023).

67 Ibid.

68 Joe Bukuras, "Biden DOJ recommends no jail time for attack on Catholic church in Washington state," *Catholic News Agency* (April 13, 2023), https://www.catholicnewsagency.com/news /254083/biden-doj-recommends-no-jail-time-for-attack-on-catho lic-church-in-washington-state (May 23, 2023).

69 Kaylee McGhee White, "With Mark Houck, as with Jack Phillips, the persecution is the whole point," *Washington Examiner* (Jan. 31, 2023).

70 Seung Min Kim, "Biden vows abortion legislation as top priority next year," Associated Press (Oct. 18, 2022), https://apnews.com /article/abortion-2022-midterm-elections-biden-health-congress -f3ffadd1d55625a4af7b87f6b691fbbc (May 23, 2023).

71 Tommy Pigott, "The Most Extreme Abortion Bill in History," Republican National Committee (May 11, 2022), https://gop .com/rapid-response/the-most-extreme-abortion-bill-in-history / (May 23, 2023).

72 Jayme Chandler and Kyle Morris, "Backlash builds after Dems vote to legalize abortion up to birth," Fox News (May 17, 2022), https:// wwwb.foxnews.com/politics/backlash-builds-after-democrats-vote -legalize-abortion-until-birth (May 23, 2023).

73 Nadine El-Bawab, "'Born-alive' bill passed by House Republicans would require care for infants born alive after failed abortion," ABC News (Jan. 12, 2023), https://abcnews.go.com/US/born-alive -bill-passed-house-republicans-require-care/story?id=96389440 (May 23, 2023).

74 Ibid.

75 "How FDR lost his brief war on the Supreme Court," National Constitution Center (Feb. 5, 2023), https://constitutioncenter.org /blog/how-fdr-lost-his-brief-war-on-the-supreme-court-2 (May 24, 2023).

76 Ibid.

77 Kermit Roosevelt III, "I Spent 7 Months Studying Supreme Court Reform. We Need to Pack the Court Now," *Time* (Dec. 10,

2021), https://time.com/6127193/supreme-court-reform-expansion / (May 24, 2023).

78 Ibid.

79 Ibid.

80 Ibid.

81 Amy Howe, "Jackson's financial disclosure reveals additional income in previous years," *ScotusBlog* (Sept. 15, 2022), https://www.scotus blog.com/2022/09/jacksons-financial-disclosure-reveals-additional -income-in-previous-years/ (May 24, 2023).

82 Luke Rosiak, "Liberal SCOTUS Justice Took $3M from Book Publisher, Didn't Recuse from Its Cases," *Daily Wire* (May 3, 2023), https://www.dailywire.com/news/liberal-scotus-justice-took-3m -from-book-publisher-didnt-recuse-from-its-cases (May 24, 2023).

83 Ibid.

84 Kaylee McGhee White, "Do not let Democrats whitewash what they did to Brett Kavanaugh," *Washington Examiner* (March 24, 2022), https://www.washingtonexaminer.com/opinion/do-not-let -democrats-whitewash-what-they-did-to-brett-kavanaugh (May 24, 2023).

85 Ibid.

86 H.R. 2584, 117th Cong. (2021).

87 Kaelan Deese, "FBI says man accused in plot to assassinate Kavanaugh was 'shooting for 3' justices," *Washington Examiner* (July 28, 2022), https://www.washingtonexaminer.com/policy/courts/man-in -plot-assassinate-kavanaugh-was-shooting-for-3-justices (May 24, 2023).

88 Mary Margaret Olohan, "Biden DOJ 'Actively' Tried to 'Dissuade' Marshals from Enforcing the Law to Protect Supreme Court Justices, Senators Say," *Daily Signal* (May 4, 2023), https://www.daily signal.com/2023/05/04/senator-britt-biden-admin-willfully-chose -not-enforce-law-protecting-supreme-cout-justices/ (May 24, 2023).

89 Abigail Adcox, "Justice Brett Kavanaugh harassed by protesters while dining in Washington," *Washington Examiner* (July 8, 2022), https://www.washingtonexaminer.com/news/justice-brett-kavana ugh-harassed-protesters-restaurant-dc (May 24, 2023).

90 Dan McLaughlin, "Democrats Need to Call Off Targeting Supreme Court Justices after Armed Assassin Arrested at Kavanaugh's House," *National Review* (June 8, 2022), https://www.nationalreview.com/corner/democrats-need-to-call-off-targeting-supreme-court-justices-after-armed-assassin-arrested-at-kavanaughs-house/ (May 24, 2023).

91 Kaelan Deese, "Garland unaware US marshals told to 'avoid' protester arrests outside justices' homes," *Washington Examiner* (March 29, 2023), https://www.washingtonexaminer.com/policy/courts/garland-unaware-us-marshals-told-to-avoid-protester-arrests (May 24, 2023).

92 Ibid.

93 Victor Nava, "Samuel Alito claims he has 'pretty good idea' who leaked Dobbs draft, says it made justices 'targets of assassination,'" *New York Post* (April 28, 2023), https://nypost.com/2023/04/28/justice-alito-i-have-pretty-good-idea-who-leaked-dobbs-draft/ (May 24, 2023).

94 Woodrow Wilson, *Constitutional Government in the United States* (New York: Columbia University Press, 1908).

95 Ibid., 167.

96 Ibid., 167–68.

97 Ibid., 172.

98 Ibid., 193.

99 Kermit Roosevelt III, "I Spent 7 Months Studying Supreme Court Reform."

100 Wilfred U. Codrington III, "The Electoral College's Racist Origins," Brennan Center for Justice (April 1, 2020), https://www.brennancenter.org/our-work/analysis-opinion/electoral-colleges-racist-origins (May 24, 2023).

101 Allen Guelzo and James H. Hulme, "In Defense of the Electoral College," *In Picking the President: Understanding the Electoral College* (Grand Forks: The Digital Press at the University of North Dakota, 2017), https://cupola.gettysburg.edu/cgi/viewcontent.cgi?article=1095&context=cwfac (May 24, 2023).

102 Ibid.

103 Hans A. von Spakovsky, "Destroying the Electoral College: The Anti-Federalist National Popular Vote Scheme," Heritage Founda-

tion (February 19, 2020), https://www.heritage.org/sites/default
/files/2020-02/LM260.pdf (May 24, 2023).

104 Ibid.

105 Ibid.

106 "Restoring and Protecting Our Democracy," Democrats.org,
https://democrats.org/where-we-stand/party-platform/restoring-and
-strengthening-our-democracy/ (May 24, 2023).

107 "The Facts About H.R. 1: The "For the People Act of 2021," Heritage Foundation (Feb. 21, 2021), https://www.heritage.org/sites
/default/files/2021-02/FS_199.pdf (May 24, 2023).

108 Hans A. von Spakovsky, "H.R. 1/For the People Act Imperils Free
and Fair Elections. Here Are the Worst 8 Parts," Heritage Foundation (March 16, 2021), https://www.heritage.org/election-integrity
/commentary/hr-1for-the-people-act-imperils-free-and-fair-elec
tions-here-are-the (May 24, 2023).

109 Raymond Aron, *Democracy and Totalitarianism: A Theory of Political
Systems* (New York: Praeger, 1965), 200.

110 "The Nation's Fiscal Health: Road Map Needed to Address Projected
Unsustainable Debt Levels" (U.S. Government Accountability
Office), https://www.gao.gov/products/gao-23-106201 (May 8, 2023).

111 Ibid.

112 "Fourteenth Amendment Section 4, Constitution Annotated,
Congress.goc, Library of Congress," https://constitution.congress
.gov/browse/amendment-14/#:~:text=Section%204%20Public%20
Debt&text=But%20neither%20the%20United%20States,be%20
held%20illegal%20and%20void.

113 "The Heritage Guide to the Constitution," The Heritage Foundation https://www.heritage.org/constitution.

114 "Debt ceiling crisis: Biden says he thinks he has authority to use
14th Amendment," *The Hill* (May 21, 2023), https://thehill
.com/homenews/administration/4014068-biden-says-he-thinks
-he-has-authority-to-use-14th-amendment-on-debt-ceiling
/#:~:text=President%20Biden%20on%20Sunday%20said,if%20
he%20went%20that%20route.

115 "Former Biden adviser Tribe: Just use the 14th Amendment now,"
Politico (May 10, 2023), https://www.politico.com/news/2023/05
/10/biden-adviser-14th-amendment-00096300.

116 Laurence H. Tribe, "A Ceiling We Can't Wish Away," *New York Times* (July 7, 2011), https://www.nytimes.com/2011/07/08/opin ion/08tribe.html.

117 Ibid.

118 "Raskin: Biden has a 'constitutional command' on debt," *Politico* (May 10, 2023) https://www.politico.com/news/2023/05 /10/raskin-biden-has-a-constitutional-command-on-debt -00096177#:~:text=One%20of%20Capitol%20Hill's%20 highest,on%20the%20nation's%20debt%20obligations.

119 Alexander Bolton, "Democrats press Biden to use 14th Amendment on debt ceiling," *The Hill* (May 14, 2023), https://thehill.com/home news/senate/4003076-democrats-press-biden-to-use-14th-amend ment-on-debt-ceiling/.

120 Ibid.

121 Friedrich A. Hayek, *The Road to Serfdom*, 172–73.

122 Naomi Lin, "Biden's 2024 'freedom' campaign a redux of 2020 with or without Trump," *Washington Examiner* (April 26, 2023), https:// www.washingtonexaminer.com/news/white-house/biden-2024 -reelection-campaign-freedom-trump.

CHAPTER EIGHT: STALIN WOULD BE PROUD

1 "The Nation's Fiscal Health: Road Map Needed to Address Projected Unsustainable Debt Levels" (U.S. Government Accountability Office, May 8, 2023), https://www.gao.gov/product /gao-23-106201.

2 Eric Holder to Jen Psaki: "Hard to see how Trump will not be convicted" (MSNBC, June 11, 2023), https://www.youtube.com /watch?v=GgEJQbmoUH8.

3 https://www.politico.com/story/2019/01/07/congress-house-demo crats-trump-subpoenas-oversight-1082563.

4 Attorney General William Barr, "Letter to Congress Summarizing Special Counsel Robert Mueller's Report," March 24, 2019, https:// www.documentcloud.org/documents/5779689-Mueller-report-con clusions-from-AG-Barr.html?embed=true&responsive=false&side bar=false (June 11, 2023).

5 Brianna Herlihy, "Durham report: FBI displayed 'markedly different'

treatment of Clinton, Trump campaigns," Fox News, May 15, 2023, https://www.foxnews.com/politics/durham-report-fbi-displayed -markedly-different-treatment-clinton-trump-campaigns (June 11, 2023).

6 Ibid.

7 Kristina Wong, "Durham: Obama, Biden Briefed in 2016 on Clinton's Plan to Link Trump to Russia—Still Pushed Collusion Hoax," *Breitbart*, May 15, 2023, https://www.breitbart.com/politics/2023/05 /15/durham-obama-biden-briefed-2016-clintons-plan-link-trump -russia-still-pushed-collusion-hoax/ (June 11, 2023).

8 Hans A. von Spakovsky, "Will New York Times, Washington Post Return Pulitzer for Misleading Russia Collusion Stories?" Heritage Foundation, Dec. 13, 2021, https://www.heritage.org/civil-society /commentary/will-new-york-times-washington-post-return-pulitzer -misleading-russia (June 11, 2023).

9 Brooke Singman, "Clinton campaign paid to 'infiltrate' Trump Tower, White House servers to link Trump to Russia, Durham finds" (February 12, 2022), https://www.foxnews.com/politics/clin ton-campaign-paid-infiltrate-trump-tower-white-house-servers .https://www.foxnews.com/politics/clinton-campaign-paid-infil trate-trump-tower-white-house-servers.

10 Kerry Pickett, "'Saw everything': Alleged whistleblower Eric Ciaramella had extensive access in Trump White House," *Washington Examiner*, Nov. 11, 2019, https://www.washingtonexaminer.com /news/saw-everything-alleged-whistleblower-eric-ciaramella-had -extensive-access-in-trumps-white-house (June 11, 2023).

11 Eric Trickey, "When America's Most Prominent Socialist Was Jailed for Speaking Out Against World War I," *Smithsonian*, June 15, 2018, https://www.smithsonianmag.com/history/fiery-socialist-challenged -nations-role-wwi-180969386/ (June 11, 2023).

12 Ibid.

13 Judicial Watch v. Nat. Archives and Records Admin. (Case No. 10 -1834, D.D.C. 2012), https://casetext.com/case/judicial-watch-inc -v-natl-archives-records-admin (June 11, 2023).

14 John Solomon, "Old case over audio tapes in Bill Clinton's sock drawer could impact Mar-a-Lago search dispute," *Just the News*, Aug. 17, 2022, https://justthenews.com/politics-policy/all-things

-trump/old-case-over-audio-tapes-bill-clintons-sock-drawer-could
-impact (June 11, 2023).

15 David B. Rivkin Jr. and Lee A. Casey, "The Trump Warrant Had No Legal Basis," *Wall Street Journal*, Aug. 22, 2022, https://www.wsj.com/articles/the-trump-warrant-had-no-legal-basis-mar-a-lago-affidavit-presidential-records-act-archivist-custody-classified-fbi-garland-11661170684 (June 11, 2023).

16 Ibid.

17 Alan Dershowitz, "The Most Dangerous Indictment in History," *Newsweek*, June 9, 2023, https://www.newsweek.com/most-dangerous-indictment-history-opinion-1805579 (June 11, 2023).

18 Ibid.

19 Kelly Garrity, "Lawmakers react to Trump indictment news," *Politico*, June 8, 2023, https://www.politico.com/news/2023/06/08/lawmakers-react-trump-indictment-00101170 (June 11, 2023).

20 "A Destructive Trump indictment," *Wall Street Journal*, June 9, 2023, https://www.wsj.com/articles/donald-trump-indictment-classified-documents-jack-smith-mar-a-lago-biden-justice-department-81591082 (June 11, 2023).

21 https://heavy.com/news/tony-bobulinski/.

22 Ibid.

23 https://nypost.com/2022/07/27/hunter-bidens-biz-partner-called-joe-biden-the-big-guy-in-panic-over-laptop/.

24 https://www.foxnews.com/politics/biden-campaign-blinken-orchestrated-intel-letter-discredit-hunter-biden-laptop-story-ex-cia-official-says.

25 https://www.foxnews.com/politics/biden-allegedly-paid-5-million-by-burisma-executive.

26 https://www.washingtonexaminer.com/news/push-to-disqualify-trump-from-2024-using-14th-amendment.

27 David Carton, "Trump Lawyers Targeted by Dark Money Group" *The American Spectator* (June 18, 2023), https://spectator.org/trump-lawyers-targeted-by-dark-money-group/.

EPILOGUE

1 22-592 Arizona v. Mayorkas (May 8, 2023), https://www.suprem
ecourt.gov/opinions/22pdf/22-592_5hd5.pdf.

2 Ibid.

3 Ibid.